# *Justice as Healing*

# Reflections on *Justice as Healing*

*Justice as Healing* offers a bountiful harvest of insights of 29 Indigenous voices—emanating from almost as many distinct Indigenous cultures—as well as five Indigenous organizations and 15 non-Indigenous contributors, at once expressing both diverse and common views about the nature of Aboriginal justice, its underlying values and worldviews, its paradigmatic differences with western justice, its parallels and divergences with contemporary restorative justice, and its applicability to healing wounds of mass systemic harm, both past and present.

Adding yet another layer of complexity and richness to *Justice as Healing*'s fulsome yield, we hear from traditional Elders and chiefs, philosophers and educators, lawyers and judges, elected officials and educators, artists and community members, a pipe carrier and lodge keeper, and from international consultants and a UN official.

This exciting compilation is a landmark work. Although the international restorative justice movement has engendered an abundance of publications in the last thirty-odd years of its existence, precious few are devoted to Indigenous justice. Even fewer offer an anthology of so many diverse Indigenous authors as this volume does.

The collection also breaks new ground because, while the recent spate of restorative justice literature includes works focused on truth commissions in South America, Africa, and Europe in post-conflict contexts, few, if any, explore how we might apply reconciliatory justice in the context of historic and ongoing mass social harm here in North America. *Justice as Healing* is one of the first to initiate this extraordinary conversation.

*Justice as Healing* is of enormous significance for yet another reason. The essential questions restorative justice asks of practitioners are: How are we to become peacemakers skilled in reconciliation? How are we to become healers of the social body? To say the least, those of us socialized in the modernist justice paradigm are total neophytes in these matters. These are very new and very different questions for us. Yet adversarial justice is not even ten centuries old, and for most of human history, we have practiced restorative-type justice, *not* adversarial justice. Thus, far from new, these questions are actually ages-old for humanity. Surviving the devastation wrought by the onslaught of hierarchies of power over the last five centuries, there remains a millennia-old and vast human heritage of know-how about peacemaking. We are deeply honored that the authors are willing to begin to share it with non-Indigenous peoples through publications like *Justice as Healing*. It helps us remember. May it be the first of many more harvests to come, arising from all the earth's directions.

*Fania E. Davis*

*Since receiving her law degree from the University of California, Berkeley in 1979, principal investigator Fania E. Davis has been practicing as a civil rights trial lawyer in California. In 2003, she received her Ph.D. from the California Institute of Integral Studies with a research focus on the Indigenous paradigm. While enrolled in the Ph.D. program, she studied with traditional Elders and Healers in Africa, the South Pacific, and North America.*

. . . .

For those of us working with justice, peacebuilding, and approaches to deep-rooted conflict, *Justice as Healing* could not have arrived at a more opportune moment. Frankly, our fields, heavy laden as they are with modern techniques and demands for fast solutions, are in desperate need of innovation, insight, and, in a word, wisdom. What better place to turn than the ageless wisdom of Indigenous ways—the pool that has always been there reflecting its light but which, lamentably, has too often been ignored and far too rarely been sought, expressed, and truly understood on its own terms and in their own words.

This book is a gift from that pool of patient wisdom. It brings together more than any one book I have seen a range of Indigenous voices, writers, and insight about centuries old and ever new approaches for helping the sisters of Justice and Healing walk together. One can but express appreciation for the accessibilty and timeliness of this contribution. In the chanting words of the Southwest: beauty before us, beauty around us, with beauty it is finished.

*John Paul Lederach*
*Professor of International Peacebuilding*
*Kroc Institute, University of Notre Dame*

# Justice as Healing:
# Indigenous Ways

· · · ·

*Wanda D. McCaslin*

EDITOR

*Living Justice Press*

ST. PAUL, MINNESOTA 55105

2005

Living Justice Press
St. Paul, Minnesota

For information about permission to reproduce selections from this book, please write to:
Permissions, Living Justice Press, 2093 Juliet Avenue, St. Paul, MN 55105

Publisher's Cataloguing-in-Publication
(Provided by Quality Books, Inc.)

Justice as healing : indigenous ways / Wanda D. McCaslin,
    editor. —1st ed.
        p.   cm.
    Includes index.
    Compilation of articles published in Justice as healing : a newsletter on aboriginal
concepts of justice from 1995 to 2004, produced by the Native Law Centre of Canada,
located at the University of Saskatchewan, Saskatoon.
        LCCN 2005921376
        ISBN 0-9721886-1-4

    1. Criminal justice, Administration of—Canada.    2. Alternatives to imprisonment—
Canada.    3. Indians of North America—Legal status, laws, etc.—Canada.    4. Indigenous
peoples—Legal status, laws, etc.—Canada.    I. McCaslin, Wanda D.    II. University of
Saskatchewan. Native Law Centre.

KE7722.C75J87 2005          364.971
                    QBI05-200031


            10  09  08  07  06  05     5  4  3  2  1


            Copyediting by Cathy Broberg
            Cover design by David Spohn
        Interior design by Wendy Holdman
    Composition at Prism Publishing Center, Minneapolis, Minnesota

# Dedicated

To the Indigenous people of Mother Earth who work every day to create a meaningful difference for our peoples. Our advocates face the daunting task of resisting colonization as they seek and celebrate our justice traditions. Their unwavering commitment to a new and respectful paradigm is inspiring.

This book is also dedicated to the memories of our community members who have suffered and continue to endure horrific violence and harm against our children, women, and men. May they come to know that people of our past, present, and future walk the journey toward justice as healing.

# Expressing Our Gratitude for Support

We at Living Justice Press are deeply grateful to those who have made this book financially possible. The Fund for Nonviolence (Santa Cruz, California), the Sisters of Charity of the Blessed Virgin Mary (Chicago, Illinois), and Yvonne Sexton of the Sexton Foundation (Grey Eagle, Minnesota) gave us most generous grants that have enabled us to proceed with this project. We have received generous support from individuals as well, including Jeannine and Mike Baden, Mary Joy Breton, Ernest J. Breton, Ruth Newman, Loretta Draths, and Christopher Largent.

Kay Pranis, our board chairperson, also made a generous donation to honor the memory of Doug Hall, who died on 24 October 2004. Besides being a former president of the Minneapolis chapter of the NAACP and cofounder of the Legal Rights Center in Minneapolis, Minnesota, Mr. Hall was a lifelong advocate for Native Peoples and was among the lawyers who defended American Indian Movement leaders and others who were arrested by the United States government during the occupation of Wounded Knee in 1973.

# Contents

**Chapter 2: Resisting Justice as Force**

## II. The Healing Process: Being a Good Relative

**Chapter 3: Healing Worldviews**

**Chapter 4: Respecting Community**

**Chapter 5: Community Peacemaking**

## III. *The Healing Process: Relying on Our Own Ways*

### Chapter 6: Responding to Harm's Legacy

## Chapter 7: Shape-Shifting Systems

## Chapter 8: Honoring Healing Paths

# Foreword

Probing the relationship between the Indigenous populations of this continent and its colonizers has been a major part of the curricular designs and many models of Indian Studies, the scholarship I've called my major interest for over thirty years. That fact is what makes this anthology, *Justice as Healing: Indigenous Ways*, a powerful, essential clarion call which will help us grasp the very real goal of seeking justice for the colonized. Justice must be achieved before reconciliation between Whites and Indians can occur, and that justice must be determined by Indians who for the first time are finding their voices. This book meets the urgent demand toward those ends by telling the stories of the oppressed, enabling powerful forms of resistance to emerge, exploring the intersection of imperialism, research, and ways of knowing.

Part 1, Truth, Reclamation, and Resistance examines the 500 years of history and ideology of the West. Part 2 sets in place family and tribal theory as a prelude to problem solving. The third part of the book, "relying on our own ways," describes alternative structures and validates the right and obligation of the people themselves to carry out their own solutions through the work of judges, family counselors, commissions, federations, and communities.

Well conceived and brilliantly written by people who know what they are talking about, *Justice as Healing* shows us that our responsibilities are not about control and supremacy but, rather, about how to value our lives and make them whole. This book is critical reading for the whole world of activists and scholars who are worried about the outcomes of brutal colonization of past centuries and want to act on their own most fundamental right to determine their own destinies.

*Elizabeth Cook-Lynn*
*Professor Emerita, EWU, Cheney, WA 99004*
*Visiting Professor of Indian Studies,*
*ASU, Tempe, AZ 85202*
*Scholar, Poet, Essayist, and Novelist*
*Enrolled Member: Crow Creek Sioux Tribe,*
*Ft. Thompson, SD*

# Preface

This book is compiled from articles published in *Justice as Healing: A Newsletter on Aboriginal Concepts of Justice* from 1995 to 2004. *Justice as Healing* is produced by the Native Law Centre of Canada, located at the University of Saskatchewan, Saskatoon.

Serving as editor over the last five years, I am delighted to celebrate the newsletter's first decade of work, especially since the newsletter has involved collaboration with so many strong Aboriginal voices here in Saskatchewan as well as around the world. A leading purpose of our newsletter is to provide a forum for hearing these Indigenous voices and their consistent call for completely different paradigms of "justice"—paradigms that are founded on Indigenous teachings and traditions and that nurture us as peoples and communities.

So much good work is being done at both decolonizing the justice system and charting a return to ways that are healing and natural for us. Over these ten years, *Justice as Healing* has provided a place for this work to be shared in the hopes of inspiring others. Through a diverse range of articles, dialogues have emerged, and we have learned from each other. We have learned about ways that work while we recover from histories of genocide and trauma, and we have also supported each other in affirming what most definitely does not work.

This book documents our journey, development, and stories of learning from each other. The authors have not been asked to update their articles to reflect their current thought, because we feel the path we have gone has meaning and value and can be instructive for those just beginning on a healing path. Our traditions tell us that knowing where we have been is essential for knowing where we are and where we want to go now. Accordingly, we have noted at the end of each article when it appeared in our newsletter. Only a few articles were written for this publication and did not appear in our newsletter first.

On a stylistic note, I have struggled with whether to use a formal or an informal writing style in my introductions. I have chosen a more informal, inclusive writing style, because it seems more reflective of the healing, "talking circle," restorative work that honors the human voice and allows it to emerge. As a result, I have used *we* and *our* (e.g., "issues *we* as Indigenous Peoples face" or "*our* languages and traditions") instead of *they* and *their*, which seems to shift the discussion to a more distant, academic frame. In doing so, however, I am not attempting to speak for other Indigenous Nations or to make pan-Aboriginal claims. I was taught to speak from my own experiences and background. Accordingly, the *our* does not mean that I presume to share the same languages or traditions with other peoples, but rather that we each have *our* own languages, traditions, cultures, histories, and ways. The *our* is inclusive of honoring our differences and is not intended to blur them. I feel a desire to mention this, so that I communicate within the ethical protocol that I was taught to respect.

Another reason that I chose the informal style is that Living Justice Press, located in the United States, aims to make restorative justice concepts accessible to a wider reading audience, reaching not only professional, legal, and academic readers but also families and community members. Accordingly, all the articles and selections have been edited for ease of readability and for consistency with U.S. publishing conventions.

I want to thank all of our contributors for their generosity in allowing us to republish their work. I have seen over the years how much these articles have meant to people—from lawyers and judges to community members to those caught in the justice system. I am most grateful now to share this work with the United States and international audiences. I also want to thank Denise Breton for her patience, persistence, and unwavering belief in the need for this book as well as everyone at Living Justice Press for their enthusiastic collaboration in this endeavor. I especially want to thank Kathleen Makela, who was the editor of the *Justice as Healing* newsletter in the early years. As well, special thanks goes to Sa'ke'j Youngblood Henderson, Marie Battiste, Zandra Wilson, Diane Kotschorek, and my colleagues here at the Native Law Centre for their enormous support over the years and for their generous assistance in birthing this book.

*Wanda D. McCaslin*

# List of Abbreviations

| | |
|---|---|
| CAIJ | Centre d'accès à l'information juridique |
| CIAJ | Canadian Institute for the Administration of Justice |
| CHCH | Community Holistic Circle Healing Program, Hollow Water First Nation |
| CNLR | Canadian Native Law Reporter |
| CP | Canadian Press |
| FAE | Fetal Alcohol Effect |
| FAS | Fetal Alcohol Syndrome |
| FASD | Fetal Alcohol Syndrome Disorder |
| FC | Federal Court Reports (Canada) |
| FGC | Family group conferencing |
| FSIN | Federation of Saskatchewan Indian Nations |
| NADAP | Native Alcohol and Drug Abuse Program |
| NNADAP | National Native Alcohol and Drug Abuse Program |
| NZLR | New Zealand Law Reports |
| NZPCC | New Zealand Privy Council Cases |
| OHA | Office of Hawaiian Affairs |
| RCAP | Royal Commission on Aboriginal Peoples |
| RCMP | Royal Canadian Mounted Police |
| Sask. L. Rev. | Saskatchewan Law Review |
| SCR | Supreme Court Reports (Canada) |
| UBC | University of British Columbia |
| UNCHR | United Nations Commission on Human Rights |
| UNED | Universidad Nacional de Educacion a Distancia |
| UNSWLJ | University of New South Wales Law Journal |
| WRSC(A) | Waikato Raupatu Claims Settlement (Act) |
| WWR. | Western Weekly Reports (Canada) |
| YCJA | Youth Criminal Justice Act |

# Canadian Terminology

Various terms have developed to refer to the Indigenous Peoples of Turtle Island since the time of European contact. Each term has various shades of meaning and connotation, including degrees of legal import. To help readers unfamiliar with these terms, especially as they are used by Canadian authors, we offer a rough guide to a few of the different terms.

*Aboriginal Peoples*, etymologically meaning those "from the origin" or the "original people," is used when referring in a general manner to Indigenous Peoples without reference to their specific traditions, practices, and cultures. In Canada, the term *Aboriginal* includes the Indian, Inuit, and Métis Peoples and is tied to their constitutionally protected rights. The Constitution Act, 1982, Section 35 states:

(1) The existing aboriginal and treaty rights of the aboriginal peoples of Canada are hereby recognized and affirmed.
(2) In this Act, "aboriginal peoples of Canada" includes the Indian, Inuit, and Métis peoples of Canada.

*First Nation(s)*, a term used in place of "Indian(s)," emphasizes the political and cultural dimensions of those who lived on the land from "time immemorial." When discussing specific First Nations, the name of that nation may be used (e.g., Mohawk First Nation).

*Indian* is an older term that continues to be used in legislation, government policies, or statistical analysis, including discussions of the Indian Act, status or non-status Indians, or on- or off-reserve Indians.

*Indigenous*, which the dictionary defines as those who originated in a land or live naturally in a particular region, tends to refer to the original inhabitants globally. The term has an international connotation.

*Métis* are distinct Aboriginal Peoples whose ancestors were of mixed heritage—First Nations and European. For Labrador Métis, the ancestors were of Inuit and European heritage. The term Métis Nation refers to those identified as a nation with roots in the Canadian west.

*Native* has a similar meaning to the term Indigenous or Aboriginal. It carries the meaning of belonging to a particular place by being innate to the region and having originated there.

*Peoples* is a politically charged term, because it reflects the integrity and self-determination to assert cultural distinctness, sovereignty, and autonomy. The Eurocentric, dominant societies may tolerate individual Indigenous people, but by and large they are highly resistant to recognizing "peoples" due to the implications for sovereignty that come with this recognition. The United Nations, for example, has witnessed hot debates over this issue.

# Contributors

**The Aboriginal Healing Foundation** (AHF) was established in 1998 as an independent, not-for-profit organization when it received a grant of $350 million from the Canadian government to support the healing processes of Aboriginal survivors of residential schools. The AHF was given one year to set up, four years to allocate the healing fund on a multi-year basis, and five years to monitor the projects, undertake evaluation, and submit a final report. The foundation, which is scheduled to close in 2009, received $40 million in the 2005 federal budget. This is not enough to extend all the projects that are currently funded or to call for new applications. It will, however, allow the Aboriginal Healing Foundation to continue to work with various Aboriginal healing programs to address the physical, emotional, and sexual abuse of First Nations people in the residential schools: "Ours is a holistic approach. Our goal is to help create, reinforce, and sustain conditions conducive to healing, reconciliation, and self-determination. We are committed to addressing the legacy of abuse in all its forms and manifestations—direct, indirect, and intergenerational—by building on the strengths and resiliency of Aboriginal people. . . . [We] support the full participation of all Aboriginal people, including Métis, Inuit, and First Nations, both on and off reserves, and both status and non-status, in effective healing processes relevant to our diverse needs and circumstances."

**S. James Anaya** is the James J. Lenoir Professor of Human Rights Law and Policy at the James E. Rogers College of Law, the University of Arizona, where he teaches and writes in the fields of international human rights, Indigenous Peoples' rights, and constitutional law. He has practiced law representing Native Peoples and organizations in matters before United States courts and international institutions. Since 2003, Professor Anaya has served as Associate Justice for the Court of Appeals of the Yavapai-Prescott Indian Tribe. He is the author of *Indigenous Peoples in International Law*.

**Edward Benton Banai** is a Wisconsin Ojibway of the Fish Clan and a spiritual teacher of the Lac Court Orielles Band of the Ojibway Tribe. He is the executive director of the Red School House, St. Paul, Minnesota, and was one of its original founders in the late 1960s. He was also directly involved with the original formation of the Minneapolis American Indian Movement, which was formed in 1968 as a grassroots organization set up as a watchdog of the Minneapolis Police Department after years of harassment and racist attacks against Minneapolis' Indian community. The Red School House was one of AIM's initial "Indian Survival Schools." An early leader in culture-based curriculum as well as in Indian alternative education, Mr. Banai has achieved a long-standing ambition to set down the oral history of the Ojibway Nation with the publication of *The Mishomis Book*, which is a representation of the life he lived as a youth within the family circle. Today, Eddie Benton Banai is a respected educator, story-teller, and spiritual leader. As a member of the Midewiwin, or Grand Medicine Society, he continues his work passing on the sacred rites of this ancient Ojibway Religion.

**Russel Lawrence Barsh** is the director of the Center for the Study of Coast Salish Environments, Samish Indian Nation (Anacortes, Washington), and is an adjunct professor of law at the Institute for Law and Society at New York University. A graduate of Harvard Law School, he has been an associate professor of Native American Studies at the University of Lethbridge (1993–2000) and an associate professor of Business, Government, and Society at the University of Washington (1974–1984). Over the past twenty-five years, Professor Barsh has been involved in a variety of projects dealing with Indigenous Peoples of Canada and abroad. His book, *Effective Negotiation by Indigenous Peoples*, was published by the International Labour Organisation in 1997.

**Marie Battiste,** a Mi'kmaq from Unama'kik (Cape Breton, Nova Scotia) and a graduate of Harvard and Stanford, is a professor in the Indian and Northern Education Program at the University of Saskatchewan. She is also a United Nations technical expert on the guidelines for protecting Indigenous heritage. She coauthored *Protecting Indigenous Knowledge and Heritage: A Global Challenge* and is the editor of several books, including *First Nations Education in Canada: The Circle Unfolds* and *Reclaiming Indigenous Voice and Vision*. A Mi'kmaw educator from the Chapel Island First Nation, Professor Battiste is internationally known for her research interests in Aboriginal languages, epistemology, curriculum, cognitive imperialism, and research ethics. Her research and experience working in First Nations schools in administration, curriculum development, and Aboriginal languages have provided a solid foundation for addressing the postcolonial challenges for the next century.

**Larissa Behrendt** is an internationally renowned Aboriginal woman and scholar as well as a professor of Law and Indigenous Studies and the director of the Jumbunna Indigenous House of Learning at the University of Technology, Sydney. In addition, Dr. Behrendt is the director of Ngiya, the National Institute of Indigenous Law, Policy and Practice. Her books include *Achieving Social Justice: Indigenous Rights and Australia's Future and Dispute Resolution in Aboriginal Communities.*

**George Blue Bird** is a Lakota language speaker, writer, and artist. Describing himself, he says: "I am from the Pine Ridge reservation in South Dakota, and I have a great concern for tribal people who are searching for their ancestral roots. This is where I belong, and I will teach this to everyone who enters the great tribal circle of life."

**Judie Bopp** is a cofounder of Four Worlds International and is a director of the Four Worlds Centre for Development Learning. She is a specialist in curriculum design and organizational transformation. She has worked in Asia, the South Pacific, Africa, the former Soviet Union, the Caribbean, and Indigenous North America. She has recently coauthored (with Michael Bopp) two books, the first related to community-based sexual-abuse intervention and the other concerning building sustainable communities.

**Michael Bopp** is also a cofounder of Four Worlds International and is a director of the Four Worlds Centre for Development Learning. He is a specialist in participatory change and development processes and, with Judie Bopp, has worked in community development internationally. He has published extensively and conducted trainings on human systems transformations, community health, research methodology, and learning for social change.

**John Borrows** is Anishinabe and a member of the Chippewa of the Nawash First Nation. He was appointed to the Faculty of Law as Professor and Law

Foundation Chair of the Aboriginal Justice and Governance in 2001. Prior to joining the faculty, he taught at the University of Toronto, the University of British Columbia as the director of the First Nations Law Program, and at Osgoode Hall Law School as the director of the Intensive Program in Lands, Resources, and First Nations Governments. He was also a visiting professor at Arizona State University and the executive director of the Indian Legal Program. His research interests include Aboriginal law, constitutional law, and natural resources and environmental law.

**Yvonne Boyer** is the former director of programs for the Aboriginal Healing Foundation in Ottawa and is now legal and policy adviser at NAHO, the National Aboriginal Health Organization. A Métis born and raised in Moose Jaw, Saskatchewan, she has obtained her LL.B., LL.M and is a member of the Law Society of Saskatchewan and the Law Society of Upper Canada. She is also the former director of justice at the Saskatoon Tribal Council, where she worked closely with the Aboriginal Elders in the Saskatoon Tribal Council as well as with justice officials to support circles as alternatives to the courts.

**Denise C. Breton,** a Breton Celt in ancestry, white American in upbringing, taught at the University of Delaware's philosophy department for nearly twenty years. She coauthored four books, including *The Paradigm Conspiracy: Why Our Social Systems Violate Human Potential and How We Can Change Them* and *The Mystic Heart of Justice: Restoring Wholeness in a Broken World.* In 2002, she cofounded Living Justice Press (LJP), a nonprofit publisher devoted to restorative justice. She currently serves as LJP's executive director.

**William Commanda** is the traditional Algonquin Elder from Kitigan Zibi, Quebec. The great-grandson of Pakinawatik, Elder Commanda is Keeper of three Wampum Belts of historic importance, including the Seven Fires Prophecy Wampum Belt. He was chief of the Kitigan Zibi Reserve for over nineteen years, a guide, trapper and woodsman, a birch bark canoe maker, and craftsman of international renown. In 1995, he led the Sunbow Five Walk for Mother Earth, bringing together representatives of the five symbolic races of man (red, white, yellow, black, and brown) whose concern for the healing of the Earth surpassed racial or religious divisions. Sunbow was a seven-and-a-half-month "Walk for Mother Earth" from the Atlantic to the Pacific Oceans. Elder Commanda is a respected spokesperson and spiritual leader at national and international gatherings. He participates regularly in United Nations peace and spiritual vigils and is acknowledged internationally for his work in promoting interracial and intercultural harmony, justice, and respect for Mother Earth.

**The Commission on First Nations and Métis Peoples and Justice Reform** was chaired by Willie Littlechild, a member of the Ermineskin Cree Nation. Established in November 2001, the commission was directed to "include in its scope of consideration all components of the criminal justice system including, but not limited to, policing, courts, prosecutions, alternative measures, access to legal counsel, corrections (including community corrections), youth justice, community justice processes, and victims services." The Executive Summary of the Final Report, issued 21 June 2004, states:

> As the Commission began its work, it became obvious that justice and all that [the] term evokes is much more than policing, courts, and the myriad of institutions that have been developed. The Commissioners learned that the issues facing First Nations and Métis people—and the reasons they come into conflict with the justice system—are rooted in failures in the areas of education, health, and economic development. . . . It was with this desire to address the issue of First Nations and Métis people and the justice system from a holistic point of view that the Commission undertook its mandate.

**Michael Cousins** is a member of the Mohawk Nation, Wolf Clan, Six Nations of the Grand River. He holds a B.A. from Wilfred Laurier, an LL.B. from the University of Saskatchewan, and an M.A. in criminology from Simon Fraser. He has published in the areas of First Nations' hunting and fishing rights and Aboriginal justice as well as lectured on legal and First Nations studies topics. He sat on various boards and committees related to Aboriginal resources at each of the universities he attended. Over the last ten years, he has worked in the areas of Aboriginal justice, hunting and fishing rights, Aboriginal child welfare and social services, and First Nations policing. In his spare time, Michael enjoys carving in the traditional Haudenosaunee style and form.

**Erica-Irene A. Daes,** a Greek, served as the Chairperson-Rapporteur for the Working Group on Indigenous Populations. She is a member of a United

Nations Sub-Commission to Protect Minorities, the chair of the UN Working Group on Indigenous Populations, and a collaboratrice of the Hellenic Institute of International and Foreign Law. She has authored a number of publications dealing with war crimes, self-determination for minorities and their treatment in Europe, a draft constitution for a new Europe, and an international bill of human rights.

**Harley Eagle** is a Dakota of the Oceti Sakowin Oyate, born in Saskatoon, Saskatchewan. Living in Winnipeg, Manitoba, he is the codirector of the Mennonite Central Committee's (MCC) anti-racism program in the United States and in Canada. He is also the co-coordinator of Aboriginal work for MCC Canada. He lived and worked on Pine Ridge Reservation for seven years and has conducted seminars on antiracism, restorative justice, circles, and peacemaking throughout the United States and Canada.

**The Federation of Saskatchewan Indian Nations (FSIN)** represents seventy-four First Nations in Saskatchewan. "The Federation is committed to honoring the Spirit and Intent of the Treaties as well as the promotion, protection, and implementation of Treaties that were made with the First Nations more than a century ago." On 16 April 1982, Saskatchewan chiefs agreed to form Canada's first Indian Legislative Assembly—a true Federation of Nations. The chiefs thereby gained control of the executive and administrative functions of First Nations government at the band, tribal council, and provincial level. The first Legislative Assembly of the Chiefs of Saskatchewan was held on 19 October 1983. Since then, Saskatchewan chiefs have made significant progress in the struggle toward recognition of treaty rights and the creation of a better future for First Nations people. For more than fifty years now, the chiefs have worked as a collective, unified voice for the protection and implementation of treaty rights. For a fuller history of the FSIN's development, see their Web site: www.fsin.com.

**Isobel M. Findlay** is an associate professor, Management and Marketing, College of Commerce, and a research scholar at the Centre for the Study of Co-operatives at the University of Saskatchewan. She is also an associate member of the Council for the Advancement of Native Development Officers (CANDO). She teaches and researches on communications, law and culture, and Aboriginal and associative organizations at the University of

Saskatchewan. She is coeditor of *Realizing Community: Multidisciplinary Perspectives* and coauthor of *Aboriginal Tenure in the Constitution of Canada*.

**Four Worlds** is an international nonprofit society with over twenty years of experience in capacity building of people and organizations for human and community development. Four Worlds emerged out of Indigenous peoples' community healing and development efforts in North America in the early 1980s. Since then, Four Worlds teams have worked extensively in rural and urban settings in every corner of North America as well as in Africa, Southeast Asia, the Pacific, the former Soviet Union, and Latin America. Four Worlds is well known for its culturally based approach to development work and for its down-to-earth articulation of principles and models to build human and community transformation. Over the past ten years, Four Worlds has conducted several national studies related to justice issues in Aboriginal communities aimed at strengthening community-based approaches, understanding and building comprehensive approaches to address root causes, and strengthening the capacity of government policy and practice to play its part. These studies and other publications are listed and in many cases free for download on their Web site. More information about Four Worlds is available from The Four Worlds Centre for Development Learning, Box 395, Cochrane, Alberta, Canada T4C 1A6 (telephone (403) 932-0882, fax (403) 932-0883, email anyone@fourworlds.ca, web site www.fourworlds.ca) or from Four Worlds International, 347 Fairmont Boulevard, Lethbridge, Alberta, Canada T1K 7J8 (telephone (403) 320-7144, fax (403) 329-8383, email 4worlds@uleth.ca, website http//home.uleth.ca/~4worlds).

**Ross Gordon Green** is a Provincial Court Judge in Yorkton, Saskatchewan, who, before his appointment, authored two books: *Justice in Aboriginal Communities: Sentencing Alternatives* and, with Kearney F. Healy, *Tough on Kids: Rethinking Approaches to Youth Justice*. His books consider the development and current state of Canadian law in regard to youth crime. He worked extensively with young offenders while he was a legal aid lawyer.

**James J. R. Guest** holds his B.A. from the University of Manitoba (1994), his LL.B. from the University of Manitoba (1997), and his LL.M. from Harvard University (1998). Mr. Guest is a former law clerk of the Mashantucket Pequot Tribal Nation.

**Kearney F. Healy** is the coauthor (with Ross Gordon Green) of *Tough on Kids: Rethinking Approaches to Youth Justice*. He authored a chapter on youth court in *Critical Criminology in Canada: Breaking the Links Between Marginality and Condemnation*, edited by B. Schissel and C. Brooks. His works make a powerful case for shifting to restorative justice, especially in view of the testimony of young people and the very real human costs they pay in the current system. He has dealt with many young offenders as a legal aid lawyer. He currently works with Legal Aid in Saskatoon.

**James Sa'ke'j Youngblood Henderson** is Chickasaw, born to the Bear Clan of the Chickasaw Nation and Cheyenne Tribe in Oklahoma. He is one of the leading tribal philosophers, advocates, and strategists for North American Native Peoples. In 1974, he was one of the first Native scholars to receive a juris doctorate in law from Harvard Law School. After graduation, he sought through scholarship and litigation to restore Aboriginal culture, institutions, and rights. During the constitutional process in Canada from 1978 to 1993, he served as a constitutional adviser for the Assembly of First Nations and the Mi'kmaq Nation. He is currently a member of the University of Saskatchewan's College of Law and is research director of the Native Law Centre of Canada. He is the author and editor of many books, including *Mi'kmaq Concordat; The Road: Indian Tribes and Political Liberty; Aboriginal Tenure in the Constitution of Canada; Continuing Poundmaker and Riel's Quest,* and with Marie Battiste, *Protecting Indigenous Knowledge and Heritage*.

**The Hollow Water First Nation and their program of Community Holistic Circle Healing (CHCH)** has received international acclaim for their work with sexual abuse in their community by using a traditional, community-based, holistic approach. The Hollow Water First Nation is an Ojibway community located one hundred fifty miles northeast of Winnipeg in Manitoba on a status Indian Reserve. In 1984, a resource team was formed to work on healing and development. It was comprised of political leaders, service providers, and a strong base of community volunteers.

Before 1986, alcohol and drug abuse loomed large as a problem, as did unemployment and the need to educate children in the cultural ways of their people. In 1986, however, personal disclosures revealed that extensive sexual abuse had been going on for many years but that talking about it was taboo. Indeed, most of the members of the resource group had been affected. The community realized they must face significant personal healing work if they were to succeed in the political and economic realms. The Community Holistic Circle Healing program developed to support these healing processes based on traditional teachings and practices. Today, Hollow Water enjoys a fairly high level of sobriety (around 80 percent), and they continue to actively deal with sexual abuse issues.

**Bria Huculak** is a Provincial Court Judge of Saskatchewan. She obtained her LL.B. from the University of Saskatchewan and her LL.M. (Hon.) from the University of Auckland, New Zealand, in 1983. Judge Huculak was the Legal Director of the Saskatchewan Legal Aid Commission, Saskatoon Rural Office, prior to being appointed to the bench in January 1992. Judge Huculak has worked extensively in restorative justice at the local, national, and international levels.

**Harold Johnson,** LL.B., LL.M., is a Cree from northern Saskatchewan. He obtained his bachelor degree in law from the University of Saskatchewan in 1995 and a master degree in law from Harvard University in 1996. Today Harold runs a small private law practice in La Ronge and is active in environmental issues affecting the north. He continues to operate his family trapline and is a commercial fisherman. He teaches sociology to First Nations students of the Saskatchewan Institute of Arts, Science and Technology. He is a director of the research group, Keewatin Visions. Harold's writing includes a work of fiction entitled *Billy Tinker* that was shortlisted for two Saskatchewan book awards in 2002. His next work of fiction will be launched in the fall of 2005. He is also an editor of the *Indigenous Justice Magazine*.

**Robert Joseph,** LL.B, LL.M., is a New Zealander through Ngāti Paretekawa, Ngāti Te Kohera, Ngāti Kahungunu, Ngāti Rangitane, and Welsh Jewish ancestry. He is also a Ph.D. candidate and legal researcher at the School of Law, Te Matahauariki Institute, University of Waikato, New Zealand.

**Phil Lane Jr.** is a Dakota-Chickasaw who is both a traditional pipe carrier and sweat lodge keeper. He has worked with Indigenous Peoples in North and South America, Micronesia, Southeast Asia, and Hawaii. In addition to being an award-winning film producer, he is a cofounder and international coordinator of the Four Worlds family of organizations. He is also president of Four Directions International and serves as chairman of Four Directions Information Systems Corporation, an Aboriginal information technology initiative. He also served on the faculty of the University of Lethbridge for fifteen years.

**Gloria Lee** is the PAGC (Prince Albert Grand Council) Justice Director and the past research and curriculum developer for the Saskatchewan Indian Institute of Technologies. Ms. Lee is of Cree ancestry from the Pelican Lake area and received her Bachelor of Law Degree in 2003. Ms. Lee is also an artist, and some of her work hangs in the College of Law at the University of Saskatchewan.

**J. Wilton ("Willie") Littlechild,** O.C., Q.C., I.P.C., a member of the Ermineskin Cree Nation, acquired his law degree from the University of Alberta in 1976. Mr. Littlechild was the first Treaty Indian in Alberta to graduate with a law degree and the first Treaty Indian elected to Canadian Parliament. He is an outstanding athlete who continues to be heavily involved as an organizer in sporting events and was inducted into four Sports halls of fame. He received the Order of Canada in 1999.

As a member of Parliament (1988–1993), Mr. Littlechild served on several senior committees in the House of Commons and was a parliamentary delegate to the United Nations. At the international level, he organized a coalition of Indigenous Nations that sought and gained consultative status with the Economic and Social Council of the United Nations and has now been appointed by the ECOSOC President to the United Nations Permanent Forum for Indigenous Peoples. He has been recognized as Queen's Counsel and Indigenous Peoples Counsel by the legal profession. Mr. Littlechild speaks Cree, English, and French.

**L. S. Tony Mandamin** is Ojibway from the Wikwemikong First Nation in Ontario and has been a member of the Alberta Law Society since 1983. He was appointed judge to the Tsuu T'ina First Nation provincial court in Alberta in 1999 and has been instrumental in the development of the Tsuu T'ina Peacemaking Court.

**Wanda D. McCaslin,** a Métis from northern Saskatchewan, obtained her B.A. in political science and her LL.B. from the University of Saskatchewan.

After being accepted as a member of the Law Society of Saskatchewan, she worked with a private law firm and later with Saskatchewan legal aid. Since 1999, Ms. McCaslin has served as the Law Foundation of Saskatchewan Research Officer with the Native Law Centre of Canada. Her work includes editing the newsletter *Justice as Healing*, coordinating the Young Professionals International, and lecturing with the College of Law. Throughout her career, Aboriginal issues have been central to her work. Ms. McCaslin has presented in the area of Aboriginal justice, case law analysis, and international Indigenous matters. In addition to her legal and academic work, she has been actively involved with Aboriginal community empowerment initiatives in the area of healing, restorative justice, housing, and youth.

**Lorna June McCue** is a Dzakaza (hereditary chief) of the Ned'u'ten People of the Lake Babine Nation. She is an assistant professor and director of First Nations Legal Studies at the University of British Columbia as well as the chair for the First Nations Law Committee at the UBC. She is an advisory council member and chair for Environmental and Aboriginal Guardianship and Legal Education Program (EAGLE). Professor McCue's areas of interest include legal issues relating to Indigenous Peoples, treaty making, self-determination, decolonization, and negotiations, and she has lectured and written extensively in these areas.

**Ada Pecos Melton** is an enrolled member of the Pueblo of Jemez in New Mexico and, for over ten years, has been president of the American Indian Development Associates (AIDA), a totally Indian-owned technical assistance, training, and research firm. She provides training to Native Nations in program and public policy development as well as research. In particular, she focuses on strengthening Indigenous methods of conflict resolution and peacekeeping to address the issues of crime, delinquency, violence, and victimization throughout Indian country. Her public service has included work as a probation officer, court administrator, and director of juvenile programs. In 1995, she took a one-year sabbatical to establish the American Indian and Alaska Native Desk in the U.S. Department of Justice, Office of Justice Programs, to increase tribal access to federal funding, programs, training, and technical assistance. In 1991, she was a fellow under the Asia Foundation and studied Indigenous justice systems in five South Pacific Islands. She serves on the American Correctional Association's Subcommittee on Cultural

Diversity and is a member of the National Tribal Advisory Committee of the National Tribal Justice Resource Center.

**Patricia A. Monture-Angus** is a Mohawk woman who, having obtained her degree in law, is now a professor at the Department of Sociology at the University of Saskatchewan. She is a passionate advocate for Indigenous people and a dedicated activist. She is currently the Special Advisor on Indigenous Initiatives to the University of Saskatchewan's Dean of Arts and Science. Her books include *Thunder in My Soul: A Mohawk Woman Speaks* and *Journeying Forward: Dreaming First Nations' Independence*.

**Ted Moses** is presently the Grand Chief of the Grand Council of the Crees (Eeyou Istchee). Before being elected Grand Chief in August 1999, he was the Cree Ambassador to the United Nations for the Grand Council of the Crees. Born on his parent's Eastmain trapline and educated at Ryerson and McGill University, Chief Moses's commitment to Aboriginal human rights has been lifelong. Dr. Moses began his career as a leader in his own community, initially as Band manager in Eastmain and eventually as Chief of Eastmain. Prior to his first term as Grand Chief in 1984, he took part in the negotiations of the Cree Naskapi (of Quebec) Act, Canada's first local self-government legislation. He was instrumental in winning consultative status for the Grand Council of the Crees from the United Nations in 1987. In January of 1989, Chief Moses was elected as the Rapporteur for the United Nations meeting on the *Effects of Racism and Racial Discrimination on the Social and Economic Relations between Indigenous Peoples and States*.

As Ambassador, he has continued to play a vital role in the ongoing work at the United Nations of obtaining recognition in international law of the rights of the world's Indigenous peoples. He has made submissions to the United Nations that resulted in the UN's very important decision that Canada's policy of "extinguishment" of Aboriginal rights violates Canada's international treaty obligations. He also made the submission that led to Canada's acknowledgment that Indigenous peoples have the right of self-determination in international law, a stipulation that is already beginning to have a positive effect on Aboriginal case law in Canada.

On 7 February 2002, Grand Chief Moses signed an agreement with Quebec Premier Landry, establishing a new nation-to-nation relationship between the Quebec Crees and the government of Quebec. For the first time

ever in Canada, this agreement begins to implement one of the most fundamental principles of self-determination—the right of Indigenous peoples to
benefit from the natural resources on their own lands.

**Julian Norris,** born and raised in Europe, is the program coordinator and
an instructor for Guiding Spirit: Renaissance Training for Youth Workers.
Trained in anthropology and wilderness guiding, he brings over fifteen years
experience of working in the field of experiential and initiatory education.
He is the cofounder of the Ghost River Rediscovery and Guiding Spirit Programs. He has also developed and presently directs the Rediscovery International Foundation's Wilderness Skills Training program.

**Monica One-spot** is the executive director of the Tsuu T'ina Stoney Corrections Society. She is also the Tsuu T'ina Crime Prevention Coordinator and
works with Judge Tony Mandamin at the Tsuu T'ina Peacemaking Court,
established in 1999.

**Steven Point** is program alumnus of the Program of Legal Studies for Na-
tive People and was director of the Native Law Program in the Faculty of
Law at the University of British Columbia. In 2005 he was appointed as
Chief Commissioner of the British Columbia Treaty Commission. He has
been a judge to the Provincial Court of British Columbia since 1999 and prior
to that time, served as Tribal Chairman of the Sto:lo Nation and Chief of the
Skowkale First Nation. In addition to being a chiefs' representative for the
Sto:lo Nation Government House from 1994 to 1998, he has a long history
of working for Sto:lo people and communities. He encouraged the revival of
traditional singing and dancing by his involvement in Sto:lo longhouses and
by serving as a committee member for the Chilliwack PowWow. He also was
an instructor of Native Law at the University of Saskatchewan and was a
recipient of the National Aboriginal Achievement Award, 2000.

**Rupert Ross,** an assistant Crown attorney for the district of Kenora, Ontario, works closely with the Ojibway and Cree Peoples in northwestern Ontario to make court systems more responsive to the needs of their communities. Portions of his book *Dancing with a Ghost: Exploring Indian Reality* first
appeared under the more self-explanatory title "Leaving Our White Eyes Behind: The Sentencing of Native Accused." His second book, *Returning to the*

*Teachings: Exploring Aboriginal Justice*, is used extensively to introduce non-Natives to how Indigenous people and communities often conceive of justice. Mr. Ross has practiced and explored restorative processes since 1990.

**Royal Commission on Aboriginal Peoples (RCAP):** Because the RCAP plays a significant role in Canada with respect to Aboriginal Peoples, it may be useful to non-Canadians to learn about it—how the Canadian government is responding to the Aboriginal Peoples who live within its borders. Founded on the premise that there can be no peace or harmony unless there is justice, the RCAP was established on 26 August 1991 with four Aboriginal and three non-Aboriginal commissioners and was given a comprehensive mandate by the Canadian Parliament:

> The Commission of Inquiry should investigate the evolution of the relationship among aboriginal peoples (Indian, Inuit and Métis), the Canadian government, and Canadian society as a whole. It should propose specific solutions, rooted in domestic and international experience, to the problems which have plagued those relationships and which confront aboriginal peoples today. The Commission should examine all issues that it deems to be relevant to any or all of the aboriginal peoples of Canada. . . .

On its Web site, the RCAP frames the 1996 release of its five-volume, four-thousand-page final report as follows:

> In four years of consultations, research, and reflection, we have come to see clearly that the problems that plague the relationship cannot be addressed exclusively or primarily as Aboriginal issues. The questions we probed during our inquiry and the solutions that emerged from our deliberations led us back insistently to examine the premises on which Canadian law and government institutions are founded and the human values that Canadians see as the core of their identity.
>
> The analysis we present and the avenues of reconciliation we propose in this and the other four volumes of our report do not attempt to resolve the so-called "Aboriginal" problem. Identifying it as an Aboriginal problem inevitably places the onus on Aboriginal people to desist from "troublesome behaviour." It is an assimilationist

approach, the kind that has been attempted repeatedly in the past, seeking to eradicate Aboriginal language, culture, and political institutions from the face of Canada and to absorb Aboriginal people into the body politic—so that there are no discernible Aboriginal people and thus, no Aboriginal problem.

Our report proposes instead that the relationship between Aboriginal and non-Aboriginal people in Canada be restructured fundamentally and grounded in ethical principles to which all participants subscribe freely.

The necessity of restructuring is made evident by a frank assessment of past relations. We urge Canadians to consider anew the character of the Aboriginal nations that have inhabited these lands from time immemorial; to reflect on the way the Aboriginal nations in most circumstances welcomed the first newcomers in friendship; to ask themselves how the newcomers responded to that generous gesture by gaining control of their lands and resources and treating them as inferior and uncivilized; and how they were designated as wards of the federal government like children incapable of looking after themselves. Canadians should reflect too on how we moved them from place to place to make way for "progress," "development," and "settlement," and how we took their children from them and tried to make them over in our image.

This is not an attractive picture, and we do not wish to dwell on it. But it is sometimes necessary to look back in order to move forward. The co-operative relationships that generally characterized the first contact between Aboriginal and non-Aboriginal people must be restored, and we believe that understanding just how, when, and why things started to go wrong will help achieve this goal.

(For further information about the RCAP, see article 3: "Residential Schools and the Intergenerational Legacy of Abuse," note 2.)

**Ellery Starlight** is from the Tsuu T'ina Nation, located southwest of Calgary, Alberta. He serves as the Tsuu T'ina Peacemaker Coordinator at the Tsuu T'ina Peacemaking Court. He attended the Resource Management Assistant Program at the Alberta Vocational Centre in Grouard, Alberta, where he gained environmental experience with Alberta Fish and Wildlife.

Mr. Starlight is active in helping First Nations people protect the environment from chemical contamination.

**Juan Marcellus Tauri** is a criminologist and member of the Ngati Porou iwi (tribe) of the East Coast of the North Island. Juan has been researching and publishing in the area of Indigenous justice issues in New Zealand, Australia, and Canada and on State/Indigenous relations and politics for the past ten years.

**Nin Tomas,** a senior Maori academic, is a member of the faculty of Law at the University of Auckland and teaches public law as well. She is editor of the *Journal of Maori Legal Writing*, which is produced by Te Tai Haruru—the Maori academic section of Auckland Faculty of Law. She is descended from the Maori Iwi of Te Rarawa, Te Aupouri, Ngati Kahu, Te Hikutu, and Taranaki. Her teaching and research are comparative, generally between Maori and Pakeha conceptualizations of law, the legal process and justice, and their application by the judiciary. Her specific research interests are the concepts of "property" and "ownership" and its application to Indigenous Peoples in the areas of natural resources and other cultural property, and the development of alternative justice systems.

**M. E. Turpel-Lafond** is a member of the Muskeg Lake First Nation. She became the first Aboriginal woman to be named to the Saskatchewan bench in March 1998. Her academic credentials include a B.A. from Carleton University, an LL.B. from Osgoode Hall Law School, an LL.M. from Cambridge University, and an S.J.D. from Harvard. Judge Turpel-Lafond ran her own law practice in Nova Scotia and Saskatchewan and served as a professor of law at Dalhousie University. She has also lectured at the University of Toronto, the University of Notre Dame, and held the position of Aboriginal Scholar at the University of Saskatchewan in 1995–96. She has served as legal counsel and consultant to the Federation of Saskatchewan Indian Nations and the Assembly of First Nations. She also served on the Royal Commission on Aboriginal People and the Native Women's Association of Canada.

**Edward C. Valandra,** born and raised on the Rosebud Sioux Reservation, is Sicangu Lakota (enrolled) and an assistant professor in the Native American Studies Department at the University of California at Davis. Previously, he taught at Sinte Gleska University and Oglala Lakota College. He is an associate fellow with the University of Nebraska's Center for Great Plains. Having served on the Rosebud Sioux Tribal Council between 1985 and 1989, he recently served on the Constitutional Task Force for the Sicangu Oyate during his Nation's 2004 Constitutional Convention. He also serves on the Great Plains Restoration Council and was the Rosebud Sioux Tribe's representative to the Intertribal Bison Cooperative between 1996 and 2001. He participated in the Makato Wokiksuye Iyanka Pi (Blue Earth Run To Remember) in 2003 and the Manipi Hena Owasin Wicunkiksuye Pi (Remember Those Who Walked) in 2004. His book, *Not Without Our Consent: The Lakota Resistance to Termination, 1950–1959*, focuses on the termination era in the United States and the infamous Public Law 83–280.

**Warren Weir** (MPA) is an assistant professor in the Department of Management and Marketing and the chair of the MBA Specialization in Indigenous Management at the College of Commerce, the University of Saskatchewan. Professor Weir specializes in Aboriginal organizations and Indigenous community economic development and teaches a number of Indigenous MBA Management Courses, including the Management of Contemporary Aboriginal Organizations. Currently, he is researching Aboriginal cooperatives in Saskatchewan.

**The World Council of Indigenous Peoples** began in 1975, when the Nordic Saami Council and other Indigenous groups held a conference in Copenhagen for the final preparations of the World Council of Indigenous Peoples (WCIP). A strategy, budget, and delegation of experts were adopted. Aslak Nils Sara, an experienced Saami political activist, was elected to the delegation as a representative of Europe and Greenland. The WCIP's goal was to establish a formal relationship to the United Nations and to have concepts of Aboriginal rights accepted internationally as basic economic and political rights of Indigenous Peoples. The WCIP proved to be a powerful force in Indigenous politics until it dissolved in 1996 due to internal conflict. Before its dissolution, the WCIP accomplished two major functions: it gave its members concrete experience in international politics, and it presented Indigenous politics to the United Nations.

**Robert Yazzie** grew up in a traditional area of the Navajo Nation. He graduated from Oberlin College in 1973 and obtained his J.D. from the University of New Mexico School of Law in 1982. Following his graduation, he practiced law in the Navajo Nation courts, acted as a Navajo-English interpreter in U.S. District Court, and served as a consultant to law firms. After seven years as presiding judge of the district court in Window Rock, Arizona, he was appointed Chief Justice of the Navajo Nation in 1992. Throughout, he has been a powerful force in integrating traditional Navajo law and peacemaking techniques into the Navajo Nation's court system. Chief Justice Yazzie has lectured extensively on Navajo justice to judges, academics, and even prison wardens. He will devote his "retirement" years to the education of Indian youth and the concerns of Indigenous Peoples in other countries.

**James W. Zion** is a lawyer and a Domestic Abuse Commissioner in the Crownpoint (Navajo Nation) Family Court. Living in Albuquerque, New Mexico, he is a longtime advocate of Indigenous rights and has written many pieces on Indigenous customary law, the rights of Indigenous Peoples in international law, and restorative justice. He represented the National Indian Youth Council and the Navajo Working Group for Human Rights at the Expert Seminar on Indigenous People and the Administration of Justice in Madrid, Spain, November 2003.

# Justice as Healing

. . . .

# *Introduction*

## Exploring Justice as Healing

*James Sa'ke'j Youngblood Henderson and Wanda D. McCaslin*

Eurocentric thought proposes many theories about justice and punishment.[1] The biblical approach of equivalence *(lex talionis)* and nineteenth-century British theories of intolerable wrongs, deterrence, and retribution *(vergeltung)* form the dominant theories of punishment in Canadian society. They try to ensure that certain individuals physically suffer for their human weaknesses, conduct, and mistakes—big and small. These approaches have not been adequate at curtailing crime or even expressing solidarity with the victim.

In March 1994, the federal and provincial justice ministers reached a consensus on the problems that Aboriginal Peoples face in the Canadian criminal justice system. They agreed (a) that the Canadian criminal justice system had failed and is failing the Aboriginal people; (b) that a new holistic approach to criminal justice, based on Aboriginal values, practices, and traditions, is essential to Aboriginal justice reform; and (c) that the Aboriginal concept of justice as healing should be reflected in the general justice system. This statement is a good beginning for renewing the Canadian criminal justice system.

From our experiences, most Aboriginal Peoples have never understood the exotic passion of Eurocentric society for labeling people as criminals and then making them suffer. The modern Canadian criminal justice system displays the Eurocentric elite's intolerance of human frailties and justifies a theory of social control by violence. In the past, Aboriginal Peoples have argued that the contrived code of conduct of another time—a code that has clearly failed Aboriginal Peoples—could not be the measure of all societies. That is, the cultural remedies of Aboriginal societies cannot be reconciled with the idea that justice is only to be reasoned about and not to be felt. Now others are sharing these thoughts. Many scholars and practitioners are wondering why the Criminal Code's sentencing provisions punish people instead of attempting to heal them.[2] Why, they wonder, have they not thought much about this?

Our past struggles with deterrence, sentencing, punishment, and preventive strategies in the Canadian criminal justice system have shown us that the most successful programs have been built on empowering Aboriginal languages, ceremonies, traditions, and values. Now these pillars of Aboriginal culture are being seen as theories that could bring about a transformation in justice from punishment to healing.

While we must not allow others to appropriate our cultural values and processes, Aboriginal Peoples must assist this transformation by articulating, renewing, and living their vision of justice as healing. It will not be easy. Canadian society seems to want their worldview, yet this is not an objective standard. Such a standard is, after all, the ultimate in subjectivity.

Justice as healing is an old tradition in Aboriginal thought and society. Now, after our experiences with colonialism, racism, domination, and oppression, we have returned to Aboriginal jurisprudence as a foundation for contemporary remedies. The systematic deprivation of Aboriginal ownership of land and resources, Aboriginal wealth and income, as well as our culture, human dignity, and social position have placed difficult demands on our traditional values and rituals. We need to explore our visions of justice as healing in their totality.

Specifically, we need to look at existing therapeutic treatments to determine whether these tools promote assimilation or cultural integrity. We need to ponder why the justice system refuses to treat our people as fully human—why it chooses instead to dehumanize us as deviant organisms or sick minds that need rehabilitation. We have to consider the relationship of punishment to human rights. We need to think seriously about replacing criminal law with tort and remedies that promote Aboriginal values. In other words, we need to rethink justice from our traditional ways.

Some of the current theories of social justice that focus on how material resources, income, or positions of reward and prestige are distributed apply to part of our situation. Yet focusing on distributive justice continues to hide and reinforce the systemic domination of Aboriginal Peoples. Indeed, this focus is often the source of our problems with how justice is administered.[3] While the proper distribution of benefits and burdens is important to Aboriginal Peoples, this issue should not be used to validate the colonial structures and contexts that determine modern distributive patterns and decision-making.

Our holistic approaches to justice as healing are crucial to resolving our experiences with colonial oppression, domination, and racism. This requires us to begin the complex task of decolonizing Canadian law, which means displacing and eventually eliminating the systemic domination of Aboriginal Peoples. To do this, we have to understand the six explicate processes of systemic oppression exercised by governments: violence, exploitation, marginalization, powerlessness, cognitive imperialism, and terror.

Additionally, we have to confront the more complex implicate context of colonial oppression and domination. At the center of this implicate context is the denial of these cognitive differences and how they have created group oppression. In 1989, a UN seminar on how racism and racial discrimination affects the social and economic relations between the Aboriginal Peoples and modern states concluded that racism toward Indigenous Peoples was a new form of global racism—a racism that assumes the guise of state theories about cultural and biological superiority. These theories have then been used to justify rejecting the legitimacy or viability of Indigenous People's own values and institutions.[4]

In articulating justice as a form of healing, Aboriginal Peoples are not trying to construct an abstract or universal theory of justice in the Eurocentric tradition. In other words, we are not obsessed with constructing a universal, normative theory of justice or adopting a Eurocentric theory of rational ideas about the good and the just. Instead, we are attempting to grasp the wisdom of our Elders, to define ourselves, to articulate a certain way of healing, and to apply it to our traumatic experiences.

Many Aboriginal people are working to create forms and processes for healing themselves based on their knowledge, traditions, and values. This effort will create many methods of healing and views of justice, reflective of our cultural diversity. While there is no single theory of Aboriginal justice, a common theme affirms the foundation of our knowledge, our people, and ourselves. The goal of healing is not to assimilate to the other but rather to allow ourselves to live in a world as Aboriginal people who feel connected with our unique, shared culture. We do not want to be healed in a manner that would make us feel disconnected from our identities or feel that our identities are better suited to other societies.

We feel it is important that our visions of justice as healing be founded on our knowledge and language—rooted in our experiences and feelings of our knowledge, jurisprudence, and language—as well as be founded on our experiences and feelings of wrongs and indignation. These emotions cannot be avoided in creating our vision of justice. Our vision of justice is to be based on Aboriginal knowledge about the nature of humans, our society, and our linguistic mode of understanding the ecology. We cannot simply borrow the Eurocentric versions of human nature or psychology or society, since they are not based on our wisdom, knowledge, or language. They have never known who we are.

Our visions of justice as healing, embedded as they are in Aboriginal traditions, are concerned with equitable processes or ceremonies to resolve conflicts more than with substantive rules. When Aboriginals say a certain behavior or rule is wrong, they are constructing a cultural vision of justice. Our vision of justice as healing recognizes that when an appropriate healing process is clear but is not followed, expressions of abhorrence at the wrong and demands for justice are often subtle ways of tolerating wrongs. When we look for visions of justice, we should look at the best in our traditions of raising children, rather than consult Eurocentric books on justice. While we should be willing to dialogue about grand systematic European theories of justice in modern society, we should also clarify their failures and how they differ from our visions.

When we begin to formulate a view of our true identity, we are inevitably forced to understand our past oppression as well as to decolonize the criminal justice system. We need to acknowledge and affirm our worldview, language, consciousness, and order. Our vision of justice as healing requires that we understand the importance of our worldviews or landscapes, instead of validating a social theory of individualism. Our traditions and values emphasize the beauty of distinct consciousness and orders. We should not repress them for formal equality with our oppressor's values.

Indeed, we must acknowledge that equal treatment under the law arose from the idea of fairness and that this idea presupposes differences. If everything were the same, fairness would be a moot point. Yet contemporary notions of equality have a difficult time acknowledging or affirming the right of Aboriginal people to be different. Instead, they attempt to suppress all differences for a universal pretense of equality. Pretense is no substitute for knowing who we are. Knowing the value of having an authentic identity and learning how our traditional values can put us on the path of healing are far more important than validating alien ideas of justice.

The following pages explore healing paths. Varied as the paths may be, they are most successful when they are most rooted in our traditional values. We have described the first phase of the healing process as "Speaking the Truth." The authors name some of the realities of our lives, based as these realities are on our histories. The articles in chapter 1, "Calls to Reclaim Our Circles," address our history head-on and offer a clear call for us to assert our identities not only as survivors of genocide but as Aboriginal Peoples, supported by heritages that ensure our healing. In chapter 2, "Resisting Justice as Force," the articles challenge the notion that justice can be established through punishment. Force is not the Indigenous way of achieving balance and harmony in families and communities.

"Being a Good Relative" describes a second phase of healing. "We are all related" is a core teaching of Indigenous Peoples, and this truth of relatedness forms the backbone of healing. Just as harm occurs when we are not mindful of how we are related, so are we healed as we live more mindfully of our relatedness. This awareness is not reducible to specific techniques or practices. Instead, it constitutes our worldview, which then permeates every aspect of our lives and societies.

In chapter 3, "Healing Worldviews," the authors explore Indigenous worldviews of connectedness and show how they translate into healing paradigms of justice—paradigms that have operated and been successful for millennia. Central to these paradigms is the role of community, as the articles in chapter 4, "Respecting Community," discuss. As Aboriginal people, we hold our communities in our hearts wherever we go. It is painful to be separated from them, and it is painful for us when they are in pain. Our healing and their healing are interwoven. The articles in chapter 5, "Community Peacemaking," describe how communities are creating different ways to heal as communities and to use the healing power of being in community to heal their members who are in pain.

We have described the last phase of healing that this book explores as

"Relying on Our Own Ways." Given all that Indigenous Peoples have faced over the last few centuries, our challenge in healing today is to reclaim our heritage, jurisprudence, and knowledge as our foundation for responding to whatever arises. Whereas colonization would divorce us from our own ways, healing restores our rootedness in who we are as Indigenous Peoples, and this rootedness in our own ways empowers us to heal from harms and to survive.

The articles in chapter 6, "Responding to Harm's Legacy," consider how we as Aboriginal Peoples can most effectively respond to the legacy of genocidal harms that we have suffered. We need to protect our knowledge and culture. We need to demand that our history be acknowledged and that the immense harms against us not be denied. And we need to find paths through which these harms can be repaired—not superficially but substantively.

Relying on our own ways also involves decolonizing ourselves, and in the field of justice, decolonizing the criminal justice system insofar as it affects us. As the articles in chapter 7, "Shape-Shifting Systems," testify, decolonizing justice systems is beset with traps that would neutralize our efforts and try to appropriate our ways to perpetuate the established structures of colonial control. Yet some efforts at transforming the current system are making inroads and forming more therapeutic practices that can benefit our people or at least reduce their suffering.

Chapter 8, "Honoring Healing Paths," presents a range of examples of how communities are forging healing paths adapted to their needs, resources, and circumstances. Each community is different, and so how a community takes steps toward healing will be unique and different as well. Patterns do emerge, though, for how communities experience the ups and downs of healing, as the last article in this chapter discusses. These patterns seem to reflect the seasons and the four directions, which are so central to many of our teachings.

The book closes with a reflection on the larger challenges of restorative justice; namely, to apply what has been learned from practicing restorative justice values in individual cases to healing peoples, societies, and nations. Tackling the roots of harm—racism, colonization, historical harms, their ongoing legacies, and a win-lose cultural paradigm—poses a necessary and much needed next step for restorative justice.

*Notes*

1. Robert M. Baird and Stuart E. Rosenbaum, *Philosophy of Punishment* (Buffalo, NY: Prometheus, 1988).

2. See R. Gosse, J. Youngblood Henderson, and R. Carter, eds., *Continuing Poundmaker and Riel's Quest: Presentations Made at a Conference on Aboriginal Peoples and Justice* (Saskatoon: Purich, 1994).

3. *Royal Commission on the Donald Marshall Jr. Prosecution* (1989); *Report of the Aboriginal Justice of Inquiry of Manitoba* (1991); *Justice on Trial: Report of the Task Force on the Criminal Justice System and Its Impact on Indian and Métis People of Alberta* (1991); *Report of the Saskatchewan Indian Justice Review Committee* (1992).

4. *Report of the United Nations Seminar on the Effects of Racism and Racial Discrimination on the Social and Economic Relations between Indigenous Peoples and the States,* Commission on Human Rights, 45th Sess., UN Doc E/CN.4/1989/22 (1989). See Russel L. Barsh, "United Nations Seminar on Indigenous Peoples and States" (1989) 83 (3) *American Journal of International Law,* 599.

. . . .

*This introduction is based on an article by James Sa'ke'j Youngblood Henderson published in the very first issue of* Justice as Healing *(1995).*

# I
. . . .

## The Healing Process: Speaking the Truth

This text tells stories of courage. It also exposes experiences that should inspire great shame in the hearts of the perpetrators. It is my hope that by breaking the silence, meaningful and systemic change will occur within my lifetime. This change will occur when we all begin to accept our responsibilities and begin to examine more fully the contours of all oppression.

PATRICIA MONTURE-ANGUS
*Thunder in My Soul: A Mohawk Woman Speaks*

# Introduction: Naming Realities of Life

*Wanda D. McCaslin*

Aboriginal Peoples face certain realities of life—realities that are unique to our cultures and traditions, our histories, our communities, and our oppressive experiences with the dominant society. It makes sense to begin the healing journey with naming some of these realities. For one thing, it is good to know where we are as we step to the future. For another, it helps to know what we're actually dealing with—what we face. Then, of course, it is good to know the larger context of how we got to where we are. Why are we struggling with these issues? What histories brought us to this point?

People often try to minimize the pain and suffering that our ancestors suffered by viewing them as "mere history," as if this history has little to do with today's reality or as if the historical patterns of harm no longer exist. The patterns of abuse and harm do exist today, not only as today's reality but also as multigenerational legacies that will extend into the future, unless the patterns are changed. These legacies have everything to do with the problems we face in our families and communities.

The articles in this first section focus on the realities of our past and present. They frame the task of justice in terms of what needs to be healed. Here—and throughout the book—Aboriginal as well as non-Aboriginal authors name colonialism as the root pattern of harm. "When we talk about colonialism in the modern world," Chief Justice Robert Yazzie writes, "we are really talking about the conquest and control of nonwhite, non-European peoples. . . . [Colonialism] is a triangle of power in which the people at the top claim they have the right to control the people at the bottom."[1] John Boersig, the former director of the University of Newcastle's Legal Centre, discusses the meaning of *colonialism*:

> [Ania] Loomba defines "colonialism" as "the conquest and control of other people's land and goods." This process is one which involves physical invasion of another's land, the destruction of pre-existing social and cultural structures, an assumption of political and economic

control, the establishment of social relations based on racial inferiority, and the weakening of resistance to allow control of society. In this manner, therefore, colonialism can be seen as insinuating imperial control throughout every aspect of society and culture.[2]

Whereas many people in the dominant society rationalize this "imperial control" as being benevolent, fair, and even helpful—as trying to do the best for "the poor, unfortunate Aboriginal people"—the authors handily demolish this colonizer view. The impact of colonialism was and continues to be devastating not only to the physical existence of Indigenous Peoples and cultures but also to our mental, emotional, and spiritual being. James Sa'ke'j Youngblood Henderson writes:

> Four hundred years of colonialism around the Earth was a process of conscious choice supported by manipulated facts on the part of the colonizers. These 400 years have had tragic consequences for Indigenous peoples. The consequences are more than mere conquest or the exercise of tyrannical power, slavery, and genocide; they go to forced cognitive extinction. After the British treaties, the colonizers created a systemic colonialism and racism that estranged Indigenous peoples from their beliefs, languages, families, and identities; that deprived Indigenous peoples of their dignity, their confidence, their souls, and even their shadows.[3]

Moreover, colonialism is not simple or one-dimensional but complex and multifaceted. Its tentacles reach into countless areas of Indigenous life. Professor Youngblood Henderson writes:

> Systemic colonization cannot be reduced to one essential definition or a unified phenomenon; instances of oppression operate together as a collective consciousness and infect most modern theory. [The philosopher Iris] Young asserts that there are at least five faces of oppression: exploitation, marginalization, powerlessness, cultural imperialism, and violence. [Historian Lise] Noël argues that we must look at many levels of domination and oppression, since a person and a group can be oppressed or dominated in many different ways.[4]

The following articles "speak the truth" about these realities of colonialism. Chapter 1, "Calls to Reclaim Our Circles," begins with a statement by Lorna June McCue, a Dzakaza (hereditary chief) of the Ned'u'ten, who speaks the truth about how every aspect of her people's life and culture has been under attack and now suffers. Her people are in pain. The Aboriginal Healing Foundation speaks the truth about residential school abuse and its intergenerational legacies.

Addressing the historical context, Dr. Edward C. Valandra provides intimate snapshots from the Oceti Sakowin Oyate's history of how racist colonization has worked relentlessly to degrade Native Peoples in the United States. It stereotypes Native people as savages, Native cultures as uncivilized, Native suffering as unworthy of restitution, and inherent Native self-determination as inconsequential. It does these things in order to justify genocide and atrocities too horrific to conceptualize at times, such as the 1862 Dakota Death March, the focus of George Blue Bird's poem. Neither is racist colonization only in the past. It is very much alive in the dominant society, from the classroom to federal and state governments to the international and global spheres. As Harley Eagle observes, if restorative justice were understood as a way of life, these harms against peoples and their systemic consequences would be on the table and a central focus of the healing work, but they're not.

With these realities of oppression, though, are the realities of revitalization and healing among Native Peoples, as expressed in the Declaration of the World Council of Indigenous Peoples. Although the opportunity is always there for non-Natives to seek genuine reconciliation by first making things right, Professor Valandra and Professor McCue observe that we as Native Peoples are not waiting for this to happen before we get on with our own healing. We are engaging our traditional ways, reclaiming our heritages, asserting our inherent self-determination, and steadily moving beyond the confines imposed by our colonizers. Professor McCue affirms that Aboriginal Peoples are keenly aware of our responsibility to pass our traditions on to our children. In fulfilling this role, we reclaim justice not in a colonizer sense but in the traditional sense of preserving peace and harmony in our communities.

Chapter 2, "Resisting Justice as Force," compares these two concepts of justice. Ross Gordon Green and Kearney F. Healey suggest that Natives and non-Natives actually find common ground on matters of justice. Both more or less agree on the nature of wrongs. Indigenous youth convicted of violent crimes, for example, agree that harming others is wrong. The concepts of justice part company when it comes to deciding what to do about wrongs. The Indigenous response is to engage everyone affected in healing, so that the underlying causes of the harm can be addressed. This healing model calls for a holistic approach that teaches children "how to be a good relative" in their earliest years.

The colonial concept of justice generates a very different response to harms. Harold Johnson traces its history and shows it to be rooted in force and punishment, first by the church, then by the state. Because "justice" is forcibly imposed, it is intrinsically violent and oppressive. The problem is not *who* imposes force and punishment but the model itself. Whether a non-Native or a Native carries out colonizer justice, the effect will be the same, and it will not be "peace and good order."

Yet for millennia, conquering states and colonizers have known that trying to establish justice through violence and oppression does not go over well with the colonized. One colonizer response is to appeal to values of equality and fairness to make colonizing methods seem legitimate and just. In his two articles, James W. Zion responds to these appeals. Whereas genuine equality involves respecting and honoring differences, the colonizing practice of "equality" does not do this. With respect to Native Peoples, it basically says: "Indians will be treated equally insofar as they stop being Indians." This model of justice enforces conformity in the name of achieving fairness.

In turn, colonizer fairness means imposing "one law for all." But whose law is the one to be imposed? Who is favored and who is constrained by the "one law"? Historically, as Mr. Zion explains, given the obvious problems with trying to impose the conqueror's law on the conquered, European law has actually had numerous precedents for legal pluralism. Yet these practices have fallen short of honoring the inherent right of peoples to self-determination. Instead, colonizer states have used and still use slogans appealing to equality and fairness to justify their domination—to make the case that force, violence, and punishment are necessary to establish fair and equal justice.

By naming where we are, how we got here, what we face as peoples, and why we face what we do, we root ourselves in the realities of our lives as Indigenous Peoples. From there, we can explore how we are developing paths of meaningful change and healing.

## Notes

1. Robert Yazzie, "Indigenous Peoples and Postcolonial Colonialism," *Reclaiming Indigenous Voice and Vision*, ed. Marie Battiste (Vancouver, B.C.: UBC Press, 2000), 39, 43.

2. John Boersig, "Indigenous Youth and the Criminal Justice System," *Justice as Healing* (2003) 8:2, 8, n. 8. He quotes Ania Loomba, *Colonialism/Post-colonialism* (London: Routledge, 1998), 2. See also James S. Frideres, *Native People in Canada: Contemporary Conflicts*, 2nd ed. (Scarborough, ON: Prentice-Hall, 1983), 295–320.

3. James Sa'ke'j Youngblood Henderson, "The Context of the State of Nature," *Reclaiming Indigenous Voice and Vision*, 29.

4. Ibid., 30.

# Engaging a Healing Context

*Denise C. Breton*

Some of the material in the following section is unconventional. Views are expressed from a discourse that is rarely heard among non-Natives, even though such views are freely expressed and widely shared in many Native communities—as well as in many communities of color.

If you are a non-Native reader who is unfamiliar with this subject matter, you may find it uncomfortable. You may experience difficult, unsettling emotions. You may also find yourself rethinking many things.

From a healing perspective, these reactions are healthy in the larger process of transforming the social context that has generated harms in Native societies and among peoples of color for generations. Non-Natives who have reflected on the racism and colonialism inside us, for example, tend to identify these reactions with the cultural programming we have received since birth. These difficult emotions can serve as signs of unconscious, internalized white conditioning being triggered and brought to the surface, so that we can look at it, see how it has affected our psyches and hurt others, and let it go.

The assumption, of course, is that we are more than our cultural programming. When the beliefs, attitudes, and emotional habits internalized from our social environment set us up to conduct ourselves in disrespectful, hurtful, or oppressive ways, we have the option to tap the "more" that we are and to become more receptive to views that we may find personally challenging. Our capacity to listen expands. In this context, difficult emotions and our inner processing of them are to be welcomed. Such emotions can be used quite constructively in dismantling racism and colonialism and in helping us to become the kind of people and society we most want to be.

Even so, our internalized programming around these particular issues is complex and tenacious, and we often identify ourselves with how we have been raised to think. As a result, emotional reactions can hinder our ability to grasp what is actually being expressed. Personal issues and past experiences can be triggered. Sometimes it takes more than one read-through to take in the "truth-telling." Although struggling with the material in these ways can be demanding for readers, it can also be transformative.

The most unfruitful response, from a healing perspective, would be for non-Native readers to dismiss what is expressed or refuse to deal with it altogether. It is this particular use of white privilege that has contributed to such a gap in awareness in the first place. The fact that Natives often "speak the truth" in these ways and that non-Natives often are unfamiliar with this level of truth-telling suggests where the healing process might start; namely, with hearing voices and views that are often not heard.

Some pain is inherent in this process—both in telling hard realities and in hearing them. Yet healing is often painful. Surgeons inflict huge pain to effect healing. Therapists work similarly. Healing psychological wounds often begins with uncovering traumatizing experiences—facing them and then engaging in various forms of grieving for what has happened.

The goal of the following articles is every bit as challenging—to heal the wounds of whole peoples and cultures, as well as to confront the mind-sets and systems that continue to inflict these wounds. This healing process calls on our best self-reflective skills. If strong emotions start surfacing, readers might ask themselves: "What are these emotions about? Where do they come from? What might the emotions reveal not only about what I'm reading but also about me, the reader, and about the society I have been socialized to accept? How might these emotions serve to promote changes in my awareness?"

Harley Eagle, a Dakota who conducts programs on anti-racism, has observed in his work that the challenge for many non-Natives is to "listen without reacting." He notices that he himself sometimes forgets how unfamiliar non-Natives can be with views and feelings that are commonly shared and taken for granted among Natives. The more non-Natives can stay in a listening place, he says, the easier it becomes for them to "get to that place of hearing what Native folks have to say."

With a self-reflective, listening approach, the different responses to the material—upsetting, disorienting, or confusing though they may be—can be framed in a transformative context. The coming together of recurring Native understandings with recurring non-Native reactions to them can be a good thing, precisely because it is potentially so constructive in effecting deeper shifts.

# Warriors of Justice and Healing

*James Sa'ke'j Youngblood Henderson*

Since the Aboriginal legal scholar Professor Gloria Valencia-Weber of the University of New Mexico introduced the idea of Aboriginal lawyers as warriors of justice and healing, we have been expanding on her idea. For example, I am fond of Vaclav Havel's thoughts on "word arrows":

> Words that electrify society with their freedom and truthfulness are matched by words that mesmerize, deceive, enflame, madden, beguile, words that are harmful—lethal, even. The word as arrow.[1]

Another example is the Western Apache's teaching of stories as arrows. Nick Thompson, a Western Apache, taught linguist Keith Basso about this tradition of stories. Basso wrote:

> So someone stalks you and tells a story about what happened long ago. It doesn't matter if other people are around—you're going to know he's aiming that story at you. All of a sudden it *hits* you! It's like an arrow, they say. Sometimes it just bounces off—it's too soft and you don't think about anything. But when it's strong, it goes in deep and starts working on your mind right away. . . .
>
> Then you feel weak, real weak, like you are sick. You don't want to eat or talk to anyone. That story is working on you now. You keep thinking about it. That story is changing you now, making you want to live right. That story is making you want to replace yourself. You think only of what you did and what was wrong and you don't like it. So you want to live better. After a while, you don't like to think of what you did wrong. So you try to forget that story. You try to pull that arrow out. You think it won't hurt anymore, because now you want to live right. . . . Even so, that place will keep on stalking you.[2]

*Notes*

1. "Words on Words," *New York Review of Books*, 18 January 1990, 11.
2. Keith Basso, "Stalking with Stories: Names, Places and Moral Narratives among the Western Apache," *Antaaeus* 57 (Autumn 1986): 95–97.

. . . .

*This article was published in* Justice as Healing *(1995). The editor would like to thank James Sa'ke'j Youngblood Henderson for permission to publish his work.*

CHAPTER 1

. . . .

# Calls to Reclaim Our Circles

## Treaty-Making from an Indigenous Perspective: A Ned'u'ten-Canadian Treaty Model

*Lorna June McCue*

As a Dzakaza (hereditary chief), I see my people and ancestral territory in pain. I see our traditional governing system, the *bah'lats*, low in power and spirit. I see my people unbalanced, not living in harmony, and sad. They are distrustful of their own kind. I see Ned'u'ten territory pillaged, rivers polluted, forests and medicines depleted, and the population of animals decreased. I see money and unhealthy capitalistic values eroding Ned'u'ten principles of respect and bestowing wealth to all the people. I see many of my people on skid row in downtown Vancouver, dying from substance abuse. I see Elders drunk or dying young from heart disease, diabetes, and cancer. I see children being abused. I see my people being fooled again. Self-determination can be a painful process when your people are in pain already.

I have seen how Canada has dispossessed my people in the past. I see how Canada continues to oppress my people today. I see how Canada plans to continue the colonization of my people in the future. I see how Canada tries to claim legitimacy to Ned'u'ten territory. I see all her masks. I see Canada racing to innocence as I remove those masks and reveal her true identity.

As a Dzakaza, I have the responsibility of respecting my name, territory, and clan relations. It is also my responsibility to ensure that "the way we do things" is passed on to my children and generations after. I have used my conventional training and knowledge of my people's ways to develop a way to remove the pain my people feel and for Canadians to wipe away the shame that clings to their name. It is my gift to both of you.

This thesis proposes a way to bring peace to the Ned'u'ten and Canada.

It is a study that reflects my perspective as a Dzakaza and scholar. It is also a critical assessment of how Canada has used Doctrines of Dispossession to hurt my people, to hurt my land. The right to self-determination and right to decolonization are two frameworks that I use to release the pain that my people feel, to liberate their spirits, and to wipe away the shame of Canada's name in Ned'u'ten territory. It is my hope to convince you that a healthy relationship can be established between the Ned'u'ten and Canada based on how the Ned'u'ten establish peace and harmony with each other and neighboring peoples.

. . . .

*Published in* Justice as Healing *(1999) 4:1, this article served as the introduction of Professor McCue's thesis, which she submitted for a Master of Laws Degree for the Faculty of Graduate Studies (Faculty of Law) at the University of British Columbia in 1998. In full, her thesis advanced the position that the Ned'u'ten, an Indigenous People whose territories are located along Lake Babine in what is now northern British Columbia, have the right to decolonize and self-determine their political and legal status at the international level. The editor would like to thank Professor McCue for permission to publish her work.*

# Residential Schools and the Intergenerational Legacy of Abuse

## *The Aboriginal Healing Foundation*

Residential schools officially operated in Canada between 1892 and 1969 through arrangements between the Canadian government and the Roman Catholic Church, the Church of England (or Anglican Church), the Methodist (or United) Church, and the Presbyterian Church. Enforcing the government's assimilation policy and the missionary agenda of the churches, the schools strove to alienate children from their families, communities, and cultures. The schools forced children to abandon their cultural and spiritual ways, imposed foreign religious practices on them, punished students for speaking their languages, and, in many cases, provided only marginal training or education.

As late as the 1950s, more than 40 percent of the schools' teaching staff had no professional training. The underfunding of the system left the children living in squalor and poverty, without suitable facilities, clothing, or food. Although the government officially withdrew its support of these schools in 1969, a few of the schools continued operating throughout the 1960s, 1970s, and 1980s. Akaitcho Hall in Yellowknife did not close until the 1990s.

Generations of Aboriginal children sent to these schools faced a strict and often damaging policy of assimilation. Physical, emotional, and sexual abuse were rampant, and little was done to stop the abuse, punish the abusers, or improve conditions. Instead, the Department of Indian Affairs attempted to deny and cover up the problems.

According to the Royal Commission on Aboriginal Peoples (RCAP) report, there was "a pronounced and persistent reluctance on the part of the department to deal forcefully with incidents of abuse, to dismiss, as was its right, or to lay charges against school staff who abused the children."[1]

Physical and sexual abuse in residential schools put children in a situation where they continually felt trauma but had no way to release their feelings. This release would have helped them resolve the trauma. Most children in residential schools were told that the abuse was their own fault. Children who saw other children abused in the schools also felt trauma, because they were helpless to stop the abuse.

Not everyone who went to a residential school was sexually or physically abused, but all who attended felt the impact of that abuse. Indeed, the impact of the residential schools has been felt in every segment of Aboriginal societies.

Unresolved trauma continues to affect individuals, families, and communities. Intergenerational or multigenerational trauma happens when the effects of trauma are not resolved in one generation, allowing patterns of abuse to continue. The patterns of abuse that are passed from one generation to the next include not only physical and sexual abuse but also low self-esteem, anger, depression, violence, addictions, unhealthy relationships, fear, shame, compulsiveness, lack of good parenting skills, body pain, and panic attacks.

Breaking the cycle of abuse that began in residential schools is essential if Aboriginal communities are to be healthy, loving places in which children can be raised with love. Stopping abuse and helping families learn how they can support their own well-being is the dream of many Aboriginal people, and it is what the mission statement of the Aboriginal Healing Foundation is all about.

## The Aboriginal Healing Foundation

After years of resistance, protest, and activism on the part of many Aboriginal people and others, the first major steps toward healing began. The churches involved in running the schools publicly apologized. The first to apologize was the United Church of Canada in 1986. This was followed by the apologies of the Oblate Missionaries of Mary Immaculate in 1991, the Anglican Church in 1993, and the Presbyterian Church in 1994.

Around the same time, the Royal Commission on Aboriginal Peoples was examining the issue of residential schools as part of its larger mandate, and in November 1996, its final report was released. Included in the report was a section outlining research and findings on residential schools and containing three recommendations specific to residential schools.

Finally, the government took its first step when a "reconciliation" statement and a healing strategy were announced in 1998. On 7 January 1998, the federal government announced *Gathering Strength: Canada's Aboriginal*

*Action Plan*, a strategy to begin a process of reconciliation and renewal with Aboriginal Peoples.[2]

## Notes

1. Royal Commission on Aboriginal Peoples (RCAP) Report (Ottawa, Ont.: Indian and Northern Affairs Canada, 1996), 369.

2. Editor's note: Non-Canadian readers may find some background information helpful. According to the Library of Parliament's Web site: "The RCAP issued its final report in November 1996. The five-volume, 4,000-page report covered a vast range of issues; its 440 recommendations called for sweeping changes to the relationship between Aboriginal and non-Aboriginal people and governments in Canada. In response, Aboriginal communities and organizations pressed for action on the recommendations.

"The report centered on a vision of a new relationship, founded on the recognition of Aboriginal peoples as self-governing nations with a unique place in Canada. It set out a 20-year agenda for change, recommending new legislation and institutions, additional resources, a redistribution of land, and the rebuilding of Aboriginal nations, governments, and communities.

"Recognizing that autonomy is not realistic without significant community development, RCAP called for early action in four areas: healing, economic development, human resources development, and the building of Aboriginal institutions. The Commission's implementation strategy proposed that governments increase spending to reach $1.5 billion by Year 5 of the strategy, and $2 billion in the subsequent 15 years. The report argued that the additional investment over 20 years would save money in the long term.

"The Royal Commission report was generally welcomed by Aboriginal groups, although not without some disagreement, and generated expectations for a government response. It received significant media attention upon its release, but faded from the public agenda in the ensuing months. In December 1996, the Prime Minister said that the government needed time to study the recommendations and would not issue a response prior to a general election. The then Minister of Indian Affairs stated that it would be difficult to increase spending to the level proposed by the Commission. In April 1997, the Assembly of First Nations held a national day of protest to express its anger over perceived government inaction and the refusal of the Prime Minister to meet with First Nations leaders to discuss the report.

"In January 1998, the government responded to the RCAP report. *Gathering Strength: Canada's Aboriginal Action Plan* set out a policy framework for future government action based on four objectives, each encompassing a number of elements."

This included the establishment of the Aboriginal Healing Foundation with its $350 million healing fund. See the Canadian Library of Parliament's Web site: www.parl. gc.ca/information/library/PRBpubs/prb9924-e.htm

. . . .

*This article was published in* Justice as Healing *(1999) 4:4 and is reprinted here with the permission of the Aboriginal Healing Foundation.*

# Decolonizing "Truth": Restoring More than Justice

*Edward C. Valandra*

## Colonial Oppression as Trauma

Trauma. The word carries immense weight in reconciliation and in reparative and restorative justice circles. Trauma conjures up horrific images and feelings of deep, unresolved pain for both those on the receiving end of harm and those who inflict it. In both cases, guilt, shame, misdirected anger, and outright rage, though hidden from the public eye, find outlets in destructive behaviors. These behaviors range from the individual struggling with an addiction to unhealthy patterns of relationships to a society that, through its basic institutions, inculcates violence as a way of life, most blatantly as the killing of civilians in the name of "national interest."

For Native Peoples, being dispossessed of our homelands through imperialism constitutes the greatest form of trauma, from which we have not recovered. Furthermore, colonialism—as a project of this imperialism perpetrated initially by Europeans and now Americans—remains a major cause of trauma for Native Peoples. Indeed, an honest view of the Native experience with colonialism can only be described in one word: holocaust. To argue otherwise maintains an important feature of the colonial project: outright denial. As recently as January 2003, many Americans, despite clear historical evidence to the contrary, thought that terms such as *imperialism* or *imperialists, colonialism* or *colonialists,* and *occupation* or *occupiers* did not apply to them. But the unprovoked attack against the Iraqi people and the subsequent occupation of Iraq by the Americans changed that, piercing the bubble of denial.

It may seem as if I digress from discussing trauma to Native Peoples when I speak of the invasion of Iraq. However, the American conduct toward the Iraqi people feels unnervingly familiar to Natives. When asked by *The Circle,* a Native newspaper serving Minneapolis–St. Paul, Minnesota, about my thoughts on the one-month-old war against Iraq, I remarked, "Native people understand what the Iraqi people are going through. Native

Americans know about pre-emptive strikes, regime change, assets in trust, American occupation. . . . [M]y advice to the Iraqi people is 'hold on to your wallet.' . . . When they [the white leadership] talk about genocide or repression by a brutal regime [like Saddam Hussein's] . . . that's our history [too, but with the Americans]." This view, popular or not, contains hard-to-dispute truths that are basic to discussing the traumas Native Peoples have experienced. These truths are also central to healing among Natives and to a possible reconciliation with our *wasicu* colonizers, the American people.

## Genocide Is THE Trauma

When I drive from the Rosebud Reservation to Mni Luzahan, I sometimes travel through the Pine Ridge Reservation. Having my share of relatives and friends living there, I stop for a chat, catch up on the latest happenings, and share what is going on within my tiospaye (see the *Glossary* at the end of this article). But then there is another visit that I sometimes make, namely, to Wounded Knee, where at least 300 unarmed Lakota women, children, and men were ruthlessly butchered by American soldiers in December 1890. Even after 110 years, it is a painful place. We still mourn at the mass grave. We still leave prayer offerings. My nation's grief over this massacre is immeasurable, and so is our anger and rage at this senseless murder of people, especially defenseless Elders, women, and children.

But Wounded Knee is not the only time when my people have cruelly suffered and died at American hands. When driving between St. Paul, Minnesota, and the Rosebud Reservation, I stop at Mankato, Minnesota, to honor the thirty-eight Dakota patriots who were hanged in December 1862. This public execution is the largest revenge killing of its kind carried out in the United States. Moreover, the hanging is part of a larger story. At Fort Snelling, Minnesota, approximately 1,700 Dakota, primarily women and children, were interned. This mass internment is arguably the forerunner of both the concentration camps and the detention centers of modern times. In November 1862 prior to their internment, these 1,700 Dakota were forcibly marched along a route that is part of my drive. Our oral tradition describes this horrific 150-mile march: "An unknown number of men, women, and children died along the way from beatings and other assaults perpetrated by both [American] soldiery and [white] citizens. Dakota people of today still do not know what became of their bodies."

Our colonizers have perpetrated many other horrific acts (both historic and contemporary) against us, the Oceti Sakowin Oyate. It is these acts that inform our understanding of what a white leader like George W. Bush really means when he brags to his fellow colonizers about bringing "American justice" to those who resist imperialism. A candid assessment of the wasicu attitude toward Native Peoples readily shows that they always believed Native Peoples to be expendable in order to preserve their Master Narrative as Occupier.[1]

Not surprisingly, this Native holocaust receives very little attention from colonial-based institutions. An education, public or private, in the United States grudgingly concedes that Columbus did not "discover" America but avoids talking about genocide. For example, using qualified terminology, such as "Indian Removal," textbooks minimize the ethnic-cleansing of thousands of Native Peoples east of the Mississippi River. By contrast, the Cherokee People who were on the receiving end of this policy—and who to this day still suffer from it—have a more appropriate and descriptive term: "The Trail of Tears."

The horrific truth of this ethnic cleansing of the Cherokee people—the truth that textbooks avoid telling—staggers the imagination and closely parallels the Germans' twentieth-century policy toward the Jews:[2]

> This history of this removal . . . may well exceed in weight of the grief and pathos any other passage in American history. Even the much-sung exile of the Acadians falls far behind it in its sum of death and misery. Under [General Winfield] Scott's orders, the troops were disposed at various points throughout the Cherokee country, where stockade forts were erected for gathering in and holding the Indians preparatory to removal. From these, squads of troops were sent to search out with rifle and bayonet every small cabin hidden away in the coves or by the sides of the mountain streams, to seize and bring in as prisoners all the occupants, however or wherever they might be found.
>
> Families at dinner were startled by the sudden gleams of bayonets in the doorway and rose up to be driven with blows and oaths along the weary miles of trail that led to the stockade. Men were seized in their field or going along the road, women were taken from their wheels and children from their play. In many cases . . . they saw their homes in flames, fired by the lawless rabble that followed on the heels

of the soldiers to loot and pillage. So keen were these outlaws on the
scent that in some instances they were driving off the cattle and other
stock of the Indians almost before the soldiers had fairly started their
owners in the other direction. . . . To prevent escape [of the Cherokee]
the soldiers had been ordered to approach and surround each house,
so far as possible, to come upon the occupants without warning.[3]

These and countless other actions by the colonizers to exterminate Native
Peoples go untold and unquestioned. In fact, when these acts are recounted,
they are viewed as a given—something unfortunate but nonetheless accepted—
under the rubric of manifest destiny or Darwin's "survival of the fittest."

Like the Cherokee, my people have experienced their share of lethal
Native-hating from the wasicu. Successful armed resistance to the annexation of our land from around 1850 to 1877 provided white imperialists with
an excuse to commit genocide as *the* final solution to their vexing "Sioux
Problem." In his governor's address to Minnesota's state legislators, white
leader Alexander Ramsey declared in September 1862 that, "The Sioux Indians [Dakota] of Minnesota must be exterminated or driven forever beyond
the borders of the state." Following Ramsey's ethnic-cleansing call, ordinary
Americans in Minnesota, like the ordinary Germans who answered Hitler's
call to exterminate Jews seventy years later, saw to it that any Dakota found
in the state became prime candidates for white bloodlust.

Not long after Ramsey declared his ethnic-cleansing policy, white military leaders believed a display of deadly force would intimidate the Oceti
Sakowin Oyate. Hence, white general Patrick Connor issued a directive to the
3,100 American soldiers in the 1865 Powder River expedition: "You will not
receive overtures of peace or submission from Indians [Lakota, Cheyenne,
and Arapaho] but will attack and kill every male Indian over twelve years of
age." Successful resistance by the Oceti Sakowin Oyate ended this expedition, but it furthered a campaign to subjugate us. In December 1866, after
the Oceti Sakowin Oyate led a stunning defeat of the Americans, another
white military leader, William Sherman, wrote to his white superior, President Grant: "We [the white colonizers] must act with vindictive earnestness
against the Sioux, even to their extermination, men, women, and children."

In the wasicu version of these events, the Oceti Sakowin Oyate are portrayed
as the ruthless perpetrators who deserve to be killed for having commit-

ted terrible harms against the poor, innocent white "pioneers and settlers." This version disregards the factual record, which shows that ordinary whites were *regularly* violating all norms of human decency—breaking treaties, trespassing, stealing property, committing murder, and carrying out other depredations—and that we (along with other Native Peoples) were simply defending ourselves against extermination.

When wasicu are confronted with this horrific record, their standard reply is to dismiss this period as an aberration or simply as an unenlightened episode in the colonizer's otherwise glorious history. At other times, like the notorious Abu Ghraib prison scandal in Iraq, far too many wasicu use the "few bad apples" line to explain away atrocities and to absolve themselves of any responsibility. The use of the "bad apple" line is not unknown to the Oceti Sakowin Oyate. We have many stories of the torture and death that occurred in white-run boarding schools, white-run insane asylums, white-run hospitals, white-run prisons, and white border towns. By invoking the "few bad apples" dodge, our colonizers somehow fail to admit or acknowledge their role in these institutions. In other words, white society and its imperial system turns a blind eye to the homicide or torture of colonized people.

Reality, of course, bites deep into the occupier's sanitized story of their "pioneering and settling" of Native North America. Because Oceti Sakowin Oyate patriots continue to challenge the Americans' presence in our land, the cultural programming of a latter-day Ramsey, Connor, and Sherman to kill Indians can reemerge, as it did in 1973. Once again, our colonizers' response to our acts of self-determination at Wounded Knee was to militarily prepare for invasion. In addition to the "17 APCs, 130,000 rounds of M-16 ammunition, 41,000 rounds of M-1 ammunition, 24,000 flares, 12 M-79 grenade launchers, 600 cases of C-S gas, 100 rounds of M-40 high explosives, as well as helicopters, Phantom jets, and personnel" made available to its surrogates,[4] the military also "had billeted a fully uniformed and armed assault unit on twenty-four hour alert."[5]

The authorization to use this much lethal force against the comparatively defenseless Native Peoples at Wounded Knee reaffirmed the American aphorism that "the only good Indian is a dead Indian." It also reminded a dismayed world that, for Native Peoples, physical extermination is our constant companion.[6] In the post-termination era (1968–present), rather than subjugating us, this invasion served as a political watershed and rekindled our national desire to end our colonization.

Despite the overwhelming record documenting the Oceti Sakowin Oyate's claim that a holocaust transpired—and is transpiring—here in Native North America, another typical reaction by our colonizers is to victimize those subjected to the holocaust with misrepresentations. For example, the official line characterizes the 1890 Wounded Knee Massacre as a "battle." As evidence, colonizers cite the twenty-nine Congressional Medals of Honor bestowed upon the "brave" American soldiers who waged that "fight," perhaps making this so-called battle the most highly awarded in U.S. military history. With so many medal-of-honor recipients, how could Wounded Knee be anything but a battle, right?

Not so. Many of our ancestors survived the soldiers' butchery and lived to tell about it. Based on the survivors' accounts, the Oceti Sakowin Oyate's oral tradition of what happened at Wounded Knee differs remarkably from the official record of our colonizers. The scant candid testimony that does exist about Wounded Knee among those colonizers who were at the scene and who were willing to speak corroborates our claim that Wounded Knee was not merely an "unfortunate incident." Their voices support the larger claim that a policy of genocide was directed against the Oceti Sakowin Oyate. First Lieutenant James D. Mann, for instance, admitted on his deathbed that by yelling "Fire men! Fire!" he gave the order to shoot indiscriminately into the Lakota who were encircled by the soldiers.[7]

The night before the massacre, the soldiers who would participate in the next day's slaughter purchased whiskey from Edward Assay, a white Indian trader.[8] Another man, a freighter, confessed to Reverend James Garvey that he never forgave himself for delivering the whiskey to the soldiers.[9] Several years later, the bodies of the dead soldiers were exhumed from their initial graves at Wounded Knee to be reburied elsewhere. These corpses told their own gruesome story: "The attending physician expected to find only the bones but was shocked to find bodies intact after so many years. His only explanation for this . . . [was] that the soldiers had consumed large quantities of alcohol and the alcohol preserved the bodies."[10]

Naturally, the Oceti Sakowin Oyate assume that apologists will name alcohol as the culprit and thus once again deflect responsibility away from the American empire. Yet a competing story—our story—to the occupier's narrative remains. A mass murder of women, children, and men at Wounded Knee occurred and constitutes, at the very least, a revenge killing for a real battle in which nearly 300 wasicu soldiers died at the hands of the Lakota, Cheyenne, and Arapaho fourteen years earlier.

In light of the statements by Ramsey, Connor, and Sherman, however, the 1890 massacre at Wounded Knee constitutes far more. It represents a calculated, strategic action on our colonizers' part to commit genocide. With the exception of the United States and a handful of other countries, the world has come to understand genocide or the extermination of a people in a precise way. This internationally agreed-upon understanding forms a basis for talking about a Native holocaust and explains why our colonizers refuse to accept that a holocaust ever occurred.

Shortly after World War II ended, the "civilized" world learned, much to its "morbid fascination,"[11] how the Germans had committed atrocities that, over a span of a few years, caused the physical extermination of about 6,000,000 Jews. Responding to the outcry against this massive premeditated killing, the American, British, French, and Russian governments had, as victors, established the Nuremberg Tribunal. The main purpose of this tribunal was to prosecute the Germans responsible for these atrocities, and subsequently several Germans were held to account for the Jewish Holocaust. The tribunal convicted and sentenced them for committing the greatest of all crimes against humanity: genocide. Not long after the tribunal ended its work, the United Nations took up the question of genocide. A genocide treaty was eventually adopted by the UN Assembly in 1948. For the Oceti Sakowin Oyate, however, the UN's adoption began a real nightmare: the Americans' unwillingness to comply with the genocide treaty. We *know* why.

It is the definition of genocide that most worries the occupiers of our land. Article II of the treaty defines genocide "as resulting from the following categories or acts committed with the intent to destroy, in whole or in part, a national, ethnical [sic], racial, or religious group":

1. killing members of a group;
2. causing serious bodily or mental harm to members of the group;
3. deliberately inflicting on the group conditions of life calculated to bring about its physical destruction in whole or in part;

4. imposing measures intended to prevent births within the group; and

5. forcibly transferring children of the group to another group.

The Oceti Sakowin Oyate can easily produce a list of grievances perpetrated by ordinary whites and their leaders that fall within each of the five categories or that represent combinations thereof. Of the first recognized act, the 1854 Blue Water and the 1890 Wounded Knee massacres are but two of the more well-known killings. Critics, of course, dismiss these massacres as beyond the treaty's scope. Because they happened a long time ago, the colonizers' descendants presumably cannot be held accountable. Well, this attempt to flee responsibility collapses, because acts of genocide have no statute of limitation, especially when these acts have intergenerational consequences.

Moreover, the Oceti Sakowin Oyates' independence movement in the early 1970s broke through the colonial facade of respecting human rights. Our colonizers called in the proverbial "cavalry," reminding us that the time is not past when "Indian killing" can be a national pastime. Much to our discomfort, the Oceti Sakowin Oyate are now watching our colonizers refit the "hostile Indian" image to the "Arab or Muslim terrorists" of today. Here again, "killing members of a group" remains entirely acceptable to Americans in promoting their "national" interests.

As for the other genocide categories, our oral tradition reveals that our colonizers have waged and continue to wage a campaign of terror throughout our homeland. During the 1970s, this terrorism did not preclude killing our traditional Lakota people who viewed the American occupation of our homeland as illegal or those who wanted our colonizers to honor the 1868 Treaty of Fort Laramie. Traditional people who moved away from the Indian Reorganization Act (IRA) governments politically and toward self-determination were silenced through intimidation.[12] Indeed, the colonial administration (the FBI, U.S. Marshals, the BIA, the military, South Dakota, and the courts) refused to fully investigate, apprehend, indict, or prosecute those who threatened our families with physical harm, death, or some other form of reprisal (e.g., incarceration). Such conduct by our colonizers contributed to the atmosphere of terror.

Understandably, the five acts that constitute the crime of genocide make a colonizer like the United States, given its horrific behavior toward Native

Peoples, feel—as it should—more than a bit uncomfortable. However, two of the treaty's articles, Articles III and IX, are without question unbearable for our colonizers. Article III makes genocidal acts punishable crimes. These acts include

1. genocide itself;
2. the conspiracy to commit genocide;
3. the direct and public incitement to commit genocide;
4. the attempt to commit genocide; and
5. complicity in genocide.

Together, Articles II and III frame our understanding of how the international community judges a state and its nationals for engaging in genocide. However, it is Article IX that our colonizers most fear. This article provides that questions or disputes surrounding the treaty's interpretation, application (which includes a state's responsibility for genocide), and fulfillment can be submitted to the International Court of Justice (ICJ). For many Natives and others who have studied the genocide treaty, this article is key.

Not surprisingly, our colonizers "ratified" the treaty on one blanket condition; namely, that they reserve unto themselves the right of exemption from any of the treaty's provisions. In particular, our colonizers have exempted themselves from Article IX. Vine Deloria Jr. wryly commented that this acrobatic political move would have allowed even Germany to go scot-free for the atrocities it had committed against the Jews.[13] In effect, by "ratifying" the genocide treaty so conditionally, our colonizers proclaimed to a stunned world their right to engage in genocidal conduct against the Oceti Sakowin Oyate as well as every other Native nation. This stance by the Americans is indeed a Native Peoples' nightmare and must be rebuked.

Given that our colonizers have now manipulated the ratification of a document so fundamental as the right to exist as peoples, how do we proceed? Before tackling this question, we must ponder a more basic question: Are our colonizers so spiritually and morally bankrupt that they lack a "making-it-right" sensibility whenever it involves Native Peoples? With few exceptions, the Oceti Sakowin Oyate will emphatically answer "yes." Such brutal honesty comes at a price, though. It exposes our colonizers' epic settlement story—their reason for being here—to be nothing more than a self-serving fable. How can such a fable justify the cost our colonizers have extracted from us?

This truth-telling invariably makes them defensive, which they express as either extreme anger or denial or both.

## Truth and Reconciliation: The Antidote for Colonizers

From time to time, though, a colonizer or two (so far, never enough to reach a critical mass for change in dealing with Native Peoples) has struggled with this basic question of moral bankruptcy. For instance, during the heyday of the termination era, hundreds of thousands of Natives were forced into mainstream society so that our colonizers could carry out a massive land grab. Harold Fey, a white writer and an editor for *The Christian Century*, was disturbed at what he saw happening to Native Peoples. In March 1955, Fey, with sarcasm, posed some unsettling questions to his fellow settlers:

> Why don't the Indians trust us? We mean well toward them. We want them to succeed. Indeed, we would be glad if the Indians were just like ourselves, and what more could they desire than that? We are not like some nations we could mention—deceivers, slave-drivers, treaty-breakers. We are upright people, and it irritates us a little to have to say so. Some of us are in the habit of referring to the United States as a Christian nation. So if the Indian does not trust us, it must be because he has some unfortunate defect in his own character, such as innate suspicion. If so, that is something we should help him overcome. . . . These things we say to ourselves to calm the uneasiness which clings to the fact that we are not trusted by the original Americans, who have known us longer than anybody else.[14]

Nearly fifty years have passed since Fey posed these questions, and yet his challenge remains unmet. What are our colonizers willing to do in order to start building a much-needed trust? We still await an *authentic* dialogue with our colonizers, one that would even begin to address the numerous harms, past and present, perpetrated against the Oceti Sakowin Oyate.

To be sure, others since Fey have wrestled with the Colonial Question with respect to Native Peoples. In February 1990, white leader George Mickelson (South Dakota governor) proclaimed a year of reconciliation:

WHEREAS, As the State of South Dakota celebrates the beginning of its second century, we must also remember that statehood was a very sad time for the Native American; and,

WHEREAS, Two tragic events, the killing of Sitting Bull, on December 15, 1890, and the Wounded Knee massacre on December 29, 1890, occurred just 13 months after South Dakota became a state; and,

WHEREAS, The anniversary of these tragic conflicts, as well as the celebration of 100 years of statehood, offer an opportunity for South Dakotans to learn more about the life and culture of the Dakota-Lakota people; and,

WHEREAS, Strife between the cultures in South Dakota has, for 100 years, been of grave concern and continues to be of great concern; and,

WHEREAS, Any improvement in cultural understanding in the past can be attributed to the work of the Indian and non-Indian people of South Dakota who have striven to understand our differences and to educate those of us who have grown up together but who have never made the effort to bridge the cultural gap; and,

WHEREAS, A statewide effort to develop trust and respect between Indians and non-Indians can, and must, include participation from the private and public sector, from churches and church associations, from tribal and state governments, and from individuals and community organizations; and,

WHEREAS, That mutuality of interest provides a sound basis for constructive change, given a shared commitment to achieving our goals of equal opportunity, social justice and economic prosperity; and,

WHEREAS, By celebrating our cultural differences and drawing on those differences for the betterment of all, we can create a new respect among our citizens:

NOW, THEREFORE, I, GEORGE S. MICKELSON, Governor of the State of South Dakota, do hereby proclaim, with the advice and consent of the state's tribal leaders, 1990 as a

YEAR OF RECONCILIATION

in South Dakota, and call on our citizens, both Indian and non-Indian, to look for every opportunity to lay aside fears and mistrust, to build friendships, to join together and take part in shared cultural activities, to learn about one another, to have fun with one another, and to begin a process of mutual respect and understanding that will continue to grow into South Dakota's second hundred years.

Without flinching, the governor noted that the resident colonizers had just finished "celebrating" *their* 100 years of statehood, and I suppose statehood was, to put it mildly, "a very sad time" for my people. After all, prior to South Dakota's establishment as a state on 2 November 1889, the colonizers' ancestors had cleared a path to present-day statehood by imposing two illegal partitions of our 26,000,000-acre homeland, shown on older maps as the Great Sioux Reservation. These two partitions resulted in the dubious "annexation" of our homeland by our colonizer(s).

The first partition occurred in February 1877. To this day, the 7,300,000 acres of partitioned land are officially acknowledged as stolen property, and as stolen property the Oceti Sakowin Oyate demand its rightful return. The colonizers, however, view the land's return as antithetical to their Occupier Narrative, and so instead of returning the 7.3 million acres, they have insulted us by offering money to justify their theft.

Despite this 128-year (and still counting) wrongful taking, despite the commercial development of the land, and despite the restrictions placed on our access to it, the Oceti Sakowin Oyate maintain their relationship to He Sapa. Unlike our colonizers, we are intimately familiar with He Sapa's many ancient places, calling them either Wamaka Ognaka Onakizin or Tatanka Tacante.[15] Indeed, He Sapa is fondly known as "the heart of our home, and the home of our heart."[16] Because of our love for He Sapa—and to underscore the unhealed wound between us and our colonizers—we continually refuse to accept any of the monetary compensation that our colonizers have offered for their admitted theft of our land. As the center of our spiritual universe, He Sapa is not for sale, and we remain committed to its rightful return.

The second partition, called the Great Sioux Agreement Act, happened in March 1889, eight months before Dakota Territory became the two states of South and North Dakota. With 18,700,000 acres remaining of the Great Sioux Reservation, our colonizers wanted between 9,000,000 to 11,000,000 acres of the reservation "opened." One colonizer admitted why a second partition was desired just twelve years after the first one: "One of the obstacles to achieving [South Dakota] Statehood was the huge reservation separating the Black Hills and the settlements easts [sic] of the Missouri River. With the news that the Dakota Indians had agreed to sell eleven million acres of land for $1.25 an acre, South Dakota became a state on November 2, 1889."[17] Depicting the Oceti Sakowin Oyate (the "Dakota Indians") as an "obstacle," the colonizer's story is obviously skewed against my people, and our response to this lie is our usual refrain: "So what else is new?"

The one story purposely omitted from the lie concerns the "land sale" and how it came about. Not surprisingly, the Occupier Narrative fails to explain what made us "agree to sell" so much land in the first place. Fortunately, Deloria fills in the crucial information:

> Some years after the great plains wars, pressure grew to allot the Great Sioux reservation which extended over almost all of western South Dakota. Thousands of [land] hungry whites demanded that the vast reservation be allotted and the surplus lands be opened to white settlement. Thus it was that General Crook, "Three Stars[,]" was sent out to negotiate the Great Sioux Agreement of 1889. With Crook sitting at the table[,] the Sioux were reminded that if they didn't agree to cede their lands[,] the Army would come in and exterminate them. In spite of such pressure by the United States government[,] less than 10 per cent of the adult males signed the paper agreeing to the cession.
>
> Claiming total accord [with Article 12 of the 1868 Ft. Laramie Treaty], the negotiators rushed to Washington and pushed the agreement through Congress as a statute.[18]

In other words, the critical and contested point about these two land partitions—"ceded land" in colonial-speak—concerns their legal status. Article 12 of the 1868 Fort Laramie Treaty is clear about what the Oceti Sakowin Oyate require before any land cession could be considered valid:

> No treaty for the cession of any portion or part of the [Great Sioux] reservation herein described which may be held in common shall be of any validity or force as against the said Indians ["Sioux Nation" in

colonial-speak], unless executed and signed by at least three-fourths of all the adult male Indians.

In the case of both partitionings, our colonizers utterly failed to obtain our consent, and any claim of legality is pure fiction. Without our approval, then, the Oceti Sakowin Oyate position is that the resident colonizers are illegal aliens and that their state, carved from the Great Sioux Reservation, is illegitimate.

The greatest difficulty of reconciliation, therefore, is that our colonizers— with whom we have sometimes developed close relationships—fail to see themselves as perpetuators or agents of the status quo. In an 11 March 1990 editorial, four weeks after the governor proposed reconciliation, the *Rapid City Journal* informed its readership that Mickelson "opposed negotiations to give land back to the Sioux." Here, again, we are not surprised by how our colonizers frame the land return debate, missing the bigger picture necessary for reconciliation. "To give land back" assumes that the land rightfully belonged to our colonizers, but the record shows otherwise. Because the land in question is stolen property, *the only thing our colonizers are in a position to do is to return—not to give back—the stolen property.*

No doubt, what I have just written will offend many people, including my own to some degree.[19] Yet an inescapable component of reconciliation is a commitment to truth-telling. On 6 April 1990, not long after the February 1990 proclamation, Ada Deer, chair of the Native American Rights Fund (NARF), responded to a *New York Times* article on South Dakota's attempt at reconciliation. Addressing Jack Rosenthal, the page editor for the newspaper, Ada Deer commended Mickelson for issuing the proclamation, but she admonished both peoples with a reminder that more is needed than recognizing the existence of a problem: "If this is to be a sincere effort toward genuine reconciliation, the historic and compelling injustices involving broken treaties and broken promises must be addressed. Let us remember that actions speak louder than words."[20]

Moreover, Deer eloquently elaborated what sincerity and genuineness might, on the part of our colonizers, really entail:

> The first step that must be taken by the State to begin this healing process is to honor the terms of the treaties which guaranteed that

the Black Hills would remain part of the land of the Great Sioux Nation. Federal legislation to return federally held land in the Black Hills must be supported to close this open wound bleeding the bodies, minds and spirits of the Sioux people. Second, the State must recognize the sovereignty of each tribal government in South Dakota. This means respecting their authority and right to govern their land and peoples without State encroachment.

These and other issues underlying the historic tensions between Indians and non-Indians in South Dakota must be seriously addressed. We must not permit South Dakota to proclaim the desire for *harmony* in theory while doing nothing in *practice*. . . . Will South Dakota and its people demonstrate their humanity by showing their compassion and making a commitment to resolving these longstanding injustices?[21]

The wording of Mickelson's proclamation, however, reveals why his efforts would fall short of such genuine reconciliation. Most likely, he was taking his cue from his fellow colonizers who desired something less than the decolonized truth.

By May 1990, the much-heralded "Year of Reconciliation" showed clear signs of failure, precisely because our colonizers failed to heed Deer's warning that reconciliation must "go beyond organizing pow-wows and feel-good feasts."[22] The state's Reconciliation Commission set up by Mickelson dodged contentious issues, such as land return or the political reform of colonization, and instead promoted warm-fuzzy projects, such as public education campaigns on various topics of interest. By contrast, the South Dakota Peace and Justice Center (SDPJC) planned a series of authentic dialogues between the colonizers and the Oceti Sakowin Oyate.[23] These initial dialogues produced the not-too-surprising litmus test that the Oceti Sakowin Oyate use to gauge the sincerity of reconciliation: land return as the core issue between our two peoples.

## Wasiglaki Istamni Yanpi

From this discussion about the historic relationship between the Oceti Sakowin Oyate and our colonizers and the ongoing impact of this history on contemporary relations, the ill-fated 1990 proclamation and the subsequent activities revealed how far our colonizers are from any meaningful reconciliation. Desmond Tutu, chair of South Africa's Truth and Reconciliation Commission, believes reconciliation is, at its best, a two-way street. The apology, the contrition, the confession, and the reparations are all to be borne by the perpetrator(s), and only then can the victim(s) move toward forgiveness.

While I believe this to be true—that reconciliation must begin with the colonizers—it does not mean we are hostages to their moral awakening, if indeed this should ever occur. We do not have to wait patiently and hope for a time when the colonizers-as-perpetrators will finally come to their senses. No, not even the most venerable Tutu believed in doing that. Such passivity would invite more abuse by not holding the perpetrators accountable.

So, in spite of our colonizers' unwillingness to engage in true reconciliation, we initiated our own healing from within the center of our nation's heart. The most well-known healing-from-within for the Oceti Sakowin Oyate happened in December 1990, exactly 100 years after the soldiers murdered our people at Wounded Knee. The Si Tanka Wokiksuye Ride retraced a route that the Si Tanka Oyate took after Tatanka Iyotaka, a beloved leader, was killed by wasicu surrogates on 15 December 1890 for resisting colonization. The purpose of this ride was "to bring the survivors of Chief Big Foot [Big Foot's people] out of mourning in 1990."[24] Standing among the hundreds of people at the massive burial site on that bitterly cold December day in 1990, I watched and prayed as the procession of riders rode their horses toward the mass grave. As the riders gathered at the grave, the emotions of immense grief, pain, and rage that we collectively experienced that day over the senseless slaughter of defenseless women, children, and men was as real and unbearable for us as it was for our ancestors on that same date a century before.

It was difficult to be there, to acknowledge what had happened to us as a people, and to honor those who have suffered since. The ride accomplished far more than it intended, however. Once all the riders and waiting crowd were gathered together, a Wiping of the Tears took place. Normally, this ceremony is conducted by community members for individuals or families who are in mourning over the loss of a loved one. The ceremony encourages the individual or family to participate once again in the community's life. It is our way of saying compassionately to a person in profound grief that she or he is deeply missed by the community and that without her or his participation in community activities, the community is, in some intangible way, less whole.

In other words, the long-term grieving of one community member affects the whole community, and the Wiping of the Tears heals that grief.

Yet because we had experienced not only an individual and family loss but also a national loss as a result of trauma-by-colonization, we had no precedent for conducting a Wiping of the Tears ceremony of such magnitude. Who, we wondered, could wipe the tears of a nation? The Si Tatanka Wokiksuye Ride provided the answer to this difficult question. For the first time in our nation's memory, this ceremony was conducted by the traumatized for the traumatized. From that day onward, knowing that we survived the greatest of all holocausts in human history—namely, the 500-year unrelenting genocide of Native Peoples in North America—the Oceti Sakowin had returned. The holocaust is by no means over. It is still being waged, but we no longer suffer within the silence of our pain and anger. Indeed, our colonizers are increasingly unsettled by our national resilience and national revitalization. Our very existence and survival are testaments that stand to haunt and confound them.

For example, as the quincentennial of Columbus's invasion was approaching and our colonizers were busily preparing to celebrate, the Oceti Sakowin Oyate's voice rose above the hoopla, reminding them that they were celebrating 500 years of genocide and that true reconciliation remained an unfinished task. When asked by the SDPJC what we had to say to our colonizers in 1992, Cheryl Crazy Bull explained how truth-telling can undo oppression:

Conciliation. That is the word for whose image I search in 1992. We Indigenous people are presenting the truth about the genocide which occurs in Indian country. We must disclose the truth about the historic genocide in which millions of us have been killed by white people. We must relate how tribally specific cultural knowledge is lost or distorted due to white oppression.... We must reveal to white people how we experience poverty and poor living conditions void of beauty and connection to the Earth as one of the many masks which genocide wears.... These forms of genocide which we experience are not our own creation. They come to us from the Europeans who have been seeking to conquer and control us during the hundreds of years since the arrival of Columbus on our lands.... The process of conciliation—acceptance—is one of healing and learning. It is opening your eyes and ears to see us and hear the voices of Native peoples. It is stopping the individuals and institutions who oppress Native peoples. . . . Conciliation is not achieved without anger, sorrow, and pain. We who come from Unci Maka, our Grandmother Earth, have everything to gain by living in balance and harmony with all creation. The only thing we have to lose is our lives.[25]

This quincentennial statement represents an example of how the Oceti Sakowin Oyate's truth-telling has continued since December 1990. My people have conducted other truth-telling events, such as the Makato Wokiksuye Iyanka Pi and the Manipi Hena Owasin Wicunkiksuye Pi. The former is a 90-mile relay that is run annually in December from Fort Snelling to Mankato. The latter is a 150-mile walk that approximates the route of the 1,700 Dakota women, children, and men who were force-marched from the Lower Sioux Reservation to Mankato to Fort Snelling. This walk is held in November, and its 150th year is currently being planned. The purpose for these events is the internal healing they provide for the Oceti Sakowin Oyate, since an important aspect of our healing includes telling the truth about the shameful ethnic-cleansing behavior of our colonizers.

When other opportunities arise, my people are quick to respond, since we take the responsibility to heal through truth-telling seriously. For instance, a "Call to the Oceti Sakowin" flyer was sent out in September 2004 to enlist our people and others in constructively engaging our colonizers around their bicentennial reenactment of their so-called Lewis and Clark Expedition. This reenactment celebrates American colonial occupation. The call powerfully challenged the wasicu narrative around the expedition—a narrative that has never allowed our voice to emerge:

> In the 1800's the Lakota encountered the Wasicu . . . Lewis & Clark Expedition. Now, America is holding a re-enactment of Lewis & Clark. . . . The U.S. has never addressed the stolen land, disease, genocide, & our sacred He Sapa (Black Hills).
>
> If the re-enactment continues on without the consent of the Lakota, just as our ancestors stood against the Lewis & Clark Expedition entry into Lakota territory, we, the descendants of the Free

Lakota, will make a stand to tell the world about the 1851 & 1868 Ft. Laramie Treaties & how America fails to abide by its own laws.

When we encounter the Lewis & Clark re-enactment of the original trespass, we call to all freedom thinking people of the Oceti Sakowin & all of our allies to stand in a sacred manner with a sovereign heart & send our message to the world: Honor the U.S. treaties with indigenous people on Turtle Island.

Such calls for direct action upset our colonizers, especially since their most recent imperialist expedition, the military occupation of Iraq, still begs for a resolution. One can imagine that Americans, as Fey noted, do in fact get more than a little irritated at having to say to the world that they really are an upright people and that they are not like "those others" who deceive the world. I guess, too, it is even more irritating to our wasicu colonizers when we point out that, "Well, yes, Saddam Hussein may have violated several UN resolutions as white leader George W. Bush alleged, but what about the nearly 400 treaties that the *American people* have unilaterally and arbitrarily broken with the hundreds of Native nations?" In other words, the existence and testimony of Native Peoples lay bare the hypocrisy and disingenuous-ness of our colonizers. Though our colonizers label others as "evil-doers," "thugs," or "killers," these labels fit them perfectly.

## Restorative Worthiness and Decolonization

On 11 September the wasicu watched the destruction of the World Trade Center's twin towers by a handful of men with utter disbelief. In the days that followed, our colonizers invoked Pearl Harbor to emotionally frame what had just happened to them, but one would have to go back further than 7 December 1941 to find an event that had a comparable emotional impact. On 25 June 1876, the news of nearly 300 American soldiers dying within ninety minutes, the first-ever capture of the U.S. colors in battle, and the death of Custer—a hero of "legendary" fame among whites—stunned the colonizers in much the same way as the collapse of the Twin Towers did. Af-ter all, our colonizers were in the cant of celebrating—albeit at a time when post-civil war politics were threatening to undo the Union—their 100 years of "independence." Thousands of spectators had flocked to the Centennial

Exhibition in Philadelphia that opened on 10 May and were treated to the imperial themes of "manifest destiny" and the "progress" of white civilization. The colonizers were also engulfed in a presidential contest that, for the first time ever, would award the office to a candidate who lost the popular vote but won the electoral college.

In this intense glow of white hubris, the startling news that a preemptive American strike against anti-colonial forces had ended in disaster was met with complete dismay. There was an automatic, 11-September-like call for vengeance and an all-out retaliation against the Oceti Sakowin Oyate. This "righteous call" overlooked the fact that my people, like other nonwestern or colonized peoples since, had had the temerity to resist subjugation.

What is the relevance of this story to the larger discussion of trauma, reconciliation, and reparative or restorative justice? As the colonizers helplessly witnessed the destruction of their World Trade Center and the damage to their Pentagon as well as learned that either their White House or their Capitol had been targeted, they experienced a little of what it means to be traumatized. After all, the colonizers' primary economic, military, and political icons were being assaulted. Because their emotional and psychological well-being have been intimately tied to these icons, the colonizers felt—much as their ancestors believed as they reacted to the Oceti Sakowin Oyates' defeat of Custer in the summer of 1876—that their "way of life" was being fundamentally called into question.

Indeed, almost all the white students in one of my classes that September morning were frightened and expressed a well-known "this isn't really happening" trauma response. They wanted to talk about "their" feelings. As I have said, we of the Oceti Sakowin Oyate do not miss opportunities for truth-telling, and 11 September provided one of my more memorable moments of teaching. As the white students were expressing their fears, I purposely redirected the discussion, stating that, as a Native, I understood something about the experience of trauma. I mentioned the destruction of our cultural and spiritual icons and social institutions—our way of life—through unprovoked attacks against my people by the Americans. Feeling empowered, Black students spoke eloquently of their ongoing emotional struggles over slavery, Jim Crow, racial profiling, and now incarceration at the hands of whites. Other nonwhite students expressed similar feelings about how they felt in a society that condones racist behaviors.

Before long, the white students' emotions shifted from anxiety to anger precisely because we did not privilege their trauma. Their trauma on that day did not receive any more attention than anyone else's, neither was their trauma treated as somehow special simply because they were white. No, much to the colonizers' angst, their trauma was not viewed as different, and *that* is evidently what upset them the most. The lesson learned through the shared truth-telling that day showed many people of color just how long a journey the colonizers would have to travel before reconciliation, reparations, or restorative justice would have any real chance of success.

Sadly, in the years following this lesson, it seems our colonizers have learned little about anyone's trauma but their own. In the aftermath of 11 September, the so-called public rallied to support the victims' families through various relief measures. From an Oceti Sakowin Oyate perspective, Angela Cavender Wilson addressed what one measure—the September 11th Victims' Compensation Fund—means to non-Natives on one hand and to Native Peoples on the other:

> By the time the deadline for filing passed, 95% of the victims [individuals or relatives of deceased individuals who were killed or physically injured as a result of the . . . aircraft crashes of September 11, 2001] applied for their piece of the government compensation program. Save the voices who rejected the government offer and are pursuing lawsuits seeking accountability for their suffering, there has been no public outcry regarding the use of federal funds to compensate these families. Indeed, the victims of 9-11 have been deemed worthy, their suffering understandable, and their need for compensation justified.[26]

State compensation satisfies the public's sense of duty and justice to aid those—the worthy victims—who directly suffered from the events of 11 September. Yet U.S. history discloses many millions of victims of white terrorist acts. Wilson uses this history to examine the law's corollary messages about who is worthy of compensation and who is not:

> If American compensation to victims of suffering is a measure of worthiness, then the Indigenous Peoples in the United States who

have suffered acts of terrorism on our lands, persons, and resources too numerous to count are apparently considered unworthy. . . . [T]he pain suffered by Indigenous Peoples in the United States has been forgotten, considered a thing of the past, and become normalized. Rather than acknowledging that there has been a terrible wrong, colonization has imposed on us responsibility for our own pain. We have been taught that our current predicament is a consequence of our own shortcomings, that we are to blame. While policies of genocide, ethnic cleansing, and ethnocide have been perpetuated against us, and our lands and resources have been threatened decade after decade, century after century, we are taught that we are to blame or that we should just get over it. There has been no adequate formal body to address our suffering or acknowledgment that we have been wronged by the policies of the United States.[27]

Other compensatory measures taken by white leaders on behalf of their "people," like the preemptive military attack against innocent Iraqi people, demonstrate our colonizers' firm belief that their pain and suffering are second to none and therefore that the pain and suffering that they have experienced must be paid for not only with money but also with the resources and blood of others. At their core, these 11-September-inspired measures are straightforward acts of vengeance against those who dare to resist American hegemony and hubris in their homelands. The Oceti Sakowin Oyate recognize the pattern. We know of what we speak, for after more than a century, we are still resisting American colonization.

Moreover, while we firmly believe in reconciliation and reparative or restorative justice, we have yet to receive any genuine or sincere acknowledgment from our perpetrators—the wasicu—for the egregious harms they have committed and continue to commit against us Native Peoples. Even so, like the freighter who genuinely and sincerely confessed to having never forgiven himself for delivering the whiskey to the soldiers, our colonizers may one day find it within themselves to do the same. I suspect at some future time when this happens—when our former colonizers (yes, former) come to their senses and want to confess, apologize, ask for forgiveness, and be reconciled with us—it will be because the world they inhabit has drastically changed.

Herein lies the tragedy for our colonizers. The Oceti Sakowin Oyate will not have waited for that day but will long since have gone forward in our revitalization. As time passes, what our former colonizers do or fail to do will have virtually no impact on us either way. The paths of healing and de-colonization could be shared, but we will not allow either path to be slowed by our colonizers' failure to acknowledge our worthiness as human beings. The window for engaging in genuinely reconciliatory process is open but closing. The permanent loss of this opportunity is the greatest risk our present day colonizers take by failing to act now.

## Notes

1. See Richard Drinnon, *Facing West: The Metaphysics of Indian-Hating and Empire-Building* (New York: New American Library, 1980). He establishes racism as the critical link between Euramericans' "settlement" in Native North America and their expansionism on a global scale.

2. See Daniel Johan Goldhagen, *Hitler's Willing Executioners: Ordinary Germans and the Holocaust* (New York: Random House, 1996) and Ward Churchill, *A Little Matter of Genocide: Holocaust and Denial in the Americas 1492 to Present* (San Francisco: City Lights Books, 1997). These are parallel works, showing normal, everyday people as participants in holocausts. Goldhagen shows ordinary Germans as perpetrators against the Jews, while Churchill shows ordinary Americans as perpetrators against Natives.

Also, see Elizabeth Cook-Lynn, *Anti-Indianism in Modern America: A Voice from Tatekeya's Earth* (Urbana, IL: University of Illinois Press, 2001). She equates anti-Indianism in North America with Germany's anti-Semitism under Hitler.

3. James Mooney, *Myths of the Cherokee*, Part I, 19th Annual Report (Washington: Bureau of American Ethnology, 1900), 130.

4. Rex Weyler, *Blood of the Land: The Government and Corporate War against the American Indian Movement* (New York: Everest House Publishers, 1982), 81.

5. Ibid.

6. White military leader Sheridan is credited with the statement: "The only good Indians I ever saw were dead."

7. Renee Sansom Flood's 14 April 1990 letter to Legia Spicer, director of South Dakota Peace and Justice Center.

8. Ibid.

9. Ibid.

10. Ibid.

11. This characterization is Vine Deloria's.

12. These "governments" came about in 1934 when Congress, the legislative body of our colonizers, enacted the Indian Reorganization Act. Section 16 of the act provides that Native communities can organize governments under a constitution.

However, these governments require the "Manner of Review" in which any actions (e.g., ordinances) are subject to review and approval by our colonizers. Our colonizers applied this exact governmental blueprint to the Iraqi people.

13. Vine Deloria, Jr., *Behind the Trail of Broken Treaties: An Indian Declaration of Independence* (Dell Publishing Co., 1974), 242.

14. "Our National Indian Policy," *The Christian Century*, 30 March 1955, 72 (13): 395.

15. See S. Bradley Bill, 705, section 11. These two designations are generic names for specific ceremonial or sacred sites.

16. David Blue Thunder's statement, see Ronald Goodman, *Lakota Star Knowledge* (Rosebud Sioux Reservation: Sinte Gleska University, 1992), 14.

17. Don C. Clowser, *Dakota Indian Treaties: From Nomad To Reservation* (Deadwood, SD: Don C. Clowser, 1974), 245.

18. Vine Deloria, Jr., *Of Utmost Good Faith* (San Francisco: Straight Arrow Books, 1971), 52.

19. Being brainwashed by colonization, we excuse the shortcomings of our colonial masters and become uncomfortable when confronted with the truth about them. As colonial subjects, we are often employed by our colonizers to dismiss or marginalize those who support an anti-colonial agenda, such as reconciliation. But this is another story.

20. Deer's 6 April 1990 letter to Rosenthal.

21. Ibid.

22. Ibid.

23. Founded in 1979, the South Dakota Peace and Justice Center is a statewide organization whose members support work on social issues from a spiritual foundation.

24. Debra White Plume, "Voices from Bridger," *Si Tanka Wokiksuye Wowapi*, 30 March 1990 (1)(3): 1.

25. "Reconciliation," (Watertown, SD: South Dakota Peace and Justice Center, n.d.), 4.

26. "Reviewing Our Suffering: Indigenous Decolonization and a United States Truth Commission" (Unpublished manuscript, 2004), 1–2.

27. Ibid., 2.


## Glossary

**He Sapa**: Black Hills.
**Makato Wokiksuye Iyanka Pi**: Blue Earth Run To Remember.
**Manipi Hena Owasin Wicunkiksuye Pi**: Remember Those Who Walked.

**Mni Luzahan Wakpa**: Swift Water. A traditional gathering place of the Oceti Sakowin Oyate in the He Sapa, now occupied by wasicu and called Rapid City.

**Oceti Sakowin Oyate**: People of Seven Council Fires. These terms describe our socio-political organization. We comprise the Sisitunwan, Wahpekute, Wahpetunwan, Mdewakantunwan, Ihanktunwan, Ihanktunwani, and Titunwan. The first four Fires reside in the eastern part of our traditional homeland and speak Dakota. The next two Fires reside in the central portion of our homeland and speak Nakota. The last Fire resides in the western part of our homeland and speaks Lakota.

**Si Tanka Oyate Wokiksuye**: Remembering Big Foot's People.

**Tatanka Iyotaka**: Sitting Buffalo. A Hunkpapa Lakota who helped lead the Oceti Sakowin Oyate at the Battle of the Little Big Horn and who was later assassinated on 15 December 1890 by U.S. surrogates. Erroneously translated as Sitting Bull.

**Tatanka TaCante**: The Heart of the Buffalo. A term denoting traditional or ceremonial sites located within the He Sapa.

**Tiospaye**: Related Community. The Oceti Sakowin kinship system's basic unit of community and local governance. Sometimes translated as extended family.

**Wamaka Ognaka Onakizin**: The Sanctuary of Everything That Is. A term denoting a space for living things who have a sacred relationship with the Oceti Sakowin Oyate.

**Wasicu**: Fat Takers. A term describing the behavior of whites or Americans. In Oceti Sakowin Oyate thought and philosophy, "taking the fat" connotes hoarding beyond what is necessary, being stingy. It also connotes a glib tongue, dishonesty, and mercenary habits.

**Wasigla Ki Istamni Yanpi**: Wiping of the Tears. A ceremony conducted for persons grieving from the trauma experienced by the loss of a loved one.

· · · ·

*First appearing in this book, this article elaborates Professor Valandra's presentation on the genocide of Native Peoples at the National Association of Ethnic Studies conference in Chicago 24 March 2005. The editor would like to thank Professor Valandra for permission to publish his work.*

# Hearing the Hard Stuff

*Harley Eagle*

*Because the preceding article may be challenging and controversial for many read-ers, the following response to it from another Native man—a person neck-deep in the work of restorative justice and anti-racism in both the United States and Canada—provides a telling perspective. Harley Eagle, who to date has not met or spoken with Edward Valandra, writes:*

Well, what can I say about the article other than excellent! Edward articu-lates well what we would often hear from a whole cross section of folks on Pine Ridge. Also, from my own personal ties to the history, his article echoes my own sentiments.

I guess why I feel it is vital to tell this story—and why it is vital for the restorative justice movement to hear it—comes from my own perception of how we as Native People work at decolonization. That process involves how we must find that safe and appropriate way of viewing our own personal life's journey and that of our Peoples and how they fit into the history of coloni-zation. We must see how our current existence is influenced by the overall dastardly plans of colonization, thereby exposing the lies that tell us that we are predisposed to the whole gamut of unhealthy lifestyles and are inferior simply because we are Native. We must begin to look at the colonizing pro-cess through the lens of our cultural teachings and values, which also hold keys to our healing journey.

When we do that, we begin to see that the so-called civilization process of colonization does not match the hype. We must look at the results, rather than the intentions. And certainly the history as we are taught it in most dominant-society educational systems does not make sense. Decolonization in my mind involves exposing the lies in popular history and rewriting his-tory to better match the overall truth from all perspectives. Edward's article does just that from his perspective as a strong, healthy Lakota man who knows 'his-story' well.

So here is my perspective on why an article like Edward's is so vital to this project. One of the issues I have struggled with for years now with the restorative justice movement—and I have also heard this from other First Nations communities and people—is that the movement in general does not understand that restorative justice comes from a different worldview. Restorative ways work in conjunction with all aspects of life found in that worldview. The worldview I refer to, of course, is found in most Indigenous Nations throughout the world. For the sake of brevity, it can be said to be about balance and the interconnection of all things found in this living universe.

The frustration with the movement is that restorative justice is often seen as something to simply be inserted into the current systems. But if one truly looks at the Indigenous Nations who held this worldview and their ways of dealing with conflict in a restorative fashion, then one also has to look at how these Nations came to be in the sad state that many of them are in today, and why, for the most part, they no longer adhere to these ancient ways.

So that brings us back to the "truth telling" that Edward's article is doing. If the movement truly wants to be restorative in its essence, then it must work at restoring or healing conflict on all levels. This, I think, is truly doing justice to the Indigenous worldviews from which the movement originated. Once again, we must take a hard look at the results of the restorative justice movement, not the intentions, especially from a First Nations perspective. Restorative justice looks at individual conflicts, but if folks understood that restorative justice is a way of life, then they would realize that it must help move both Aboriginal Peoples and whites out of the colonizing system we still live with. If restorative justice were truly a way of life for people, then we would see that and experience that, but we're not.

. . . .

*The editor would like to thank Harley Eagle for permission to publish his correspondence.*

# Wicakute Omanikiyapi:
# Dakota Death March, November 7–13, 1862

*George Blue Bird*

Minnesota's ancestral tribal warriors
were removed from physical sight
by a secret plan
which would not allow them
to see these seven days
of extreme belligerent hate
and outright genocide
perpetrated
against
their families and relatives.

      Almost two thousand of their people
      were ordered to begin walking
      at gunpoint
      in a death march
      over four miles long.

      They were being moved militarily
      from their homelands
      under political orders
      issued by President Lincoln
      and Governor Ramsey.

Concentration camp personnel at Mankato
were not prepared
to handle those who'd been burned
with boiling hot water
that was thrown

deliberately
onto old people and children
who were weak
and unable
to keep themselves moving.

      Skin actually peeled off
      from their wounds
      and when this happened
      everyone
      bit their back teeth down.

      These horrible and immense pains
      diminished
      with each night's arrival of sleep
      but this healing
      only lasted for a little while.

Several selections took place each morning
and whoever was chosen
would receive
premeditated forms of torture
and isolated whippings
that were implemented
as a means
of psychological warfare
and complete
malicious oppression.

      A respected grandmother
      could sense that she was going to die
      and so she spoke
      her last words of honor
      to those who would remember her.

Her precious life was put to an end
later that day
in a shameful killing
of repeated stabbings
by soldiers with sabers and knives.

Fort Snelling was built as a structure
to intimidate and torment
all indigenous and natural prisoners
with punishment systems
that included
deprivation of food
and sanctions
which reduced everybody
down to unreasonable declarations
of survival.

It was here in this place of hostility
that many beautiful mothers
in their powers
were able
to unite everyone with comfort.

Grandparents and little children
visited and told stories
amongst each other
while others
believed in their prayers.

. . . .

*The editor is most grateful to Mr. Blue Bird for permission to publish this poem.*

# Indigenous Peoples and Human Rights

## Declaration of the World Council of Indigenous Peoples

We are the Indigenous Peoples, we are a People
with a consciousness of culture and race,
on the edge of each country's borders and
marginal to each country's citizenship.
And rising up after centuries of oppression,
evoking the greatness of our ancestors,
in the memory of our Indigenous martyrs,
and in home to the counsel of our wise Elders:
We vow to control again our destiny and
recover our complete humanity and
pride in being Indigenous People.

. . . .

*This declaration was published in* Justice as Healing *(2000) 5:2.*

· · · ·

# CHAPTER 2

# Resisting Justice as Force

## Aboriginal Notions of Justice:
## Questioning Relationships of Force

*Ross Gordon Green and Kearney F. Healy*

Philosophical differences are often cited between the British-based views and practices of the conventional Canadian justice system and those of Aboriginal Peoples. Professor James (Sa'ke'j) Youngblood Henderson, the director of the Native Law Centre at the University of Saskatchewan, spoke to these differences at a 1999 national convention of Canadian judges. He discussed Britain's inability to successfully transfer its criminal justice system to the Indigenous people in its colonies:

> Far from being a Canadian anomaly, these conclusions are global. The failure of imposed foreign criminal jurisdiction system over Indigenous nations has haunted each British colony's legal system. In recent decades, every commonwealth country that has studied the problem has reached similar conclusions: the British legal system is not succeeding with Aboriginal peoples. The failure is a function of relationships of force rather than justice.

That relationships of force produce negative effects makes sense in light of the ineffectiveness of criminal punishment. While our clients generally dislike custody, their return rate is high. In our experience, the harsher these youths are treated by justice officials, the farther they get from the mainstream. Their families attest that the longer they are in custody, the worse they are when they finally return home. To state the obvious, our clients and their families agree that the use of punitive force to change these youths has been unsuccessful. When victims learn that the person charged has previously been before the youth court, even sentenced to custody, they wonder if the custody was too short, or they question whether custody works at all. In total, this "relationship of force" is not reducing recidivism or making for safer communities.

Professor Henderson was careful to say that the failure was not a failure of justice. Indeed, there is "no real cultural conflict as to the definition of [many] criminal behaviors," as "[t]heft, assault causing injury, sexual abuse [and] domestic violence" all "violate contemporary and traditional Aboriginal norms just as surely as they violate non-Aboriginal norms."[1] The philosophical beliefs and senses of justice among Aboriginal people are thought to have remained intact. What has failed is the way criminal law has been imposed on Indigenous people.

We can relate Professor Henderson's words to many of the Aboriginal clients we represent. On the one hand, these youths genuinely do not believe in harming others. Yet they are often thrust into situations where the force of circumstance causes their actions. A young Aboriginal woman who had frequently appeared in youth court in her early teens spoke about the effect of circumstances when asked if it might be beneficial for judges to meet with young people outside of court and learn about their lives:

> I think it would be good for the judges to actually understand, if they saw the youth where they are living, and understand the circumstances they are facing and what environment they are living in. If they saw them in the jail system, if they actually saw them as kids, as children, as young people, they're not there because of some violent crime. They're there because of circumstances that made them do it. Just actually talk to them and see them as a person and not a number.[2]

A number of youth held in custody in Saskatoon in September 2002 were asked: "Do you think it's okay to hurt others?" Sixteen out of eighteen replied no, it was not all right, including those charged with violent offenses. Most thought that a negative answer was so obvious they doubted the question's seriousness. The remaining two answered that it was okay but did so in a manner that implied that their answers should not be trusted. In researching this book, in-depth interviews with other youth, including those convicted of violent offenses, revealed a unanimous agreement that harming others was wrong.

Professor Patricia Monture-Angus of the University of Saskatchewan is a respected scholar who has spoken and written widely about Aboriginal concepts of justice. She has explained how, historically, Aboriginal societies had no need of a specialized group of criminal practitioners, specialized techniques, or even a specialized body of knowledge. This, she said, could be explained by a focus on healthy relationships, well-educated children, and high standards of character. She explained that in "the Mohawk language, when we say law . . . it really means 'the way to live together most nicely.'"[3] Law, she said,

> is about retaining, teaching, and maintaining good relationships. . . .
> What we can reclaim is the values that created a system where the
> abuses did not occur. We can recover our own system of law, law
> that has as its centre the family and kinship relations. We must be
> generous with ourselves and kind as well, as we discover how to live
> again as healthy and disciplined individuals. We must know that
> the dominant system of government will also be kind and generous
> to us as we heal from five hundred years of oppression. We must
> be patient with each other as we learn to live in a decolonized way
> again . . . this means looking further than the mere creation of so-
> called Aboriginal or tribal courts. . . . Alternatives are merely small
> add-ons to the existing system, which stands ready with the full
> force of its adversarial and punishment-oriented values if the "nice"
> solution does not work.[4]

Professor Monture-Angus told the audience that "our law is family law" and urged those present to go "home, pick up your responsibilities and do it now." In particular, she said, "[W]hen you know of abuses from political corruption to the abuse of women and children occurring within your community or within your own family, do not turn the other way."[5]

In drawing connections between Aboriginal concepts of justice and the variety of nonpunitive views existing in the broader society, it is worth remembering that, throughout human history, criminal law has often served to protect powerful elites. For example, criminal law in Imperial Rome had much to do with stabilizing the Roman Empire. Nero, branding the early Christians as criminals, was acting to consolidate his power. The Romans quickly learned to employ criminal sanction as a way of protecting their empire. As a result, criminal law and the use of force became inextricably linked. But just as Canadian Aboriginal voices have come to question this potentially harmful connection, so too have others across national lines and across history.

## Notes

1. Address to CAIJ, "Social Context for Aboriginal Peoples of Canada" (1999). See Jeremy Webber, "Relations of Force and Relations of Justice: The Emergence of Normative Community between Colonists and Aboriginal Peoples" (1995) 33 Osgoode Hall L.J. 623; M. Jackson, "Locking Up Natives in Canada" (1988–89), 23 U.B.C. L.Rev. 215 (article originally prepared as a report of the Canadian Bar Association Committee on Imprisonment and Release in June 1988), 215–16.

2. Interview with S. N. (18 December 2002) Saskatoon, Saskatchewan.

3. P. Monture-Okanee [P. Monture-Angus], "Thinking about Aboriginal Justice: Myths and Revolution" in R. Gosse, J. Youngblood Henderson, and R. Carter, eds., *Continuing Poundmaker's and Riel's Quest* (Saskatoon: Purich, 1994), 194, 222, 127.

4. Ibid.

5. Ibid., 229.

. . . .

*Published in* Justice as Healing *(2003) 8:4, this article provides excerpts from chapter 4 of Ross Green and Kearney Healy's book* Tough on Kids: Rethinking Approaches to Youth Justice *(Saskatoon: Purich Publishing., 2003). The editor would like to thank the authors and publisher for granting permission to reprint these excerpts.*

# Promises Worth Keeping

*Harold Johnson*

Intrinsic to colonial justice is the concept of punishment. This idea has roots in English history. The earliest written laws of England are contained in Aethelberht's code. Aethelberht I of Kent was supposedly converted to Christianity by St. Augustine in about 600 CE. Upon conversion, Aethelberht drafted a code wherein, instead of resorting to feuds to settle disputes, the parties had the option to settle for fixed sums of money. If one person killed another, the deceased's kin, house, or church could demand a code-determined amount proportionate to the worth of the deceased. The Christian church encouraged this early alternative to the feud and private dispute settlement, not only because the church had a problem with people both fighting a feud and upholding Christian values, but also because it provided a windfall for the church. Aethelberht's code demanded the highest payments for dead priests and actions against the church.

The Christian concept of penance played a huge role in the development of a concept of criminal law. A wrongdoer had to pay penance to cover the sin of his crime. The shift was subtle but evolutionary. The penance was, of course, paid not to the kin of the victim but to the church. These rewards gained from processing criminals soon led the church to establish its own courts. The concept of a fine was well established in the ecclesiastical courts and in canon law before the king took over those courts and claimed the proceeds for himself.

Today, all fines are paid to the Crown. The victims and their families are forgotten in the modern machinery of the criminal justice system. The ideological constructs of the criminal justice system have evolved slowly from penance to punishment, which continues to be the major factor in sentencing principles. However, the dominant underlying motivation remains economic.

Whereas Aethelberht set in motion the economically motivated evolution of state jurisdiction over the criminal, thereby taking jurisdiction away from the community, later generations have certainly perfected the system.

With the development of capitalism, criminal law underwent a major revolution. The factory and the penitentiary are similar institutions. Each operates according to strict rules of conduct and authority. Each operates under strict rules of time. The factory processes materials, and the penitentiary processes Indians.

Economics dominates thought in this century. With the collapse of the Soviet Socialist Union, cowboy capitalism has been left to dominate the world agenda. There are no imagined alternatives. The political right dominates, and the left, if not dead, is stalled. The criminal justice system, like all other systems in the industrial world, is affected by the move to the right. The only arguments that are listened to when discussing the criminal justice system are economic: "It costs *x* to keep an Indian in jail for a year."

Treaties No. 6 and No. 7 hold a promise of Indian maintenance of "peace and good order." That Indians "aid and assist the officers of Her Majesty in bringing to justice and punishment any Indian" requires the Indians to participate in the economics of the criminal justice system. If the Indians participate by aiding and assisting the officers of her Majesty, they undermine their ability to maintain peace and good order amongst themselves. When Indians who have been processed in the industrial penal institutions are released, they require community resources to return to a way of life where they can participate in peace and good order.

The more the Indians aid and assist the criminal justice system, the more they destroy their ability to maintain peace and good order. When the Indians reach a point where they are no longer able to maintain peace and good order, they are completely wedded to aiding and assisting the officers of Her Majesty in punishing. In order to re-achieve peace and good order, the Indians must stop aiding and assisting the officers of Her Majesty. The Indians must stop participating in the economics of justice and punishment and focus their limited resources on maintaining peace and good order.

Peace and good order cannot compete with justice and punishment in the economic arena. They are diametrically opposed principles. Justice and punishment are the values of a hierarchy. Ultimate peace and good order can be achieved only in an anarchy, which exists without hierarchy of any kind. In a true anarchy, people live together without oppression. The argument against anarchy, of course, is that without authority, competing interests would cause anarchy to deteriorate into chaos. Nevertheless, if anarchy could be maintained, it would, until deterioration, be ultimate peace and good order. By contrast, whenever hierarchy is imposed—whether through benevolent democracy, despotic tyranny, or economic democracy—it results in some form of oppression. According to hierarchical thinking, oppression through the imposition of justice and punishment is necessary to achieve a semblance of peace and good order.

Yet peace and good order cannot exist in an oppressive state. The act of oppressing by imposing punishment destroys the peace. It is not good order to use violence to maintain the appearance of order. Punishment is violence. Incarceration is violence. The violence of incarceration maintains and is maintained by the economic system of the industrial capitalist criminal justice system.

We are left with the problem of participating, aiding, and assisting hierarchy in an attempt to re-create peace and good order. Yet the criminal justice system's use of violent punishment has decimated our communities. Do we break our treaty promise to keep peace and good order, or do we break our treaty promise to aid and assist? The answer is, of course, economic. If we are denied the resources to heal the incarcerated, we will not be able to maintain peace and good order.

. . . .

*This article was published in* Justice as Healing *(1997) 2:1. The editor would like to thank Harold Johnson for permission to publish his work.*

# Punishment versus Healing:
# How Does Traditional Indian Law Work?

*James W. Zion*

Many people are skeptical of justice methods that do not have punishment as their driving force. For that reason, there is a great deal of disbelief about the effectiveness of traditional Indian law, and there are many who are leery of the growing restorative justice movement as well. One of the difficulties with "law" as it is viewed in Canada and the United States (two English common-law jurisdictions) is that it is dominated by legal positivism. Legal positivism defines *law* as "a rule laid down for the guidance of an intelligent being by an intelligent being having power over him."[1] Western law is built on the relationship of "superiors" to "inferiors."

This is relevant to Indians and their nations within the modern states of the Western hemisphere, because conquest itself may create law as we know it. Franz Oppenheimer holds, "[L]aw in the strict sense is found only where one group has conquered another and remains in the territory of the conquered as a dominant caste or class. The resulting social stratification is then rationalized, the inferior group is subjected to punishment for any infringement of the interests of their superiors, and thus formal law comes into being."[2] This sort of relationship feeds political oppression, which, according to Eli Sagan, "is easier when there is a racial or cultural distinction between the masters and the oppressed. Tyranny will be harsher in a state established through conquest of one people by another than in a state where all share the same language, culture, and history."[3]

There is a contradiction in the ways Canadian and American law view Indians and their nations. Given these definitions of law and their consequences in states created by conquest, states try to treat Indians as "equals" in democratic societies without honoring their rights as Indians. We see attempts to maintain societies where "all share the same language, culture, and history" through civil rights legislation or court rulings. Yet the legislation and rulings deny Indian values because they do not fit an equal protection model, reject that Indian nations hold jurisdiction over non-Indians, impose English-only legislation, and void affirmative action programs.

Of course, we all know that history is written by the oppressor and not by the oppressed. Legal positivism is a dangerous and racist doctrine.[4] We must remember that contemporary Canadian and U.S. "Indian law" is the product of social Darwinists who strongly influenced nineteenth-century thought at a time when the foundations of present-day Indian law were established. While Canada attempts to create a multicultural society, the United States is dominated by a white, male, Protestant, authoritarian power structure.

By contrast, most Indian societies are genuinely egalitarian in nature. They do not rely on artificial and imposed "equality." For example, a great deal of traditional Indian law is distributive justice: the notion that people should share limited resources.[5] We see this in Potlatch and Giveaway ceremonies, as well as in the way Indians look to their relatives for help when they have problems. Most traditional justice methods are based on talking things out to reach consensus. Whereas a great deal of the early (Anglo) literature on Indian justice methods stresses retribution, punishment, revenge, and strong institutions such as "chiefs,"[6] powerful councils, and soldier societies, these may have been caused by pushing groups of Indians away from their original homes into new environments.[7] More recent research (especially by Indian writers) shows that most methods of traditional Indian justice were based on consensus and equality.

Another distinction between Western and Indian justice is the role of religion or spirituality. Modern constitutional provisions on the separation of church and state make it difficult for Western justice to use religion or spirituality in dispute resolution. Traditional Indian justice depends on it. Indian spirituality is essential to traditional dispute resolution, because the Indian worldview integrates spiritual beings with everyday life, and these spiritual beings can help in addressing conflicts.

Western law does not attempt to reach into the mind or deal with psychological injuries, much less seek spiritual help in doing this. Traditional Indian law does, and that is why it heals. Most disputes occur because of bad attitudes, feelings, or thinking. Whereas we use "head thinking" about others to handle our conflicts, traditional Indian processes move people to "heart thinking" and empathy with others.[8] When an injury creates a dispute, anger and hurt naturally follow. People experience cognitive dissonance, which happens when the mind creates excuses and justifications to avoid shame.[9]

Most traditional Indian justice methods address cognitive dissonance and shame. They do not make a sharp distinction between "victim" and "offender."[10] Instead, they involve the relatives of both. They use a talking-out process among relatives (by both blood and clan) to reach a practical consensus about what to do about a problem. They use ceremony and prayer to bond people to the process and to involve the spirits both in forming the path to a solution and in making the decision binding. The process gets to the bottom of things.

Most Indigenous Peoples have a word to describe group and person solidarity, or as Justice Raymond D. Austin of the Navajo Nation Supreme Court puts it, "freedom with responsibility." The Navajo word for it is *k'e*, the Lakota term is *tiospaye*, and the Zulu word is *ubuntu*. Indigenous Peoples believe in individual freedom, but it is exercised in the context of the group. Indigenous justice uses respect, consensus, solidarity, mutuality, interdependent relationships, reciprocity, and even love as the means to heal in traditional justice methods. These values bind the individual to the group and the group to supporting the individual. We do not see these values at work in Canadian or American courts or legislatures.

In sum, Indian thought is sophisticated. It is humanist, and humanism is a value that has been lost in the current social Darwinist climate. Indian law uses emotions and feelings, whereas rationalist thought rejects them. Thomas Aquinas said that law is a "rule of reason," but he also reminded us that humans possess both reason and emotion. Emotion was thrown out the window in the structure of modern Western law as found in the United States and Canada.

Whereas Western law is based on punishment, Indian law[11] is based on healing. The problem with many contemporary justice initiatives directed at Indians is that they are integrationist and ultimately assimilationist. Assimilation is a genocidal and ethnocidal force that is not yet prohibited by human rights law, but it should be. Indian justice works because it heals. It should not be taken captive by a legal system based on force, as with circle sentencing dominated by a judge or family group conferencing directed by a non-Indian police officer. Indian justice should stand on its own, and if the

Western systems of power, force, and authority wish to utilize Indian methods in their own way, they should do so.

We must take a close look at the institutions and rules that dominate in North America and realize that there are alternatives—methods that heal. We must recognize the forces of authoritarianism, social Darwinism, and racism in today's political and legal discourse and reject them in favor of multiculturalism and humanism. Canada seems to be headed in that direction, while the United States is still affected by its sad history of slavery, criminal exile, and race conflict. In the United States, a small white elite holds most of the power and money and struggles to maintain its dominance through repressive law. Both Canada and the United States have a lot to learn from traditional Indian law and its foundations in genuine equality, respect, humanity, and spirituality.

## Notes

1. Edwin W. Patterson, *Jurisprudence: Men and Ideas of the Law* (Brooklyn, NY: Foundation Press, 1953), 85 (quoting John Austin, an English academic and legal philosopher who lived from 1790 through 1859).

2. Howard Becker and Harry Elmer Barnes, *Social Thought from Lore to Science*, 3rd ed. (New York: Dover Publications, 1961), 30.

3. Eli Sagan, *At the Dawn of Tyranny: The Origins of Individualism, Political Oppression and the State* (New York: Alfred A. Knopf, 1985), 278.

4. See, e.g., Curtis A. Bradley and Jack L. Goldsmith, "Customary International Law as Federal Common Law: A Critique of the Modern Position," *Harvard Law Review* 816 (1997), 110. Bradley and Goldsmith warn Americans that the United Nations is creating new customary law and human rights norms that may be applied by U.S. courts and thus override the prerogative of Congress to deny human rights. Accordingly, they say, we should change our reading of the supremacy and treaty clauses of the U.S. Constitution to reaffirm the power of Congress to do so. This is legal positivism at its worst. The theories of parliamentary supremacy and the devolution of authority from a parliament or legislature are a species of the genus.

5. I think that the Black culture(s) of North America retain a great deal of their Indigenous thought. For example, a few years ago I had the pleasure of hearing Lani Guinier, the "Quota Queen," whose nomination as the head of the Civil Rights Division of the U.S. Department of Justice was shot down by right-wing Republicans and a cowardly president. She explained her theory of proportional representation in legislatures in a simple way. She said they are based on the simple concept of

"sharing." See Lani Guinier, *The Tyranny of the Majority: Fundamental Fairness in Representative Democracy* (New York: The Free Press, 1994).

6. The office of "chief" as a domineering and authoritarian figure was, of course, invented by the Europeans.

7. The essays in R. Brian Ferguson and Neil L. Whitehead, eds., *War in the Tribal Zone: Expanding States and Indigenous Warfare* (Santa Fe, NM: School of American Research Press, 1992) clearly point that out. Indians suffer from five centuries of warfare, and they suffer from mass post-traumatic stress disorder as a result. That makes the healing component of traditional Indian law even more important.

8. This is the thesis of Laurie Melchin Grohowski, "Cognitive-Affective Model of Reconciliation (CAMR)" (M.A. thesis based on a study of Navajo peacemaking) (cited with permission).

9. For a definition of cognitive dissonance, see Elliot Aronson, *The Social Animal*, 7th ed. (Santa Cruz: University of California Press, 1995), 178. Psychiatrist James Gilligan maintains that "The emotion of shame is the primary or ultimate cause of all violence, whether toward others or toward self." Violence, he says, is designed to replace shame with pride to prevent "the individual from being overwhelmed by the feeling of shame." James Gilligan, *Violence: Our Deadly Epidemic and Its Causes* (New York: Grosset/Putnam Books, 1996), 110.

10. For example, in one Navajo peacemaking case, "as a reticent teenager explained why she was causing such disharmony in a troubled home, she broke down, saying she desperately wanted to stop drinking. Then she dropped a bombshell—another family member had been molesting her. The courtroom silenced. The peacemaker declared the need for a follow-up with the accused. A look of relief, even a few smiles, crossed family members' faces. One by one, they effusively thanked [peacemaker Ruthie] Alexius." Vince Bielski, "The Navajo Model," *California Lawyer* (November 1995), 39. Peacemaker liaison Betty Donald of the Tuba City (Navajo Nation) District Court says that such situations are common.

11. That is, "Indian law" in the sense of the laws of Indians. The "Indian law" texts we see in law schools teach the law of the oppressor and not that of the oppressed subjects of that corpus of law.

. . . .

*This article was published in* Justice as Healing *(1997) 2:3. The editor would like to thank James W. Zion for permission to publish his work.*

# The "One Law for All" Myth

*James W. Zion*

## Introduction

The United Nations Expert Seminar on the Administration of Justice and Indigenous Peoples was held in Madrid, Spain, on 12–14 November 2003. The primary purpose of the gathering was to advise the special rapporteur Rodolfo Stavenhagen of Mexico "on the situation of human rights and fundamental freedoms of Indigenous people" and on the administration of justice and Indigenous Peoples in order to contribute to his report on these subjects to the United Nations Commission on Human Rights during its upcoming 2004 meeting.[1]

On the first day of the seminar, Mr. Stavenhagen posed two important questions to the experts sitting before him. First, how would they respond to a tradition of one law for everyone? Second, if states accepted the legal systems of Indigenous Peoples, how would the Indigenous Peoples guarantee individual rights in their communities, particularly the rights of Indigenous women?[2]

The seminar was held in a climate where some state parties were attempting to block or weaken the Draft Declaration on the Rights of Indigenous Peoples. As a result, the seminar offered a fresh approach to "standards-setting" procedures for elaborating international declarations and conventions on human rights in the United Nations.[3] These procedures were established following the adoption of the Universal Declaration of Human Rights in 1948. People realized that a consensus document with very general provisions adopted during the Cold War had to be more specific in naming human rights standards, usually stated in declarations and conventions, that member states had to adopt and follow.

Unfortunately, the human rights standards-setting discourse was changed for Indigenous Peoples in the discussions of the Draft Declaration. Some state representatives argued that Indigenous Peoples shouldn't have "rights" at all—only unenforceable and meaningless "aspirations," wishes, and nice stuff said about them. Alternatively, we need a body of official statements that can begin to be used as evidence of international *customary* law. We also need expert seminars that permit Indigenous representatives to educate special rapporteurs on how to develop Indigenous rights (as "rights") in reports that can serve as viable alternatives to the stalled declaration process.

The role of international litigation was also discussed as a means to set standards. Obviously, we must find alternatives to the negotiated declarations and conventions, given how states are obstructing that process.

This article will address the special rapporteur's question about the "one law for all" tradition to show that it is a myth, a slogan without concrete meaning, a pretext for refusing to acknowledge Indigenous law and institutions, and an assertion that is actually contrary to the history of Western law. This piece will trace the sources of recognizing the law of "The Other" as well as the origins of the "one law for all" slogan. It will show how "law" has been used to block recognition of Indigenous law and why it is falsely or incorrectly applied this way given the history of legal pluralism.

## The Origins of Recognition

There is a theory that "law" is actually about domination. Some thinkers hold that "law in the strict sense is found only where one group has conquered another and remains in the territory of the conquered as a dominant caste or class. The resulting social stratification is then rationalized, the inferior group is subjected to punishment for any infringement of the interests of their superiors, and thus formal law comes into being."[4]

It should be no surprise that the "one law for all" slogan comes from Rome, one of the first empires that had to struggle with what to do about law and conquered peoples. The empires and colonial powers that followed faced the same problems. "It was a general principle which marked early Roman policy in Italy to allow a subject community to retain its own municipal laws and to administer justice between its own citizens, so far as this was consistent with a state of subjection to Rome."[5]

Rome had to deal with Indigenous populations in its empire, and one of the most dramatic examples of the application of that policy was the trial and execution of Jesus Christ. Matthew relates that following his arrest, Christ was brought before the high priest Caiaphas and the scribes and Elders, and they tried and condemned him. The next day, he was brought before

Pilate, the Roman governor, who said, "I am innocent of the blood of this just person; [but] see ye to it [Christ's execution].[6] That is a precedent for the acknowledgment of Indigenous legal systems and their decisions, because it is an example of the recognition and enforcement of a judgment of a "tribal" court by a state system. Given the prominence of the case of Christ as stating the rule of recognition, it is strange that it is still being debated as something new.

The Roman policy carried over into the law of another world empire, that of Spain, beginning in 1492 with the fall of Grenada and the grant of a charter of exploration to Columbus. Spain had several diverse cultures—Christian, Moslem, and Jewish, and different ethnic groups that populated the Iberian Peninsula. Spain was—and is—an aggregation of different regions with diverse populations and languages, and it has a history of struggles to maintain a centralized national "Spanish" state in the face of cultural pluralism.[7]

Following the complete reconquest of Spain by Christians in 1492, the national legal system that emerged was based on the beliefs that "there was a natural law binding on all people and peoples whoever they might be," and there was "a variety of human observance, all of it permissible so long as it did not conflict with" natural law and Ius Gentium [the law of peoples or nations]. Natural law was described as "a common body of law and custom that might be found in the practices of all peoples."[8] Based upon these principles, when Christians retook control of Spain, "Moslems were allowed to live under their own law and custom and to resort to their own courts for matters concerning themselves."[9]

When the Spanish occupied the New World, they recognized Indian laws and courts as well.[10] On 6 August 1555, Emperor Don Carlos (Charles V) and Queen Dona Juana ("Jane the Insane of Spain," Charles's mother) issued a decree that "ordered and commanded" that "the laws and good customs" of Indians, along with their "usages and customs," "be kept and executed."[11] This recognition principle was firmly entrenched in *Derecho Indiano* (Spanish Indian Law), but it was lost when new states emerged in Latin America following the period of revolutions.

After England split from the Catholic Church, it too entered the field of colonialism, and, as other empires had done, it addressed the problem of what a conquering force attempting reconstruction after war (e.g., Afghanistan and Iraq) had to do in order to administer law for conquered peoples. The British created Native or village courts to recruit Indigenous leaders to apply Indigenous customary law as instruments of control, replicating the recognition policy.[12]

The emerging empire of the United States of America faced the same dilemmas of conquest as it expanded across a continent (and around the globe, at the close of the nineteenth century) and asserted control over Indigenous colonial populations. In 1872, during the period when American Indians were confined on reservations, the United States needed a new policy of legal colonialism. A Presbyterian missionary suggested that the Secretary of the Interior follow the British model of using native Sepoys in India to serve as police in the place of soldiers, who were "intemperate and immoral men, exerting the worst influence on Indians."[13] This suggestion was followed, and the first Navajo police officers were appointed in August of that year.[14]

Ten years later, in 1882, a newly appointed Secretary of the Interior expanded on the idea of using Natives in a legal system and ordered the creation of Indian courts with special regulations for Indians. These came into existence in April of 1883.[15] While Indians were involved in a justice system, they were only captive actors in it, and it was overseen by non-Indian Indian agents on each reservation.

Therefore, the concept of the recognition of Indigenous law and institutions is an ancient one, beginning in Roman law. It was carried forward in the empires of Spain and the emerging nation-states that continued to exercise colonial control over Indigenous Peoples. Although we are said to be in an era of post-colonialism, the colonial relationship between Indigenous Peoples and modern states remains, and the same dilemma of how empires can control Indigenous populations remains as well.

This brief overview shows that recognizing disparate and multiple Indigenous laws and legal systems is a fundamental policy of Western law. It is also a principle of customary international law, given the uniformity and consistency of state practice.[16]

In Madrid, an American academic marveled at the fact that American Indian leaders hold out tribal courts as an example of the possibilities for Indigenous justice around the world, when they began as instruments of control. That is a dilemma that arises from this historical record of state recognition of Indigenous law and institutions as a means of dominance and control.

As we think out how Indigenous Peoples—and the states that dominate them—can shift from a paradigm of law as domination and hegemony to a paradigm of law based on respect for human rights and egalitarianism, we need to look at precedents from the past and consider how we can use them in positive ways. Indigenous law does not have to be law created by others, and the same holds true of legal institutions. Some of the presentations in Madrid showed that Indigenous customary law and traditional institutions still exist and operate, although they were driven underground when modern state legal systems and population dominance suppressed traditional Indigenous justice.

Today, we are challenged to recognize Indigenous law based on respect rather than dominance. We are also challenged to change how we articulate standards for recognizing Indigenous law and institutions, which require equal and appropriate inclusions of Indigenous Peoples in state systems.

## Origins: The Misrepresentation of a Philosopher

The research for this article began on 28 September 2003 with a "Google" search of the phrase "one law for all." It returned 1,829 hits. A review of Web pages from the search showed that the phrase is usually asserted as a rhetorical slogan and argument-stopper, with no consideration of its origin and original meaning and context.

Marcus Aurelius, a second-century Roman emperor and Stoic philosopher, thanked one of his brothers for teaching him to value "the conception of the state with one law for all, based upon individual equality and freedom of speech, and of a sovereignty which prizes above all things the liberty of the subject."[17]

We often hear the "one law for all" part of the emperor-philosopher's valued concept, but we are not told about its moorings or realize that there are preconditions to the application of the principle. The word *sovereignty* is horribly abused by the "one law for all" mob, although it is actually based on the same foundations. That is, the sovereignty of the state (including Indigenous states), expressed in law, must address equality, free speech, and (above all things) the liberty of the subject, if we use Marcus Aurelius's principles.

Equality was very much on the agenda of the expert seminar in Madrid, where Indigenous lawyers pointed out that there is a lack of equality for Indigenous Peoples in most state legal systems. In fact, affirmative discrimination against the Indigenous Peoples was represented at the seminar. Are

Indigenous Peoples "equal" in state systems, and do their laws and institutions have equal status with state law?

We often overlook the fact that *liberty* is an ancient term that refers to the ability of distinct peoples to govern their own affairs. The 1537 papal bull *Sublimis Deus* stated, "We hereby declare that the said Indians . . . must not be deprived of their freedom and their possessions . . . [and] they must be left to enjoy their freedom and their possessions."[18]

As for "free speech," the experts gathered in Madrid from Indigenous perspectives (Navajo, Aymara, and other Indigenous cultures) explained that free speech includes traditional Indigenous methods of speaking and talking things out to resolve disputes. People who assert that there must be "one law for all" and use the catchphrase as a barrier to Indigenous law and institutions overlook these considerations and the original context of the term with its clear preconditions.

### Abuse of the Phrase

In 1986, the Law Reform Commission of the Commonwealth of Australia published a parliamentary paper on the recognition of Aboriginal customary laws. In reviewing the arguments against recognition, it referenced "Divisiveness and the 'One Law,'" which claimed that recognition "would be divisive or an affront to public opinion."[19] "Proponents of these views argue that there should be 'one law for all,' and that the goal should be 'social equality for Aborigines with the concept of racial unity and integration.'"[20] Nonetheless, the commission found that recognition, supported by the doctrine of legal pluralism, "is necessarily desirable."[21]

One of the leading Indigenous or Aboriginal rights issues in Canada is the establishment of First Nations justice systems, and the Lake Babine Nation of British Columbia is encountering resistance to its efforts to do just that. Opponents of the Lake Babine Nation denounce "alternative justice systems as a violation of the principle of 'one law for all.'"[22]

Another example of the misuse of the phrase can be found in the objections to the effective implementation of the Maori Treaty of Waitangi. Opponents argue that the treaty has a "one law for all" requirement—namely, Pakeah (Anglo) law.[23] The Google search revealed several other cases where "one law for all" was used as an unchallenged objection to Indigenous rights.

Aside from bluster, sloganeering, and use of the phrase to filibuster Indigenous rights, are there examples of reasoned applications of the concept? When the Supreme Court of Canada addressed the legality of the succession of Quebec in 1998, it reviewed the concepts of constitutionalism and the rule of law. It concluded that "the rule of law is supreme over acts of both government and private persons. There is, in short, one law for all."[24] In the case of *Rose Bear v. Attorney General of Canada*, the federal court said that the "one law for all" principle was violated when status Indians employed on reserves were barred from paying into a national retirement plan, while other Canadians could do so since 1988.[25]

There are few illustrations of the practical application of the term, and they are largely meaningless. They, too, fail to put the phrase in the original context stated by Marcus Aurelius, which involves examining problems of equality, free speech, and (political) liberty. The phrase is a slogan thrown out loosely in political forums, and it appears as dicta used to reinforce nice-sounding ideas in judicial opinions. It seldom has concrete meaning.[26] Can we approach the myth from another perspective?

## Legal Pluralism

Both the experts and the special rapporteur in Madrid referred to "legal pluralism" as a basis for the recognition and coexistence of diverse laws and legal systems in modern states. Several examples of developing state law principles dealing with Indigenous Peoples referenced the existence of multicultural societies throughout the world. "Legal pluralism" is a fairly modern term, but it encompasses centuries of actual practice. Harold J. Berman wrote a masterful history of the Western legal tradition's formation.[27] Throughout, he relates the struggles of the state to free itself from institutionalized religion, the struggles of those in religious institutions to free themselves from the control of the state, and the rise of the modern state through law and competing claims of cities and merchants to free themselves of centralized control. In other words, Berman shows the fact of legal pluralism throughout medieval and modern history.

Today, we see the claims of Indigenous Peoples to autonomy ("liberty"), self-determination ("liberty" again—a customary international law right), and different forms of group rights, echoed in libertarian, "polycentric law," free market, and even anarchist arguments. All of these claims assert that centralized authority and control are counterproductive to human initiative and growth.[28] The recognition of Indigenous law and institutions is part of a larger trend toward more inclusive democracy and local autonomy. This requires the devolution of decision-making authority, including shifts in the recognition of such authority.

## Conclusion

From the trial of Christ to the disproportionate numbers of Indigenous individuals in jails and prison due to state discrimination, we see the "one law for all" argument proven false. It is a sound bite that has little meaning when examined in light of history, consistent state practice, and its original context. Different laws and institutions can co-exist to address the common goals of equality, free speech, and liberty, and the modern legal pluralism movement reinforces this possibility.

The right of Indigenous Peoples to have their own law and institutions— and their rights to equality and freedom from discrimination in state justice systems—are international human rights that are particular to them. In a larger sense, though, these rights are international customary rights that can be claimed by many different kinds of groups. After all, *democracy*—another term subject to misrepresentation and misuse—means inclusion, voice, local control, participation, and effective self-determination. As we re-examine the role of the central state in light of technological advances, and as we take a fresh look at the term *democracy*, we see that diversity, co-participation, and distinctness in multicultural societies are not only possible but are keys to the future of humanity. This is the traditional meaning of the term *liberty*, and we can hope that it is making a comeback.

I attempted to answer Special Rapporteur Rodolfo Stavenhagen's two important questions in Madrid. He is obviously aware that Indigenous thinkers must counter two false assertions thrown out to block definitive statements of Indigenous human rights. "One law for all," the first false assertion, is merely a slogan, on par with the ads that assert that one thing or another is a "cure all."

The second false assertion claims that Indigenous Peoples care little about individual rights and particularly the rights of women. However, considering that we have not begun to examine the fact that Indigenous law, as pre-state law, is based on individual dignity and participation,[29] it is quite wrong to raise this specter. Traditional Indigenous law and its forms are the product of a high degree of individualism and a resulting respect for individuals. The lesson for the West is that you cannot have one law for all if you forget about equality, effective free speech in the form of talking out one's own problems, and the political liberty to solve your own problems in a context of legal pluralism and self-determination. As has been said by many authors in *Justice as Healing*, law must be based upon healing. Accordingly, we must reject the "one law for all" myth, based as it is on dominance, if healing is to begin.

## Notes

1. Stevenhagen was appointed under Commission on Human Rights Resolution No. 2001/57, UNCHR 76th meeting, 24 April 2001. The specific seminar issues included "the implementation of recent legislation related to the rights of Indigenous Peoples at the national level; best practices of how to combine Indigenous customary systems with the national legal system; examples of discrimination in the access to the administration of justice and particularly how this affects Indigenous women; juvenile justice; and how individual and group rights of Indigenous Peoples are protected in the various legal systems." Office of the United Nations High Commissioner for Human Rights and Universidad Nacional de Educacion a Distancia (UNED), *Expert Seminar on Indigenous People and the Administration of Justice* (announcement).

2. The author was present. This article does not address the special rapporteur's second question, but the author suggested that the assertion that Indigenous Peoples deny women's rights is false and a pretext for inaction, and that Indigenous women should address that issue themselves, refute it, or raise problems to be addressed.

3. For a discussion of the specific application of standards-setting to Indigenous Peoples, see Sarah Pritchard, Aboriginal and Torres Strait Islander Commission, *Setting International Standards: An Analysis of the United Nations Draft Declaration on the Rights of Indigenous Peoples*, 2nd ed. (1998).

4. Howard Becker and Harry Elmer Barnes, *Social Thought from Lore to Science*, 3rd ed. (New York: Dover Publications, 1961), 30 (citing German sociologist Franz Oppenheimer on the nature of the State). For an examination of state formation and tyranny ("an abuse of hierarchy"), see also Eli Sagan, *At the Dawn of Tyranny: The Origins of Individualism, Political Oppression and the State* (New York: Alfred A. Knopf, 1985). While this definition of law may be exaggerated, it typifies the relationship between modern states and Indigenous Peoples.

5. William C. Morey, *Outlines of Roman Law* (New York: American Book Company, 1900), 64.

6. Matthew 26:66, 27:1–24 (King James).

7. See John A. Crow, *Spain: The Root and the Flower* (Berkeley: University of California Press, 1985). The book gives a cultural history of Spain that shows an ongoing struggle between local autonomy and central authority.

8. Woodrow Borah, *Justice by Insurance: The General Indian Court of Colonial Mexico and the Legal Aides of the Half-Real,* (Berkeley: University of California Press, 1983), 6.

9. Ibid., 7. The principle of recognition has roots in Islamic law as well as Roman law. See Patricia Seed, *Ceremonies of Possession in Europe's Conquest of the New World 1492–1640* (Cambridge: Cambridge University Press, 1995), 69–99 (relating Spanish and Moorish doctrines of recognition).

10. Borah, *Justice by Insurance,* 8, 21–22.

11. Donald Juneau, "The Light of Dead Stars," 11(1) *American Indian L. Rev.* 1, 13 (with the text of the decree in English and Spanish).

12. A. St.J. Hannigan, "The Imposition of Western Law Forms Upon Primitive Societies," 4(1) *Comparative Studies in Society and History* 1 (1961).

13. Norman J. Bender, *New Hope for the Indians: The Grant Peace Policy and the Navajos in the 1879s* (Albuquerque: University of New Mexico Press, 1989), 81.

14. Ibid.

15. See William T. Hagan, *Indian Police and Judges* (New Haven, CT: Yale University Press, 1966) (a standard history of those institutions).

16. This point is argued at greater length in James W. Zion and Robert Yazzie, "Indigenous Law in the Wake of Conquest," *Boston College International and Comparative L. Rev.* 55 (1997): 20. This article focuses on the recognition of Indian law when it is applied in state fora and not simply state tolerance of Indigenous law and institutions.

17. Robert Royal, "Who Put the West in Western Civilization?" *The Intercollegiate Review* 3, 8 (Spring 1988) (quoting Marcus Aurelius).

18. Pontifical Commission on Justice and Peace, *The Church and Racism: Towards a More Fraternal Society* at para. 3 (1988). The usual translation of the bull is that Indians have the right to "liberty and property," showing the use of the medieval term as political liberty. The bull also states that any action to deprive Indians of liberty or property is null and void. See also Robert John Araujo, "The Catholic Neo-Scholastic Contribution to Human Rights: The Natural Law Foundation," *Ave Maria L. Rev.* 1(1) 159 (2003) (a more detailed account of concepts of justice and liberty by the Attaché to the Permanent Observer Mission of the Holy See to the United Nations).

19. Law Reform Commission, Parliament of the Commonwealth of Australia, Report No. 31, *The Recognition of Aboriginal Customary Laws,* vol. 1 at 88, at para, 118 (1986).

20. Ibid. That echoes the definition of "law" that began this piece in terms of

the hegemony of one cultural group over others under the guise of racial unity and so-called integration. The same kind of appeal to one race—a "raza unida" or mixed-blood society—is also being used to deny recognition and effectively recognize diversity of Latin Countries. (One of the complaints is that, although several countries, particularly in South America, have constitutional amendments that officially recognize multiculturalism, they have not been effectively implemented in legislation. Mexico was not mentioned, but its infamous recent constitutional amendments also recognize multiculturalism.)

21. Ibid. The concept of legal pluralism will be addressed below.

22. Jo-Anne Fisk and Betty Patrick, *Cis dideen kat—When the Plumes Rise* (Vancouver: UBC Press, 2000), 9.

23. See Stephen Franks, M.P., "The Treaty of Waitangi and Colour Blind Property Rights" 11, n. 15, New Zealand Law Conference, Christchurch (October 2001) (paper advocating an interpretation of the treaty to uphold "classical property rights" as enunciated in English common law).

24. Reference re: Succession of Quebec [1998] S.C.R. at para. 71.

25. *Rose Bear v. Attorney General of Canada* [2002] F.C. 356, at para. 74.

26. For an additional illustration of that fact, see a law review article using the phrase in its title, Jeremy Waldron, "One Law for All? The Logic of Cultural Accommodation," 59 *Wash. and Lee L. Rev.* 3 (2002) (examining logical problems in making a given rule of law and then establishing exceptions that could swallow it).

27. Harold J. Berman, *Law and Revolution: The Formation of the Western Legal Tradition* (Cambridge, MA: Harvard University Press, 1983).

28. The "Bible" many utilize to reinforce such arguments appears to be Robert C. Ellickson, *Order without Law: How Neighbors Settle Disputes* (Cambridge, MA: Harvard University Press, 1991). Libertarians often point to traditional Indian law as an example of societies that do very well without state law.

29. The participatory democracy and inclusion-based principles are apparent in one survey of customary American Indian law. Bruce L. Benson, "An Evolutionary Contractarian View of Primitive Law: The Institutions and Incentives Arising Under Customary American Indian Law," 5 *Review of Austrian Economics* 65 (1991). Benson marvels at the beauty and individual rights-protecting nature of the traditional American Indian law as he surveyed and then compared it with imposed systems and asked why Indians don't return to their original justice forms.

. . . .

*This article was published in* Justice as Healing *(2003) 8:4. The editor would like to thank James W. Zion for permission to publish his work.*

# II
· · · ·

# *The Healing Process:*
# *Being a Good Relative*

What is an offender? It is someone who shows little regard for right relationships. That person has little respect for others. Navajos say of such a person, "He acts as if he has no relatives." So, what do you do when someone acts as if they have no relatives? You bring in the relatives!

CHIEF JUSTICE ROBERT YAZZIE

# Introduction: Reweaving the Fabrics of Life

*Wanda D. McCaslin*

Speaking the truth about where we are raises the call for healing. In response to this truth-telling, Indigenous people turn to the fabrics of our lives for help; namely, to our relationships with our families and communities as well as with the Creator and the natural and spirit worlds. This second phase of the healing process encourages not just "offenders" but all those affected to become more mindful of how profoundly connected we are. Among Aboriginal Peoples, our relatives—from the closest to the most extended—are our life's blood. Without them, our lives are not properly balanced, and it is easy to fall into unbalanced ways. As Chief Justice Yazzie says, acting as if we have no relatives is how hurtful behavior arises. The Indigenous response is not to sever our ties even more by sending people off to prison but to rebuild the bonds that hold us on a good path.

Non-Aboriginal people often misunderstand our healing processes. Accustomed to majority-rule democracy, Western thought constructs a hierarchy in which the community wields power over the individual. This power-over way of thinking appeals to force—strength in numbers—to enforce conformity. Thinking from this model, non-Aboriginal people tend to construe our restorative processes as simply a matter of the community putting social pressure on an offender to correct his or her ways, essentially by shaming the person into compliance. Familiar with the power-over approach of the criminal justice system, they assume Indigenous processes work similarly by using force and coercion—albeit a sociological, shaming kind rather than a physical, punitive sort—to make offenders change.

This is not how we understand healing processes. True, given the multigenerational effects of trauma and oppression that we face in our communities, force and coercion are sometimes necessary. Community pressure does play a role, of course, and in the presence of their families and communities, offenders do feel shame for having hurt others, especially since their relatives share responsibility for the harms done. Though force, shaming, and coercion may stabilize an event, they are not the essence of our healing processes, neither do they characterize traditional law relationships between communities and their members. Force and coercion are not fundamentally how we make our societies, communities, and people harmonious; therefore they cannot provide the means we use to repair harms.

Instead, when hurts occur, we are instructed to go back to what makes our families and communities strong in the first place: we work to rebuild the bonds of mutual responsibilities that hold us together in a good way. These bonds are forged not in force but in respect, in an honest appreciation of each person as a valued member of the community, and in a trust that we each have a sacredness that guides us.

Law is embedded in our ways of thinking, living, and being. For Indigenous Peoples, law is far more than rules to be obeyed. Law is found within our language, customs, and practices. It is found within the carefully balanced relations of our clan systems and our extended families. It is also found in ceremonies and rituals. Law is a whole way of life. Through countless means, our traditions teach us how to be respectful of others and mindful of how our actions affect them.

In other words, to exist as Indigenous Peoples is to live our law, which holds us in balance. Our communities are a part of the law, and our community members—be they Elders, respected leaders, family, or even our youth—protect law by preserving our cultures' worldviews and ways. These are not passed on through lectures or written codes. Instead, law is modeled for us daily through our languages, customs, behavior, and relationships. The closer we stay to our traditional ways, the more we internalize our law and its values, so that they exist among us as a natural, everyday expectation of what it means to "be a good relative"—not only with each other but with all beings. Law is a part of us as we go about our lives, and in turn we seek to express our law through everything we do.

When imbalances occur, our communities have customarily responded according to traditional healing processes in order to make things right. These processes seek to right harms without coercion. The Navajo maxim "It's up to him" expresses the respect for others that we bring to our peacemaking processes. The best and most effective solutions come from those involved, because then the members commit to making those solutions work. Forced, imposed "solutions" are much less effective.

Looking beyond those immediately involved, Indigenous people tend to interpret hurtful actions less individualistically and more as signs of imbalances within the community as a whole—imbalances that affect everyone. In this sense, offenders help the community by drawing attention to imbalances, especially when they have become a functionally invisible "norm." Offenders serve the community in the way that canaries served miners: they alert our communities to dangers. Their actions tell us that the essential fabric of the community is starting to unravel and needs mending. Sometimes it takes an event of crime to jolt us into addressing harmful patterns in our midst. Instead of placing all the blame on the offender, our traditions acknowledge that everyone in the community has played some role in the patterns that culminated in hurtful actions. The responsibility for harms is distributed and shared. Doing justice requires a community.

On yet deeper levels, Indigenous healing processes address the root causes of imbalance. Our cultures have been under attack from colonizers for generations and remain so. Hence, our communities use "crime" as opportunities to do the hard and complex work of decolonization. To heal, we must confront multigenerationally internalized trauma, oppression, colonized attitudes and habits, racism, pressures to assimilate, and the ongoing denigration of people and cultures. Because we have internalized many of these destructive patterns, harms make us confront how we are acting them out—not on the colonizers but in most cases on each other.

The Hollow Water First Nation on Lake Winnipeg, for example, uses community holistic healing circles to deal with sexual assaults on family members. Their work is controversial among some people in the criminal justice and domestic violence fields, because it is so demanding and must be done with such care and attention. But as the Hollow Water community explains, the alternatives are either looking the other way on rampant sexual abuse or having their people sent off to prison, which is another form of genocide and ethnocide.

Whatever aspects of harm we face, our communities are central to how we respond to them. For us, healing is about bringing the community back into the picture. It is about communities finding their own solutions. Communities can view problems as opportunities for seeing more clearly how we have drifted out of balance. The challenges give us a chance to work toward a balance that grows from our traditions and is not imposed from without. When others use our challenges as an excuse to impose their ways, we are weakened. Specifically, when the criminal justice system steps in and imposes "solutions," it is not only highly disrespectful but highly damaging as well. By contrast, when we deal with harms in Indigenous ways, all communities—Aboriginal and non-Aboriginal—can grow stronger. Respecting our communities and our inherently existing powers of self-determination are what justice as healing requires.

The articles in part 2 explore this core phase of the healing process. Chapter 3: "Healing Worldviews" explores both the philosophies underlying a healing concept of justice and how these philosophies translate into different practices. The "Teachings of the Seven Prophets: The Seven Fires" frames the healing process in an immense context of change that encompasses many generations. Conveying how much is at stake for all peoples, the Seven Teachings call on the best in everyone to choose wisely.

In "Defining Traditional Healing," Gloria Lee sketches the overall philosophy of Indigenous healing and its spiritual roots, explaining that this approach applies to healing social harms as much as it does to healing bodies. In her article, "Indigenous Justice Systems and Tribal Society," Ada Pecos Melton shows the clear difference between Indigenous and Western models of justice and then outlines the range of restorative practices that tribal societies are currently using to deal with crime.

The next three articles explore how different Native Peoples respond to harms based on their traditions. In "Healing as Justice: The Navajo Response to Crime," Chief Justice Robert Yazzie gives an overview of the Navajo peacemaking process—the *Hozhooji Naat'aanii* or the "Justice and Harmony Ceremony"—explaining its rootedness in the clan system and traditional Navajo values and ways. Nin Tomas discusses Maori justice and how it functions on the *marae*, the Maori formal meeting place. Finally, Michael Cousins presents the Haudenosaunee approach to preserving community harmony, from the overall Haudenosaunee worldview to their traditional ways of handling specific crimes.

Chapter 4, "Respecting Community," begins with Judge Bria Huculak's article "From the Power to Punish to the Power to Heal." Judge Huculak underscores the failure of punishment to bring positive change for either offenders or their communities. Active herself for many years in introducing restorative justice practices in Saskatchewan, she calls for a profound shift to more community-based alternatives to the criminal justice system. In "Evaluating the Quality of Justice," Russel L. Barsh argues that what we as a society want from a justice system will determine how we approach evaluating it. If all we want is deterrence, then we will evaluate our justice systems in terms of "law and order." However, if society wants a system that is just and is experienced as such by all those involved, then we will evaluate our ways of responding to crime in terms of the quality of relations that are achieved. Finally, in "Throwing the Baby Eagle Out of the Nest," John Borrows draws from his own experiences to urge Aboriginal people, especially professionals whose work has carried them into the dominant society, to stay connected to their original home communities as much as possible.

Chapter 5, "Community Peacemaking," shares the experiences of different communities as they practice community-based peacemaking. "A Healing Circle in the Innu Community of Sheshashit" presents the report of a healing circle conducted for a case in the Newfoundland Supreme Court. The next two articles—"Aboriginal Community Healing in Action: The Hollow Water Approach" by Rupert Ross and "The Sentencing Circle: Seeds of a Community Healing Process," a report given by the Hollow Water First Nations Community Holistic Circle Healing—discuss the work of the Hollow Water community and its use of healing circles to deal with sexual abuse. In the history of the *Justice as Healing* newsletter, these articles are among the ones most requested for reprints. In "Community-Based Justice Initiatives of the Saskatoon Tribal Council," Yvonne Boyer discusses some of the different community-based restorative justice programs that the Saskatoon Tribal Council has developed to meet the diverse needs of its people, both on and off reserve. Judge Steven Point's article, "Alternative Justice: Testing the Waters," closes this section with a very personal account of his journey as an Aboriginal judge from the courtroom to a sentencing circle to a community peacemaking ceremony.

· · · ·

# CHAPTER 3

# *Healing Worldviews*

## Teachings of the Seven Prophets: The Seven Fires

*A Traditional Story Written Down by Edward Benton Banai
and Read by Elder William Commanda*

Seven prophets came to Anishinabe. They came at a time when the people were living a full and peaceful life on the northeastern coast of North America. These prophets left the people with seven predictions of what the future would bring. Each of the prophecies was called a fire, and each fire referred to a particular era in the future. Thus, the teachings of the seven prophets are now called the "Seven Fires."

The first prophet said to the people, "In the time of the First Fire, the Anishinabe Nation will rise up and follow the sacred shell of the Midewiwin Lodge. The Midewiwin Lodge will serve as a rallying point for the people, and its traditional ways will be the source of much strength. The Sacred Megis will lead the way to the chosen ground of the Anishinabe. You are to look for a turtle-shaped island that is linked to the purification of the earth. You will find such an island at the beginning and end of your journey. There will be seven stopping places along the way. You will know the chosen ground has been reached when you come to a land where food grows on water. If you do not move, you will be destroyed."

The second prophet told the people, "You will know the Second Fire, because at this time the Nation will be camped by a large body of water. In this time, the direction of the Sacred Shell will be lost. The Midewiwin will diminish in strength. A boy will be born to point the way back to the traditional ways. He will show the direction to the stepping stones to the future of the Anishinabe people."

The third prophet said to the people, "In the Third Fire, the Anishinabe will find the path to their chosen ground, a land in the west to which they must move their families. This will be the land where food grows on water."

The Fourth Fire was originally given to the people by two prophets. They came as one. They told of the coming of the light-skinned race.

One of the prophets said, "You will know the future of our people by the face the light-skinned race wears. If they come wearing the face of brotherhood, then there will come a time of wonderful change for generations to come. They will bring new knowledge and articles that can be joined with the knowledge of this country. In this way, two nations will join to make a mighty nation. This new nation will be joined by two more, so that four will form the mightiest nation of all. You will know the face of the brotherhood if the light-skinned race comes carrying no weapons, if they come bearing only their knowledge and a handshake."

The other prophet said, "Beware if the light-skinned race comes wearing the face of death. You must be careful because the face of brotherhood and the face of death look very much alike. If they come carrying a weapon . . . beware. If they come in suffering . . . they could fool you. Their hearts may be filled with greed for the riches of this land. If they are indeed your brothers, let them prove it. Do not accept them in total trust. You shall know that the face they wear is one of death if the rivers run with poison and the fish become unfit to eat. You shall know them by these many things."

The fifth prophet said, "In the time of the Fifth Fire, there will come a time of great struggle that will grip the lives of all Native people. At the warning of this Fire, there will come among the people one who holds a promise of great joy and salvation. If the people accept this promise of a new way and abandon the old teachings, then the struggle of the Fifth Fire will be with the people for many generations. The promise that comes will prove to be a false promise. All those who accept this promise will cause the near destruction of the people."

The prophet of the Sixth Fire said, "In the time of the Sixth Fire, it will be evident that the promise of the Fifth Fire came in a false way. Those deceived by this promise will take their children away from the teachings of the Elders. Grandsons and granddaughters will turn against the Elders. In this way the Elders will lose their reason for living. . . . They will lose their purpose in life. At this time a new sickness will come among the people. The balance of many people will be disturbed. The cup of life will almost be spilled. The cup of life will almost become the cup of grief."

At the time of these predictions, many people scoffed at the prophets. They then had medicines to keep away sickness. They were then healthy and happy as a people. These were the people who chose to stay behind in the great migration of the Anishinabe. These people were the first to have contact with the light-skinned race. They would suffer most.

When the Fifth Fire came to pass, a great struggle did indeed grip the lives of all Native people. The light-skinned race launched a military attack on the Indian people throughout the country aimed at taking away their land and their independence as a free and sovereign people. It is now felt that the false promise that came at the end of the Fifth Fire was the materials and riches embodied in the way of life of the light-skinned race. Those who abandoned the ancient ways and accepted this new promise were a big factor in causing the near destruction of the Native people of this land.

When the Sixth Fire came to be, the words of the prophet rang true as children were taken away from the teachings of the Elders. The boarding school era of "civilizing" Indian children had begun. The Indian language and religion were taken from the children. The people started dying at an early age. . . . They had lost their will to live and their purpose in living.

In the confusing times of the Sixth Fire, it is said that a group of visionaries came among the Anishinabe. They gathered all the priests of the Midewiwin Lodge. They told the priests that the Midewiwin Way was in danger of being destroyed. They gathered all the sacred bundles. They gathered all the scrolls that recorded the ceremonies. All these things were placed in a hollowed-out log from the Ironwood tree. Men were lowered over a cliff by long ropes. They dug a hole in the cliff and buried the log where no one could find it. Thus the teachings of the Elders were hidden out of sight but not out of memory. It was said that when the time came that the Indian people could practice their religion without fear, a little boy would dream where the Ironwood log, full of the sacred bundles and scrolls, was buried. He would lead his people to the place.

The seventh prophet that came to the people long ago was said to be different from the other prophets. He was young and had a strange light in his eyes.

He said, "In the time of the Seventh Fire, New People will emerge. They will retrace their steps to find what was left by the trail. Their steps will take them to the Elders, whom they will ask to guide them on their journey. But many of the Elders will have fallen asleep. They will awaken to this new time with nothing to offer. Some of the Elders will be silent out of fear. Some of the Elders will be silent because no one will ask anything of them. The New People will have to be careful in how they approach the Elders. The task of the New People will not be easy.

"If the New People will remain strong in their quest, the Water Drum of the Midewiwin Lodge will again sound its voice. There will be a rebirth of the Anishinabe Nation and a rekindling of old flames. The Sacred Fire will again be lit.

"It is at this time that the light-skinned race will be given a choice between two roads. If they choose the right road, then the Seventh Fire will light the Eighth and final Fire, an eternal Fire of peace, love, brotherhood and sisterhood. If the light-skinned race makes the wrong choice of the roads, then the destruction that they brought with them in coming to this country will come back at them and cause much suffering and death to all the Earth's people."

Traditional Mide people of Ojibway and people from other nations have interpreted the "two roads" that face the light-skinned race as the road to technology and the other road to spiritualism. They feel that the road to technology represents a continuation of headlong rush to technological development. This is the road that has led to modern society, to a damaged and seared Earth. Could it be that the road to technology represents a rush to destruction? The road to spirituality represents the slower path that traditional Native people have traveled and are now seeking again. The Earth is not scorched on this trail. The grass is still growing there.

The prophet of the Fourth Fire spoke of a time when "two nations will join to make a mighty nation." He was speaking of the coming of the light-skinned race and the face of brotherhood that the light skinned Brother could be wearing. It is obvious from the history of this country that this was not the face worn by the light-skinned race as a whole. That mighty nation spoken of in the Fourth Fire has never been formed.

If the Natural people of the Earth could just wear the face of brotherhood, we might be able to deliver our society from the road to destruction. Could we make the two roads that today represent two clashing worldviews come together to form a mighty nation? Could a Nation be formed that is guided by respect for all living things? Are we the New People of the Seventh Fire?

. . . .

*Published in* Justice as Healing *(1997) 2:2, this story was read by Elder William Commanda at the Aboriginal Justice Learning Network Constituency Meeting of Elders, policy makers, and academics on 16 and 17 April 1997 in Aylmer, Quebec. The story is found in* The Mishomis Book: The Voice of the Ojibway *by Edward Benton Banai (St. Paul, Minnesota: Indian Country Press, 1979). The book is available for purchase from Indian Country Communications Inc., 8558 N Country Road K, Hayward, WI 54843; telephone (715) 634-5226. We are grateful to Elder Commanda, Elder Banai, and Indian Country Press for permission to reprint it here.*

## 12

# Defining Traditional Healing

*Gloria Lee*

### The Approach of Traditional Healing[1]

The four elements of the person are the spiritual, emotional, physical, and mental. Disease or bodily ailment is traditionally viewed as the physical manifestation of a weakness—a symptom of something deeper. The weakness may come from the spiritual, emotional, or psychological aspects of a person. When a person is afflicted with a disease, the traditional view is that the disease exists to offer the individual a teaching. The teaching will ultimately be about oneself, but the person may choose to deal only with the physical manifestation of the weakness—the symptom—and not address its root. If the person chooses to treat only the symptom and ignores the teaching that is being offered, then the disease will return. Physical manifestations may continue to appear until the individual accepts the teaching.

The weakness is caused by our being out of balance or out of center, and there can be many reasons for being out of balance. These reasons may involve, for example, working too much in one area, overworking on the job, being too greedy, or wanting too much—in other words, not attending to the many parts of ourselves, our lives, and our families in a balanced way. If we do not pay attention to all these aspects, then we will become unbalanced. That is when an illness may appear to remind us that we are overlooking some area. We may also become out of balance when we do not receive the appropriate teachings from our Elders. This happens when a First Nation's culture has been hidden to protect it from total loss.

There are traditional ways of dealing with illnesses. With the support of Elders and the assistance of Healers and Elder apprentices, we can find the right healing for an illness and an explanation for why it happened in the first place. If we ignore this explanation and continue with the same behavior or activity that is said to have caused the illness, then the illness will return because we continue to be out of balance. Being out of balance happens whenever we have not lived a "careful" life.

Traditional Healers say that much of what they do involves sorting out the jumble of disorder that they find in and around the patient. The disorder has many causes, but primarily it is caused by not living life in a good way. The job of the Healer, simply put, is to help reorder the elements of the person and to explain why and how disorder occurred. The Healer then explains how to ensure that the illness does not return.

Families turned to a Healer when they determined that an illness was an "Indian" illness:

> When people discuss a particular case of illness, identifying the probable cause was often a central topic. Indeed, when the cause of a particular illness was not readily apparent, individuals would commonly note that the illness "just didn't occur for no reason." In conversations about serious or complex cases, several different explanations may be discussed.[2]

Understanding the cause of an illness or some observable behavior was important in finding the appropriate treatment:

> "Indian" illnesses are those which can be explained by reference to a potentially observable event. These include such things as colds, fevers, and respiratory infections, like bronchitis, attributed to exposure to excessive cold, or to being overheated and catching a chill; and stomach aches or diarrhea that come from overeating."[3]

A Healer can determine if these physical manifestations are actually due to a spiritual or emotional imbalance; this is part of the diagnosis.

Understanding healing begins with the Elders and what they have to teach, which comes from the Creator. Because traditional healing is within each of us, we are all capable of healing ourselves. Sometimes, though, we need the help and support of others, such as Elders, Healers, and helpers. Healing begins with one's own center. For this reason, we are ultimately responsible for our own well-being.[4]

This traditional approach to healing is reflected in Aboriginal discussions about the meaning of justice. For example, the *Report of the Aboriginal Justice Inquiry of Manitoba* states:

The dominant society tries to control actions it considers potentially
or actually harmful to society as a whole, to individuals or to the
wrongdoers themselves by interdiction, enforcement or apprehen-
sion. . . . The emphasis is on the punishment of the deviant as a
means of making that person conform, or as a means of protecting
other members of society.

The purpose of a justice system in an Aboriginal society is to
restore the peace and equilibrium within the community, and to reconcile the accused with his or her own conscience and with the individual or family who has been wronged. This is a primary difference.
It is a difference that significantly challenges the appropriateness
of the present legal system for Aboriginal people in the resolution
of conflict, the reconciliation and the maintenance of community
harmony and good orders.[5]

From the First Nations' understanding, the Euro-Canadian concept of
justice is too narrow and confining. It doesn't appreciate all the elements involved in a holistic perspective of justice. The Euro-Canadian justice model
primarily delivers punishment for wrongdoing. Justice is understood as
maintaining or administering what is righteous by determining rewards or
punishments. Justice is also discussed as having the quality of being just,
impartial, or fair.

The First Nations' philosophy of justice offers a vastly expanded understanding of justice, so much so that what is meant does not even mean *justice*
anymore. There is no English word for the First Nations' holistic understanding of justice. Aboriginal people inherently have a higher standard and
fuller concept of what is required to make things right. This understanding is
guided by the spiritual realm and the teachings of the Creator. These teachings are sometimes referred to as natural laws. The following excerpt from
a report by the Federation of Saskatchewan Indian Nations' Justice Unit
entitled *Historical/Customary First Nations Law Practices—The Natural Law*
reflects this understanding:

The teachings of our culture tell us that we as Aboriginal people
were placed here by our Creator, the same Creator who is responsible for all of Creation. This of course includes all nations, regardless of race. Each nation was provided with a means of communi-

cation to the Creator, or as some would call it, a faith or religion from which to follow. These various religions are considered gifts to mankind and are to be treated with respect by all. Therefore, for one nation to denounce or show disrespect to another faith is, in essence, committing an act of disrespect to the Creator, even though it is done unintentionally. Once we, as a Nation of people, begin to acknowledge the existence of one Creator, a teaching of respect for mankind emerges.

If one chooses to accept or acknowledge this concept, one can easily see that our culture, customs, and traditions were also provided to us by the Creator. We are told that our culture is based on the natural law and that the natural law is connected to the natural universe. Long ago our ancestors had a clear understanding of the natural law and they understood how all things were interconnected. It was understood by our ancestors that when one walked with disrespect, their own spirit paid with retribution. Even by insulting the smallest child, one insulted their own spirit. Such acts were considered an abuse or violation of the natural law and the individual was obligated to correct the wrongdoing through service to mankind.

We have been told that such teachings have not been a part of our people, as a nation, for several hundred years. This is not to suggest that natural law has diminished, for the natural law is constant and does not change. Rather, our own understanding and practice of the natural law as a whole nation has diminished. This is not intended to discourage First Nations people, as we are told that we as a nation are entering a new cycle of life, which will bring increased harmony and balance. As we learn more about our traditional past, we will be challenged to the degree that we will doubt our own ability to learn. We are to have faith in our Creator and the power of the Spirit and to continue no matter how it is perceived.

The natural law, as we know it, is connected to the natural universe, which is comprised of positive and negative energy forces. Our white brothers and sisters understand this concept to a certain degree; however, they have chosen to acknowledge it in a different manner, namely, in scientific terms. At times, they have chosen to direct these energies in a negative fashion, i.e., splitting of the atom, thus allowing the creation of atomic weapons. We have, on the other hand, chosen to acknowledge and respect these energy forces in accordance with our traditions, for even the negative energy that is present in the universe can show us the beauty of love. The negative energy is used as a balance to maintain harmony within and, by doing so, can provide a greater understanding of love. We are told that as humans, we have to maintain that balance.[6]

This brief introduction to natural law is not a complete explanation. It does, however, give a sense that natural law encompasses the workings of the universe (physics) and emotions, such as love, all of which are guided by the power of the Creator. The Euro-Canadian understanding of justice does not consider either physics or love.

## The Cultural and Religious Contexts

The way individuals choose to relate to the Creator and to all of Creation determines how they perceive justice and view restorative justice. The natural laws of Aboriginal Peoples and the state laws of non-Aboriginal people are inherently different, based on fundamentally different beliefs and values. As a result, they are in ongoing conflict.

In a position paper, the Hollow Water Community Holistic Circle Healing discusses the meaning of justice, how different cultural perspectives define justice, the cultural orientation of their First Nation's perspective on justice, and how this orientation is radically different from the Euro-Canadian model, which is based on Christian ideas. As they explain, culture and values are central in determining the concept of justice that a society or community will accept and develop:

A community's justice system reflects its culture and values, which are often entrenched in its religion. In comparing the Hollow Water notions of justice with those of the Euro-Canadian system, it is easy to perceive the religious roots.

The overriding rationale for the use of traditional teachings for Community Holistic Circle Healing (CHCH) is found in the importance of healing, which has an important spiritual significance due to the need to unite all aspects of a person's being: the physical, the spiritual, the mental, and the emotional elements. For CHCH, the act of sexual abuse clearly indicates a lack of balance in all aspects of a person's being.

Because the spiritual being is integrally interwoven into the relationship with the Creator, a lack of balance in the spiritual being has an impact on the relationship with the Creator.

While it can perhaps be over-simplifying a very complex process, it can be said that justice for CHCH is restoring the balance.

This implies, for the "justice process" of CHCH, not only a consideration of the imbalance that led to the wrongful act, but also the external forces that caused the imbalance, as well as the consequences of the act. One would be foolish to think, for example, that an act of sexual abuse would not affect the spiritual balance of the victim. Justice then would include righting that imbalance as well.

One can easily see the role of Christianity in the concepts of the Canadian justice system. Christianity is a "top down" system with God at the top. In the Old Testament at least, God smote those who offended him. Christians pay for their sins with God doling out the punishment.

In our [criminal] justice system, the role of God is played by the judge. Christianity is founded on the notion of free will. People choose to sin and are held accountable for that choice. Sinners are punished.

This context, translated into the Canadian system, makes justice focus on very simple issues. Free will in the justice system is translated into *mens rea* (guilty mind). It forms the most important concept in our justice system. It allows us to focus our attention on a single act.

We never need to ask "Why?" because that answer is always supplied to us through the precepts. The presence of *mens rea* means the accused chose to commit the act, and that's all we need to know. The offender is then held blameworthy, ready to be punished.

The result of the fact-finding approach in a justice system which seeks to lay blame on an individual is to pit the offender and the victim against one another, thus further exacerbating the harm that has come between them.

Having established guilt, we then invoke the wisdom of experts, i.e., complete strangers to the protagonists, to advise us as to the implications of the wrongdoing.

The only time we look beyond the offender is in the punishment stage. But this is only to determine what caused the offender to go wrong. (We already know this because of our free will concept.)

It arises in a concept called general deterrence. Simply put, this amounts to punishing the offender for an offence someone else might commit in the future. No doubt the rationale for this can be traced back to the concept of "original sin" which in essence makes us responsible for the sins of others.

In Christianity, the ultimate punishment is Hell. In our justice system, it is jail, a place similar to Hell where we organized the gathering of wrongdoers to cohabit with one another. It is not a place designed to make the offender a better person, but simply to punish him for his wrongful acts, just like Hell.

It is not far removed from the eye for an eye concept of justice, about which Gandhi once said, if we practice an eye for an eye as justice, soon we will all end up blind.

Recent trends would lead one to the conclusion that popular notions of justice are not moving away from the view that offenders deserve to have great amounts of suffering inflicted upon them in the name of justice.

When one considers the two systems from this perspective, it is easier to understand the underlying causes of the tensions between them. If one accepts that the respective views of justice—and the systems that have evolved around those views—are founded on the underlying belief structure of the culture, then it follows that each culture will have difficulty perceiving the merits of the other's approach to justice. It is difficult to accept as valid that which does not conform to one's fundamental beliefs. Even more problematic is the effort to inflict on one culture the justice system, and thus the underlying belief structure, of the other culture. Where the underlying belief structures are fundamentally inconsistent, the justice system of the one cannot work for the other, for in their eyes, what is being delivered is not justice."[7]

## The Relationship between Healing Justice and Canadian Justice

In his article *Justice and Aboriginal People*, James Dumont describes the Aboriginal concept of justice:

> The Anishinabe way of expressing the concept of justice is gwaik/ minodjiwi/dibaakonagwin (literally, "right and respectful judgment"). On the one side hovers the forever, unchanging, and always-truth of the Creator, governed by the guardian of the Creator's law, who is strict and unbending. On the other side is the ever-changing, moving, and unfolding truth of the human reality within the Creation, which is governed by a guardian who is kind, compassionate, and forgiving. In between these two is the law of balance and harmony toward which humankind must strive: this quest is governed by integrity, humility, and respect. Justice is the pursuit of a true judgement required to re-establish equilibrium and harmony in relationship, family, and society—a judgement which is gwaik: straight and honest, while at the same time being minidjiwin: respectful of the integrity of all persons, both the wronged and the wrongdoer.[8]

The quality of justice that Dumont expresses sets a high standard, primarily because Aboriginal justice is guided by the Creator's natural law. Humans must abide by the order of things as it was originally laid out. In many First Nations, the Elders speak of the retribution that the spirit pays in the spirit world and the retribution that the human must pay in this physical world. The concept of punishment or retribution is present; the difference between Aboriginal justice and Euro-Canadian justice is that in the Aboriginal view, punishment is determined by natural law and the Creator, not by human beings. Dumont goes on to state that:

> The Anishinabe justice system is one that leans toward wise counsel, compensation, restitution, rehabilitation, reconciliation, and balance, rather than obligatory correction, retribution, punishment, penance, and confinement. As a people whose spirit and psyche revolve around a core of vision and wholeness that is governed by respect, it is natural that a system of justice evolved that, in desiring to promote and effect right behavior, not only attends to balance and

reconciliation of the whole, but does so by honoring and respecting the inherent dignity of the individual.[9]

For a better understanding of the First Nations' value system and worldview and how these influence the meaning of words and phrases, I recommend Judge Murray Sinclair's article "Aboriginal Peoples, Justice and the Law" in *Continuing Poundmaker's and Riel's Quest.*[10]

The process of traditional healing is similar to the process called restorative justice. They share some common goals, such as to reconcile parties in conflict and to restore balance and harmony through understanding traditional teachings and ceremonies. Because of these similarities, it is important to learn more about traditional healing.

Yet traditional healing and Canadian justice remain estranged. The great hope is that these two ways of understanding and doing things might be reconciled, or at the very least, might find a way to acknowledge some common goals. As with any reconciliation that brings understanding, respect, and acceptance, we will continue to look for common ground as we explore these two paradigms from a First Nations' perspective.

## Notes

1. The information in this section was obtained through the oral tradition given by Elders Mary Lee, Danny Musqua, Henry Ross, and others, except where otherwise noted.

2. Linda C. Garro, "Ways of Talking about Illness in a Manitoba Anishinabe (Ojibway) Community," in *Circumpolar Health* no. 90, 226.

3. Ibid., 226.

4. These concepts and others are discussed further by Edward A. Connors, Registered Mohawk Psychologist, in "How Well We Can See the Whole Will Determine How Well We Are and How Well We Can Become," in Sue Deranger, *Culturally Specific Helping with First Nations People*, 1996.

5. A. C. Hamilton and C. M. Sinclair, *Report of the Manitoba Justice Inquiry* (Winnipeg, Manitoba: Queen's Printer, 1990), 22.

6. FSIN—Justice Unit, *Historical/Customary Law, First Nations Law Practices: The Natural Law* (December 1995), 3–4. This text is respectfully included with permission.

7. This section is respectfully included with permission from the Hollow Water Community Holistic Circle Healing CHCH Discussion Paper.

8. James Dumont, "Justice and Aboriginal People" in the Royal Commission on Aboriginal Peoples, *Bridging the Cultural Divide: A Report on Aboriginal Peoples and the Criminal Justice System in Canada* (Ottawa: Queen's Printer, 1996), 69.

9. Ibid., 69.

10. Judge M. Sinclair, "Aboriginal Peoples, Justice and the Law" in R. Gosse, J. Youngblood Henderson, and R. Carter, eds., *Continuing Poundmaker and Riel's Quest: Presentations Made at a Conference on Aboriginal Peoples and Justice* (Saskatoon: Purich, 1994), 173–84.

. . . .

*Published in* Justice as Healing *(1996) 1:4, this article is an excerpt from Ms. Lee's academic paper prepared for a Native Studies research course with the University of Saskatchewan under the advisement of Patricia Monture-Angus. The editor is grateful to Ms. Lee for permission to reprint her work.*

# Indigenous Justice Systems and Tribal Society

*Ada Pecos Melton*

Many contemporary tribal communities have dual justice systems. One is based on what can be called an American paradigm of justice; the other is based on what can be called an Indigenous paradigm.

The American paradigm has its roots in the worldview of Europeans. It is based on a retributive philosophy that is hierarchical, adversarial, punitive, and guided by codified laws and written rules, procedures, and guidelines.[1] The vertical power structure is upward with decision-making limited to a few. According to its retributive philosophy, because the victim has suffered, the criminal should suffer as well. Its premise is that criminals are wicked people who are responsible for their actions and deserve to be punished.[2] Punishment is used to appease the victim, to satisfy society's desire for revenge, and to reconcile the offender to the community by paying a debt to society. It does not offer a reduction in future crime or reparation to victims.

The Indigenous justice paradigm is based on a holistic philosophy and the worldview of the Aboriginal inhabitants of North America. These systems are guided by unwritten customary laws, traditions, and practices that are learned primarily by example and through the oral teachings of tribal Elders.[3] In the holistic philosophy, the circle of justice connects everyone involved with a problem or conflict on a continuum that focuses everyone on the same center. The center of the circle represents the underlying issues that need to be resolved to attain peace and harmony for the individuals and the community. The continuum represents the entire process, from disclosing problems, to discussing and resolving them, to making amends and restoring relationships. These methods are based on concepts of restorative and reparative justice as well as on the principles of healing and living in harmony with all beings and with nature.[4]

Restorative principles refer to the mending process needed to renew damaged personal and communal relationships. The victim is the focal point, and the goal is to heal and renew the victim's physical, emotional, mental, and spiritual well-being. The mending process involves deliberate acts by the offender to regain dignity and trust and to return to a healthy physical, emotional, mental, and spiritual state. These are necessary for the offender and victim to save face and to restore personal and communal harmony.

Reparative principles refer to the process of making things right for oneself and those affected by the offender's behavior. To repair relationships, the offender must make amends by apologizing, asking forgiveness, making restitution, and demonstrating a sincerity to make things right. The communal aspect views crime as a natural human error that requires corrective intervention by families and Elders or tribal leaders. Offenders remain an integral part of the community because of their important role in defining the boundaries of appropriate and inappropriate behavior and the consequences associated with misconduct.

In the American justice paradigm, the separation of powers and the separation of church and state are two essential doctrines designed to ensure that justice is uncontaminated by politics and religion. By contrast, for many tribes, law and justice are part of a whole that prescribes a way of life. Invoking the spiritual realm through prayer is essential throughout the Indigenous process. Restoring spirituality and cleansing one's soul are essential to the healing process for everyone involved in a conflict. Therefore, these separation doctrines are difficult for tribes to embrace; many find it impossible to make such distinctions. Whether this is good or bad is not the point. It is, however, an example of the resistance of Indigenous people to accept doctrines or paradigms that contradict their holistic philosophy of life.

## Law as a Way of Life

The concept of law as a way of life makes law a living concept that one comes to know and understand through experience. Law, as life, is linked to the elaborate relationships in many tribal communities. In some tribes, law is exemplified by tribal divisions that represent legal systems, since they prescribe the individual and kin relationships of members and the responsibilities individual and group members have to one another and to the community.[5]

For example, in several Pueblo tribes, a person is born into one of two *moieties*, or tribal divisions, decided by patrilineal lines. A woman can change membership only through marriage, when she joins her husband's moiety. Males generally cannot change their moiety, unless it is done during childhood through adoption or if their mother remarries into the opposite moiety.

This illustrates how tribal law becomes a way of life that is set in motion at birth and continues through an individual's life and death.

The Indigenous approach to justice requires that problems be handled in their entirety. Conflicts are not fragmented nor is the process compartmentalized into the stages of preadjudication, pretrial, adjudication, and sentencing. Such divisions hinder the resolution process for victims and offenders and delay the process of restoring relationships and communal harmony. The Indigenous approach examines all the contributing factors, so those involved can address the issues that led to the problem. Everyone affected by a problem participates in the process.

This distributive aspect generalizes individual misconduct or criminal behavior to the offender's wider kin group, hence there is a wider sharing of blame and guilt. The offender, along with his or her kinsfolk, are held accountable and responsible for correcting behavior and repairing relationships.[6]

## Indigenous Systems Today

The status of tribes as sovereign nations are both preconstitutional and extraconstitutional. Tribes continue to possess four key characteristics of their sovereign status: a distinctive permanent population; a defined territory with identifiable borders; a government that exercises authority over territory and population; and the capacity to enter into government-to-government relationships with other nation-states.[7]

The administration of justice, law, and order is a function of government retained by the tribes as sovereign nations. It is within this realm that Indigenous justice systems exist. Although there have been many efforts to limit the jurisdiction of tribal justice systems,[8] tribes retain the authority to determine the legal structure and forums that they use in administering justice and to determine the relationship of that legal structure with other governing bodies. Tribes have personal jurisdiction over their members and non-member Indians, territorial jurisdiction over their lands, and subject-matter jurisdiction over such areas as criminal, juvenile, and civil matters. In the United States, while limited by the Indian Civil Rights Act (1968) in sentencing,[9] tribes have concurrent jurisdiction over the felony crimes enumerated under the Major Crimes Act (1885).[10]

The forums for handling disputes differ for each tribe. These include varying combinations of family and community forums, traditional courts, quasi-modern courts, and modern tribal courts.

*Family forums*, such as family gatherings and talking circles, are facilitated by family Elders or community leaders. Matters usually involve family problems, marital conflicts, juvenile misconduct, violent or abusive behavior, parental misconduct, or property disputes. These family forums use customary laws, sanctions, and practices. Individuals are summoned to these gatherings following traditional protocols initiated by the chosen Elder. For example, in Pueblo communities, the gathering is convened by the aggrieved person's family, which must personally notify the accused and his or her family of the time and place of the gathering.

Generally, Elders are selected as spokespersons responsible for opening and closing the meetings with prayers. During the meeting, each side has an opportunity to speak. The victim may speak on his or her own behalf, and the family may help express the victim's issues. Extended family members often serve as spokespersons if the victim is very young or vulnerable. Similarly, a spokesperson may be designated to speak on behalf of the accused, especially if the accused is a juvenile or if other circumstances prevent the accused from speaking. When the family forum cannot resolve a conflict, the matter may be pursued elsewhere. Offenders must comply with the family forum's agreements, and their behavior is monitored by the families involved. Whether decisions and agreements are recorded is the family's decision.

*Community forums* require more formal procedures than family forums, but they draw on the families' willingness to discuss the issues, events, or accusations. These forums are mediated by tribal officials or representatives. Some tribes have citizen boards that serve as peacemakers or facilitators. Again, customary laws, sanctions, and practices are used. Tribal representatives give notice personally to the individuals and families involved. Usually, this is all that is necessary to compel individuals to meet in both the family and community forums. When necessary, tribal officials may provide a personal escort to the gathering place. In some tribal communities, notice may be sent by mail.

In community forums, the tribal representative acts as a facilitator and participates in the resolution process along with the offender and the victim and their families. As with the family forum, prayers are said at the beginning and at closure. An unresolved matter may be taken to the next level, but tribes may or may not offer an appeal process for the community forum. In the Navajo peacemaker system, formal charges in the Navajo district court may be filed. In some Pueblo communities, matters may be pursued through the traditional court. Once again, offenders must comply with the outcome, and they are monitored by the families and tribal officials.

*Traditional courts* incorporate some modern Western judicial practices to handle criminal, civil, traffic, and juvenile matters, but the process is similar to community forums. These courts exist in tribal communities that have retained an Indigenous government structure, such as the Southwest Pueblos. Matters are initiated through written criminal or civil complaints or petitions. Relatives often accompany defendants to the hearings.

Generally, anyone with a legitimate interest in the case may participate, from arraignment through sentencing. Heads of tribal government preside and are guided by customary laws and sanctions. In some cases, written criminal codes with prescribed sanctions may be used. Offenders must comply with the outcome; they are monitored by the tribal officials with assistance from the families. If offenders do not comply, more punitive actions may result, such as arrest and confinement.

Defendants are notified in writing of hearings, proceedings, and outcomes. Although rare, matters may be appealed to the tribal council. In some tribes where a dual system exists, interaction between the modern American court and the traditional court is prohibited. That is, one may not pursue a matter in both lower-level courts. However, an appeal from either court may be heard by the tribal council, which serves as the appellate court. Generally, courts record the proceedings and issue written judgment orders.

*Quasi-modern tribal courts* are based on the Anglo-American legal model. These courts handle criminal, civil, traffic, domestic relations, and juvenile matters. Written codes, rules, procedures, and guidelines are used, and lay judges preside. Some tribes limit the types of cases handled by these courts. For instance, land disputes are handled in several Pueblo communities by family and community forums. As in traditional courts, noncompliance by offenders may result in more punitive sanctions. These are courts of record, and appellate systems are in place.

*Modern tribal courts* mirror American courts. Guided by written codes, rules, procedures, and guidelines, they handle criminal, civil, traffic, domestic relations, and juvenile matters. They are presided over by law-trained judges and often exist in tribal communities that have a constitutional government. As with traditional courts and quasi-modern tribal courts, non-compliance by offenders may once again result in more punitive sanctions, such as arrest and confinement. Like quasi-modern tribal courts, these are courts of record and include appellate systems.

Some of the quasi-modern and modern courts use Indigenous justice methods as an alternative resolution process for juvenile delinquency, child custody, victim-offender cases, and civil matters. The trend of tribal courts is to use the family and community forums for highly interpersonal matters, either as a diversion alternative, as part of sentencing, or for victim-offender mediation. Some are court-annexed programs, such as the Alternatives for First Time Youth Offenders Program, sponsored by the Laguna Pueblo tribal court in New Mexico. Under this program, juvenile offenders are referred to the village officers, who hold a community forum. The court may make recommendations for resolving the matter, or village officers may handle the resolution informally. By working together, the court and village officers address problems at the local village level and intervene early to prevent further delinquency.

## Characteristics of Indigenous Law

The law of Indigenous societies is commonly referred to as *customary law, Indigenous law, Native law,* and *tribal* or *Native law ways.* All of these refer to the same concept.

*Customary law* is generally derived from custom. Custom in this sense means a long-established practice that has acquired the force of law by common adoption or acquiescence; it does not vary.[11]

*Tribal common law* is based on the values, mores, and norms of a tribe and is expressed in its customs, traditions, and practices. In some tribes, the tribal common law has been set out over time in different court decisions and written opinions and has become case law.[12] In several Pueblo communities, the matrilineal system holds that property belongs to the female. In a divorce or separation, property is divided according to the matrilineal definitions of property ownership and is written into the decisions of the traditional or tribal court. Similarly, Navajo courts incorporate Navajo common law in decisions in probate, criminal, and child custody cases and in marital conflicts.[13]

For many tribes along the northwest coast, such as the Yurok, customary laws dictate where families can conduct their fishing, hunting, and gathering. These areas are passed down from one generation to the next. When someone fishes in another family's area, it is considered an affront to the entire family. By custom, the wronged family convenes a family forum about the proper way to handle the matter and to request compensation. Compensation may be with fish, fishing gear, feathers, hides, beadwork, traditional clothing, or other forms of payment.

In several Pueblo communities, the *fiscale*, who is responsible for maintaining the peace and overseeing the welfare of children and youth, has the customary role of administering discipline. It is a general practice for parents to summon the fiscale when their children are unruly or misbehaving. This person advises the children about the consequences of their misconduct and may reprimand them or refer them and their parents to services, such as counseling.

In many tribes, information, beliefs, and customs are handed down orally or by example generation to generation.[4] For example, the Minto Tribal Court of Alaska includes a segment in the resolution process dedicated to "traditional counseling" by the facilitator or presiding judge. Similarly, the traditional courts of the Pueblos and the "talking to" in the Navajo peacemaking system include a general practice of "advising" or "giving." This segment is traditionally set aside for the spokespersons or tribal officials to speak of community values, mores, and the consequences of misbehavior or misconduct. Often these are conveyed in parables or creation narratives and beliefs. Advice is given about harboring vengeful feelings, and everyone is encouraged to renew relationships.

## The Indigenous Justice Process

Indigenous methods of conflict resolution include traditional dispute resolution, peacemaking, talking circles, family or community gatherings, and traditional mediation, described only by the language of the tribal community. All of these refer to methods for resolving problems and to the methods of restorative and reparative justice. The structure of relationships in many tribal communities is paramount to a legal system, exemplified by the clan system. Tribal law determines clan identification, which is often matrilineal.

In Pueblo communities, moiety and clan affiliations determine which group an individual will dance, sing, or hunt for in social activities; which religious or medicine groups one may join; which political positions one may hold; whom one may court or marry; or what property one may own. The clan system regulates the behavior of its members. The interlocking relationships in tribal communities often determine how problems are handled.

For example, in many tribal communities, parents and the extended family are expected to nurture, supervise, and discipline their children. When parental misconduct occurs, such as with physical or sexual abuse or neglect, the parents and extended family convene through the leadership of an Elder to address the matter. In a minor case of physical abuse or neglect, the family forum is used. This forum extensively invokes the distributive aspect of responsibility to ensure the children's protection and to monitor and enforce proper parental behavior and responsibility, which the family regulates. More serious cases may involve tribal officials.

In family and community forums and in traditional courts, those accused of wrongdoing must give a verbal account of their involvement in an incident, whether or not they admit to the accusations.[15] This verbal account is key to discovering the factors leading to the problem. The offender's family and relatives must also participate, since they may have to explain the offender's misconduct, especially when some type of victimization has occurred. For example, parents may be admonished for not providing proper discipline and supervision for children who vandalized or destroyed property. Relatives may be criticized for allowing a son or brother to abuse his wife or children.

Holding offenders and their families verbally accountable is essential to expressing remorse to the victims and their families. Face-to-face exchanges of apologies and forgiveness empower victims to confront their offenders and to convey their pain and anguish. Offenders are made accountable for their behavior. They must face the people whom they have hurt, explain themselves, ask forgiveness, and take full responsibility for making amends. Observing and hearing the apologies helps victims and their families to discern the offenders' sincerity and to move toward forgiveness and healing. Forgiveness is strongly suggested, but it is not essential for victims to begin healing.

The restorative aspect frequently involves using rituals to cleanse the offender's spirit and soul of the bad forces that caused the person to behave offensively. Ceremonial sweats, fastings, purifications, and other methods are used to begin the healing and cleansing process. This process is necessary for victims, offenders, and their families to regain their mental, spiritual, and emotional well-being and to restore family and communal harmony.[16]

The agreements reached in family and community forums are binding. The same interlocking obligations established in individual and community relationships compel participants to comply. This method of achieving compliance and enforcement is an important aspect of Indigenous systems, because it leaves little need for coercion. Just because offenders accept punishment, though, does not guarantee they will hold themselves accountable. Therefore, offenders must perform outward acts to show they are taking responsibility for correcting their behavior. Maintaining offender accountability is essential to ensuring their compliance with decisions and to preventing further criminal or other hurtful behavior. The fact that those who were affected by the offender's behavior are the ones who decide which punitive sanctions are needed and who then apply them makes the process all the more effective in changing offending behavior.

Historically, there is little evidence of penal systems in tribal communities. This remains true today, although many people now express a need for secure confinement facilities to address serious and violent crimes. Tribal communities continue to use many customary sanctions to appease victims and to safeguard against vengeance. These include public ridicule, public shaming, whippings, temporary and permanent banishment, withdrawing citizenship rights, financial and labor restitution, and community service. Some tribes still temporarily or permanently banish individuals who commit serious or violent crimes. According to custom, the Warm Springs Tribes in Oregon refer lawbreakers to the "whipman," who may whip a person for misconduct. The Laguna Alternatives for First Time Youth Offenders Program use community service quite extensively.

Tribal communities also use the Indigenous process for victimless offenses, such as problems between parents and children, individual misconduct, or alcohol abuse. Family members who are affected by the offender's behavior or who are concerned with his or her welfare may participate. Many tribal people view crime, delinquency, and other deviant behaviors as symptoms of bigger family problems. Including parents, siblings, and other extended family members engages those most familiar with the situation in helping to correct and prevent more serious crimes.

The Indigenous process can often be extremely uncomfortable and emotional because everyone affected participates. That is why facilitators and organizers take great care to provide a safe environment for whatever needs to be discussed. The distributive nature of this process engages the extended family as a resource for the offender, the victim, and the community. The community joins in the effort to resolve problems, to ensure compliance, to provide protection, and to retain ownership of the problems.[17]

## Preserving Indigenous Systems

Tribes face the inevitable conflict created by two justice paradigms competing for existence in one community. Many Americans believe that the law is something to be applied and that justice is something to be administered. In contrast, tribes traditionally believe that law is a way of life and that justice is a part of the life process. For one paradigm to exist, it must convert people to follow it.

Although it appears that tribal courts follow the Anglo-American legal system, many adhere to the traditional values of the tribal justice system. Tribes have been wary of the ethnocentric view of the Western colonizers. The colonizers have devalued tribal legal structures and worked to replace them with an imported Western system.[18] Tribes were also required to participate in the Anglo-American legal system in order to protect their lands and people, but they did so without trusting or believing in it. Because the federal government imposed this foreign system on tribes, its efforts to convert them was thwarted.

Discontent with the efforts of modern tribal courts to address the crime, delinquency, and social and economic problems in tribal communities has driven the tribes' efforts to strengthen and retraditionalize tribal justice systems. Their discontent is joined by the dominant culture's current disillusionment with justice in this country, raising doubts about retributive justice and moving people toward a more restorative framework.[19]

This emerging restorative perspective for the American justice system is characterized by adherence to distinctly restorative values. For example, the process of responding to crime includes all the affected parties—offenders, victims, and the community. Government and local communities play complementary roles in that response. Accountability is based on offenders understanding the harm caused by their offense, accepting responsibility for that harm, and repairing it. These and other values of restorative justice guide professionals in using sanctions appropriately and equitably and ensuring that offenders make amends to victims and the community.[20]

Converting to the American justice paradigm is a difficult choice for tribes, particularly those with a functional Indigenous justice system. For many, full conversion is not possible because the Indigenous justice paradigm is too powerful to abandon. Moreover, the strong adversarial features of the American justice paradigm will always conflict with the communal nature of most tribes. For these reasons, the inherently restorative and reparative features of the Indigenous justice paradigm will continue to be more appealing to the majority of tribal people.

Nonetheless, tribes need to identify their community strengths and views on justice, law, and order. The role of non-Indians is to assist and support the tribes in strengthening their justice systems and to suppress the urge to take over or replace them. Tribes have the sovereign and cultural right to explain, interpret, change, enact, and apply their own laws—oral and written—through whatever mechanisms they choose. It is their responsibility to teach the knowledge and skills embedded in their Indigenous paradigm to their young. American Indian and Alaskan Native people have the clearest understanding of their Indigenous law ways because they live them. They must be the messengers of this law to preserve its integrity, authority, power, and meaning to the people.

The many intrusions to the tribal way of life have interfered with the natural evolution of the Indigenous justice paradigm, yet though it has been slowed, it has never stopped. The resurgence among tribes to strengthen and retraditionalize their judiciaries has rejuvenated the evolutionary process. While mainstream society is in the midst of shifting from a retributive to a restorative justice model, many tribes are strengthening their Indigenous paradigm. In doing so, they are empowering themselves to provide a justice system that has meaning to the people they serve and that has the power to perpetuate what was preserved by the ancestors and passed on by the Elders as testimony of their commitment to the future of tribes. Contemporary

American Indian and Alaskan Native people are now faced with making the same commitment to preserve the Indigenous justice system that the Elders maintained and to find ways to perpetuate it.

## Notes

1. Robert Yazzie, "Life Comes from It: Navajo Justice Concepts," Legal Education Series, *Alternatives in Dispute Resolution and Traditional Peacemaking* (Petaluma, CA: National Indian Justice Center, 1993); and Richard Falk, *International Jurisdiction: Horizontal and Vertical Conceptions of Legal Order*, 32, Temple L.Q. 295 (1959).

2. Travis, *Introduction to Criminal Justice*, 2nd ed. (Cincinnati: Anderson Publishing, 1995); and Neubauer, *America's Courts and the Criminal Justice System*, 2nd ed. (Monterey: Brooks/Cole Publishing, 1984).

3. Yazzie, "Life Comes from It"; Tso, "Decision Making in Tribal Courts," 31, *Arizona L. Rev.* (1989); and Zion, "Searching for Indian Common Law," in Morse and Woodman, eds., *Indigenous Law and the State* (Dordrecht, Holland: Foris Publications, 1988).

4. Yazzie, "Life Comes from It," 4.

5. Connors and Brady, "Alaska Native Traditional Dispute Resolution," paper presented at the National Conference on Traditional Peacemaking and Modern Tribal Justice Systems in Albuquerque, New Mexico; Tribal Justice Center (1986), "Indian Jurisprudence and Mediation the Indian Way: A Case Review of the Saddle Lake Tribal Justice System," paper presented at the Conference on Mediation in Winnipeg, Manitoba.

6. Melton, "Traditional and Contemporary Tribal Law Enforcement: A Comparative Analysis," paper presented at the Western Social Science Association, 31st Annual Conference in Albuquerque, New Mexico (1989).

7. Valencia-Weber and Zuni, pre-publication draft (1995), "Domestic Violence and Tribal Protection of Indigenous Women in the United States" *St. Johns University Law Review* (forthcoming).

8. See the establishment of the Court of Indian Offenses in 1883; the unilateral imposition of law and order codes in 1884; passage of the Major Crimes Act, 18 U.S.C. §1153 (1885, Stipp. 1986); the Indian Country Crimes Act, 18 U.S.C. §1152 (1817); the Assimilative Crimes Act, 30 Stat. 717 (1898); Public Law 83-280, Indians-Criminal Offenses and Civil Causes-State Jurisdiction, 18 U.S.C. § 1162, 25 U.S.C. §§ 1321-1326, 28 U.S.C. § 1360; the Indian Civil Rights Act, 25 U.S.C. § 1301 1303 (1968, Suppl. 1986); and Supreme Court decisions such as *Oliphant v. Suquamish Indian Tribe*, 435 U.S. 191; and *Duro v. Reina*, et al., 110 S.Ct. 2953.

9. Indian Civil Rights Act, ibid., 18, imposes certain protections and limitations

on tribal authority and, as amended in 1986, limits criminal punishment to one-year imprisonment and a $5,000 fine.

10. Major Crimes Act, 18.

11. Zuni, "Justice Based on Indigenous Concepts," paper presented at the Indigenous Justice Conference (1992).

12. Austin, "Incorporating Tribal Customs and Traditions into Tribal Court Decisions," paper presented at the Federal Indian Bar Association: Indian Law Conference in Albuquerque, New Mexico (1992).

13. Zuni, "Justice Based on Indigenous Concepts," 25.

14. Ibid.

15. Melton, "Traditional and Contemporary Tribal Law Enforcement," 16.

16. Bluehouse and James Zion, "Hozhooji Naaliannii: The Navajo Justice and Harmony Ceremony," 10 *Mediation Q.* 327 (1993).

17. Canadian Institute for Conflict Resolution, "Report to the Council of Akwesasne Concerning a Peacemaking Process," Ottawa, Canada (1990).

18. Mohawk, Prologue, in Wallace, *The White Roots of Peace* (Philadelphia: University of Pennsylvania Press, 1946).

19. "Victims Seeking Fairness, Not Revenge: Toward Restorative Justice," *Federal Probation* (September 1989); Van Ness, "Restorative Justice," in *Criminal Justice, Restitution, and Reconciliation,* ed. Galaway and Hudson (Monsey, NJ: Willow Tree Press, 1990).

20. Bazemore and Umbreit, "Balanced and Restorative Justice: Program Summary," Office of Juvenile Justice and Delinquency Prevention (October 1994).

. . . .

*Published in* Justice as Healing *(2001) 6:1, this article appeared first in* Judicature 79:3, *the journal of the American Judicature Society. The editor would like to thank Ada Pecos Melton and the publisher for their permission to reprint the work.*

## Healing as Justice: The Navajo Response to Crime

*Chief Justice Robert Yazzie*

As Navajos always do, I introduce myself by clan so you will know who I am. I am of the Folded Arm Clan. I was born for the Bitter Water Clan. Most people don't realize it, but when Navajos introduce themselves that way, they are actually performing a *legal* ceremony that has to be with healing. You will see what I mean as I go along.

### Indians, Anthills, and Stereotypes

Many people think they know what the word *law* means. But when you speak of the Indian version of "traditional law" or "Indian common law," you lose them; they don't have the slightest idea what you mean. Two summers ago, a six-state conference of state judges asked me to speak on Navajo common law. After my talk, Jim Zion, our court solicitor, dashed outside to have a cigarette. He overheard two Wyoming judges talking. The first judge said, "What did you think of Chief Justice Yazzie's presentation on Navajo common law?" The second laughed and said, "He didn't mention staking people to anthills." Obviously the judges saw too many Western movies.

Unfortunately, there is a popular stereotype that Indian justice is rough justice—that Indians used punishments such as staking people to anthills, running them through a gauntlet of people armed with clubs, or stringing an offender (usually shown in the movies as a white offender) up in the sun to bake. That is unfortunate. One of the reasons I want to speak at this important conference is that people such as myself, Indian leaders, need to do more to educate the general American public about Indian ways.

### Definition of Law

One definition of *law* states that law is composed of three things: norms, institutions, and force. A *norm* is a feeling of "ought." One ought to do this and ought not to do that. A norm becomes a law when it is enforced by an institution, such as a court or the police. Many definitions insist that without force or the ability to punish, there can be no law. The Anglo definition of *law* insists on visible institutions, such as courts and punishment. This type of law can only hurt; it cannot heal.

When I first heard this definition, I felt something was missing. I asked the person who gave me the definition if human emotions should be a part of the definition. Aren't emotions a part of the process? Shouldn't they be? If so, how?

When the Navajo courts define law, we must consider *norms*. Norms are values and shared feelings about the way to do things. Sometimes Navajo say, "Do things in a good way." As Indians, we know what it means to do things in a good way. Therefore, the people's shared feelings fill in that broad term of *law* to give it meaning. We must also consider moral values in the definition of law. Too often, people reject the word *morality* because of its religious overtones. But it means something more: it is shared feelings about the right path. To complete the definition of law, the traditional Indian "institutions" must be included: family; clan; ceremonial bodies or societies; and even people dealing with each other.

For example, an anthropologist by the name of Downs mentions the case of a man who stole a woman's blanket and jewelry at a dance so he could sell them and buy wine. The woman suspected the man and confronted him the next day. He immediately admitted what he had done and gave the woman enough sheep to make up for the loss. What were those two Navajos doing? They were applying norms, values, moral principles, and emotions in the institution of addressing each other in a good way. The woman asked about the loss of her blanket and jewelry. The man replied honestly and offered *nalyeeh*, or compensation. The man did things in "the good way," because this is a shared value.

## Is Punishment Necessary for Law?

European explorers often said, "Indians have no law." Why? They couldn't see police; they didn't find courts; they didn't see uniforms, jails, and all the trappings of power. But they also couldn't see the clan mothers, who are so important to our Native legal institutions.

A clan is built on relationships. In the Navajo way, we trace our clan membership through our mothers, and we are "born for" our father's clan.

My introduction of myself by clan simply identified who I am within our traditional legal system, so that you will know your relationship to me. I may be a thousand miles away from Navajo land, but I still introduce myself by clan. Why is clan relationship so important? We Navajos say of people such as yourselves—who may be strangers—"Treat strangers like they were a relative." We deal with each other in ways to avoid confrontation and the use of force. Force, coercion, and the ability to punish are not necessary to have law.

Many people seem to be turning away from law as coercion and are looking to restorative and reparative principles. *Restorative* is defined as "the process for renewing damaged personal and community relationships." *Reparative* is defined as "the process of making things right for those affected by an offender's behavior." In other words, *how* can we help victims? We use only one word for both ideas: peacemaking. The Navajo term is *Hozhooji Naat'aanii*. Because it is difficult to translate its concepts into English completely, I will simply describe it as "talking things out in a good way."

## "Talking Things Out"

The traditional Navajo response to crime is *not* staking the offender to an anthill. It is to talk the problem out with respect. In traditional Navajo society, everyone is equal. There is no strong "chief" who hears a dispute and makes a decision for others. In fact, the idea of someone with power and authority making decisions for others is entirely contrary to Navajo morals. We believe in a high degree of freedom, but we call it "freedom with responsibility," to use the words of our Associate Justice Raymond D. Austin.

What is an offender? It is someone who shows little regard for right relationships. That person has little respect for others. Navajos say of such a person, "He acts as if he has no relatives." So, what do you do when someone acts as if they have no relatives? You bring in the relatives! Victim rights are an important issue. What do you do about them? There, too, you bring in the relatives.

Vincent Craig, our chief probation officer, once told me a story. He said that an oral history came down to him saying that in the old days, many young women became pregnant while herding sheep. The woman's family would then approach the man's family to talk out a settlement. That is what I mean by bringing in the relatives.

## Leadership, Leaders, and Judges

Does the Navajo practice of talking things out mean that we don't have any kind of civil leadership? Certainly not. But our leadership works differently from Western ways. In an Anglo courtroom, a judge may use his or her wisdom to announce the reasons for a decision, but the judge never speaks to or counsels the parties. There, judges know the law and make decisions for others.

In the traditional Navajo way, when someone has a problem, we can appoint a peacemaker to handle it. The peacemaker uses the "talking out" process to address the problem. Who is invited to attend the discussions? The victim and his or her family. The offender and his or her family. Friends, neighbors, and anyone else who is involved in the matter or affected by it will be invited to attend or simply may attend as well.

The ones who have the problem are actually the "judge." That is, the people involved in a dispute make the decision themselves. I say "people involved" in a dispute, because a dispute affects everyone. If, for example, someone hurts me, my family is involved in the dispute because I am hurt. If I hurt someone else and I am obliged to pay compensation to make up for the injury, my family is involved because they have a responsibility to help pay the compensation. This is one of the ways the Navajo clan works as a legal system.

Who are the peacemakers? Navajo wise persons, whom we call *naat'aanii*. Others call them an Elder. The term refers to someone who speaks well, plans well, and bears himself or herself well. These persons use their wisdom to counsel and provide guidance; they encourage parties to talk out their problems but do not make decisions for others. They help plan decisions through guidance, but they don't make the decisions.

Navajo women were naat'aanii too. They still are. This challenges another stereotype; namely, that Indian men are the strong, dominant leaders. A naat'aanii is not a "chief." A naat'aanii isn't just an adviser. A naat'aanii is someone considered so wise in his or her community that people listen. Today, we call a naat'aanii a peacemaker. We have over 250 of them in 110 local communities called "chapters."

## The Healing Way

Our traditional Navajo justice ceremony is called *Hozhooji Naat'aanii*. Many Navajo words have no corresponding term in English. I will say simply that this term refers to talking and planning in order to restore damaged relationships, guided by a person with wisdom who helps plan things to regain *K'e* (respect). Hozhooji Naat'aanii is the "Justice and Harmony Ceremony," and it is a healing ceremony.

The procedure is fairly simple. Its elements are (1) prayer; (2) expressing feelings; (3) "the lecture"; (4) discussion; (5) reconciliation; and (6) consensus.

*1. Prayer.* A traditional prayer puts people in the right frame of mind for the talking out. Often, a peacemaker will choose an Elder to say it. Beginning this way is important, because the Indian world is not solely a material world. In Indian belief, the people of the spirit world are very much a part of daily life and actively participate in it. You can ask them for help. Prayer is the way you seek guidance and help. Put in a more material or Western way, prayer helps set the tone and make people more receptive. Even Alcoholics Anonymous speaks of "the Higher Power."

*2. Expressing feelings.* After prayer, everyone has a say about what happened. They also express how *they feel* about what happened. When talking about the process of the Navajo Peacemaker Court, we like to say that the most important piece of paper in the procedure is the tissue for drying tears. That's because emotions are on the table. Opinion evidence is freely allowed within the bounds of saying things in a respectful way.

For example, imagine the situation of someone who has whiplash because a drunk driver rear-ended him at a stop sign. What happens if the injured driver wants to tell the court about his or her pain and anger from being injured? "Objection!" "Sustained."

Navajo peacemaking has a place for people to express how they feel without rules of evidence to quiet them. In Western courtrooms, a person is not allowed to express how he or she feels. Yet expressing emotions is an essential part of healing. In peacemaking, you must know how I feel, and I must know how you feel. That is part of making or restoring a healthy relationship. This corrects another big stereotype about Indians; namely, that we have no emotions—that we bear everything with a calm, stoic face. That is not so. Indians' emotions are very important, and we express them.

*3. "The lecture."* When the prayers have been said, when emotions have been expressed, and when people have told their stories, it is time for guidance from our naat'aanii. We have "the lecture." That's when the peacemaker does some teaching. Again, we use our wise people in a way that is different from how Western courts use their wise people—judges. The peacemaker will relate parts of the *Hajine Bahane*, our creation lore, and apply it to the problem. The old "stories" are actually a form of precedent that everyone respects. That is why peacemaking is not "mediation." Most mediators are called "neutrals," which means they don't express an opinion about the problem they are handling. Peacemakers have very definite opinions about what they hear while talking things out.

By offering guidance from our stories, traditions, and ceremonies and applying them to the situation, our peacemakers teach the law. We know these are laws. They are binding because we have been reared in them. Indians don't store their law in books; they keep it in their minds and hearts. Everyone knows the law.

4. *Discussion.* Who participates in peacemaking? The parties themselves (who are the "judges"), a leader and planner (naat'aanii), and relatives. Having relatives participate in the process is fundamental. Consider the following example: A young Navajo woman took a man to court in a paternity action for child support. The man denied that he was the father. It was his word against hers, and most Navajos can't afford blood tests. The judge sent the case to the peacemaker court. The couple's parents attended. The discussion was no longer about whether the man was the father, but what the families were going to do for the well-being of their child. Those grandparents knew what was going on all the time. It is hard to hide things in a small community.

Family participation is a part of the healing process because it gets past denial. Denial—the psychological barrier that underlies most cases of child abuse, alcohol-related crime, family violence, sexual abuse, and driving while intoxicated—is the act of people refusing to face reality or own up to their actions.

In a recent peacemaking involving domestic violence that took place in our Tuba City court, the male batterer's sister came in with him. The defendant was full of denial; he made light of his actions; and he blamed his wife for the whole thing. It was the man's *sister* who straightened him out. She told him he was violent and that he must do something about his emotional state and his drinking—to stop making excuses for his *own* actions. She told him the traditional principles that he violated—that Navajos believe in the dignity of women, so you must not hurt them. She then offered to help him. She broke down his barrier of denial and used her influence as a sister to deal with the underlying problems. See how relatives get the job done?

The discussion phase also gets at the *causes* of problems. For example, the judge in our Ramah district learned about post-traumatic stress disorder (PTSD), a psychological condition that creates fear and mistrust and results in violent conduct. She started having her probation and parole officer check offenders' records for military service and PTSD. Sure enough, most of the assault defendants in front of her were war veterans. She also found that the children of vets with the ailment were accused of delinquency. The parents were teaching their children to be suspicious and violent. The judge started sending these people to traditional Navajo curing ceremonies designed to deal with the psychological injury that comes from military conflict.

I must add that *all* Indians suffer from a form of mass post-traumatic stress disorder because of the trauma caused by attempts to kill our culture and government. One study indicates that PTSD underlies a great deal of alcohol-related crime, violence, and abuse.

**5. *Reconciliation.*** If you operate a "winner take all" system of justice, expect ongoing problems. If you have a system that works toward reconciliation, you may resolve the conflicts that underlie ongoing problems. For example, a couple got a divorce in the Tuba City court in 1978. For years, the woman, who had custody of their child, returned to court month after month to attempt to get child support. Month after month, the man complained that his visitation with his son was too limited. The family judge got tired of that family living in his courtroom, so he sent the case to the Navajo peacemaker court. When the couple was allowed to talk about their problems—the woman's need for child support and the man's need to be with his son—the situation changed. Now the man pays his child support because he knows his son needs it. The man gets to see his son whenever he wants, and he often stays at the woman's house while she and her second husband are out of town.

Navajo justice is restorative justice. It restores people to good relationships with each other. That is particularly necessary in Navajo land, because people tend to live together in small communities, and clan relatives have disputes with each other. Unlike the law in Florida, Navajos can't divorce their relatives.

**6. *Consensus*.** Finally, based upon the prayer, venting, discussion, and knowledge of the traditional way of doing things, the people themselves usually reach a consensus about what to do. Planning is actually a central Navajo justice concept, and the people plan a very practical resolution to the problem. Today, we put it in writing, and the parties sign it.

Consensus is what makes our justice and harmony ceremony—peacemaking—a healing process. Navajos believe in a greater degree of equality than you will find in Canadian and American law. What does it mean when people are equal? Navajos believe it is wrong to use coercion, so the legal process requires consensus among equals. Each person enters peacemaking as an equal and participates as an equal due to consensus. Decisions in peacemaking are a product of agreement, which is sometimes urged by the naat'aannii.

Navajos also believe in equality in outcome. Most often, this means a form of sharing where people either lower their demands or do what they might not otherwise do. In one peacemaking case that involved a truck killing some sheep on the road, the grandfather of the driver agreed to pay for the damage done to the pickup truck and to give the herders a few rams and ewes. You would not get that result in a Canadian or American court where liability is based on fault. In our sheep case, the parties all compromised for an outcome that benefited everyone.

## "The Traditional Probation Officer"

How do we know that the parties will stick to the agreement? Our sentencing policy uses the concept of a "traditional probation officer." Let me explain it this way: In the Navajo way of thinking, when someone "acts as if they had no relatives," relatives have certain responsibilities. It is shameful to have a relative who acts out against others. That hurts *your* relationships with others. So, you assume responsibility for your relative's actions. The same holds true for victims. If my relative is hurt, I have a responsibility to step in and help.

There is an action verb in our policy that is important to understand. It is *nalyeeh*. You can translate it a couple of different ways. It can be translated as "restitution" or "reparation." Articles on Indigenous traditional law often use that translation. However, those are nouns, aren't they? I said an action verb. The other translation is that it is a "demand to be made whole." It is also a demand to enter into a respectful discussion of the hurt. The aim of nalyeeh is not punishment or the correction of a person. That would violate the Navajo maxim "It's up to him." Instead, the aim is correction of the *action*. It is to cure the harm caused by bad conduct.

People will negotiate the amount of nalyeeh, but that can be symbolic only. Recently, we got a call from a Colorado probation officer. He interviewed a young Navajo woman who was the victim of a sex offense and asked her what she wanted. She said, "Six horses." He called us to ask us what she was talking about. She was demanding nalyeeh, and six horses were the symbol of her injury and what she felt her honor required. The negotiation is the talking-out process I described. At the end, although the relationship of the parties is the most important topic of discussion, a payment is often required to seal the successful conclusion of the problem and to make the victim whole.

The offender's relatives play a very important part in nalyeeh. It is they who actually pay the money, horses, or goods. Once they have done that, they will keep an eye on the offender to make certain that he or she will not offend again. Our policy provides for a peace bond, signed by relatives, for this purpose.

In a case where a non-Indian court intervened and disrupted the negotiations, the families of three young men who raped a young Navajo woman were about to transfer twenty-one head of cows to the victim's family. A state court had jurisdiction, and it refused to enforce the agreement. The woman was shamed by not having a public symbol of her innocence delivered to her home, and she got nothing. If the traditional arrangement had been followed, the young men would have been on very strict probation by their own families. I do not know what finally happened.

In sum, we want the families of offenders to take responsibility for their relative and the families of victims to speak along with their relative. In a situation where a victim is afraid to face the perpetrator, the victim's relatives can do the talking.

There is something else important about the traditional probation officer concept. In 1892, Western courts were imposed on Navajos. This told Navajos that they were not competent to solve their own problems. The other aspect of the traditional probation officer concept is that we want communities to reassume their proper role in resolving community problems.

## Anglo Law and Peacemaking

As I have come to understand both the law I learned in law school and the law I learned in Navajo ceremonies, I can begin to see the difference between the two systems. Anglo law is built on authority, rank, and obedience in the face of punishment. Navajo common law is built on relationships, traditions, emotions, and methods of dealing with each other in a good way. We have a hard time translating our legal terms into English, because there are no English words for what we are talking about. Words carry connotations, and non-Navajos have a hard time understanding the connotations of what we are talking about in our legal language. I will give a few examples.

The dynamic of Navajo justice that makes the "talking out" in peacemaking work is called *k'e*. It has to do with the importance of relationships. It is a deeply embedded feeling we have of our responsibilities to others and our duty to live in good relations with them. It produces consensus and healing. Where does it come from? For example, when a baby first shows signs of awareness of his or her surroundings and laughs, that is a joyful event. The first person to hear a baby laugh must sponsor a ceremony to celebrate. All of the baby's relatives attend, and the baby's awareness opens to a world of relatives and relationships. That is where the baby first learns about k'e. Sometimes the word *k'e* is translated as "solidarity," but that doesn't get at the deep connotations that the word has for us as Navajos.

Another example is the *kinaalda* or a woman's puberty ceremony. It stresses the importance of women and teaches their dignity. It is our domestic violence law.

The word *hozho* is often translated as "harmony." Again, it doesn't convey the deep meaning we understand. It means "the perfect state." It means "there is a place for everything in reality, and there is hozho or harmony when everything is in its proper place, functioning well with everything else." It is the goal of peacemaking—our justice and harmony ceremony. Our teachings and beliefs, including the ones I mentioned a few moments ago, are designed to guide people to that state. Traditional Indian justice works because it is a community view of life, not an individual "win-lose" process.

## Peacemaking in the Criminal Justice System

The two systems—Anglo and Navajo—can be used together. In Navajo courts, our sentencing policy provides for peacemaking before a charge is filed, after one is filed, before sentencing, and after sentencing. I will describe how this works.

Many courts have diversion programs in the prosecutor's office, which send people into some form of community justice in place of filing charges. Most often, deferred prosecution is used as the incentive. We had a demonstration program in our Chinle court where we diverted DWI [drinking while impaired] cases into peacemaking, and it was very successful. We found that the talking-out process works in changing attitudes about drinking and driving. Our judges can also divert into peacemaking at the time of plea.

I think we have a good way to address victims' rights by using peacemaking to recommend a sentence. The victims can choose whether to participate or not, yet they often do. The parties then reach a consensus about a sentence and recommend it to the judge. I want to stress that when I say "consensus," I mean that everyone has to agree. What, you might say, if the victim is being coerced? That is why we have the victim's relatives attend. Does that mean that the defendant has a slim chance of a favorable outcome? His or her relatives get to speak too. Also, our peacemaker has an opinion and will have some influence on the decision. While peacemakers do not make a decision or impose one, they have an important say about how things should be concluded.

Why would you use peacemaking after a sentence has been imposed? Most courts use the suspended imposition of sentence, suspended execution of sentence, or probation to get defendants into treatment programs or to get them to pay restitution or to do community service. Sometimes that works, and sometimes it doesn't. We all know the defendant who attends the alcohol or counseling program only because a possible jail sentence is hanging out there. You know how they look: their arms are folded with an angry stare; their barriers are up. In peacemaking, however, you can make a defendant *want* to go into alcohol treatment or counseling.

There is a fifth use of peacemaking I haven't mentioned. The Navajo Nation is 25,000 square miles big. It is bigger than nine states of the United States. It's something like the Texan who said that it took him three days to drive across his ranch. A Navajo replied, "Yeah, I once had a truck like that too." We don't have enough police to patrol that large an area. In fact, most Indian nations have a police force only half the size of a normal rural police force.

Most of our peacemaking cases are walk-ins where the people themselves bring the case. Rather than call the police, many people call a peacemaker.

People are using peacemaking for family squabbles, alcohol-related behavior, family violence, and even such controversial things as sex offenses. It works.

## Conclusion

In August 1555, Holy Roman Emperor Charles the Fifth ordered the Spanish to "honor and obey" the "laws and good customs of Indians." The Spanish couldn't—or wouldn't—understand them, so things went downhill from there.

In 1883, the U.S. Supreme Court said that traditional Indian criminal law was the binding law, not state or territorial law. Congress couldn't understand it, so it imposed a federal criminal law on Indians—trying them by strangers outside their homelands.

In 1899, the U.S. Supreme Court ruled that traditional Indian law applied in probate court. The Bureau of Indian Affairs didn't understand (or didn't *want* to understand) traditional probate, so in 1910, it gave the Secretary of the Interior the power to decide Indian estates under state law. We have only just begun.

Think of what America and Canada know about Indian common law. It is only the tip of the proverbial iceberg. Both governments are afraid of what is underneath the water. Think of the Canadian icebreaker approaching; it wants to push our iceberg out into the warm waters to melt. That is assimilation. The U.S. icebreaker wants to blow up the iceberg. It's too big. It's too big to melt, and it's too big to be blown up. In fact, as Indians regain their legal traditions, it's growing. We found that we *can* use traditional methods in a modern court system. We are ahead of the curve when it comes to restorative or reparative justice. We call it peacemaking.

The final point I want to make is this: Peacemaking is also good horse sense. I like that Anglo expression, because we Navajos *love* horses. We see that our ancestors were pretty smart. They had human dynamics figured out and knew psychology long before Freud.

Peacemaking simply taps the wisdom of our communities. It involves communities in the process and responds to their needs. It makes offenders look at themselves and at the consequences of their actions. Whereas many victim-assistance programs forget that victims have families, peacemaking engages the families as one of the best resources for help. That's the Navajo response to crime in a nutshell: it gives justice by offering healing.

## Glossary

**Hajine Bahane**: Navajo creation story.

**Hozho**: Harmony. The perfect state. There is a place for everything in reality, and there is hozho or harmony when everything is in its proper place, functioning well with everything else.

**Hozhooji Naat'aanii**: Talking things out in a good way. Justice and Harmony Ceremony.

**K'e**: The importance of relationships. A deeply embedded feeling of our responsibilities to others and our duty to live in good relations with them.

**Kinaalda**: A woman's puberty ceremony stressing the importance of women and teaching their dignity. A domestic violence law.

**Naat'aanii**: A peacemaker. Someone who is considered so wise in his or her community that people listen.

**Nalyeeh**: (v.) A demand to be made whole. A demand to enter into a respectful discussion of the hurt. Restitution, reparation, compensation.

. . . .

*This article combines two articles by Chief Justice Yazzie that were published in* Justice as Healing. *One was published in 1995 and the other in 1998 (3:2). The second article was based on a speech delivered by Chief Justice Yazzie at the National Symposium entitled "Sentencing: The Judicial Response to Crime" at the American Judicature Society in San Diego, California, on 2–3 November 1997. We are grateful to Chief Justice Yazzie for permission to publish his work.*

# 15

# Maori Justice—The Marae as a Forum for Justice

*Nin Tomas*

Hutia te rito o te harakeke
Kei hea te ko'mako e ko
Ki mai ki au
He aha te mea nul o te ao
Maku e ki atu
He tangata, he tangata, he tangata

*Pluck out the central part of the flax bush*
*Where will the Korimako be heard*
*If you were to ask*
*What is the greatest thing of this world*
*I would reply*
*It is people, it is people, it is people*

This Whakatauki (proverb) speaks of the flax bush that grows in Aotearoa, providing a source of weaving materials and medicine for Maori people. The "rito" is the central shoot that produces the new growth of the flax. If this is removed, then the bush cannot grow; it must, eventually, wither and die. The Korimako is a bird that thrives on the nourishment that the flax bush supplies. Its voice is often heard calling from within the flax. If the rito is removed and the flax dies, how will the Korimako sustain its existence? Likewise, if that part of us which is central to our existence as Maori people be taken away, how can we sustain ourselves?

Ko Whangatauatia te Maunga     *Whangatauatia is my mountain*
Ko Karirikura te Moana     *Karirikura is my sea*
Ko Tinana te Waka     *Tinana is my ancestral canoe*
Ko Tumoana te Tangata     *Tumoana is the chiefly ancestor*
Ko Te Rarawa te Iwi     *Te Rarawa is my tribe*
Ka tu ake tenei kaikorero!     *This speaker stands!*

In May and June of this year, I was fortunate to spend time in Vancouver with the Sparrow whanau (family) and in Saskatoon with the Monture-Angus whanau. During this time, we spoke of what it would be like to deal with issues of justice among ourselves and in a manner that arises from within our own cultures. I have given much thought to this, and here is my response as a Maori woman, a daughter of Papatuanuku (earth mother) and Ranginui (skyfather).

Justice wears many different faces, and yet in essence it is constant and, just like the flax bush, essential to our existence. When our actions are in accordance with Pono (truth) and Tika (moral rightness), then justice is done. Justice is the means by which we, as humans, keep our world balanced. Its measure is the sense of harmony and well-being felt by the individual and reflected in his or her actions within the community. Justice, then, is a communal asset of great value to the spiritual and physical well-being of any community. The ultimate product of justice is social stability based on consent by consensus.

Justice produces equilibrium. In order for equilibrium to exist, there is a pathway—Ko Te Ara Tika (the right road) that Maori seeking justice for themselves and others must follow. It is paved with traditional principles—indicators and measures of true and proper behavior—crafted by our ancestors as they journeyed through the cosmos and into Te Ao Marama (the physical world).

These principles remind us of the Whakapapa (genealogical) links of humans to the rest of the world, which we must constantly strengthen with our actions. We do this by acknowledging and respecting Tikanga Maori (Maori concepts and principles) in our daily living. Only when Maori people act in accordance with Tikanga can we live balanced, trouble-free lives, secure in the knowledge that we are fulfilling our duties to our past, our present, and our future generations.

Maori principles for life are broad. They are heavily laden with obligation to other people and serve to position each individual within the wider universe that we carry within us. These principles include

Pono (truth)—so that our actions must be true to the worldview we
   as Maori hold of the universe;
Tika (rightness)—our actions must be in accordance with the truth
   of our worldview;

Whakapapa (genealogy)—our actions must recognize our un-
   severable spiritual and physical relationships with the rest of
   the world; and
Whanaungatanga (interrelatedness)—our actions must show that
   we uphold and reaffirm our relationships with other people and
   with the rest of the world.

In order to achieve this, there are at least three basic spiritual concepts that
Maori recognize and draw upon in daily life. They are Wairua (spirituality)—
that part of our existence which is not physical:

Tapu—the authority that is located in all things, being placed there
   by our Gods;
Mana (prestige and dignity)—the way in which spiritual authority
   manifests itself so as to be perceivable by others; and
Mauri (life essence)—that which links all things spiritually and is
   the source of our own life essence.

The Marae (formal Maori meeting place) is where these principles
are most fully expressed. It is here that they are reflected in art form and
through speech in the Whare Nui (meeting house). "Ko te reo te haa wairua
o te Iwi Maori" (Language is the spiritual breath of Maori people) is evident
when Maori gather to discuss important issues on the Marae. We are tribal
people, and although we share a common language, we have separate ances-
tries and relationships to the land to whom we are related. Iwi (tribe), Hapu
(sub-tribe), and Whanau (extended family) often have their own meeting
houses, each house representing a tribal ancestor. The front of the house is
the head, the side gables represent arms spread to embrace people entering
the body, the Tahuhu (central ridge-pole) is the backbone, and the Heke
(rafters) form the ribs. Inside the house, we are within the body of our ancestor, safe and protected.

The meeting house is a repository of knowledge and Whakapapa. Inside
the house, the universe that we each carry within us is portrayed in Whakairo
(carving) that represents the Maori worldview:

   ⋆ the Gods are given form, each in their own domain;
   ⋆ the ancestral pathways are laid out for us to see;

+ the journey from birth to death and toward wisdom and learning is captured in art form;
+ the unbreakable linkages between Gods, humans, and the rest of the world finds expression.

This is an environment in which a world in balance is expressed—where the spiritual aspects of life are physically portrayed in Whakairo as a series of guidelines for the actions of humans. It is an environment in which the inherent Tapu (spiritual power) of the Gods can be acknowledged, in which human Mana (prestige and dignity) can be restored, and the healing of a weakened Mauri (life essence) can begin. It is the doorway through which many Maori step in order to journey upon Te Ara Tika.

Ko te reo Maori (the Maori language) is another vehicle by which spirituality finds expression for Maori. As Manuhiri (visitors) approach the Marae, they are welcomed with a Karanga, a call in which their ancestry, their Tapu, and the purpose of their visit are articulated by the local Tangata Whenua (people of the land) and to which the Manuhiri generally respond. The Tapu of the two sides remains separate, and they do not touch. Once inside the Whare (house), Tangata Whenua begin the process of Whaikoorero (formal speech-making) in which, through reciting ancestral events, the two sides weave their Wairua, through Korero, back and forth. When the process is complete, the two sides hongi (press noses), thus sharing their Mauri (spiritual essence), and dispelling the separating Tapu. Now the subject of the meeting can be addressed as a single issue affecting the whole group.

In Aotearoa, a hara (wrong) has occurred that affects and considerably weakens our Whanaungatanga links. Increasingly, accounts are surfacing of our Kaumatua (male Elders who are holders of knowledge and guardians of the Marae) sexually abusing our Tamariki (children). Often the abuse surfaces only when children become adults and have the confidence to speak out. Some Kaumatua try to justify their hara by using as historical precedent the creation story in which Tane, the first Maori male, mated with his daughter to produce humans. Others blame alcohol. Others still simply deny that it happened, accusing the accuser of lying.

In this type of situation, the Pakeha (European) courts are of little use. The best they can achieve is the temporary removal of the perpetrator from the community. They do little to remove the disease afflicting the abuser and even less to heal the spiritual havoc that the victim and relations have suffered—a contamination that will be passed to future generations.

Tauiwi ('strangers') laws do not deal with sexual abuse in a way that allows the community to restore its equilibrium and harmony. The process of healing cannot begin in a courtroom that is presided over by a stranger speaking a strange language and that does not allow the full participation of the victim and his or her whanau and the accused and his or her whanau. The removal and incarceration of perpetrators, while it may provide temporary respite for victims, does not heal the pain and disease that remains festering within the community. As one woman who suffered repeated sexual attacks from several of her Kaitiaki has publicly stated, she would rather be raped again than be subjected to the legal process and its humiliating evidential requirements. This woman was not satisfied with the legal process; she wanted—and received—justice on the Marae.

The Marae provides a forum in which healing can occur for all the people who are affected by sexual abuse and where it can be acknowledged that everyone is a victim in some way. I say this not to minimize the hara or to protect the perpetrators but to acknowledge that the Maori community as a whole is affected by the sexual abuse of its children, and, this being so, must be able to participate in the healing process.

On the Marae, all members of the community are able to take part. Discussions are based on an acceptance of the Tapu that resides in all things, the Mana that emanates from all things, the Mauri that provides the spiritual and physical health of all things, the Whanaungatanga that exists between all things, and the Whakapapa of the particular group as related to their spiritual ancestors. The process of discussion is one of weaving together and strengthening Whakapapa links through our acceptance of obligations toward our human relations and our acknowledgment of actions that do not uphold these obligations.

When people are able to see themselves as part of the fabric of life, when they are able to identify those to whom they are closely related, when they are able to see themselves as the present manifestation of a long and unbroken physical and spiritual process, then healing can begin. Utu (restoration of balance) may require physical and spiritual actions to be taken in order to initiate the healing process for the victim, so that harmony can be restored to the family and community.

For the victims of sexual abuse (and other hara) and their abusers, the Marae process is that which, once completed, begins the healing process. It allows our people to follow in the footsteps of our ancestors, traveling Te Ara Tika. As I understand it, the Marae and the Whare-Nui have been left as entrances—ways to Te Ara Tika, Te Ara Tika being the pathway to justice—and justice, like the rito of the harakeke, is what sustains us as a people.

Ehara I te mea
No naianei te aroha
No nga tupuna
Tuku iho tuku iho

*It is not from the present*
*that compassion springs*
*But from our ancestors*
*Handed down*
*Handed down*

## Glossary

**Aotearoa**: The Maori name for New Zealand.
**Hapu**: Sub-tribe.
**Hara**: Wrong.
**Harakeke**: Flax bush.
**Heke**: Rafters of the meeting house.
**Hongi**: To press noses.
**Iwi**: Tribe.
**Kaitiaki**: Guardian.
**Karanga**: A call that articulates a visitor's ancestry, their Tapu, and the purpose of their visit.
**Kaumatua**: Male Elders who are holders of knowledge and guardians of the Marae.
**Korero**: Speech, i.e., to talk or to say.
**Korimako**: A bird that thrives on the nourishment the flax bush supplies.
**Ko Te Ara Tika**: The right road.
**Ko te reo Maori**: The Maori language.
**"Ko te reo te haa wairua o te Iwi Maori"**: Language is the spiritual breath of Maori people.

**Mana**: Prestige and dignity.
**Manuhiri**: Visitors.
**Marae**: Formal Maori meeting place.
**Mauri**: Life essence, that which links all things spiritually.
**Pakeha**: Europeans.
**Papatuanuku**: Earth Mother.
**Pono**: Truth.
**Ranginui**: Skyfather.
**Rito**: The central shoot that produces the new growth of the flax.
**Tahuhu**: Central ridge-pole of the meeting house.
**Tamariki**: Children.
**Tane**: The first Maori male.
**Tangata** Whenua: People of the land.
**Tapu**: Spiritual power, the authority that is located in all things.
**Tauiwi**: Strangers.
**Te Ao Marama**: The physical world.
**Te Ara Tika**: Pathway to justice.
**Tika**: Moral rightness.
**Tikanga Maori**: Maori concepts and principles.
**Utu**: Restoration of balance.
**Wairua**: Spirituality, that part of our existence which is not physical.
**Whaikoorero**: Formal speech-making.
**Whakairo**: Carving.
**Whakapapa**: Genealogy.
**Whakatauki**: A proverb.
**Whanau**: Family.
**Whanaungatanga**: Interrelatedness.
**Whare**: House.
**Whare Nui**: Meeting house.

. . . .

*This article was published in* Justice as Healing *(1996) 1:4. The editor is grateful to Nin Tomas for permission to reprint her work.*

# 16

# Aboriginal Justice:
# A Haudenosaunee Approach

*Michael Cousins*

## Introduction

Most of the current inquiries into the causes and prevention of crime are framed by the European tradition. Not surprisingly, the resulting theories and explanations reflect a viewpoint that is shaped by the scientific method. This method uses empirical studies and quantitative data to explain criminal acts and to help prevent them. Yet crime remains a significant problem in Western societies. I contend that Western societies would benefit significantly from examining the methods that non-European societies have historically used to regulate criminal behavior.

The traditional methods that the Haudenosaunee[1] use, for example, ensure a relatively crime-free social order.[2] The Iroquois may well be the most studied Aboriginal Peoples of North America in regard to the social, political, and ceremonial aspects of their cultures. However, few if any studies have analyzed why crime is so rare within their communities. Neither do they explore why the Great Law of Peace[3] developed or how it works together with the Haudenosaunee perception of reality to inhibit antisocial acts.

To fill this gap in understanding, I will discuss the Iroquoian worldview, the founding of the Great Law, how this framework regulates criminal behavior, and how it identifies offenses and sanctions.

What I present here is based on traditional Haudenosaunee (Six Nations of the Grand River)[4] oral teachings[5] that have been given to me, combined with my study of the accounts of early European explorers, historians, and anthropologists. It may not be in complete agreement with other Haudenosaunee Nation or traditional understandings, since cultural variations do exist. I do not claim to speak for all Haudenosaunee Peoples or for an Aboriginal perspective in general.

## Traditional Haudenosaunee Methods of Social Control

To understand why a society uses certain methods to control antisocial or criminal behavior, we must first understand the society's worldview and cultural and spiritual practices. Without this context, we would undoubtedly perceive its social control methods through our own cultural contexts. In other words, we would see and interpret the practices through a distorted lens. To avoid such misrepresentations, I will begin with a very basic[6] description of traditional Haudenosaunee views on material and spiritual reality.

## A Haudenosaunee Worldview

The fundamental difference between a Haudenosaunee worldview and a Euro-Canadian outlook is that the Haudenosaunee worldview gives a holistic, contextual, and cyclical or circular way of understanding, whereas the Euro-Canadian outlook presents a linear, time-bound way of thinking. In a Haudenosaunee world, all things have been placed here through the will or direction of the Creator or the Master of Life; therefore all things have a distinct purpose.[7] They are of equal value, although they may have different forms and functions. Every material object (such as rocks, trees, or water) and every nonmaterial energy (such as wind) has a spirit or life force that allows it to exist. It is through this spirit or life force that all things are integrally connected. Those things that take a similar form (such as humans or other mammals) have a somewhat deeper connection, because they share similar experiences and understandings. No single thing or force has a more inherent value or more beneficial purpose to serve, since all things exist in order for all other things to exist.

Ultimately, human beings have been gifted with life to evolve spiritually through the material experience. The experiences we encounter in life are either of our own creation (the law of free will), another person's creation (that person's free will), things that occur through the will of the Creator (spiritual law), or different combinations of these. Experiences do not happen by accident. All occurrences have purpose and meaning.

When we create our own experiences, we are responsible and accountable for the outcome of those experiences, since we are responsible for our own will and actions. When the Creator wills certain events into our lives in order to forward our personal growth or to provide assistance in something, we are responsible for how we respond to these events. However, we are also given additional assistance from our Spirit Guides, who are with us constantly.

If we are subjected to an experience because of another person's will, the spiritual law takes this into account.[8] If the outcome of the experience and its impact on us are not within the divine plan for us, Spirit Guide intervention will occur to change the outcome, so that it will be in accordance with the divine plan.[9] An individual's divine plan includes many different experiences. Some of these may be extremely difficult to endure, but they are definitely in the interest of that person's personal growth and evolution. When we view experiences through this spiritual framework, life takes on a completely different meaning and is appreciated from a very different perspective.

Though we view life through a spiritual framework, we must also exist in the material world and interact with it. We observe the physical realities of the world as operating in a cyclical manner. The days, the seasons, and life and death all run in a cycle; they repeat themselves. Time is also experienced this way. Each day or each moment is not viewed in a linear way with an endpoint but rather as a continuation of a cycle. A new day could be said to be the same day repeating itself but with changes in the physical realities that occur throughout the cycle of day and night. The physical realities and their changes move within their own cycles, which are integrally linked to the day/night cycle.

In order for this cyclical reality to continue, everything that occurs at any given moment must have a diametric opposite. Day/night, life/death, warm/cold are all examples of this concept, and neither side of these polarities can exist without the other. In a Haudenosaunee understanding, the opposite is not seen as something negative. These realities just are. They exist as necessities of creation—necessary for the continuation of material existence.

This concept also applies to human beings. Awake/asleep, hungry/full, and happy/sad are good examples. However, we have something that allows us a measure of control over our experiences. That factor is free will. Free will allows humans to make choices that release us from acting in a purely instinctual or impulsive manner. Being gifted with free will gives us the responsibility to use it in a commendable manner. People who use free will commendably treat all things with honor and respect. For them, other people's well-being is as important, if not more so, than their own. Personal desires and gratification are not overriding objectives.

In meeting our material needs, we make some act of gratitude toward the material objects (e.g., food, medicinal plants) and the Creator for meeting our needs. Our duties and responsibilities to others (human and nonhuman), as opposed to personal needs and rights, are foremost in our considerations. If we do not use free will in an honorable manner, we become significantly out of balance with one or more of the four aspects[10] that constitute the whole of who we are, and we must do whatever is necessary to rebalance ourselves.

Rebalancing often requires some form of mental, emotional, physical, and spiritual sacrifice. A Cleansing (Sweatlodge) Ritual, fasting, prayer, and meditation are examples. These may be considered fairly significant forms of suffering, but the suffering is sacrificial—a way of making personal amends for our negative or hurtful actions. They are attempts to put things back into balance (personal and external) and to establish a clear and integral connection to the spiritual realm.[11]

Through continued ritual sacrifice, we develop a deeper insight into ourselves and others (healing) and a fuller understanding of how vitally important our interconnection and interdependency with all material entities truly are.

This dramatic change in our perceptions and actions affects material reality. People who act in inappropriate or hurtful ways are fully responsible for taking the necessary action to restore their balance—or to ask for help and guidance if they don't know how to do this. If they choose not to rebalance themselves, they will remain in conflict with spiritual and natural law, which eventually has serious consequences.

Natural law also has a powerful influence in the traditional Haudenosaunee understanding. Those who choose to ignore it or toil against it often suffer grave repercussions. Natural law is not particularly forgiving, nor does it discriminate. For example, anyone who tries to survive in winter without adequate shelter or clothing will die. If we don't pay attention at the edge of a cliff, we may fall and be killed or seriously hurt. These results follow no matter who we are or what our station in life may be.

Conversely, when we follow the rules of natural law, this law sustains life. If we plant corn and tend it sufficiently, it will grow to produce the food we need. In the material world, certain acts bring certain results. From natural law, we learn to be aware, to observe the effects of certain acts or omissions, to understand the limitations of human existence, and to accept that certain things will be whether we like them or not.

According to a Haudenosaunee understanding of spiritual and material realities, both realities exist united with the other. All things have a life force or spiritual energy that gives rise to a material form. In the physical world, both the spiritual and material exist together as a part of one another. The material cannot exist without the spiritual energy as its foundation. Human beings are both at the same time—spiritual *and* material entities—as are all other material existences. In the material world, people are "humans being," while in the spiritual world, they are "being human." This understanding of the connection between material and spiritual forms the basis of the Haudenosaunee world perspective. In conjunction with the Great Law, it forms the basis for a mutually respectful way of life within Haudenosaunee societies.[12]

## The Great Law of Peace

The most significant and influential event in Haudenosaunee history was the founding of the Great Law of Peace.[13] This Great Law was bestowed on the Haudenosaunee by Tekanawita [hereafter "the Peacemaker"][14] in order to advance a cooperative and peaceful coexistence among the Five Nations.

Before the Great Law was introduced, the Haudenosaunee lived in a way similar to other First Nations. Each nation was an independent body with similar dialects and customs, but there was no political alliance. Each person and each nation was a law unto themselves.[15] During this period, the Iroquois often warred with each other as well as with surrounding nations. In addition, they engaged in blood feuds amid their own people and within their own nations, killing each other for any slight offense. An individual's life was not valued. Acts of revenge-killing escalated, since family members would then seek new revenge for the murdered loved one. Ultimately, some families would be completely destroyed by the cycle of vengeance.[16]

In response to this internal violence and strife, the Creator sent the Peacemaker to convince the Haudenosaunee to accept the Great Law of Peace and to establish one of the most powerful political alliances on the North American continent.

Many Iroquoian historians have attempted to date the origin of the Great Law, but there is little consensus on the matter. The traditional European historians assign a date anywhere from 1440 to 1600.[17] The late Chief Jake Thomas, an oral reciter of the Great Law and Haudenosaunee historian, asserted that it is over 2,000 years old.[18] The most recent historical and scientific analysis by Dr. Barbara Mann and Jerry Fields of the University of Toledo identifies an exact date of 31 August 1142.[19] Although there remains disagreement on the date of its founding, there is no contention that the Great Law existed as a principle regulating every element within Haudenosaunee society.

## The Regulation of "Criminal Acts"

Although the Great Law is very detailed and lengthy, it is founded on three core principles:

1. Righteousness, which means justice practiced between people and nations;
2. Health, which means soundness of mind and body and the peace that comes from them;
3. Power, which means the authority of law and customs backed by such force as is necessary for justice.[20]

Adhering to these principles and other articles of the Great Law, combined with their distinct worldview about material and spiritual realities, the Haudenosaunee have developed effective methods for restraining antisocial behavior. The interdependence that grew among the Five Nations after they accepted the Great Law played a primary role in enabling them to do this. The people learned that the welfare and interests of society as a whole are of paramount importance. This priority, in turn, led the members of Haudenosaunee society to develop relationships based on equality, respect, and regard.

The concept of individual rights, by contrast, is antithetical to this understanding. In the Haudenosaunee way, each person retains a significant measure of rights, but these rights and privileges never exceed one's duties and responsibilities to others.[21] In the Great Law,[22] duties and responsibilities outnumber individual rights. This priority keeps our members focused on acting cohesively and living in unity with one another, as opposed to seeking gain for ourselves by asserting personal rights. When we focus on the best interests of others within the clan or society, the motives of criminal behavior, such as greed or vengeance, have far fewer opportunities to develop.[23] Our leadership must also act for the good of the whole society and not for themselves. Statesmen or chiefs are required to make decisions that are in the best interests of the people as well as in the best interests of the coming seven generations. Those who fail to do so are deposed.[24]

One major factor that keeps individuals content and satisfied with this form of social organization is the practice of unanimous decision-making among the statesmen.[25] This unanimity extends beyond those who are influential or in positions of leadership. All members of Haudenosaunee society have a say on matters of national importance, and voices of dissent are properly considered.[26] If unanimity cannot be reached on a proposal, it will not become national policy.[27] This allows everyone to have a significant influence on societal matters, which in turn fosters a sense of equality within the whole of the society. This sense of equality directly influences personal decisions. Because each member shares a sense of responsibility for the good of the collective, he or she acts in a manner that is in the best interests of all.

Another feature that checks antisocial behavior is the fervent disdain of ambition for personal power. All people in the society are considered equal, and no one is compelled by a higher authority to do anything. The women hold the chieftainship titles, and they choose the chiefs based on their personal honesty, integrity, and good character.[28] Statesmen retain their positions as long as they adhere to these standards and to the Great Law.[29] Their reward is the honor and esteem of the people. Those who dishonor their position through personal ambition are punished with removal and the further humiliation of community ostracization.[30]

Holding the chiefs, who are also viewed as mentors, to the strictest standards of good character sends an unmistakable message to society about the kind of behavior that is expected from its members. It helps everyone in Haudenosaunee society develop good, acceptable values. Honesty, integrity, generosity, and other qualities are seen as beneficial to all and are the standards that individuals are expected to strive for. Those who violate these values will often be ostracized, which the Haudenosaunee consider the harshest sanction that can be imposed.[31]

The clan system prescribed by Articles 42–54 of the Great Law also regulates delinquent behavior. Under this system, the lineal descent of the people is traced through the female line. All of a woman's children become members of her clan. All people of the same clan are forbidden to marry. Further, all members of the same clan are considered relations, even if they are from another nation within the League. Therefore, a person's parents are not of the same clan, a spouse is from a different clan, and a spouse's parents are of different clans.

All Haudenosaunee members of the same clan are obliged to treat one another with hospitality and kindness. Not to do so is considered a grave misdeed. In addition, each individual is intricately linked to other clans through his or her mother's father, his or her own father, or a spouse and his or her family. In this way, an individual can undoubtedly be connected to all Haudenosaunee clans directly or indirectly.

If one commits a crime against another, therefore, there is a good possibility that the victim will be either a relation or the relation of someone close to the offender. This places an obligation on all people to treat each other with respect or to suffer the consequences of public, or even worse, familial indignation.[32]

## Specific Crimes and Sanctions

Although crime was and is rare in Haudenosaunee societies, it does occur on occasion. When transgressions of the Great Law take place, definite penalties follow to see that justice is done. The three principles of righteousness, health, and power mandated by the Peacemaker all support the concept of justice. Under these principles, justice involves ensuring that the essence of the Great Law, namely, peace and unity, prevails.

When someone acts against this divine mandate, the people carry out justice according to the Great Law and the Haudenosaunee worldview to deter[33] the offender and others from committing any further grievous acts.[34] The four antisocial or criminal acts that are known to have existed in Iroquois societies[35] are witchcraft, murder, theft, and adultery. The Haudenosaunee have dealt with these in the following ways to ensure that they remain rare occurrences.

### Witchcraft

Witchcraft [denoting the use of powers in selfish, hurtful, or destructive ways] is considered an offense against the whole nation. It is viewed as a matter of national consequence, since anyone could be the next victim.[36] Witches and wizards are believed to have the power to make people violently ill and eventually to cause death. They are also able to transform into birds or animals to escape pursuers. If cornered, they can shapeshift into rocks or rotten logs to evade capture.[37] If caught, a witch could be sentenced to death. A council is called and the witch arraigned before it in the presence of the accuser. If the witch confesses and promises to amend his or her ways, he or she is set free. If the person denies the accusation, witnesses are called and evidence given. If the evidence of guilt is established to the council's satisfaction, which has often happened, the accused would traditionally be sentenced to death. Volunteers from within the nation would then carry out the penalty.[38]

The Great Law doesn't directly address witchcraft, but those who cause sickness and death are certainly in violation of the core principles of peace and unity. Death may seem like a harsh penalty, but it has been imposed only on the unrepentant. To remain united in peace, the Haudenosaunee must make sure that the Great Law remains the guiding principle of life. Those accused will always be spared execution if they confess and pledge to amend their behavior. Amending behavior involves a process of rebalancing through some consistent form of ceremonial self-sacrifice. Only after this has occurred will the individual be accepted unconditionally back into the community. Again, as with other antisocial acts, the harshest penalties are reserved for the unrepentant. Those who are remorseful and willing to abide by the Great Law are typically forgiven for their misdeeds.[39]

### Murder

Murder is, of course, a serious offense. The Great Law refers to it in Article 20, which speaks of murder committed by a chief. Such an act is a matter of national importance, since the chiefs are considered the mentors of society. For a statesman to commit murder cannot be tolerated, and any chief who does so will be deposed and banished (often permanently) from the League. The hereditary chieftainship titles will then go to a sister family, since the title cannot be associated with bloodshed.

This policy holds true in a time of war. All chiefs are required to give up their titles temporarily before they take part in warfare.[40] Statesmen are generally held to a stricter standard in regard to delinquent acts. First, they are representatives of the Great Law, and second, Haudenosaunee societies teach acceptable conduct by example.

Murder committed by other individuals is traditionally treated differently. It is considered a private concern, and the statesmen have no authority to impose a punishment or grant a pardon. Punishment or pardon is always a matter for the families and clans involved to decide.[41] If a murder occurs between different families or clans, the council of each clan will meet to discuss a settlement. If it occurs within a specific clan, then the members of that clan will settle the issue.

Two sanctions are defined as appropriate remedies. The first is for a member of the victim's clan to execute the offender. The second is for the offender to offer a belt of white wampum to the victim's family.[42] This act is intended to forever eradicate the memory of the offense and to symbolically demonstrate that the accused is willing to confess the crime and make atonement. In addition, it represents the offender's petition seeking forgiveness from the victim's family and clan. If the second sanction of wampum is accepted, then the offender must give one hundred yards for the death of a man and two hundred yards for killing a woman.[43] Because wampum is traditionally extremely labor intensive to produce, these amounts are of considerable value. By giving these quantities to the victim's relatives, the offender intends to "put things right."

If a death occurs that would be classified as second degree murder or manslaughter, members of the victim's clan make every effort to effect a reconciliation between the aggrieved immediate family and the offender. If the offender were executed in these circumstances, this type of private retaliation could lead to the rampant blood feuds that existed before the Great Law. Because the prospect of reverting to this state of violence and chaos is to be avoided at all costs, clemency is usually the outcome.[44]

Cases of premeditated murder rarely receive the same compassion. Such acts are not tolerated within Haudenosaunee society, and the customary sanction is execution. A member of the victim's clan would traditionally be appointed to carry out the sentence—a duty that he could accept or refuse. If he accepted but the offender had fled, he would be required to complete his duty, regardless of the time or distance involved.[45]

The rationale for executing offenders in situations of premeditated murder is not primarily one of revenge. The overriding purpose is to satisfy the spirit of the victim, who cannot find peace among the departed ones (spirit world) until the soul of the offender joins him or her.[46] All members of society know that execution is the sanction for this offense, and most of those who have been condemned to it readily meet their fate without fear.[47]

Undoubtedly, executing a friend or clan/nation member is a most difficult duty to perform. The principal aim of capital punishment is to "put things right" with the victim and to reestablish the principles of peace and unity mandated by the Great Law. Achieving both ensures that the blood feuds of the past do not return or become a divisive factor within the League.

## Theft

The Great Law addresses the issue of theft in Article 107. The Article, entitled "Protection of the House," forbids anyone from entering another's home when a stick is leaning against the entrance. This signal indicates that the owners are not in residence and also warns any passers-by to keep as much distance from the dwelling as their business will permit. Although this article of the Great Law would appear to apply only to entering a residence, its scope includes the principle of respect for personal property.

Contrary to the prevailing belief that First Nations do not have a concept of personal property, the Haudenosaunee have an unmistakable understanding of ownership, along with defined sanctions for any violations of personal property. Article 44 allocates land and longhouse ownership to the women. Again, although the article speaks only to the specifics of land and longhouse ownership, the principle applies to other affairs of life. In Haudenosaunee society, all are required to respect the personal ownership of goods.[48]

Moreover, the Haudenosaunee view about those who accumulate personal property serves to keep theft a rare occurrence.[49] Although property rights do exist, the members of society traditionally have no desire to possess more than others. No social status or esteem is gained through material accumulation. Conversely, one of the greatest insults is to suggest that someone hoards material goods and does not share with others.[50] For the Haudenosaunee, generosity is a quality that is highly admired. It is common for the statesmen to own the least materially, having presented most of their goods to the people. In return, they receive the respect and esteem of the people.[51]

Since generosity is the prevailing value traditionally, theft signifies a departure from the path of integrity and therefore is considered a most despicable act. Those who steal suffer the penalty of public disregard,[52] which is considered a severe form of punishment.

The custom of generosity undoubtedly reinforces adherence to the guiding principles of peace and unity within the League. The Haudenosaunee are well aware that greed is a key motive in many crimes. Consequently, they practice traditions to prevent its development. These traditions keep the principles of the Great Law foremost in the thoughts and actions of the Haudenosaunee people.

I will end this section with a quote from L. H. Morgan, who describes the Haudenosaunee perspective in relation to theft:

> But in justice to them it must be acknowledged, that no people ever possessed a higher sense of honor and self-respect in this particular, or looked down with greater disdain upon this shameful practice, than did the Iroquois. To this day, among their descendants, this offence is almost unknown. No locks, or bolts, or private repositories were ever necessary for the protection of property amoung themselves.[53]

## Adultery

In traditional Haudenosaunee society, adultery is considered a somewhat serious antisocial or criminal act. The Iroquois do not permit polygamy. Marriage, although deemed a sacred union and permanent partnership, can be dissolved by either party by simply declaring it so. However, such a dissolution is not taken lightly, since the longstanding tradition is one of permanence.[54]

The act of adultery is considered serious because of the ease of spousal separation, coupled with the deceit and dishonesty of the deed itself. Infidelity is not seen as a sensible alternative when a divorce can be so easily obtained. Such acts display a deficiency of character and a glaring disrespect for social norms. This betrayal could also lead to significant social turmoil, conflict, and possible blood feuds if an aggrieved spouse sought vengeance. As with other crimes that violate the principles of the Great Law, adultery is not acceptable behavior.

The primary sanction for infidelity is publicly ostracizing both parties. As a deterrent, daily social denunciation keeps adultery a rare occurrence.[55]

Again, criminal sanctions are designed to ensure that everyone within the Five Nations continues to follow the principles of internal peace and unity.

## Sanctions in Light of the Great Law and the Haudenosaunee Worldview

How were these sanctions integrated with the Haudenosaunee philosophy of reality and the Great Law? The process is somewhat complex, but I will attempt to explain it briefly and simply.

### Ostracization

Being ostracized is the most widely used punitive sanction that the Five Nations give offenders. It is considered worse than a death sentence because of the daily humiliation that someone has to endure.[56] Condemnation is primarily used for theft, greed, dishonesty, confessed witchcraft, and infidelity. Ostracizing someone involves denouncing his or her "bad character," which leaves the offender feeling disconnected spiritually from the community. However, once an offender has made the necessary community and personal amends to prove his or her sincere change to having a "good character," he or she is accepted back into society.[57]

### Execution

Although execution is a defined sanction within Haudenosaunee society, it has seldom been used. The death sentence has been imposed on chiefs who consistently disregard the will of the people, commit premeditated murder, or deny the practice of witchcraft but subsequently are found guilty of it. In the case of an obstinate chief[58] and an accusation of witchcraft, execution can be prevented if the accused admits wrongdoing and repents.[59]

Although capital punishment seems barbaric to many people today, the Haudenosaunee understand death entirely differently. In their understanding of reality, the deceased return to the place of their beginning where their ancestors are waiting to greet them. The spirit world is a kinder, gentler place. To the Iroquois, death is not something to fear, nor is there any "hell" to which they can be condemned. Thus, execution is not perceived as it is in Euro-Canadian society.

However, the Haudenosaunee are well aware that each individual has been given life by the Creator and consequently has a purpose. Further, execution does not give the offender an opportunity to correct the harm he or she has done. In light of these perspectives, the death sentence is not considered an appropriate way to "put things right" and is reserved for only the most severe cases, such as premeditated murder or when offenders refuse to take responsibility for their misdeeds. The continued presence of these few individuals would only cause further harm to the community and nation.[60]

## Reparation

The most common method of responding to wrongful behavior is negotiated settlement. If an individual commits an offense, the council of that person's family or clan meets with the council of the victim's clan to discuss the matter. If the offense occurs between same-clan members, then the clan council members discuss it among themselves. The discussion results in a settlement that requires the offender to make reparations to the victim, or, in the case of murder, to the victim's family. Reparations usually consist of giving the aggrieved party something of great value, such as wampum. This type of resolution is used for many offenses that are not so injurious or malicious as to warrant harsher penalties. When the offender carries out the terms of the settlement, the offense is forever removed from the memory of the community.[61]

## Banishment

If offenders continue to engage in antisocial acts or hurtful behavior, the Haudenosaunee use banishment as a last resort.[62] Banishment has two purposes. First, it protects the community. Second, it attempts to help the offender return to a spiritual state where he or she can be socially interconnected. When people have to survive alone or are forced to live with other communities in shame, they can go through intense personal reflection that often leads to a spiritual awakening. Banishment is used, therefore, to urge offenders to make the character changes necessary to interact positively with their communities.

Banishment rarely occurs for life, and individuals often return home after a prescribed period of exile. They are allowed to remain if they have fully embraced the principles of peace and unity. The Great Law decrees that in-dividuals who have acted in disruptive manners be given three opportuni-ties to change.[63] This dictate actually applies to most sentences, including banishment.[64]

These sanctions have been developed and are always applied according to the Haudenosaunee spiritual and cultural perspective and the Great Law of Peace. All members of society are taught this perspective and the dictates of the Great Law of Peace from a very young age. To act contrary to either is considered somewhat peculiar, but the frailties and limitations that come with being human are well understood and always taken into consideration when councils must decide on an appropriate sanction. Most problems are solved without dissension or further harm.

Contrary to the general view that Aboriginal societies work out peaceful resolutions because they depend on each other for survival, the Haudeno-saunee at least come to peaceful resolutions because of their world perspec-tive and their adherence to the spiritual and material unity decreed by the Great Law. Many of the guiding principles of the Great Law can be used to create harmony not only in Haudenosaunee communities but in other so-cieties as well.

## Notes

1. Europeans referred to the Haudenosaunee as Iroquois, Five Nations, or the League. Throughout this paper, I use these terms for grammatical reasons. In English, the word Haudenosaunee, which the Iroquois use to refer to themselves, translates to "The People of the Longhouse."

2. See A. C. Parker, *Parker on the Iroquois,* vol. 3 (Syracuse: Syracuse University Press, 1968); P. A. Wallace, *The White Roots of Peace* (Philadelphia: University of Pennsylvania Press, 1946); W. B. Newell, *Crime and Justice amoung the Iroquois Na-tions* (Montreal: Caughnawaga Historical Society, 1965); L. H. Morgan, *League of the Iroquois* (New York: Burt Franklin, 1901); H. C. Colden, *The History of the Five Indian Nations of Canada, 1727,* vol. 1 (New York: Allerton Book, 1922); E. M. Chad-wick, *The People of the Longhouse* (Toronto: The Church of England Publishing Company, 1897); W. M. Beauchamp, *A History of the New York Iroquois* (New York: AMS Press, 1976); E. Kenton, *The Indians of North America* (New York: Harcourt, Brace and Co., n.d.); J. E. Seaver, *A Narrative of the Life of Mary Jemison: The White Woman of the Genesee,* 22nd ed. (New York: American Scenic and Historic Preserva-tion Society, 1925).

3. See appendix 2 in *The Great Law of Peace of the Longhouse People* (Akwesasne: White Roots of Peace, 1973).

4. The Five Nations became the Six Nations with the admission of the Tuscarora in 1724.

5. My traditional teachings have come from several different sources over different periods of time, thereby making exact date and personal references somewhat futile. To account for this, I name all references in one citation, note 12.

6. An in-depth explanation of the Haudenosaunee spiritual and material perspective would be the topic for several volumes of publication.

7. Please note that the Haudenosaunee Creation Story gives a full account of how the earth and all things on it came into being through the actions of Sky Woman and the left- and right-handed twins. I state that the Master of Life is responsible for all things on earth because it is ultimately through the life-giving force of the Master of Life that things may exist. For one account of the Creation Story, see H. Hertzberg, *The Great Tree and the Longhouse* (New York: Macmillan and Company, 1996), 16.

8. Spiritual law is contextual and takes all matters and outcomes into account.

9. Spirit Guide help and intervention is a somewhat complex matter. If an individual is acting independently with free will, Spirit Guides are not allowed to intervene in that individual's choices without the individual's consent or request. Spirit Guides cannot independently break the law of free will. In this case, all that is required for assistance is a request for help and permission to intervene. If an individual has an experience caused by external factors and not by his or her free will and the outcome is not within the person's divine plan, Spirit Guides will intervene to modify the outcome so that it ultimately corresponds with the divine plan. However, Spirit Guides will not always intervene, even if asked, since the outcome as it is may be in accordance with the divine plan. One is never really sure when intervention will occur, if at all, and on occasion severe consequences from an act of free will or external forces will still follow. This is one of the reasons why life is called the Great Mystery.

10. The four aspects of an individual are the mental, physical, emotional, and spiritual.

11. Those who have engaged in such sacrificial rituals (including myself) can attest to the powerful spiritual connection that develops through the experiences. Please note that sacrificial rituals are not the only way to gain spiritual insight and connection, but for the purposes of healing someone significantly out of balance, they may be the most effective means because of their intensity.

12. I draw upon traditional oral teachings with S. Sandy, Clanmother, Mohawk Nation; J. Thomas, Traditional Chief, Cayuga Nation; R. Maracle, Traditional Chief, Mohawk Nation; G. Hill, Pipekeeper, Mohawk Nation; L. Hill, Traditional Healer,

Mohawk Nation; R. Hill, Pipekeeper, Onondaga Nation; S. Porter, Sweatlodge conductor, Mohawk Nation; R. Longboat, Elder, Mohawk Nation (1994–2002), Six Nations of the Grand River.

13. For an edited condensed version, see appendix 1 in A. C. Parker, *Parker on the Iroquois* (Syracuse: Syracuse University Press, 1968).

14. This is done in keeping with the Haudenosaunee tradition of respect.

15. A. C. Parker, *Parker on the Iroquois*, vol. 3 (Syracuse: Syracuse University Press, 1968), 8.

16. A. C. Parker, *The Constitution of the Five Nations* (Ohsweken, Ont.: Irocrafts Ltd., 1984), 16–17.

17. P. A. Wallace, *The White Roots of Peace* (Philadelphia: University of Pennsylvania Press, 1946), 69.

18. Oral teachings (see note 12).

19. D. George-Kanentiio, "Founding date for Confederacy thought to be 1142," *TEKAWENNAKE* [Six Nations of the Grand River] (24 February 1999), 7.

20. Wallace, *White Roots of Peace*, 15.

21. W. B. Newell, *Crime and Justice Among the Iroquois Nations* (Montreal: Caughnawaga Historical Society, 1965), 35.

22. See appendix 2 in *Great Law of Peace of the Longhouse People*.

23. Oral teachings.

24. See appendix 2 in *Great Law of Peace of the Longhouse People*, article 59.

25. Ibid., articles 5, 6, 8, and 9.

26. Ibid., articles 93, 95, and 96.

27. L. H. Morgan, *League of the Iroquois* (New York: Burt Franklin, 1901), 106–7.

28. See appendix 2 in *Great Law of Peace of the Longhouse People*, article 53.

29. Ibid., articles 25 and 27.

30. H. C. Colden, *The History of the Five Indian Nations of Canada, 1727,* vol. 1 (New York: Allerton Books, 1922), 17.

31. Morgan, *League of the Iroquois*, 324.

32. Oral teachings.

33. Deterrence in this context does not necessarily mean applying highly punitive sanctions in order to deter through fear. It also includes a rehabilitative component of rebalancing the individual.

34. Oral teachings.

35. Morgan, *League of the Iroquois*, 325.

36. Newell, *Crime and Justice Among the Iroquois Nations*, 47–48.

37. W. M. Beauchamp, *Iroquois Folk Lore* (New York: AMS Press, 1976), 62–65.

38. Morgan, *League of the Iroquois*, 321–322.

39. Oral teachings.

40. See appendix 2 in *The Great Law of Peace of the Longhouse People*, article 90.

41. G. H. Loskiel, *History of the Mission of the United Brethren among the Indians of North America* (London: 1791), 133.

42. "To our forefathers, wampum was a symbolic material linked, in ancient tradition, to the Peacemaker's founding of the Haudenosaunee Confederacy. When beads were collected into strands or woven together as belts, the wampum stood for the authority of a spoken message.

"To us today, it contains the best thinking of our people from the Peacemaker to the present. It represents who we are and reminds us where we have been. Wampum means an agreement to hold onto our traditions because our history and laws are wrapped up in it. To us it is sacred—a substance with powerful healing presence.

"Wampum consists of beads made from mussel shells found along the coast of New England. White beads came from several species of whelk. The purple beads derived from the hard-shell or quahog clam . . . The wampum objects were woven on a bow-like loom. Sinew was used for the horizontal threads. Vertical strands were composed of a vegetal fiber (perhaps milkweed or hemp). Wampum was connected to the spoken word. A piece of wampum testified to the truth and importance of a message which was "read into" the object itself. A very important message, such as a treaty, required a large amount of wampum often in the form of a belt." (This explanation is taken from the Oneida Nation's Web site: http://www.oneida-nation.net/wampumexh.html.)

43. E. M. Chadwick, *The People of the Longhouse* (Toronto: The Church of England Publishing Company, 1897), 55.

44. Morgan, *League of the Iroquois*, 322–324.

45. Ibid.

46. Newell, *Crime and Justice Among the Iroquois Nations*, 57–58.

47. J. V. H. Clark, *Lights and Lines of Indian Character and Scenes of Pioneer Life* (Syracuse: E.H. Babcock and Co., 1854), 92–93.

48. Newell, *Crime and Justice Among the Iroquois Nations*, 39.

49. W. M. Beauchamp, *A History of the New York Iroquois* (New York: AMS Press, 1976), 387.

50. E. Kenton, *The Indians of North America* (New York: Harcourt, Brace and Co., n.d.), 131.

51. Colden, *The History of the Five Indian Nations of Canada*, 17.

52. Morgan, *League of the Iroquois*, 324.

53. Ibid.

54. Chadwick, *The People of the Longhouse*, 58–59.

55. J. E. Seaver, *A Narrative of the Life of Mary Jemison: The White Woman of the Genesee*, 22nd ed. (New York: American Scenic and Historic Preservation Society, 1925), 64.

56. Morgan, *League of the Iroquois*, 324.

57. Oral teachings.

58. See appendix 2 in *The Great Law of Peace of the Longhouse People*, article 59.

59. Morgan, *League of the Iroquois*, 321–322.

60. Oral teachings.

61. Chadwick, *The People of the Longhouse*, 55.

62. Clark, *Lights and Lines of Indian Character and Scenes of Pioneer Life*, 92.

63. See appendix 2 in *The Great Law of Peace of the Longhouse People*, article 59.

64. Oral teachings.

. . . .

*Published in* Justice as Healing *(2004) 9:1, this article is an excerpt from Mr. Cousins's master's thesis, entitled "The Inherent Right of the Haudenosaunee to Criminal Justice Jurisdiction in Canada," that he is currently undertaking at Simon Fraser University. The editor is grateful to Mr. Cousins for permission to reprint his work in this volume.*

# CHAPTER 4

# *Respecting Community*

## From the Power to Punish to the Power to Heal

*Judge Bria Huculak*

> The commonest technique of control in modern life
> is punishment. The pattern is familiar: if a man does
> not behave as you wish, knock him down; if a child mis-
> behaves, spank him; if the people of a country misbehave,
> bomb them. Legal and police systems are based upon
> such punishments as fines, flogging, incarceration, and
> hard labour. Religious control is exerted through pen-
> ance, threats of excommunication, and consignment to
> hell fire. Education has not wholly abandoned the birch
> rod. In everyday personal contact, we control through
> censure, snubbing, disapproval, or banishment.

B.F. SKINNER (1953)

### Punishment: A Questionable Technique

Crime remains at the forefront in the media. Recently, some murders and the allegation that young persons committed them have raised calls for harsher punishments, longer jail sentences, and the return of capital punishment. "Law and Order" is regularly on the agenda in political elections.[1]

In the Western world, Canada uses imprisonment as a sanction second only to the United States. Since its inception, the idea of using imprison-ment to punish socially disapproved behavior has concerned many and been the focus of reform movements. Yet the huge, gray, spaceship-like fortresses remain, and even greater numbers are being built to meet the demand. Imprisonment as a legal sanction has a complex conceptual base that is closely tied to the very function and purpose of law.

Through history, societies have dealt with offenders in various ways that are driven by diverse motives: punishment; deterrence (both individually and general); retribution; the protection of society; incapacitation; humanitarianism; reform; treatment; and rehabilitation. Today, contemporary authors disagree about the purpose of legal sanctions. The philosophy of punishment is a controversial, almost political subject. On one hand, Ernest Van Den Haag defines punishment as suffering or deprivation imposed by law.[2] On the other hand, Herbert L. Packer argues that punishment is for the "prevention of undesired conduct and [the] retribution of perceived wrongdoing."[3]

No doubt the concepts and methods we use in dealing with offenders reflect our underlying views of crime and "the criminal." These views are bound up with our view of humans—e.g., do we have free will, or are we determined?—which, in turn, are bound up with our views of the nature of society, culture, values, and economics. All of these concepts are reflected in the law and the other methods we use for social control.

The use of imprisonment as the leading form of punishment is a historically complex issue. Why do we still use imprisonment despite its obvious failure? What function do prisons perform? In the past two decades, various writers have grappled with these questions, e.g., Michael Foucault, Michael Ignatieff, Hay, Rotham, and Hall. These authors have offered significantly different explanations from the traditional ones. Despite almost immediate denunciation as a failure, prisons exist unabated.

Foucault viewed this "failure" from a unique perspective. He saw the system of incarceration as deeply rooted and as carrying out precise functions.[4] He argued that punishment in general is not intended to eliminate offenses but rather to distinguish, distribute, and use them. That is, punishments are intended not to render docile those who break the law but rather to assimilate them in a general tactic of subjection.

In short, penalty does not "simply check irregularities; it differentiates them." It provides them with general economy.[5] Foucault argued that the penal system in its entirety and ultimately the entire moral system result from a power relationship established by the bourgeois. Moreover, they constitute an instrument for exercising and maintaining that power. In other words, prisons are an integral part of the control apparatus of industrial capitalism.

Whatever theory one subscribes to, traditional or modern, two facts must be faced. First, it costs approximately $10 billion to operate the "justice" system, and second, it does not work.[6] Here in Canada, our justice system is seriously flawed, and it is seen as unjust and ineffective. We need people with courage to challenge the justice system and to develop an alternative vision at a time when pessimism is rampant and many have given up in despair. Community-based "restorative" justice modes give hope.

In 1992, Judge Barry Stuart, Territorial Court of the Yukon, used circle sentencing. On the basis of the *Moses* case,[7] provincial court judges in northern Saskatchewan initiated sentencing circles approximately three years ago. Since then, over one hundred individuals in many communities have benefited from the process, primarily in the north.

One consequence of using sentencing circles has been a drop in the crime rate[8] as well as a reduction in the numbers of individuals imprisoned. Another consequence is that communities are becoming engaged in a direct way. The focus shifts from retribution to restitution, reintegration, restoration, reparation, and rehabilitation—not to mention reclamation. Reclamation means returning to the community what is rightfully theirs: the ownership and responsibility for their members.

Specific criteria were developed to ensure consistency in applying sentencing circles. Specifically, the accused must agree to be referred to the sentencing circle. The accused must have deep roots in the community in which the circle is held and from which the participants are drawn. Elders or respected nonpolitical community leaders must be willing to participate. The victim must also be willing to participate—and without any coercion or pressure to do so. The court should try to determine beforehand, as best it can, if the victim is subject to battered women's syndrome. If she is, then she should have counseling and be accompanied by a support team in the circle. Disputed facts should be resolved in advance whenever possible. The case should also be one in which a court is willing to take a calculated risk and to depart from the usual range of sentencing.

The circles are held in informal settings that give everyone an opportunity to speak. Participants include the offender, the victim, their families, Elders, and other community members, as well as the judge and counsel. The goal is to reach a consensus on how to deal with the offender in the context of the community and the victim. Through the process and the group dynamics, healing starts.

The process is often painful and emotional for participants. The offender must face the victim as well as her or his own family and community. This is precisely why it is more effective.[9] The community's involvement validates Aboriginal community values within the current system.[10] It is a first and important step toward self-determination and autonomy. The sentencing circle replaces the Anglo-European-based, adversarial, punitive system with a system whose objective is to restore harmony to the community. The focus is on rehabilitation, not punishment. In this way, it provides the best hope for protecting the public.

There is no "right" model for restorative justice. Each community must find its own way and develop a model that reflects its own community values. Justice reform cannot be set apart from Aboriginal people's demands for self-determination.[11]

In some northern communities, sentencing circles are now being used in pre-charge diversion programs. The accused may be sent directly to the community for resolution, instead of being diverted from the court. Control over the process stays within the community. This practice is especially significant, because it holds the most potential for developing community-based restorative justice models. Some are concerned that this development may represent little more than "tinkering" with the justice system. What is clear, though, is that these circle practices are preferable to the "status quo." Fundamental change is necessary in the justice system, because this system has failed Aboriginal people and non-Aboriginals as well.[12] Non-Aboriginal community diversion programs based on restorative models are operating successfully.[13] These models can easily be used in urban centers for both Aboriginal and non-Aboriginal offenders.[14]

In Saskatchewan, the use of sentencing circles has now expanded to urban centers. We can also expect the pre-charge diversion community model used in the north to be used here in the future.

These models are not a panacea. They do not deal with the complex causes of crime, but they do emphasize prevention and alternatives to prison. Shifting the healing, restorative functions back to the community—both

Aboriginal and non-Aboriginal—is a start in changing the hierarchy and paternalistic structure of our justice system.[15]

We have everything to gain by being creative in economics and, more important, in the lives of individuals. We need to embrace change with an open mind. To move forward, we need to be willing to confront the hard political questions, starting with rethinking punishment and the role of penal institutions.

## Notes

1. *Globe and Mail,* July 1995. See also "Ottawa Wants New Regulations for Dealing with Violent Offenders," *Star Phoenix,* July 1995.

2. Ernest Van Den Haag, *Punishing Criminals* (New York: Basic Books, 1975), 8.

3. Herbert L. Packer, *The Limits of the Criminal Sanction* (Stanford: Stanford University Press, 1968), 26.

4. Michael Foucault, *Discipline and Punish: The Birth of a Prison* (New York: Pantheon Books, 1977).

5. Ibid.

6. Anthony Doob, "Harsher Youth Laws Too Costly: Study," Toronto (CP), *Star Phoenix,* 21 July 1995.

7. *R. v. Moses,* [1992] 3 *Canadian Native Law Reporter* 116 (Yukon Territory Court).

8. Yukon Statistics, see "Creative Justice," *Justice Report* 8, no. 4 (Spring 1992), Canadian Criminal Justice Association.

9. John Braithwaite and Stephen Mugford, "Conditions of Successful Reintegration Ceremonies," *British Journal of Criminology* 34, no. 2 (1994).

10. Note: Out of deference, I will not use the word *accommodate.*

11. Luke McNamara, *Aboriginal Peoples, the Administration of Justice and the Autonomy Agenda* (Winnipeg: Legal Research Institute of the University of Manitoba, 1993); P. Monture-Okanee and M. E. Turpel, "Aboriginal Peoples and Canadian Criminal Law: Rethinking Justice," *University of British Columbia Law Review* 26 (1992): 366.

12. Saskatchewan, *Report of the Saskatchewan Indian Justice Review* and *Report of the Saskatchewan Métis Justice Review* (Regina: Government of Saskatchewan, 1992), Chair: Judge P. Linn.

13. See "Restorative Resolutions Mediation Service," *Star Phoenix,* 20 July 1995.

14. See the New Zealand Group Family Conference Models as per Judge F. W. M. McElrea, "Restorative Justice—The New Zealand Youth Court: A Model for Development in Other Courts?" *Journal for Judicial Administration* 4 (1994): 33.

15. See Christie Jefferson, *Conquest by Law* (Ottawa: Solicitor General Canada, 1994); Joan Ryan, *Doing Things the Right Way* (Calgary: University of Calgary Press, 1995).

. . . .

*This article was published in* Justice as Healing (1995). *The editor would like to thank Judge Huculak for permission to publish her work.*

# Evaluating the Quality of Justice

*Russel L. Barsh*

Justice, like beauty, is largely in the eye of the beholder. Medieval Europe's "trial by combat" may seem loathsome and absurd in the eyes of contemporary Canadians, but their ancestors demanded the right to defend themselves by that means. Swearing oaths on Bibles or other Christian relics was once considered deeply meaningful, but now it is seen as merely quaint. What people deem just in a particular era plumbs the deepest levels of their culture. It expresses the basic principles attached to human relations.

When I asked students to define *justice*, most non-Aboriginal students referred to *equality before the law* or the application of the same rules to everyone. Most Aboriginal students used the term *harmony* or a synonym of it. To my mainstream Canadian students, the reality is life in a bureaucratic state, which manifests its justice by treating everyone at arm's-length without distinguishing among them. My Aboriginal students experience a reality of all-pervading kinship not only in the home but in economic life and politics as well. For them, justice involves minimizing the frictions of living among kinfolk and maximizing its potential synergies.

Few empirical studies have tried to measure the extent to which modern Western legal systems actually apply their rules equally. Measuring justice in the Aboriginal sense poses even greater challenges.

To think more clearly about justice, we might start by challenging the widespread tendency to confuse the term *justice* with the concept of *order*. We routinely refer to the police, criminal courts, and prisons as institutions of justice, when in fact they were clearly devised to maintain order among certain social classes—first non-Normans, later commoners, eventually the poor. Justice was an afterthought historically. It arose when the governments tried to justify their methods of imposing order on society with the developing sense of "rights" and the inevitable resistance among the people on whom order had been imposed.

Order can be maintained without any justice at all. For example, a ruthless but efficient dictatorship can impose order without any justice. Studies of the Nazi, Soviet, and South African legal systems confirm that highly repressive regimes can consistently enforce a set of laws or rules. In other words, *deterrence*, the principal tool of Western notions of order, can be achieved to some degree by extreme but bureaucratically consistent cruelty. Granted, societies that choose this path may not last for more than one or two generations.

Purportedly "objective" measures, such as recidivism and changes in the frequency of reported offenses, relate to the deterrence goal of legal systems, not to justice. Most existing subjective tests are also deterrence-oriented, such as measures of individual feelings of physical security or beliefs that "crime is being dealt with effectively." In other words, measures focused on deterrence monitor the order generated by a system of social control; they do not tell us whether just-ness is being achieved.

The challenge posed by Aboriginal Peoples is a very different one. It requires us to separate the just-ness of the responses to violence and disorder from the short-term effectiveness of those responses in reducing the quality of violence and disorder.

This alternative approach may be based on the theory that, in the *long run*, just systems lead to lower rates of violence. This is explained by a related theory that just systems of responding to harms create greater harmony and cooperation in the community long-term. In other words, the goal or payoff will be found not in lower crime rates or recidivism per se but in a more self-respecting, self-confident, and productive society made up of individuals who feel valued and not rejected. Clearly, this kind of result cannot be tested within a few years (if at all) of using an alternative legal system. At best, it may take a generation or two for these long-term goals to be realized.

In the shorter-term, how can we focus more on justness and less on deterrence? To test the perceived just-ness of institutions in the minds of all participants—victims, decision-makers, and the accused—we will have to use subjective measures that capture an individual community's values and expectations. A just legal order should seem *more* just to all participants *than the alternatives*. As a result

- Victims should feel that their pain and anger are acknowledged and more effectively addressed.

+ Decision-makers must feel that they are able to understand the needs of the parties and respond more appropriately than would be possible in mainstream adjudication.
+ Accused persons must feel that they are treated fairly and with respect and must be more willing to comply with decisions.
+ Community members who are currently observers rather than participants should nonetheless have a more positive view of the legal order.
+ People in the community as a whole should feel that, whether as victims or as the accused, they would expect to be treated more fairly and respectfully. In other words, those who are presently only potential participants should *expect* just treatment.

If the direct participants feel well served, then we can reasonably predict that decisions will hold beyond the time-horizon of our research measurements. If the community at large senses greater justice as well, then this community viewpoint will help create greater long-term community harmony and cooperation.

The most important step in evaluating alternative justice models, then, is working with communities to clarify their objectives. If a community equates justice with more effective deterrence, notwithstanding what has been said here, then its program must be evaluated using more conventional, "objective" measures, such as offense rates. However, if community members agree that their ultimate goal is just-ness and the hypothesized long-term social advantages of just-ness, then its program must be evaluated with subjective measures that indicate whether just-ness is, in fact, being achieved.

. . . .

*This article was published in* Justice as Healing (1995). *The editor would like to thank Russel L. Barsh for permission to publish his work.*

# Throwing the Baby Eagle Out of the Nest

*John Borrows*

As First Nations Peoples, we still have some distance to go to be free from the oppression we live under. While it is true that our sovereignty has not been extinguished[1] and that partial victories have occurred to facilitate our existing powers of self-determination,[2] much remains to be done.[3] The politics and laws of Canada continue to contribute to our devastation.[4] We can and must persist in our critique of colonialism, but we cannot rely on Canada alone to give us more power. Power comes from within and, though we continue to struggle for an explicit recognition of our rights, we cannot expect that the most important victories we achieve will be from any source other than ourselves.[5]

When I first started as a professor at University of British Columbia Law School, I had an interesting dream that brought this message to my attention. I had just recently moved to British Columbia from Ontario to be the director of the First Nations Law Program. I am Anishinabe, and though I really liked my work, I did not feel at home. I missed my feelings and knowledge of the land and the connections I have with friends and family. In this context, my dream occurred early one morning just before I woke up, so I remembered it very clearly as I went about my day's activities. It is not my Vision Quest dream, so I have the liberty of sharing it with you. I believe that the dream has something remarkably important to say about justice and healing within our communities. The dream unfolded in the following way.

I returned home to my reserve[6] to visit with my mother and to relax and enjoy the peace I have when I am there. One of the first things I did was to visit with my Auntie Norma and have supper with her. When we were finished our meal, we decided to drive down to the lake and take in its beauty. As we were getting close to the water, I noticed a small island just off the shore with a large pine tree growing on it. One of the limbs of the giant extended over the water toward the shore, and on the limb was a man. I wondered what he would be doing there, and I eventually noticed that he had his hands in a bundle of sticks on the branch.

When we stopped the car and got out, I realized that the man's hands were in an eagle's nest. I called out to him to stop. As I did this, he lifted a baby eaglet from inside its home and perched it on the side of the nest. My shouting had attracted attention, and people started gathering on the shore to see what was happening. At this point, I ran through the knee-deep water to get to the tree to try to prevent him from harming the bird. As I reached the trunk, he cast the small life over the side of the nest and into the water, where it drowned in the depths below. This made me quite upset, so I climbed the tree to restrain him. Just before I could reach him, he set another baby on the side of the nest, rested it there for a second, and then cast it over the side too. At this point, I was able to stop the man from further harming the nest, and we came down from the tree.

When I got to the bottom, there was a considerable number of people watching the proceedings. No one had moved or said anything. From the midst of the crowd, a band constable stepped forward and said he was arresting me for disturbing the peace. I started to protest and said, "I'm trying to help. Don't you remember me; I just came home to visit my Auntie Nor—."

He interrupted me and said, "Oh yeah, now I know you; you're John. I heard you were having supper at Norma's place tonight—now I remember. You are free to go." My dream ended, and I woke up. I boarded a plane an hour and half later and traveled to an isolated community on the central coast of British Columbia, accessible only by float plane and boat. There I had an experience that reinforced what I learned as I was sleeping, which I will return to in a moment.

Before I do this, though, I want to pause and ask, what does this dream-story teach about justice and healing? It probably teaches more than I understand right now, as there seems to be levels of symbolism that I continually discover. The first thought that occurred to me was that I could not do anything of significance to help my people if I did not remain known to my community. I must constantly keep my association and attention focused on the everyday experience of my people, if I am going to be able to do anything helpful. My people are not only the Anishinabe and my home reserve, but also the First Nations communities I participated with in British Columbia.

I believe that my dream contains this general lesson that others could consider. We must be careful not to become detached from our community in our attempts to assert our interests before the wider Canadian public.[7] If we do, we run the risk I saw in my dream that people will not accept our actions, even when our deeds are well intentioned and right. This is an incredibly heavy burden to bear, as it requires much greater effort, but it seems to be most in keeping with our structure as First Nations.

The second lesson I garnered from the dream was that there are *some* people in our own communities who are casting the power of our future away, "over the side of our nest." This is done in different ways. Children are being abused and taken away from us.[8] Women are being violated, assaulted, and excluded from community participation.[9] Community factions are encouraged, and "rivals" are destructively isolated from political, economic, and social influence.[10] Language is used that does not respect the convictions and feelings of others and offends the vision that our grandmothers and grandfathers preserved for us.[11] Some people mischaracterize the words and intentions of others in order to make their own arguments appear stronger and more persuasive.[12]

Realizing these things were happening in my communities, after my dream I had to honestly ask myself: Am I also the man in the nest? Do I, by what I write and teach, cast our future away? I believe it could be helpful for others to ponder these questions as well.

Finally, the dream taught me about what is happening in our communities when we as leaders and academics speak about justice. Figuratively speaking, our people generally stand at the edge of the issues and watch.[13] While Oka encouragingly illustrated that people will take action if pushed beyond measure, for the most part we witness silent watchfulness, as rhetoric, politics, and philosophy become increasingly disconnected from the actions and understanding of people "at home."[14] Participation in healing then occurs at a distance through the media, with little active involvement from the people it will most personally affect.

This observation is not meant to diminish the accomplishments of those who have worked tirelessly to advance our powers; we would not have even the sovereignty we do possess if it were not for them. I merely want to stress that I must add to my future actions a greater degree of our people's understanding and participation. People need to be more directly involved and feel justice move from within, and they need to be more intimately caught up in the events taking place around them. I know this is difficult when there are so many pressing issues that make it hard to look up from today's needs and participate in the vision of tomorrow. Again, this is a hard task to accomplish, but once again, it seems to be the one most in line with our requirements as Nations today.

The lure of political power, personal influence, money, tenure, self-satisfaction, and other forms of acquisitiveness make these lessons all the more difficult to learn and follow. I admit that the dream was directed to me, and therefore I am the one who must most directly heed its lessons. If others can benefit from the dream in working to restore balance within our communities, in the spirit of sharing I leave it with you.

Meditations on my dream were reinforced by the subsequent experience that I alluded to earlier. Six hours after waking, I was in the Kwagiulth village of Kingcome Inlet, home of approximately eighty Tsawataineuk people. I spent three days visiting with members of the community. At the end of my time there, I was taken to their ceremonial big house. It was an eighty- or ninety-year-old structure with beautiful house posts and carvings. It was a place to be respected. My host explained the representations that the engravings depict, and he told me the stories of their origins with visible pride.

However, as he was going around the room, he stopped at one pole and showed me where someone had taken an axe to the figure and partially de-faced it. With a note of shame, he said to me, as I remember it, "This is what our people have done in the day of their sadness. Some of us forgot who we were and turned against that which would most help us remember. Our people are beginning to recall their power, but this pole stands as a reminder that we must never again forget." When he finished his tour, I thought of the lesson of casting baby eaglets over the side of a nest.

There is still much to be written and said in legal and political discussions to persuade others that First Nations have a presently existing, inherent power of self-government. At the same time, there is much more we can be doing within our communities to reconstruct and recapture the full dignity and liberty that flows from being the Sovereign First Nations of this land. These efforts will become more effective the more a widening circle of First Nations people take responsibility and participate in these efforts. This is the best way to ensure that our children will become grandmothers and grand-fathers, so that when they get old, they too can become eagles.

## Notes

1. See Royal Commission on Aboriginal Peoples, *Partners in Confederation: Aboriginal Peoples, Self-Government and the Constitution* (Ottawa: Supply and Services, 1993).

2. See Kathy Brock, "The Politics of Aboriginal Self-Government: A Canadian Paradox," *Canadian Public Administration,* 34 (1991): 272.

3. For the most recent review of statistical measures of the impoverished conditions within First Nations, see Statistics Canada, *1991 Aboriginal People's Survey* (Ottawa: Statistics Canada, 1993).

4. For an accessible and well-written description of the problematic application of Canadian law and policy to First Nations, see, generally, A. C. Hamilton and C. M. Sinclair, *The Justice System and Aboriginal People: Report of the Aboriginal Justice Inquiry of Manitoba* (Winnipeg: Queen's Printer, 1991).

5. "As we begin to start understanding ourselves again as a people, as we start to deal with our own ceremonies, our own traditions, our own songs, I believe we will again identify for ourselves what is the true source of authority for all peoples." Gordon Peters, Ontario Region Chief, Chiefs of Ontario in Frank Cassidy, ed., *Aboriginal Self-Determination* (Lantzville: Oolichan Books, 1991).

6. Neyaashiinigmiing or Cape Croker Indian Reserve on the southwestern shores of Georgian Bay in what is now Southern Ontario.

7. One of my Nation's teachers wrote about the importance of attachment:

> There are four orders in creation. First is the physical world;
> second, the plant world; third, the animal; last, the human world.
> All four parts so intertwined that they make up one life and one
> whole existence. With less than the four orders, life and being are
> incomplete and unintelligible. *No one portion is self-sufficient or
> complete*; rather each derives its meaning from and fulfills its func-
> tions and purpose within the context of the whole of creation.

Basil Johnston, *Ojibway Heritage* (Toronto: McClelland and Stewart, 1976), 21.

8. See Lavina White and Eva Jacobs, *Report of the Aboriginal Committee, Community Panel Family and Children's Services Legislation Review in British Columbia: Liberating Our Children—Liberating Our Nations* (Victoria: Ministry of Social Services, October 1992).

9. See *Voices of Aboriginal Women: Aboriginal Women Speak Out about Violence*

(Ottawa: Canadian Council on Social Development and the Native Women's Association of Canada, 1991).

10. To examine this occurrence under the new registration procedures of the Indian Act, see *The Impacts of the 1985 Amendments to the Indian Act (Bill C-31): 1) Aboriginal Inquiry* (Ottawa: Indian and Northern Affairs, 1990).

11. I have purposely chosen not to give any citations to the abuse and disrespectful language employed in some circles. I have done this because I might be a poor judge of the motivation and effect of people's words. While I have definitely read and felt the bite of such language, I want to give others the benefit of the doubt in why they said certain things and how they were said. I have also restrained from citation here out of consideration for those who have unknowingly used such tactics and in the hopes that many people might examine their own talk and writing. Such introspections might be hindered if specific individuals were identified.

12. Ibid.

13. For example, in my community less than 10 percent of the population voted in the referendum. Many people I spoke to did not feel they had sufficient information to make an informed decision. For a statistical compilation of low voter participation rates in the referendum in status Indian communities, see *Referendum 92: Official Voting Results* (Ottawa: Chief Electoral Officer, 1992).

14. See Menno Bolt, *Surviving as Indians: The Challenge of Self-Government* (Toronto: University of Toronto Press, 1993), especially his chapter on leadership, 117–66. "Oka" refers to the action of the Mohawks in the 1990s to claim the land around the town of Oka as their own, based on the 1763 establishment of the land as Crown held in trusteeship for the Oka Indians. The Sulpician Order of the Catholic Church has been claiming the land for itself and selling it bit by bit to whites for centuries.

. . . .

*This article was published in* Justice as Healing *(1996) 1:1. The editor is grateful to John Borrows for permission to publish his work.*

. . . .

# CHAPTER 5

# Community Peacemaking

## A Healing Circle in the Innu Community of Sheshashit

### Background

During the fall of 1994, while attending a clinic on alcohol and substance abuse, Gavin Sellon told the counselors that he had committed a sexual assault the year before. On his return to Sheshashit, Labrador, Mr. Sellon went to the RCMP detachment and gave a cautioned statement in which he admitted to having had intercourse with L. R. without her consent. Mr. Sellon's disclosure came before the RCMP had begun its investigation.

The accused first appeared in provincial court on 12 June 1995. He elected to be tried in the Supreme Court, waiving the preliminary inquiry. On 9 August 1995, the matter was called in the Supreme Court, and the accused indicated that he wished to plead guilty and apply for a "sentencing circle." The Crown opposed the motion. The matter was set over to 18 December 1995 for argument, at which time Mr. Sellon withdrew his application for a sentencing circle.

However, the counsel for the accused decided to pursue an informal "healing circle" outside the courtroom setting and in the community of Sheshashit. Mr. Sellon's counsel also asked Judge O'Regan to strongly consider sentencing Sellon with a restorative rather than a punitive approach. Counsel for the Crown, on the other hand, suggested that the accused, being a non-Native, should be sentenced by the traditional court methods. Judge O'Regan told both counsels that if they wished to attend the healing circle, they could do so. He also assured them that he would give an appropriate weight to the results of the healing circle.

A report of the circle was prepared and attached as appendix A to the decision of Justice O'Regan of the Newfoundland Supreme Court: Trial Division. In considering sentencing, Judge O'Regan found that "the concern of the Crown [was] a non-issue . . . however, [he was] cognizant of the fact that [Sellon] did grow up in the community of Sheshashit and was exposed to the Innu culture and thus can benefit from the community's involvement in such things as the healing circle which he attended" (para. 14). Judge O'Regan accepted the recommendations of the healing circle and imposed a noncustodial sentence. The following is an abridged and copyedited version of appendix A.

## The Report of the Healing Circle

On Sunday, 21 January 1996, a circle was held in the Alcohol Centre in She-shashit. This circle was unique, because unlike previous circles, the participants knew that a written report about the circle would be shared with the court. The following is a report of that circle.

Those involved in planning the circle all agreed that, as the service provider, Innu Nation needs to demonstrate both to Innu and to the non-Innu public and justice system that Innu can develop and deliver services best suited to meet the needs of Innu. Not only does Innu Nation need to provide the services, but it also needs to be acknowledged as providing effective, supportive services. . . .

Therefore, we made a conscious decision to be clear about whose needs and which needs we were trying to meet through this process. We could then evaluate the effectiveness of the circle based on what we set out to do. We decided to tailor the circle to meet L.'s need for an opportunity to be heard within a supportive circle of those most directly affected by and involved with what happened between her and Gavin.

We also decided that it was not suitable or accurate to call this planned circle a "sentencing" circle. Sentencing is a justice system process to be done in court by court participants and the judge. This circle would be held as a circle of concern and support for L. and Gavin. The circle would eventually share participants' recommendations with the court for the judge to use as he saw fit. The focus, though, was on support and concern for L. and Gavin, which is why we proceeded to plan and carry out this circle. . . .

We decided that the purpose of this circle is twofold:

1. to give Gavin an opportunity to acknowledge responsibility for his actions; and
2. to give L. an opportunity to say what needed to happen for her to feel that the situation was being made more right.

Several weeks before the circle, Jack Penashue met with L. to ask her if she would be willing and able to participate in a circle with Gavin and others to deal with the incident. . . . Separate meetings were held with her father and her mother to determine their support for their daughter's decision. . . .

Once the date was set for the circle, Lyla met with Gavin Sellon to invite his participation in the circle. He was told who L. had invited and was asked if there were people he wanted to invite. . . . Gavin was given more information about the purpose of the circle and about how it was expected to proceed. . . .

When the circle convened on Sunday, there were ten participants: L.R., G.R. (L.'s mom), R.N. (L.'s sister), Gavin Sellon, Patricia Nuna (Gavin's spouse), Lynne Gregory (Gavin's mom), Apenam Pone (Gavin's stepfather), Germaine Benuen (community member), Jack Penashue (facilitator), and Lyla Andrew (facilitator).

The participants had coffee and tea before the circle started. Then all participants moved into the large meeting room and sat in a circle on the floor. With joined hands, they shared a prayer. Jack then explained the symbolism of burning sweetgrass and smudging. If participants found it meaningful, they were invited to smudge, and Jack went around the circle. He spoke Innuaimen first and then in English. When this was completed, Jack asked Lyla to explain the circle process.

She explained to participants that their conduct in the circle would be guided by their acceptance and use of four principles: honesty, kindness, sharing, and respect. Each person in turn would have the chance to speak uninterrupted. If they chose not to speak, they could pass the small "talking stone" to the next person. No one would be forced to speak. The circle would have four rounds, so each person would have four opportunities to speak.

The first round of the circle was for each participant to explain why he or she was present. The second round was for each participant to speak directly to L. and to share concern, support, and encouragement. The third round was for each participant to speak directly to Gavin and to share with him directly his or her feelings about him. The fourth round was for each participant to make recommendations to those in the circle, especially to Gavin, about what could or should be done to help bring resolution to the situation.

Before the facilitators began the rounds, they discussed the possible need for interpretation between Innuaimum and English. It was agreed that participants would speak the language of their choice, and anyone could request interpretation. Jack Penashue agreed to provide the interpretation. . . .

It is very difficult to put into words the effect and power of this circle. Participants in circles learn the power of the circle by actively participating in them. They learn that the atmosphere or feeling created by the participants is every bit as important as what is said. The following comments are those of the facilitators and Germaine Benuen, who have tried to express their impressions about the intangibles of the circle process—why it was so effective and powerful.

As the participants began arriving at the building, there was a noticeable tension among some. L. arrived with her mom and was quiet, almost sad. She spoke little and stood off to the side. Others chatted in twos or threes. All the participants seemed nervous. The facilitators had to be very direct to get participants to come into the room to start the circle. L.'s mother was the third participant to speak, and she admitted that she was scared.

The tension lessened noticeably, however, as the participants explained why they were present. It seemed to help that all the participants had an equal opportunity to say something. Even though L. did not speak in the first round, she began to appear less tense and less pressured, perhaps because she was not put on the spot to speak. In a way, we felt that both the process and the participants in the process showed respect to L. by not forcing her to speak. She certainly began to appear more confident. . . .

Another important aspect of the circle process was the emotions that the participants expressed. The facilitators had no way of knowing beforehand which emotions—whether anger, sadness, or frustration—the participants might voice or express. From previous experiences, the facilitators knew that the circle process was powerful, because honesty and emotion are an integral part of it. They also realized that how people spoke would be just as important to the impact of the circle as what people actually said. . . .

People often assume that the recommendations that circle participants make in the final round are most important to the court. . . . However, what was said in the earlier three rounds—and how that was expressed—greatly influenced and indeed shaped the recommendations that were eventually made.

Probably the most important comments that affected the final recommendations were those made by Gavin. In the first round, Gavin spoke in a clear voice and in a direct way. He said that he had come to the circle to apologize to everyone whom he had hurt by what he had done. He said that he wanted to find out what people wanted from him—what they expected from him. . . . In the round when everyone was invited to speak to L., Gavin emphasized that L. was in no way to blame for what had happened; he took full responsibility for his actions. . . .

Because of the seating, L. had the opportunity in each round to speak before Gavin. She didn't speak in the first or second rounds. In the third round, though, she spoke to Gavin, saying that she was happy he had opened up about what had happened between them. She said she would not have been strong enough to open up to others about what happened, but she was glad he had. She also told participants that she was happy to be a part of the circle. . . .

Jack began the final round by saying that he felt what needed to be said had been said. . . .

Lyla then began speaking. She said she, too, found the last round the most difficult. The earlier rounds had been difficult in their own ways, because what had been expressed was more painful. In her view, however, the difficulty they faced with making recommendations came from a sense of having to satisfy people or groups outside the circle—those who hadn't experienced what had happened inside the circle . . .

One recommendation offered to L. was that she accept and use for her own well-being the deep caring that her family has for her—that she use this care and concern to grow into being her own person. As a young mother, L. was encouraged to keep in mind the people who care for her deeply and to go to them for support and help when she needed them. At the same time, she was reminded that she is making her own choices and that she needs to choose what feels right for her. . . .

Another specific recommendation was made about Gavin. If he were placed on probation, participants recommended that he not be supervised directly by the adult probation office. Instead, he could be made accountable to the people in the community to whom he is connected. These community members would know why he was on probation and would have a real concern about how he is doing on probation. . . .

Another recommendation was directed to all of the circle participants. The suggestion was that they tell others about how the circle works based on their experience—that it is possible for someone to be held accountable by others in the community and to take responsibility for hurting another person. Each participant in the circle is connected to many other people, and we should use these connections to spread the word about the real need for us to support each other. . . .

Lynne told Gavin that she felt he needed to resolve the difficulties in his life that continue to cause him distress. She felt it wasn't for her to say what those things were, but she recommended that he continue to seek support on a regular basis . . . to reach out to people, to share his feelings and his dreams, and, with support, to start realizing his dreams. . . .

Gavin's mom then stated that she was feeling much better as a result of the circle. Before the circle, she felt that she could not reach out to the people most affected by Gavin's behavior . . . because of the court process and because of what other people might think if she tried to reach out. But now, she no longer feels stopped, and she knows she will be able to speak freely. . . .

Apenam recommended that Gavin continue to work at what Apenam knew Gavin had learned from going to the Brentwood treatment program. . . .

Participants also encouraged L. and Gavin to talk to each other—to learn again how to be comfortable around each other. Lynne said she felt it was important, if L. was able, to share how she felt about that, because in the end, her feelings about this were the most important, and we should try to know how she feels.

L. replied right away that she had no problems or difficulties talking with Gavin, sharing with him, or anything like that. She would like to do that, in fact. Everyone agreed to close the circle and, with hands joined, stood and together repeated the "serenity prayer."

At this point, the tape was turned off, and participants embraced one another as they chose. L.'s mom went over to Gavin and embraced him, but most significantly, L. and Gavin embraced one another.

. . . .

*This report was published in* Justice as Healing *(1997) 2:2 and is reprinted here with permission. For a more extensive treatment of the circle process and further ways that it can be used with the justice system, see Kay Pranis, Barry Stuart, and Mark Wedge,* Peacemaking Circles: From Crime to Community *(St. Paul, Minnesota: Living Justice Press, 2003).*

# 21

# Aboriginal Community Healing in Action:
# The Hollow Water Approach

*Rupert Ross*

Hollow Water is an Ojibway community of some six hundred people located on the east side of Lake Winnipeg, about two hundred kilometers north of Winnipeg. In 1984, a group of social service providers, concerned with the future of their young people, looked into the issues of youth substance abuse, vandalism, truancy, and suicide. After some study, the focus shifted to the children's home life when they identified intergenerational sexual abuse as the root problem. By 1987, they tackled sexual abuse head-on, creating their Community Holistic Circle Healing Program (CHCH). They presently estimate that 75 percent of Hollow Water residents are victims of sexual abuse, and 35 percent are "victimizers."

They formed a broad-based team to promote and respond to disclosures of abuse. It includes the child protection worker, the Community Health Representative, the Nurse in Charge, and the NADAP (Native Alcohol and Drug Abuse Program) worker, together with others from the RCMP, the school division, and community churches. The majority of team members are women, many of whom are volunteers.

The team members worked to break down the professional barriers between them, including separate chains of reporting and confidentiality, in order to create a coordinated response. They believed that working in isolation on separate aspects of each troubled person or family would cause further splintering when their goal was to create "whole" people. From the outset, outside professionals were seen as necessary to the project's success, but these professionals were required to "sign on" to a coordinated team approach. They also had to permit a "lay" member of the team to be with them at all times, so each could learn from the other. Community members could learn the outside professionals' skills, and the outside professionals could learn the community's approach to healing. Partnership was—and remains—the model.

They developed a detailed protocol of thirteen steps, leading from the initial disclosure to the Healing Contract to the Cleansing Ceremony. The Healing Contract, designed by the people involved in the offense or personally touched by it, requires each person to "sign on" to the task of bringing certain changes or additions to their relationships with the others. In view of the challenges involved with true healing, such contracts are expected to last more than two years. One contract is still being adhered to five years after its creation. If and when the Healing Contract is successfully completed, the Cleansing Ceremony is held to "mark a new beginning for all involved" and to "honor the victimizer for completing the healing contract process."

Criminal charges are set as soon as possible after disclosure. The victimizer can proceed either on his or her own through the criminal process or with the healing support of the team. Those who choose the latter must accept full responsibility for their acts and enter a guilty plea at the earliest opportunity. Virtually all those accused have requested the team's support, and as a result, trials are rare.

The team requests that sentencing be delayed, so they can begin their healing work and prepare a "presentence report." The report analyzes everything from the offender's state of mind, level of effort, and chance of full rehabilitation to the reactions, feelings, plans, and suggestions of all those affected. The report gives special attention to the victim, the nonoffending spouse, and the families of each. It proposes an "action plan" based on the Healing Contract. The team requests that any probation order require the victimizer's full cooperation with their healing efforts. If jail is imposed, they try to arrange regular work with the offender while in custody and to prepare everyone for the day of release.

At all times, team members work with, protect, support, teach, and encourage a wide range of people. It is their view that since many people are affected by each disclosure, all deserve assistance, and all must be involved in any process aimed at creating healthy dynamics and breaking the intergenerational chain of abuse. I watched them plan for a possible confrontation with a suspected victimizer. The detailed dispersal of team members throughout the community to support those whom disclosure would touch reminded me of a military operation in its logistical complexity.

Virtually all community team members are themselves victims of longstanding sexual abuse, primarily at the hands of family members. Their views on the dynamics of sexual abuse prevail. Even former victimizers who have been honored for completing their healing process are asked to join the team. The personal experiences of team members in the emotional, mental, physical, and spiritual complexities of sexual abuse give them extraordinary rapport with victims and victimizers alike. In circles, they share their own histories to coax others out of the anger, denial, guilt, fear, self-loathing, and hurt that must be faced. Their personal experiences also give them the patience to embark on very long processes and to see signs of progress that might escape others' notice. From their own lives, team members have gained the insight to recognize who is manipulating or hiding in denial and the toughness not to give up.

This healing process is painful, because it involves stripping away all the excuses, justifications, angers, and other defenses of each abuser. Finally, when confronted with a victim who has become strong enough to expose his or her pain in the abuser's presence, the abuser actually feels the pain that he or she created. Only then can rebuilding begin for both the abuser and the abused. The word *healing* seems like such a soft word, but the process of healing within the Hollow Water program is anything but.

When the accused finally goes to court for sentencing, the team is brutally honest about the sincerity of his or her efforts and about how much work still has to be done. This does not mean that someone accused who is still resisting the team's efforts is abandoned to jail—far from it. While Western justice systems seem to have forged an unbreakable link between "holding someone responsible for their crime" and sending them to jail, Hollow Water fiercely denies the wisdom of that connection. I will let their 1993 position paper on the issue of jail speak for itself:

> CHCH's position on the use of incarceration and its relationship to an individual's healing process has changed over time. In our initial efforts to break the vicious cycle of abuse that was occurring in our community, we took the position that we needed to promote the use of incarceration in cases that were defined as "too serious." After some time, however, we came to the conclusion that this position was adding significantly to the difficulty of what was already complex casework.
>
> As we worked through the casework difficulties that arose out of this position, we came to realize two things:

1. As we both shared our own stories of victimization and learned from our experiences in assisting others in dealing with the pain of their victimization, it became very difficult to define "too serious." The quantity or quality of pain felt by the victim, the family/ies, and the community did not seem to be directly connected to any specific acts of victimization. For example, attempts by the courts—and to a certain degree by ourselves—to define a particular victimization as "too serious" and another as "not too serious" (e.g., "only" fondling vs. actual intercourse; victim is daughter vs. victim is nephew; one victim vs. four victims) were gross over-simplifications and certainly not valid from an experiential point of view.

2. Promoting incarceration was based on and motivated by a mixture of feelings of anger, revenge, guilt, and shame on our part, as well as on our personal victimization issues, rather than on the healthy resolution of the victimization we were trying to address.

Thus, our position on the use of incarceration has shifted. At the same time, we understand how the legal system continues to use and view incarceration, namely, as punishment and deterrence for the victimizers (offenders) and protection and safety for the victim(s) and community. What the legal system seems not to understand is the complexity of the issues involved in breaking the cycle of abuse that exists in our community.

The use of judgement and punishment actually works against the healing process. An already unbalanced person is moved further out of balance.

What the threat of incarceration does do is keep people from coming forward and taking responsibility for the hurt they are causing. It reinforces the silence and therefore promotes, rather than breaks, the cycle of violence that exists. In reality, rather than making the community a safer place, the threat of jail places the community more at risk.

In order to break the cycle, we believe that victimizers must be held accountable to—as well as receive support from—those most affected by the victimization: the victim, the family/ies, and the community. Removing the victimizer from those who not only must hold him or her accountable but also are best able to do so—as well as to offer him or her support—adds complexity to the already existing dynamics of denial, guilt, and shame. When victimizers are removed, the healing process of all parties is at best delayed and most often actually deterred.

The legal system, based on principles of punishment and deterrence, as we see it, simply is not working. We cannot understand [why] the legal system doesn't see this.

Their position paper also speaks of the need to break free of court ways. The adversarial model of court proceedings does not promote healing. So, too, when defense counsel recommends both complete silence and pleas of "not guilty," the healing process is seriously impeded. Moreover, when victims are cross-examined on the witness stand, a second "victimization" occurs. In their view, "[t]he courtroom and process simply is not a safe place for the victim to address the victimization—nor is it a safe place for the victimizer to come forward and take responsibility for what has happened."

Toward the conclusion of the position paper, they state:

We do not see our present position on incarceration as either "an easy way out" for the victimizer or as the victimizer "getting away." We see it rather as establishing a very clear line of accountability between the victimizer and his or her community. What follows from that line is a process that we believe is not only much more difficult for the victimizer, but also much more likely to heal the victimization, than doing time in jail could ever be.

Our children and the community can no longer afford the price the legal system is extracting in its attempts to provide justice in our community.

Based on these views, most of Hollow Water's work takes place away from the courtroom. The team works with affected people wherever and whenever they can. Virtually all their work takes place in a circle format, opened and closed by prayers, and respects the "non-blaming" imperative that the circle demands and fosters. Only their assessments, presentence reports, and action plans have been part of court proceedings thus far. In the fall of 1993, however, they will take their circle into the courtroom so the judge can hear directly from the people, the family/ies, and the community.

· · · ·

*Published in* Justice as Healing *(1995), this article is an excerpt from Rupert Ross's discussion paper:* Dueling Paradigms? Western Criminal Justice versus Aboriginal Community Healing. *Mr. Ross's article does not represent either the thinking or the policy of any branch of government. The editor would like to thank Mr. Ross for permission to publish these excerpts. For a more extensive treatment of the circle process and examples of how it has been used with the justice system, see Kay Pranis, Barry Stuart, and Mark Wedge,* Peacemaking Circles: From Crime to Community *(St. Paul, Minnesota: Living Justice Press, 2003).*

# The Sentencing Circle:
# Seeds of a Community Healing Process

*The Hollow Water First Nations Community Holistic Circle Healing
Interim Report, 1994*

## The Sentencing Circle: Background

The seeds of the "sentencing circle" concept have been within our community since the mid-1970s. At that time, a few individuals started to look at traditional teachings and practices as a way of beginning personal healing journeys. . . .

In 1984, these personal healing journeys became the seeds of a community healing process. . . . By then, most of us occupied various social program positions in the community, and we talked about how we could better meet the needs of the individuals and families with whom we were involved as service providers. . . .

By 1989 . . . we had learned that sexual victimization was at the core of the unhealthiness of most individuals and families in our caseloads. . . . We began to look for, develop, and then apply a community healing process to address sexual victimization. This eventually became known as Community Holistic Circle Healing (CHCH).

CHCH is our attempt to take responsibility for what is happening to us. Through the power of the circle, we work to restore balance and to make our community a safe place for future generations. CHCH stems from our beliefs: (1) that victimizers are created, not born; (2) that the vicious cycle of abuse in our community must be broken—now; and (3) that, given a safe place, healing is possible and will happen.

CHCH utilizes the principles that were traditionally used to deal with matters such as victimization. The traditional way was for the community

1. to bring it out into the open;
2. to protect the victim, so as to minimally disrupt the family's and community's functioning;

3. to hold the victimizer accountable for his or her behavior; and
4. to offer the opportunity for balance to be restored to all parties of the victimization. . . .

## Rationale

In our conjunctive relationship with the legal system, we see our role as one of representing our community. We do not see ourselves as "being on the side of" either the Crown or the defense. Both represent members of our community, and the pain of both is felt in our community.

Until now, our efforts have focused on

1. helping both the Crown and the defense see the issues in the court case as the community sees them and therefore asking for their support in representing the community's interest; and
2. providing the court with a presentence report, which outlines the situation as we see it, informs the court of the work we are doing with the victimizer, and offers recommendations on how to proceed with restoring balance around the victimization.

Now, however, we believe it is time to expand the community's involvement in this process. We believe it is time for the court to hear directly from the community at the time of the sentencing. Until now, the sentencing hearing has been the point at which all of the parties of the legal system (Crown, defense, judge) and the community have come together. There have been major differences of opinion about how to proceed. As we see it, the legal system usually arrives with an agenda to punish and deter the "guilty" victimizer as the way to protect and ensure the safety of the victim and community. The community, on the other hand, arrives with an agenda to hold the victimizer accountable to the community and by this means to restore balance to all parties of the victimization.

The differences in these two agendas are seriously deterring the healing process of the community. We believe that balance is more likely to be restored if sentencing itself is more consistent in both process and content with the community's healing work. Sentencing needs to become more of a step in the healing process, rather than a diversion from it. The sentencing circle promotes this rationale.

## Purpose

The sentencing circle serves two primary purposes:

1. It promotes the community healing process by providing a forum for the community to address the parties of the victimization at the time of sentencing.
2. It allows the court to hear directly from the people most affected by the pain of the victimization.

In the past, the Crown and defense as well as we ourselves have attempted to convey this information. We believe that it is now time for the court to hear directly from the victim, the family of the victim, the victimizer, the family of the victimizer, and the community-at-large.

## Participants

The following people need to be included, if at all possible, in the sentencing circle:

1. the victim;
2. the support people working with the victim, including his or her individual worker, group workers, the psychologist, as well as members of his or her support group. If the victim is not able to attend, the individual worker may take the role of the victim's representative;
3. the family of the victim;
4. the victimizer (offender);
5. the support people working with the victimizer, including his or her individual worker, group workers, the psychologist, as well as members of his or her support group;
6. the family of the victimizer;
7. the community, which includes members of the CHCH and others from the community who wish to participate;
8. the court party, which includes the judge, Crown, and defense counsel; and
9. the RCMP, which hopefully includes the members responsible for the investigation as well as for policing our community.

## Preparing for the Sentencing Circle

The CHCH team's preparations include

1. offering tobacco to the presiding judge;
2. preparing the presentence report and distributing it to the Crown, defense, and judge;
3. meeting with the chief, mayors, and councils to develop and carry out a process for ensuring community participation;
4. holding circles with the victim, victimizer, and family/ies the day before the sentencing circle; and
5. making the sweat lodge available to any interested circle participants the evening before the sentencing circle.

The day of the sentencing circle, morning preparations include

1. a pipe ceremony;
2. hanging the flags;
3. smudging the court building;
4. placing the community drum and eagle staff in the courtroom;
5. serving breakfast to participants from outside of the community; and
6. offering tobacco for a prayer to guide the sentencing circle.

## The Structure

The courtroom seating consists of two circles: an inner and an outer one. The inner circle is for participants who wish to speak. The outer circle is for participants who prefer to observe and listen. We hope most participants choose the inner circle.

## The Sentencing Circle Process

The process of the sentencing circle unfolds through the following order:

1. personal smudges;
2. an opening prayer;
3. covering court technicalities, e.g., a confirmation of pleas;

    4. outlining the "ground rules" that govern the sentencing circle, which is done by the presiding judge;

    5. the first "go-around": why did I come today? why am I here?

    6. the second go-around: participants speak to the victim;

    7. the third go-around: participants speak to the victimizer (offender) about how the victimization has affected them, their families, and the community;

    8. the fourth go-around: participants outline their expectations to the victimizer and express their opinions about what needs to be done in order to restore balance;

    9. the judge gives a decision regarding sentencing;

    10. a closing prayer.

Following the judge's decision and the closing prayer, participants are invited to stay and use the circle for sharing and debriefing purposes.

## The Seating and Speaking Order of the Inner Circle

The judge occupies the seat at the northern point of the circle. On the judge's immediate left sit two CHCH members who serve as process facilitators. To their left sits the victimizer, followed by his or her individual worker, then four members of the CHCH team, then the victim, followed by his or her support worker, then all the other participants of the circle. The Crown and defense lawyers are seated on the judge's immediate right. The first person to speak in the circle is the person on the immediate left of the judge. Speaking follows a clockwise direction and ends with the presiding judge.

## The Rules Governing the Circle

The participants' conduct in the circle is governed by the following rules:

    1. only one person may speak at a time;

    2. the Laws of the Creator shall govern the person speaking; these laws are honesty, kindness, sharing, and respect;

    3. a person may only speak in turn; there are to be no interruptions while a person is speaking;

    4. if desired, a person may pass when it is his or her turn to speak;

    5. all other participants should be attentive to the person speaking.

## Conclusions

1. Using the sentencing circle promotes sentencing as a step in the healing process.
2. Because those most affected by the victimization are involved in the sentencing process and have input in the decision, the healing processes of individuals, family, and community are enhanced.
3. The victimizer is both held accountable and supported by those most affected by the victimization.
4. Including the formal court party affirms the conjunctive relationship between the community and the legal system, as established through the protocol with the Attorney General's Department and supported by the Federal Justice Department.

. . . .

*Published in* Justice as Healing *(1995), this article is an excerpt from appendix 3 of the* Interim Report of the Hollow Water First Nations Community Holistic Circle Healing (CHCH), *which describes the activities of CHCH for the period of 1 April 1 1993 to 9 February 1994. The editor would like to thank the authors for permission to reprint. Communities use circles to deal with conflicts and crime in many different ways according to their own traditions and the needs of a case. For a further discussion of some of these ways, see Kay Pranis, Barry Stuart, and Mark Wedge,* Peacemaking Circles: From Crime to Community *(St. Paul, Minnesota: Living Justice Press, 2003).*

# Community-Based Justice Initiatives
# of the Saskatoon Tribal Council

*Yvonne Boyer*

### Overview

The Saskatoon Tribal Council is comprised of seven First Nations in central Saskatchewan. Its population is approximately 9,000 people from three different tribal groups: Saulteaux, Cree, and Dakota. Approximately one-half of the Saskatoon Tribal Council members live in urban areas with a large transient population.

Two of the four corporations of the Saskatoon Tribal Council are directly involved with justice initiatives: STC Urban First Nations Services, Inc., and the Saskatoon Tribal Council, Inc. The first, STC Urban First Nations Services, Inc., has a mandate to provide services and programs on a status-blind basis for the Aboriginal population of Saskatoon. The second, Saskatoon Tribal Council, Inc., provides programs and services to the on-reserve population of the seven member bands. Many of the programs overlap to some degree in order to adequately serve both a nontransient and a migrating population. These programs include Education, Labor Force Development, Housing and Engineering, Finance, Human Resources Management, Justice, Health, and Social Development.

The justice program for the Saskatoon Tribal Council began in July 1997 when government funders and the Saskatoon Tribal Council signed agreements to develop community-based justice initiatives for the seven member bands and the urban services in Saskatoon. The Aboriginal urban population and the seven-member bands were keenly interested in reclaiming justice—developing a system that would work for the people whom the system has engulfed.

Many of the problems were evident from the beginning. The legacy of colonial policies have left their mark on the Aboriginal Peoples within the city of Saskatoon and among the Saskatoon Tribal Council's on-reserve members.

The residential school system has deeply wounded generations of people both on and off reserve. Many of these people are currently in the criminal justice system and are besieged not only with complacency about themselves but also with the hopelessness of knowing that future generations are likely to follow suit.

Many of the youth in the urban setting have lost their language, culture, and traditions: they do not even know which bands their parents came from, nor have they ever set foot on reserve land. The problems they face are so horrific and tragic that the condition seems unimaginable in Canada, a first-world country. These are the youths whose faces are regularly seen in court, and they make up most of the population in young offender facilities. These drifting children were born into a country whose government policies have insisted on disposing of or assimilating their parents and grandparents with the brown skin and the "savage" traditions.

One of the first steps in tackling the colossal task of building programs that would work for both youths and adults was to understand what diversion meant to those affected. The Elders are the wise ones, the ones with the memories and knowledge taught by their Elders. The only commonsense approach was to ask them to share their knowledge. In 1997, a process began to formally request their help. The process took a month and involved visiting the Elders in each reserve at their homes.

Due to the different tribal groups and unique traditions, the community justice workers in each reserve provided advice on the proper process for requesting the Elders' presence. Gifts and tobacco were given in each of the Elders' homes. On one occasion, some of the Saskatoon Tribal Council members joined in the festivities of a traditional feast to honor one of the Elders. They briefly explained what diversion meant in the current justice system. Their goal was to gain each individual Elder's trust enough to convince him or her to attend a gathering of Elders to discuss their knowledge of traditional justice.

The first Elders' gathering was held in 1997 at Wanuskewin Heritage Park just outside Saskatoon. Wanuskewin Heritage Park is considered sacred ground for tribes who have gathered at the site for centuries, as was evident by the Elders' tears, hugs, and warmth as they met one another. During a talking circle, the Elders and the participants spoke on justice issues important to them. With the permission of the Elders, the conversations at the original

circle and subsequent circles were recorded and transcribed into books. Elders' gatherings are now held twice each year at Wanuskewin Heritage Park
and have focused on sharing the Elders' knowledge of traditional justice and
what was taught to them by their Elders.

The main lessons learned at these gatherings include the following: that
showing respect is the basic law of life; that it is good to be truthful at all
times; that all races are children of the Creator; and that traditional justice
must include healing, reconciliation, accountability, respect, and kindness.
Without a foundation in these tenets, any justice program—on-reserve or
urban—is doomed to failure.

## Urban Programming: Youth Circles Program

The Youth Circles Program diverts youth from the criminal justice system
within the city of Saskatoon. In operation since October 1997, it is steadily
and rapidly growing. The process is unlike mainstream mediation programs,
which have not allowed Aboriginal youth to divert their charges through mediation. The program's planning research discovered that the reason that Aboriginal youth have been excluded is that, by the time they reach the young
offender age of twelve, they have already had so many contacts with the police that they are considered unsuitable for diversion. In accordance with the
Saskatchewan Justice Policy of diversion, the Youth Circles Program worked
to include these youth and target them, so they did not become entrenched
in the criminal justice system.

Early on, organizers realized that Aboriginal people are the ones best
suited for determining and developing programs that are culturally appropriate and sensitive to Aboriginal youths, who comprise the majority of youth
in the system. Based on the lessons taught by the Elders, including lessons
about the medicine wheel, the approach followed traditional justice ways.
Every referral involved a home study to determine which aspect of the medicine wheel was out of balance. The Aboriginal youths faced similar issues:
low self-esteem, extreme poverty, and challenges in the home life. They also
tended to struggle with one or more addictions, which can and often do lead
to problems with the law.

Our process begins with asking a youth to attend a circle voluntarily and to
take responsibility for his or her behavior. Our Elder(s) guide the circle process with the victim, the victim's family and support people, the offender and

his or her family and support group, community representatives (sometimes from the home reserve), and a professional facilitator from our program.

The circle determines the path that a youth needs to follow to rebalance his or her life, which always includes the family. If the youth's family is not capable or willing to participate, or if the family requires further support, an "artificial" family is created through the support of other youths or resources in the program. Every person is treated with equal dignity and respect.

The circle has a strong victim/offender mediation component and includes certain victim/offender reconciliation processes. Grandparents who attend the circle provide valuable input to the offender. Youths find it far more difficult to explain an offense to their grandmother than to face a judge in a robe on a bench. So, too, the impact of a youth looking a victim in the eye and saying, "I am sorry," is a powerful experience.

After everyone has had opportunities to speak through several rounds, the circle comes to a consensus about which areas of the youth's life need rebalancing. The youth has significant input into his or her own healing journey, and this input is crucial to the outcome in terms of his or her ability to change behavior. The circle defines a set of tasks or conditions to help the youth make positive changes; these tasks usually take a few months to complete.

A compelling feature of the Youth Circles Program is the follow-up care for the youth. The daily challenge, of course, is to find resources to accommodate each individual's needs. One area that consistently requires more resources is treatment for addictions. Nearly all of the youth in the Youth Circles Program have one or more addictions or have family members with serious addictions. If the physical aspect of the medicine wheel requires attention, the STC youth workers and the youth participate in basketball games with the Saskatoon City Police Team. This gives the youths an opportunity to address their physical needs as well as to break down barriers between them and the police.

Youths who have anger-management problems may attend boxing classes with our workers or other activities. Through these experiences, they learn discipline as well as a positive outlet for their anger. Another outlet is the summer canoe trip with the Saskatoon City Police Services—an activity nominated by the International Institute on Crime Prevention as one of thirty top crime-prevention strategies worldwide. The youth may also attend Elders' gatherings and pow wows. If required, some youth attend Elder counseling sessions or are referred to family counselors.

The mental aspect of the medicine wheel approach always includes education as a key component. If education is not applicable or realistic, then the youths are given work experience or training. If family issues need to be addressed, youths and their families are referred to the STC Urban First Nations Services Family Center for healing circles.

Twice during the summer, fifteen youth are taken to the Healing Lodge at Wahpeyton First Nation. The Healing Lodge houses provincial and federal male inmates who are completing the last portion of their sentences. Joined by the STC Youth Circle staff, the youths camp out for two days in a tipi and sit in a talking circle with the older inmates. The older inmates tell their little brothers about the bad choices they have made in their lives and their decision to start their healing journeys. Their sharing always affects the youths, leaving them with haunting memories. In general, the youths chosen for this trip are those who have exhibited a negative attitude or who have been involved with gang activity.

Given the youths' range of needs, the staff has to be very creative in giving them opportunities to help them rebalance themselves, which in turn brings more positive life choices. When a youth's tasks or conditions are complete, the staff returns to the court and has the charges withdrawn. Most youth retain contact with the STC Youth Circle staff.

The program is experiencing success at various levels. Presently, ten to fifteen youths who have made drastic, positive life choices have become leaders for the younger ones entering the program. These young people have been trained in mediation and serve as role models and co-facilitators in the youth circles.

When determining its "success," the Youth Circles program looks not so much at re-offense statistics as on the ability of the youth to make changes in their lives that reflect a more healthy, well-balanced lifestyle. Of the 108 cases completed in the 1998–99 fiscal year, only twelve youth have had system-generated re-offenses, and only one youth went on to commit a crime more serious than the one that originally brought him into the program.

Given these numbers, it seems clear that our processes are improving the lives of Aboriginal youth. Because of the unique needs of Aboriginal youth in urban environments, the youths must be picked up at their homes for their appointments, their family moves tracked, home visits made, transport arranged for the camping and fishing trips, as well as all the other follow-up activities managed. Without this individualized care and concentrated effort, it is unlikely that any tangible change would occur.

Changing attitudes in the criminal justice system is a slow process, though, and the funding we receive reflects this. The resources that come to us hardly compares with the amount of money our program saves in housing the youth in facilities, staffing various agencies, and providing follow-up care.

## On-Reserve Community Justice Programs

All of the seven-member bands of the Saskatoon Tribal Council have community-based justice programming. Each justice committee functions differently (as in the urban environment) according to the unique cultural and traditional requirements of the individual reserves and tribal groupings.

For all of them, the challenge has been to keep the programs running effectively with minimal funding. Other band initiatives and programs must fund the justice initiatives to keep them functioning. Every band functions at its own pace, and some programs are more developed than others. The needs for resources on each reserve vary. They depend on the population that is incarcerated or otherwise in the criminal justice system, the community's acceptance of the justice initiatives, and the overall support of the chief and council.

Many of the problems and issues on reserve are the same as those in urban areas, especially poverty, addictions, and a sense of hopelessness. On reserve, though, communities experience greater closeness, both in proximity and in relationships. With the community's input and direction, community-based justice and follow-up are easier to monitor and maintain.

Some of the justice initiatives being used on reserve include sentencing circles, healing circles, mediations (both individual and community-based), family group conferencing, community group conferencing, cautioning, re-integrations, and other dispute resolution processes. Often these methods of dispute resolution are combined. Regardless of the specific method, all processes are based on traditional justice as taught by the Elders. In brief, the Saskatoon Tribal Council communities use the following processes.

### a. Sentencing Circles

The sentencing circles hosted by the on-reserve communities have been very difficult for the community, and the very smallest steps have been considered a success. Held in 1997, the first sentencing circle was a great challenge, and it took the community nearly a year to be ready for another circle.

This first circle was held at the Prince Albert Court House. The defense counsel, police, prosecutor, victim, offender, and community supporters were present. Training sessions had been held, and the judge, prosecutor, and police had been briefed on how the circle works. The defense counsel had not been available to take calls, so the first time he appeared was at the circle itself.

The circle went as planned, yet there was a major component absent, namely, a feeling of "truthfulness" within the circle. A consensus was reached, and the judge passed the offender recommendations, which were very harsh. The victim and the offender were related, and the offense arose from a long-standing family feud that resulted in serious charges. There was no victim-offender reconciliation.

In the "debriefing" following the circle, however, it came to light that the defense counsel had forbidden the offender to say anything. This simple point corrupted the whole circle process, and the community was left to pick up the pieces, trying to salvage the positive points of the circle experience.

In a more recent sentencing circle, the judge, prosecutor, and police again attended, along with the victim, offender, supports, and three Elders. This particular community has its own Elders' peacemaking court. The Saskatoon Tribal Council only provided a facilitator and an Elder to help guide the process.

At the beginning of the circle, the sacred circle process was explained to the participants. They were told about the importance of respecting each other and the circle, why the circle proceeds in a clockwork fashion, and the importance of expressing respect by not speaking out of turn. At the gateway to the circle (the opening where participants entered), two Elders sat as gatekeepers to guard the sacred circle process.

In Aboriginal culture, Elders are treated with the utmost respect and honor. They are honored with eating first at meals. If there is only one cup of juice left, it is given to the Elder. If they need help walking, they are helped. To serve the Elders at feasts is considered an honor that must be earned. An Elder is never, ever interrupted, and the Elders' stories are considered valuable and precious.

During this particular circle, the judge and the prosecutor were constantly interrupting the Elders. The RCMP officer broke the circle by walking out. When the Elder asked her if there was anything wrong, she snapped, "It's personal," and stomped out with total disregard for the Elders and the sacred circle process that she had been given the honor to attend. The Elders and the community members were very disheartened by the actions of the judge, the RCMP officer, and the prosecutor. I personally was ashamed that the two worlds to which I belong are so far apart.

A few days ago, the justice coordinator in one of the Saskatoon Tribal Council communities asked me to help set up a sentencing circle in the fall. This particular community is advanced in their justice initiatives but realized the problems that lay ahead. The justice committee requested permission to handle the circle without the judge, defense council, prosecutor, and the police. It is unlikely that their request will be granted because of the severity of the offense. The defense counsel is a prominent criminal lawyer and has expressed to the justice committee that he wants the circle over with as quickly as possible, since "his time is money." In desperation, the community has asked me to speak to this individual to try to help him understand the circle process. I doubt that I can change this person's attitude, and the circle will once again be dishonored.

Only a handful of the sentencing circles that Saskatoon Tribal Council bands have been involved in have not been blemished somehow. While attending a sentencing circle at Muskoday First Nation, I had the opportunity to discuss the role of judges, prosecutors, and the police in sentencing circles with a very progressive judge of the Prince Albert Provincial Court. We both agreed that neither the judges, prosecutors, nor the police have any role in community-based justice.

The experiences of the Saskatoon Tribal Council bands demonstrate how true this is. Either the community must intervene before the sentencing, or it must be trusted enough to pass sentences on its own offenders in each community's own ways. As it is now, if the community diverts charges before sentencing, the charges must conform to the Saskatchewan Justice Policy of diversion, yet this severely limits which charges the communities can divert.

A more preferable route would be for communities to hold their own circles, pass sentence, and then bring the recommendations to the court. The First Nations people of the Saskatoon Tribal Council bands do not want to offend anyone by excluding them from the circle. They often agree that it is "easier" to allow themselves to be offended, so they can have some control over the lives and sentences of one of their own people and band members.

## b. Reintegration

Many Saskatoon Tribal Council band members are institutionalized in either the federal or provincial correctional centers. Muskoday First Nation wanted to arrange an early release for one young man who had been incarcerated since he was fourteen years old. At the time, he was approaching his thirty-fourth birthday and had spent twenty Christmases in prison. The community was determined to help this young man reconnect with his family on reserve and with the community he once belonged to. Chief and council met on several occasions to discuss a plan to allow a safe re-entry to his home community. The justice committee worked very hard at putting together a plan that would allow this to happen.

The process took nearly two years, even though this young man should have been paroled years before. The result was a thorough release plan prompted by a caring, committed community. In coordination with the justice committee, the young man galvanized a community to work for his release. This release plan is currently being used as a model for many other First Nations communities in the province. The young man is now settled—happy and safe in his home community.

## c. Other Dispute Resolutions

Despite some of the gloomy experiences that the justice committees have endured, many encouraging events have happened as well. Various court interventions and healing initiatives are occurring on a regular basis in each of the Saskatoon Tribal Council communities. Mediations, group conferencing that brings together both the family and the community, healing circles that prepare for more difficult cases or that support survivors of residential school abuse, proactive methods, and other creative approaches that incorporate traditional justice: all these methods are used interchangeably. As a result, the communities are slowly taking more control over their lives and their family members in the justice system.

## Summary

According to the Report of the Royal Commission on Aboriginal Peoples, the strongest message heard from the Round Table discussions was that successful justice projects must be firmly rooted in the communities they are intended to serve. Judge Robert Cawsey, chief judge of the Provincial Court of Alberta, made this point very clearly. Chairing the task force on the criminal justice system and its impact on the Indian and Métis People of Alberta, Judge Cawsey stated:

> Everything that has worked when we're dealing with Natives has come from the Natives. I don't know of anything that has worked that has been foisted upon them from above. There is no one model of justice development. This must be kept in mind while the communities and the urban centers are developing the processes that best address their own needs.
>
> Further, the process of building credibility among stakeholders and agencies within the city and the municipalities surrounding the on-reserve communities has been slow and painful. Many times, the courts, police, and the Crown have mistrusted or not had the confidence that Aboriginal people have the education, knowledge, or the ability to effectively deal with their own problems in their own ways. However, good working partnerships are developing between stakeholders and other diversion agencies in the city. These partnerships strengthen and enhance each other's abilities to further the common goal of building stable, mutually beneficial relationships that will lead to a clearer understanding and a more balanced justice system.

· · · ·

*Published in* Justice as Healing *(1999) 4:4, this paper was presented by Yvonne Boyer at the Canadian Institute for the Administration of Justice Conference entitled "Changing Punishment at the Turn of the Century" in Saskatoon, Saskatchewan, on 26–29 September 1999. The editor is grateful to Ms. Boyer for permission to publish this paper.*

# Alternative Justice: Testing the Waters

## Judge Steven Point

I have been invited here to speak to you about alternative justice, and I am grateful for the opportunity to share my experiences with you and some thoughts.

I realize that you are law students and will be leaving these classrooms someday to begin your own careers as lawyers. You will no doubt be faced with the same reality that many new lawyers face; namely, that you don't really get taught everything you will need to know to be a practicing barrister or solicitor. There are things that are left for you to discover on your own and to be assimilated into your already vast legal memory banks. For example, "legal aid billing forms" and "form letters" and "negotiating a claim out of court" are some things you may not learn about in law school. Another such matter is the relatively new—yet old—concept of restorative justice, aka alternative justice.

Maybe I am wrong on this, but I would bet that not too many schools include this yet as a formal part of law school training. When I first heard the term, it seemed vague and uncertain, and even when you hear someone explaining it, it sounds somehow made up or unreal. Perhaps this is because it is outside the conventional sources of learning. Academic writing normally comes from highly educated professionals who are well known for their published legal theories about things like "mens rea" or evidence or constitutional matters. Restorative justice, however, originated from the needs and concerns of ordinary citizens.

When I read Judge Barry Stuart's report of August 1996 entitled "Building Community Justice Partnerships: Community Peacemaking Circles—A Description of the Yukon Experience," it became clear to me that this was not a theoretical essay but rather a report based on his experiences with people. His ideas and solutions fascinated me. I have tried to follow his advice in my town of Prince Rupert where I am a sitting Provincial Court Judge.

At its base, restorative justice is a criticism of the current justice system. Whereas the movement to find alternatives to the existing system began within First Nations communities, it has grown to a search for an alternative for all Canadians. It begins with the argument that the current system is not working well: It is too expensive. It is too complex. It is not inclusive. It takes too long to get results. It ignores the needs of victims. It is adversarial in nature. It does not promote harmony or wellness in the offender's community or family. And it requires specialists to travel in and interpret the inner workings of the system. These are but a few of the complaints levied at the current justice system not only in Canada but also in the United States, Australia, Japan, and many other countries.

The central concern is that Canadians have abdicated their responsibility for managing conflicts within their families and their communities. They are now outsiders, watching a slow, incomprehensible system deliver what seems to be injustice and not justice. The system's high cost is not justified when one examines the results—the crime rate and the recidivism rate.

Supporters of restorative justice want the right to manage conflict locally through what are called peacemaking circles. The circle is made up of community members who sit together and work out a solution that is an alternative to the typical jail sentence. They see jail time as a short-term solution that only postpones addressing the real problem, which is healing the relationship between the offender and the victim. Jail is a costly solution that doesn't work. It does not bring about rehabilitation, nor does it reduce the crime rate or reduce the likelihood that one will reoffend. Restorative justice is about returning to family and community the responsibility for sustaining healthy relationships and harmony by managing conflicts locally.

If all of this sounds too "airy fairy" to you, well, at first blush, it does seem that way, but I can tell you that I am now a believer. However, I don't want to leave you with the impression that I am an expert on this subject, because I am not. Nor should you think that, because I am Aboriginal, I know any more about restorative justice methods than anyone else. But I can say that I think I understand it and am willing to give it a try. So here is what I have done so far.

First, I am aware of the sentencing principles in the Criminal Code that now have restorative justice aspects to them. I have read the *Gladue* decision and realize that, as a judge in the provincial court, I can ask for certain things regarding alternatives that may exist in First Nations communities before I sentence Aboriginal offenders. I have attended the lectures given by her

Honor Judge Turpel-Lafond in which she explains the process—the dos and don'ts of sentencing post-*Gladue*.

When I raise this issue with other players in the court system, however, they seem mystified or perhaps uncertain about what I am saying, as if I am speaking a different language or at least with an accent they cannot understand. They seem reluctant or maybe afraid to try these alternatives, such as circle sentencing.

Anyway, there I was in court one day, and it was a family matter in which the children, four of them, were now in the hands of the director for family and child services. The question was whether they should be returned to the mother, and in this process, the First Nation has a right to be heard. Counsel for the First Nation requested that we move to the community hall to allow more members to attend, since the courtroom could only accommodate twenty people. I thought, "What a good idea. Let's go to the community to hear from the people on their own turf; perhaps we can get a dialogue going about local solutions to these kinds of problems."

Well, the first issue came from the director who did not wish to attend the community hall and, if was directed to attend, would not speak. I said that that was fine, but that we were going. Then counsel for the mother asked who was going to speak—could anyone speak, and in what order? I said that I did not know, but that since it was their request, we would be following their protocol.

That afternoon, we moved the whole court—sheriffs, clerk, witnesses, and lawyers—to the local community hall where people were already gathering. It was a basketball gymnasium with one side of the room for seating. The main floor was taken up with chairs, and they had set up a semicircle of chairs for the lawyers and clerk on one side, the hereditary chiefs on the other side, and me in the middle. The chiefs wore their button blankets and cedar hats. The proceeding began with a song and prayer. The main chief then addressed the gathering in his own language and then in English. Elders in the audience also wore their button blankets and sat, watching and listening with great interest. Every now and then, someone would bring coffee to them as they sat and waited.

Then I spoke briefly about why we were there and what we hoped to accomplish. We were there to hear from the people. These children were from their community. The mother was one of their own as a family member and community member. They were all well aware of her situation and the history of the ministry's involvement. Individual members were now given an opportunity to address the court.

The other chiefs spoke first about their community and the history of their village. Then mothers took the floor to talk about how they had been taken by the ministry as children and how that had affected their lives. They spoke of how the ministry had also taken their children and how that affected them. Mothers openly wept as the lawyers and court staff watched in total silence. One speaker was the local bus driver who spoke about the mother and how the kids looked every morning. Another spoke of how helpful the mother was during funeral feast and gatherings—that she always arrived with food for the family and helped clean the home for the visitors. Other tribal chiefs spoke of how they have tried to get children returned without success. The session went on to about six o'clock, when one of the chiefs remarked that the Elders were getting tired and cold. We adjourned to the next day. The speakers came to court and continued for the entire morning speaking on behalf of the mother.

I really did not know what to expect from this approach. I didn't know if they were going to suggest a solution or not. What did occur, however, was that their feelings on the matter were heard. They held long-term resentments for past treatment by the ministry of family and children. If nothing else, they finally felt like they were a part of the process. What happened in the end was that they did develop a solution that was accepted by the ministry. I don't know if it was because of the community hall experience, but I like to believe that that experience made a difference.

What I think is all-too-often overlooked is that the dominant system of conflict resolution was brought here and imposed on the Aboriginal people who don't feel like they are part of the process. What we are beginning to hear from the mainstream is that they feel the same way but for different reasons. Alternative justice is about bringing the community back into the picture, if that is what people desire. It's about allowing communities to find their own solutions to local and ongoing problems.

The justice system cannot be all things to all people, but it can open its doors and invite others in to offer new solutions to long-term problems. A healing circle can bring in those parties who have been affected by the incident to air their concerns. The offender can hear and see the pain that he or she has caused. Other family members can accept responsibility along with the offender—important in some cases, such as those with young offenders—so that that person isn't standing alone.

Restoring the harmony becomes much more important than punishment. Reconnecting the offender with family and friends can do a lot more for the recidivism rate than yet another probation order to do community service work. Any justice system that aims at resolving conflicts is only as good as the support and respect it enjoys from the people it serves. We really need to re-examine our current system to make it user-friendly, accessible, understandable, and ultimately fair and just.

Before concluding, I would like to share another example of this process. I was in court on a youth criminal matter and about to sentence the young man when a call came in from the chief of the youth's community. She asked me to consider moving the hearing to the community to allow the Elders to participate. I agreed. Two weeks passed, and I found myself with the court staff and one sheriff on a small plane heading to a remote village on the west coast of British Columbia. The boy had pleaded guilty to cutting in half two logs that were being prepared for a feast hall. He had also thrown into the salt water two chain saws that belonged to the First Nation. The Elders wanted a public apology from the youth during a traditional feast called a "shame feast."

When we arrived, we were greeted by the chief and her father, who was the hereditary chief. He welcomed us and thanked us for coming to their community, which had no roads or cars, only a wharf for boats and planes. Inside the community hall where the court was to be held, tables were set up in a feast fashion with dishes and bread already on them. I got ready and the sheriff announced "all rise." When I entered, every seat was taken by family and community members.

Once again, the proceeding began with a prayer and a speech from the hereditary chief, and then court commenced. The young man (the accused) came forward with his family and made his public apology. The Elders listened, and then they each spoke to him. They gave him advice and thanked him for following through with their old ways. I was informed that he had had to gather the food for the meal as well as the gifts that had to be given out as part of the potlatch. He made a commitment to replace the logs from his family's land and to replace the saws.

At the end just before the meal, his grandfather spoke. He cried for his grandson and he, too, apologized to the Elders for the boy's actions. He commented how it had strained their relationship and was glad that this was now done. He crossed the floor and embraced the old chief and both wept. It was a very moving and solemn moment that seemed to last a long time. Everyone watched in silence.

After that, the meal commenced. I changed to my street clothes and joined the others at one of the tables. The boy's family began to bring out the meal, which included clams, fish, potatoes, homemade bread, fruit, and much more. Just when I thought it was over, someone got up to speak for the young man, and his family and friends openly pledged assistance—both financial and otherwise—for him to complete his obligation to the Elders. Then his family gave each guest a small gift to remind them that this happened. I still remember with laughter the moment when the sheriff asked me if he could keep his gift. I explained that he must keep it; otherwise the family would be offended.

This kind of reconciliation would not have been possible if I had merely sentenced the boy to probation and perhaps restitution. Through this ceremony, the offender reconnected to his family and to the community at large. He accepted responsibility, as did his family, for his actions. It was all very good.

My intention was to speak with you briefly about restorative justice and then to share with you two of my experiences in trying to implement what I have learned. What I discovered is that I have a lot of learn. I hope that you have learned something today. Thank you for listening. Thank you.

. . . .

*Published in* Justice as Healing *(2001) 6:1, this article is a reprint of the lecture delivered by Judge Point at the College of Law, University of Saskatchewan, on 29 January 2001. The editor would like to thank Judge Point for granting us permission to reprint his lecture.*

# III

· · · ·

# *The Healing Process:*
# *Relying on Our Own Ways*

Our tradition, our culture, speaks clearly about the concepts of judgment and punishment. They belong to the Creator. They are not ours. They are, therefore, not to be used in the way that we relate to each other. People who offend against another (victimizers) are to be viewed and related to as people who are out of balance—with themselves, their family, their community, and their Creator. A return to balance can best be accomplished through a process of accountability that includes support from the community through teaching and healing. The use of judgement and punishment actually works against the healing process. An already unbalanced person is moved further out of balance.

Hollow Water First Nation
Position on Incarceration

# Introduction: Healing in Rough Waters

*Wanda D. McCaslin*

Rough waters describe what many Indigenous Peoples face today as we seek to move in healing directions. Healing our communities from the onslaught of cognitive imperialism and colonization is a complex, sometimes confusing, and often overwhelming process. Every effort has been made to throw us off our original balance and to get us to conform to "norms" that were never ours and do not fit us.

Now, after generations of assault, many currents flow in us and in our communities. Some of the currents are clearly not ours, and yet they are in us—concepts and attitudes we have internalized from the colonizing process. These cause trouble and divisions among us. Not many of us, if any, have escaped these currents, and when they surge, we each see in the other the colonizer's shadow lurking in ourselves.

Other currents are powered by our responses to all that has happened and still happens. These currents can be rough as well, filled as they are with trauma, pain, grief, anger, and disorientation. Although these currents respond to what has been imposed on us, they are nonetheless ours, because they flow straight from who we are. In a thousand different ways, they represent our authentic Indigenous voices saying "no" to racism, colonization, oppression, degradation, and injustice. Our reactions may be intense and passionate, conflicted, or sometimes even unhealthy, misdirected, or hurtful, but if we respect them for what they are and for their role in a healing process, they can bring us together and provide opportunities for rebalancing ourselves.

Most fundamentally, we experience the deep, abiding currents of our traditions and cultures. Some Indigenous Peoples and communities feel these currents more strongly than others, depending on the access we have to Elders, traditional family structures, and culturally rooted communities. These currents align us to who we are as Indigenous Peoples. Our culture and traditions give us energy, hope, and direction as we do our best to negotiate rough waters.

Indeed, this is our challenge, namely, to respond in an Indigenous way to whatever arises, including harms. If we are disconnected from who we are, we will be out of balance in our lives and communities. Instead of turning to our Indigenous ways when troubles arise, we will resort to remedies that were designed by and for our colonizers. Yet because these are not *our* remedies, they will not address the underlying causes of our hurts and conflicts. The "solutions" they bring will be superficial and symptom-oriented at best and will extend the damage of colonization, residential schools, and assimilation at worst.

For healing, we need to rely on ways that build on the millennia-old foundations of our cultural wisdom and learning as Indigenous Peoples. Indigenous ways can restore us through an understanding of how to be in good relationship, whether it is with ourselves, our families, our communities, other Indigenous Peoples and nations, or with the peoples of the natural world. Engaging Indigenous ways of being in relationship, especially when hurts and conflicts arise, is the issue in this third section on the healing process, and it is not easy, simple, or clear-cut.

In chapter 6, "Responding to Harm's Legacy," the authors name why finding and following our own healing ways has become difficult. For one thing, the full force of modern states globally forbids us to do precisely that. In "Invoking International Law," Chief Ted Moses cites the racism that denies Indigenous Peoples the inherent rights of self-determination that other peoples energetically claim—and receive support from the world community for doing so. Similar support remains glaringly absent when we as Indigenous Peoples assert our inherent self-determination.

The more our self-determination has been systematically denied, the harder it is for us to call on our own self-healing ways when we most need them. The ongoing attack on our Aboriginal rights as people and peoples has left us disconnected in varying degrees from the daily practices that reinforce our cultural identity. As a result, we often find ourselves struggling to know who we are. In her article, "Protecting Knowledge—Traditional Resource Rights in the New Millennium: Defending Indigenous Peoples' Heritage," Erica-Irene A. Daes names this core challenge for Indigenous Peoples:

It is possible for a people to survive *physically* without knowing who they are—without knowing how to contribute the Creator's gifts to them to the world. This is what colonialism is all about: depriving a nation or people of *self-knowledge*, of full awareness and confidence in their unique contribution to the whole human symphony. Colonialism teaches people to think that they are someone else—it tries to change peoples' identities. A colonized people can free itself physically or legally—it can even become an independent or self-governing state—and yet continue to be completely colonized in its thinking.

In the excerpt from their book, *Protecting Indigenous Knowledge and Heritage: A Global Challenge,* Marie Battiste and Youngblood Henderson explain that protecting Indigenous culture is central to Indigenous survival. Valuing Indigenous knowledge and heritage is not for colonizers to do for the sake of profits or for preserving historical information. The intellectual and cultural property of Indigenous Peoples is for Indigenous Peoples to use "as a means to express ethnic autonomy and to redress exploitation."

Protecting Indigenous knowledge and heritage is supercritical, because Indigenous sovereignty remains under attack globally. In "The United States Supreme Court and Indigenous Peoples: Still a Long Way to Go toward a Therapeutic Role," S. James Anaya documents some of the U.S. Supreme Court rulings that continue the national policy of forced assimilation, which is genocide as defined by the UN treaty on genocide. The Supreme Court's rulings deny Indigenous Peoples' self-determination and refuse to consider the immense historical injustices that underlie current conflicts.

In "Denial, Acknowledgment, and Peace-Building through Reconciliatory Justice," Robert Joseph explains some of the ways that colonizing societies routinely deny injustices—past and present—to protect the status quo. Though this dogged denial poses formidable barriers to righting harms, these barriers can nonetheless be broken down through definite steps that move Indigenous Peoples and colonizers toward reconciliation. Because this reconciliation process demands transformation on the part of the colonizers, though, very few modern states and their citizenries have been willing to take these steps. New Zealand is one of the few who have taken a small step toward this path, and the successes and challenges of the *Waikato Raupatu Claims Settlement* offer considerable insights into the reconciliation process.

So far, various authors have discussed the differences between a model of justice as punishing and one of justice as healing. Underlying this, though, are two fundamentally different concepts of what law itself is. Chapter 7, "Shape-Shifting Systems," explores how this difference pervades the transition from criminal justice system dominance to Indigenous self-determination in handling hurts and conflicts.

The prevailing Eurocentric concept of law is grounded in *legal positivism*. It defines law as a set of rules and norms that become binding insofar as an authority has the power to rigidly and strictly enforce them. In democracies, this authority is made up of the majority of people, who in turn vest their power in those whom they elect to represent them and those whom the elected appoint to public offices. The rules and norms—the body of law—that this authority establishes and calls *objective rules* have no relation to moral values, natural law, or inherent order. They can be arbitrary, inequitable, and unjust, or they can be idealistic, equitable, and high-minded. Whichever, those who have the power to enforce "the law" decide which rules and norms will be treated as binding and will enforce them accordingly.

In other words, for a group who holds a power advantage to impose its laws on others is inherent in this notion of law. This is precisely how law is made, established, and legitimized according to legal positivism. It is also intrinsic to a democracy: the majority, having a power advantage, can impose its collective will on any minority. All the inequities and injustices that follow are not, therefore, unfortunate side effects or occasional deviations from an otherwise just and equitable concept of law. Exerting force on those who lack the power to resist and compelling them to obey "the norm," as they so decide it, follow from the essential meaning of law as legal positivism defines it. Indeed, if a minority has the power to resist and prevail—as those with great wealth often do—then their rules become law instead.

Given that using power imbalances to benefit some at the expense of others is inherent in the legal positivist concept of law, can this model "do justice" for more people than those who are the beneficiaries? It would seem not. Not only does the model fail to do justice for the billions of people globally who do not find themselves at the top of the power hierarchy, but also who in this scheme of law represents the peoples of the natural world? In other words, can this model of law produce "fair and equitable treatment"—"due process"—for all the beings affected, or is injustice built into this paradigm of law at its core?

The latter seems to be the case, especially given the number of patches that the system requires to achieve some semblance of justice. "Due process," for example, started as an effort to offset the inherent oppressiveness of a system of law and justice designed to favor the wealthy and powerful. Given the statistics of who is in prison, however, this patch seems not to be working. So, too, the very necessity of legal instruments—a constitution and a bill of rights—to protect individuals and minorities from the tyranny of the majority reveals an awareness of how oppressive the paradigm is from its original conception. Instead of trying to further patch an inherently oppressive model by naming every conceivable right and every category of being that requires legal protection, a better solution may be to simply rethink what law itself might mean.

In contrast to legal positivism, the Indigenous concept of law is translated as *natural law*. It understands law as inherent in the order of things, which is why law is binding. Treating others disrespectfully, for example, will not build good relations, and coercion will not be experienced as respectful treatment. Conversely, good relations are built on respect, which involves finding ways to work things out without coercion. These are natural laws; they do not need to be enforced; they just are, given the nature of relationships. Understanding natural law helps to align us with the natural order of how we are all related. Because moral and spiritual values are fundamental to the cosmic and natural order, they are fundamental to our nature as humans and to our relationships. For this reason, they are fundamental to how we understand law as well.

Indigenous Peoples adhere to a lawful way of being, not by being compelled to do so by authorities through the fear of punishment, but because following natural law is a sustainable way to live. Natural law holds us in a good relationship with each other and the natural world. To violate a lawful way of being is to embark on a path that is inherently destructive, because it leads us to act disrespectfully and hurtfully to relationships, yet it is relationships that sustain us.

The difference in these fundamental concepts of law underscores why having the legal positivist model imposed on Indigenous Peoples has been so devastating. Obviously, Indigenous Peoples are not the beneficiaries of the laws of legal positivism. These laws were not designed to favor Indigenous interests. Nor do legal positivism's laws respect the natural law and order of how we are related. The state-enforced order violates natural Indigenous ways, which are based on values such as respect, talking things out, patience, compassion, shared responsibilities, deep family and community bonds, and healing. The laws of legal positivism, by contrast, use hierarchies of power, judgment, and punishment to enforce compliance with win-lose, individualistic, exclusive, adversarial, and divisive norms. In other words, because laws are forcibly imposed on Indigenous people to benefit others and because the values behind these laws are antithetical to Indigenous ways, the laws of legal positivism invariably damage the very fabric of Indigenous lives and communities.

Can the practice of legal positivism be improved? Can restorative justice provide yet another patch? Can, for example, the criminal justice system adopt more Indigenous values, or would this quickly devolve into merely an indigenization of the current colonialist system? To be genuine, changes would have to honor Indigenous self-determination, since this is what the value of respect requires. The criminal justice system could no longer dominate. Any meaningful change would have to be achieved with Indigenous people working at the forefront. Short of this, "improvements" would be suspect—the same controlling, oppressive system hiding under "Indigenous" clothing.

To approach the issue another way, can the dominant system simply be made less force-centered and coercive, hence less disrespectful and oppressive, without changing its core paradigm? Again, it would seem not. If the core model is not changed, then the practice of force continues, though under the guise of being somehow mitigated or more benign. For those on whom force is exerted, though, guises do not hide what is actually happening: force will be experienced as force. The message will be one of disrespect. Accordingly, transformation and healing will not occur, and so patterns of harm will continue.

Abandoning the model of jurisprudence now imposed on Indigenous people seems the most reasonable route if we are interested in achieving a practice of justice that feels just, respectful, and healing to all those involved, and yet the realities of power make this unlikely, at least in the near future. That being so, and given the further realities of huge numbers of Indigenous people being incarcerated daily, our challenge is to find paths from where we are to where we want to be.

In chapter 7, "Shape-Shifting Systems," the authors wrestle with the complexities of these issues: How can we move from the realities we face under legal positivism to a practice of law that is ours and that holds us in a good way? How can we decolonize the currently colonized ways of dealing with hurtful conduct, so we can respond to harms in ways that reflect how Indigenous people understand law?

Patricia A. Monture-Angus sets the stage in "Thinking about Change." In view of the long recognized over-incarceration of Indigenous Peoples, she cites several roadblocks that governments typically use to avoid honoring First Nations' authority. Nonetheless, she argues, since the Indigenous model of justice is about healing, governments cannot prevent Indigenous Peoples from doing healing work in our own families and communities.

In "Sentencing within a Restorative Justice Paradigm: Procedural Implications of *R. v. Gladue*," Judge M. E. Turpel-Lafond discusses the implications of the 1999 watershed ruling of the Supreme Court of Canada. The Court ruled that judges must take into account the unique circumstances and systemic discrimination that Aboriginal people suffer when they sentence Aboriginal offenders. Accordingly, restorative justice principles and healing values are to be considered in every case. The actual sentence should support the healing values of Indigenous communities and, wherever possible, engage communities in helping offenders rectify their harms.

Judge Bria Huculak discusses another major acknowledgment of restorative justice principles by Canadian law in "Restorative Justice and the Youth Criminal Justice Act." The act provides opportunities to introduce a restorative justice approach with youths. Given the increasing evidence of how effective a restorative approach can be with victims, offenders, and communities, Judge Huculak encourages both the public and those in the criminal justice system to take up the "challenge to do justice differently."

The Federation of Saskatchewan Indian Nations (FSIN) makes a similar call to do justice differently in a report on their Alter-Natives to Non-Violence Initiative, entitled "Aboriginal Youth Gangs Exploration—A Community Development Process." Challenging the superficial stereotyping of youths by police, the report describes the problem of gangs as "youth disenfranchisement from family and society." With this analysis, the initiative charts a response that is rooted in First Nations communities. Moreover, it calls on governments to provide the resources necessary for this healing-oriented response to the many thousands of Indigenous youths at risk.

The next two articles challenge the "indigenization" of the criminal justice system, showing that, in the name of using culturally appropriate processes, colonial governments appropriate Indigenous culture to keep the existing systems and power hierarchies in place. In other words, Indigenous cultures are being manipulated to meet policy and administrative ends, enabling law as force—a system that is obviously failing Indigenous Peoples—to prevail. In "The Newest Old Gem: Family Group Conferencing," Gloria Lee opposes the pressure that Canadian governments have put on First Nations communities to adopt the presumably Maori-based method called "Family Group Conferencing" (FGC). Each First Nation has its own ways of responding to harms, and trying to force one Indigenous People to adopt the methods of another seriously misses the mark of showing respect and honoring First Nations' self-determination.

In "Family Group Conferencing: The Myth of Indigenous Empowerment in New Zealand," Juan Marcellus Tauri applauds Ms. Lee's analysis and goes further to critique how FGC is being used in his homeland. As it is practiced by New Zealand's neocolonial criminal justice system, FGC represents an attempt to indigenize the criminal justice system with token nods to Maori culture or with "cheap," culturally appropriated substitutes to avoid honoring authentic Maori autonomy in matters of justice.

Substantive change in how justice issues are handled begins, at the very least, with listening—discovering what Indigenous Peoples want and need to restore good relationships. The excerpts from the 2003 Interim Report and 2004 Final Report of the Commission on First Nations and Métis Peoples and Justice Reform, chaired by Willie Littlechild, present testimony gathered by the commission in dialogues with a number of Aboriginal communities. Through many voices, the speakers underscore the need for Indigenous Peoples to respond to wrongdoing in our own ways and not to have an alien concept of law and justice imposed on us. Isobel Findlay and Warren Weir conclude these excerpts with a discussion of four myths and fears about Aboriginal participation in the justice system.

Finally in this section, James J. R. Guest surveys the profound differences between Indigenous communities and the criminal justice system in their two concepts of law and justice. Given the scope of the differences, Mr. Guest questions how effective restorative justice practices can be within a criminal justice framework. The far better route, he argues, is to honor the inherent authority of Indigenous communities to develop restorative practices based on Indigenous teachings and traditions, diverse as they are.

In chapter 8, "Honoring Healing Paths," the authors describe how Indigenous communities are moving in the direction of doing precisely that. The vision of the future is not to leave the colonizer's house for a better colonizer's house; the aim is to rebuild the tipis—or long houses, hogans, iglus, pueblos, wikiups, earth lodges, wigwams, plank houses, grass houses, or chickees. In other words, the goal is to achieve justice through Indigenous ways whenever conflicts and harms arise.

In "Indian Justice: Our Vision," the FSIN presents its "Strategic Plan for Indian Justice," which incorporates the values and traditions of First Nations self-governance. The aim is to develop a justice system that will not only "promote the healing of First Nations individuals, families, and communities" but also "accommodate the cultural, geographic, and linguistic diversity of our peoples."

Indigenous languages are our life's blood—as Nin Tomas wrote, "language is the spiritual breath of Maori people"—because they embody values, knowledge, wisdom, and a sense of relationships. Being forbidden to use these languages and being subjected to justice processes in an alien tongue have been highly traumatizing for Indigenous Peoples. "Saskatchewan Holds Court in Cree" reports on the Cree Court established by Judge Gerald M. Morin, himself a fluent Cree speaker. This court is demonstrating the necessity and feasibility of adapting jurisprudence to Indigenous needs in the most fundamental way: using appropriate languages. By so doing, Judge Morin shows respect for the Cree language and ways. Moreover, the Cree Court is not only a Cree language court but also a court that adheres to peacemaking principles and so takes important steps toward transformative justice.

In "Peacemaking and the Tsuu T'ina Court," Judge L. S. Tony Mandamin, together with his colleagues Ellery Starlight and Monica One-spot, describe the Tsuu T'ina Peacemaking Court that this Dene community has developed. The court uses the peacemaking circle process for dealing with conflicts in the community. Not all of the court's cases qualify, but the many that are referred to peacemaking generate outcomes that heal and strengthen both the community and its people.

Larissa Behrendt presents an Elder-facilitated model of dispute resolution that can be used in traditional, rural, and urban Indigenous communities. An excerpt from her book, *Aboriginal Dispute Resolution: A Step towards Self-Determination and Community Autonomy*, her article proposes the format of the resolution process as well as the cultural values on which it is based. She also discusses how it can be implemented in various types of communities, including having non-Aborigines approach the Elder-based process on the community's terms for dispute resolution.

Lastly, in 2002, the First Nations Research Project on Healing in Canadian Aboriginal Communities released its final report, entitled "Mapping the Healing Journey." Drawing on in-depth consultations with six First Nations communities, this report begins with a brief description of how multigenerational trauma and abuse are manifested in Indigenous communities. The report then explores core concepts of healing and shares the voices of communities engaged in the healing work. Communities emphasize that personal healing and nation building must go hand in hand—that decolonization is the therapy most needed as the framework for personal and community transformation. Both individuals and communities heal through stages. After presenting stages of individual healing, the article closes with an analysis of the four seasons of the healing process that communities often experience. From beginning the journey (winter) to gathering momentum (spring) to hitting the wall (summer) to moving from healing to transformation (fall), the healing process in communities seems to follow a natural, intrinsic order.

The specific steps that these and many other communities take as we leave the colonizer's house to build our own dwellings will differ greatly. However, as several authors have suggested, the steps themselves are less important than the direction they move us, namely, toward justice as healing through Indigenous ways.

CHAPTER 6

. . . .

# Responding to Harm's Legacy

✻ 25

## Invoking International Law

### Chief Ted Moses

I would like to reflect today on the international recognition of the rights of the world's Indigenous Peoples. . . .

The United Nations was founded on the principle that the interests of the international community would not be bound up in the lowest common denominator of the legal systems of its member states. There would be a higher standard. States would have to acquiesce to the principle that the rights of human beings inhere in themselves and not in the state.

Unfortunately, the international community has not been completely successful in leaving behind the special interests of its members. Diplomats regularly receive instructions to vote in the United Nations so as to preserve the legal status quo of the states they represent. Then they proceed to dress this crude obedience to their ministers in a fabric of fine words expounding rights and precedents in international law. . . .

The Grand Council of the Crees first went to the United Nations in 1981. Tommy Wapachee, a Cree infant from Nemaska, had died on 11 August 1980. An epidemic of measles, gastroenteritis, and tuberculosis took the lives of eight Cree children before the end of that year.

It was not the first time disease had killed our children, but circumstances had changed. The *James Bay and Northern Quebec Agreement*, our treaty with Canada and Quebec, had promised clean water, sanitation, medical services, and clinics; yet none of these had been put in place. The sad fact was that the children would not have died if the governments had kept their promises and respected their own laws.

We went to the international community because after five years, using every means to enforce and implement the treaty, we had essentially exhausted our remedies in Canada. We went to the courts, we lobbied, we spoke to the media, we brought in engineers and doctors; but the governments waited us out. By 1981 we had nowhere to turn—except to the international community.

Some of the people here in this room today were at that meeting in Geneva in 1981. There was no working group on Indigenous populations, no Martinez-Cobo Report on discrimination against Indigenous Peoples.

In Geneva, we described our situation in Canada. Others described terrible atrocities in their own lands. Some who went to that meeting were never seen again after they went home. They were punished for telling us about their world.

Some of our Cree delegates were told: You are lucky you live in Canada where it is not that bad. I took no comfort in that. That was before Oka, and I think before Restiguche. I was not going to let Canada off the hook because it was worse somewhere else. What logic supports that kind of thinking?

I knew also that if the government of Canada could be persuaded to recognize strong international standards to protect the rights of Indigenous Peoples, then not only would our lives improve in Canada, but we would also have a means to address the terrible situations in other countries.

The 1981 meeting was one of the events that led to the eventual establishment of the working group on Indigenous populations in 1983. Establishing this working group and the International Labor Office, Convention 107 on Indigenous and Tribal Populations, were the only visible evidence that the United Nations had finally recognized our existence. That recognition was minimal. . . .

Nevertheless, we viewed the opportunity to bring the concerns of the Indigenous Peoples to the United Nations very seriously, for it offered the hope of a brand-new and badly needed means of redress for our people. The working group had two essential mandates: to review current developments concerning our peoples and to draft international standards to protect the rights of Indigenous Peoples.

The members of the working group were cautioned not to hear complaints from the hundreds of Indigenous representatives who attended its yearly five-day sessions. That, of course, is difficult. How does one review current developments in communities whose members are being systematically murdered without appearing to make complaints? How does one describe dispossession of lands without appearing to be grieved? How do you describe your rivers being dammed, communities being flooded, burial grounds flooded beneath reservoirs, hunting territories denuded of trees—how do you describe these things and not object? How do you tell this story without demanding that the international community act to protect the Indigenous Peoples?

But the states that were behind these situations were sensitive about complaints being made before the United Nations. The working group was carefully and intentionally mandated so that it could not properly hear complaints. That was the rule. The Chairman, Dr. Erica-Irene Daes, who is here with us today, would be obliged to caution the Indigenous representatives who were telling their story, "This is not a chamber of complaints," she would say. She would, nevertheless, hear the grievances, because it was impossible not to hear them in the context of current developments. . . .

It took several years to convince the members of the subcommission that the Indigenous Peoples were not necessarily minorities. Imagine the reaction when diplomats learned that in some states, the Indigenous Peoples actually constituted the majority of the population. Even in those places, the Indigenous Peoples were dispossessed, their rights were abused, and of course, they did not have a voice in government.

The working group's mandate to review developments contributed directly and substantively to the work of standard setting. It is important that this be understood. We did not work from theory or hypothesis about international law and international rights. There was nothing abstract about our work.

Indigenous people brought their experiences, their grievances, and the history of their lives and peoples to the working group. These experiences formed the basis for the proposals that eventually became the draft text.

I have said this many times, but it bears repeating: Every paragraph of the *Declaration on the Rights of Indigenous Peoples* is based on an abuse of human rights that the Indigenous Peoples have experienced. The declaration proposes remedies in the form of human rights standards.

These are not theoretical. We knew from bitter experience what needed to be in the draft. This is the unfortunate truth. And yes, every paragraph is also a demonstration that existing human rights law is not well respected.

The *Declaration on the Rights of Indigenous Peoples* is essentially an instrument that *attaches* the Indigenous Peoples to the basic human rights instruments that already exist. This should not be necessary. It has become necessary, though, because certain states—Canada, one of the most insistent—propose that the international recognition of our status and rights as Indigenous Peoples be contingent upon how this recognition would affect municipal law.

In other words, states such as Canada deny our status in international law in order to avoid recognizing the rights that this status would give Indigenous Peoples. This in itself is the most blatant form of racial discrimination, yet it is put forward as government policy without the least embarrassment.

Thus, when the Indigenous Peoples proclaim themselves to be "peoples" who are subjects of international law, there is a chorus of objections from the states—Canada, France, Brazil, India, to name a few—who believe their interests would be adversely affected by the recognition of our status.

The high-minded sentiments and objectives of the Universal Declaration and the Charter of the United Nations, which expound the rights of peoples and nations, simply vanish. Diplomats tell us: If we recognized your rights, you would declare independence, you would want your lands back, you would prevent development, you would ask for compensation, you would want to have your own laws. Where would it end?

Some states do not acknowledge this reasoning and resort instead to other strategies. Some argue that the Indigenous Peoples want special rights in international law. We are accused of seeking privileged status.

The government of Canada put this idea forward with considerable success two years ago at the Commission on Human Rights. Others, like France, argue that it is against their constitution to grant separate status to a nation within a nation.

When the French Ambassador stated this position in Geneva last year, I asked him how France could recognize the right of Quebec to leave Canada and yet not recognize that the Indigenous Peoples in Quebec have the same right if that is their choice to remain in Canada. He dismissed the objection: "You must understand, Quebec is a special situation. France is a unitary and indivisible state, and it would be contrary to our constitution to recognize the self-determination of the Indigenous populations."

How should we respond to such reasoning when it negatively influences the setting of international standards that are in themselves intended to eliminate racial discrimination and prejudice? It seems that certain states are imbued with such a pervasive belief in their own superiority and supremacy that they fail to recognize the clearly racial basis for their international policies. They use their enormous power to shape the meaning of international law, placing what I believe is a mistaken view of their own interests above all else. . . .

It is in this context that we have worked to protect the rights of the Indigenous Peoples during the past fifteen years. I have often been told that the whole effort is useless. I cannot agree. I think we have little choice but to continue to defend our rights at the international level.

We have also had the opportunity now to see how critical it is that we demand our rights without reservation. The rights of the Indigenous Peoples in Quebec have become a test case for the whole question of the rights of the world's Indigenous Peoples.

Is it possible for a mixed population of European origin to demand and exercise a right of self-determination, but for that same population to deny that the Indigenous Peoples have at least the same rights? The Quebec example clearly demonstrates a double standard based on race. In the separatists' view, Quebecois, whoever they are, have the right; Indians do not.

If it had not been for our international work, this issue would likely already have been lost. In Geneva in 1991, we raised the question of Cree rights in the context of Quebec secession from Canada. I was summoned by the Canadian Ambassador in Geneva and reprimanded, as he said, "for bringing a domestic issue to international attention. Separation will never happen; why discuss it here and make it a reality?" That is what he said.

We persisted, filing a large brief with the United Nations Commission on Human Rights in February 1992. That brief became the essence of the argument concerning our rights. It helped people understand that Indigenous Peoples must have the same status and level of recognition as all other peoples. It was no longer acceptable to propose that our right of self-determination be limited only to internal self-determination. Sometimes—and the Quebec situation demonstrates this conclusively—the Indigenous Peoples may need to be able to exercise an external right of self-determination in order to protect their most fundamental rights.

The *Draft Declaration on the Rights of Indigenous Peoples* reflects this need.... No conditions may be imposed upon the exercise of the rights of Indigenous Peoples that do not apply equally to all of the world's peoples, Indigenous or otherwise.

. . . .

*Published in* Justice as Healing *(1996) 1:3, this article provides excerpts from Ambassador Moses's keynote address at the Special Convocation held at the University of Saskatchewan on 27 June 1996, in which honorary degrees of Doctorates of Laws were granted to Erica-Irene Daes, Ted Moses, and Rigoberta Menchú Túm. The ceremony was held in conjunction with the 1996 International SSHRCC Summer Institute Cultural Restoration of Oppressed Indigenous Peoples hosted by the Aboriginal Organizing Team, University of Saskatchewan, under the direction of Dr. Marie Battiste. The editor is grateful to Chief Moses for permission to publish these excerpts.*

**26**

# Protecting Knowledge—
## Traditional Resource Rights in the New Millennium:
## Defending Indigenous Peoples' Heritage

*Erica-Irene A. Daes*

Honorable Elders, grand chiefs, chiefs, distinguished representatives of the academic family, dear students and young Indigenous persons, ladies and gentlemen, I am deeply honored by the invitation of the Union of British Columbia Indian Chiefs and the Interior Alliance to address this important gathering of Elders, chiefs, and community leaders from the northwest coast and around the world. You have given me a very great challenge, and I hope that my humble remarks today will prove helpful in some way as you continue your work on "Protecting Knowledge" over the next few days.

I would like to begin by telling a story—to share with you how I feel about the topic of our conference. This story was written by the Nahuatl (Aztec) historian Tezozomoc more than four hundred years ago and was translated into Spanish and English by the great twentieth-century Mexican scholar Miguel Leon-Portilla.

Writing just after the Spanish invasion, Tezozomoc told the story of an earlier age when the Aztecs were still a very young nation. Responding to a powerful vision or a dream, their Elders and teachers left them and traveled east toward the sun. Now this, in the words of Tezozomoc, is the song the people sang when their Elders left them:

> Will the sun shine, will it dawn?
> How will the people move, how will they stand?
> How will the earth continue?
> Who will govern us?
> Who will guide us?
> Who will show us the way?
> What will be our standard?
> What will be our measure?

What will be our pattern?
From where should we begin?
What will be our torch, our light?[1]

The story does not end there. Tezozomoc goes on to say that, in the midst of their confusion and despair, the Aztec people discovered that there were still four old men who had not gone away. Of all the Aztec people's ancient teachers and scholars, only these four shy old men were left. But with the memories of these four Elders, the Aztec people slowly reconstructed their history, their laws, their calendar, and their sciences. And as they relearned their history, they became a powerful nation.

Tezozomoc was telling a hopeful story of rediscovery and renewal to his people, who had so recently been crushed and enslaved by Spain. He was telling them that, as long as a few fragments of their heritage and history survived in the memories and hearts of their Elders, there was still hope of recovering what seemed to be lost. Indeed, he tells us, the generation that rediscovers its history and spirituality will be even more powerful than its ancestors.

I want to emphasize this important point as we begin our work together. A people's heritage really lives or dies in their hearts. Centuries of foreign occupation and oppression cannot destroy a people's heritage if they continue to cherish and believe in it. I know this is true because I am Greek and because my country survived nearly four hundred years of foreign rule by the Ottoman Empire.

But it is also true, in my experience, that a people can lose their heritage in a single generation. People who neither respect nor value their heritage can lose it—or sell it off—in no time at all. It is futile to hoard your heritage in museums and books if your children are ashamed of their parents and grandparents and only value what they see on television. I am saying this not only as a legal scholar but also as a grandmother.

Out of the love that you have for your children, it is important that you not only speak to them in your own languages and teach them your cultural knowledge, but that you earn and keep their respect. It is from love of you that your children will keep your heritage alive. Without this love and respect, there is nothing that the law can do to preserve your histories, your oral literatures, your sciences, or your artistic traditions. I have been very fortunate in my long career at the United Nations to travel to many parts of the world and visit a great many Indigenous nations and communities. I am absolutely convinced that strong, healthy, and loving families are indispensable to the survival of Indigenous cultures.

It is possible for a people to survive *physically* without knowing who they are—without knowing how to contribute the Creator's gifts to them to the world. This is what colonialism is all about: depriving a nation or people of *self-knowledge*, of full awareness and confidence in their unique contribution to the whole human symphony. Colonialism teaches people to think that they are someone else—it tries to change peoples' identities. A colonized people can free itself physically or legally—it can even become an independent or self-governing state—and yet continue to be completely colonized in its thinking.

One of the most powerful tools of colonialism is making children ashamed of their parents. Genuine decolonization can be achieved only by a means that involves the genuine, deserved love and respect of the children for their Elders and grandparents. I have seen too many tragic situations around the world where people have struggled single-mindedly for their freedom and rights, only to be overthrown by their own children who view them as obsolete or oppressive.

As we enter a new century and a new millennium, it is appropriate that we reflect carefully on the lessons to be learned from nearly one hundred years of bitter anti-colonial and anti-totalitarian struggles. Power can never completely crush a people who cherish their heritage—nor can power ever completely liberate a people who have abandoned their heritage.

In a recent collection of essays on the rise and fall of Eastern European Communism, the Czech writer Ivan Klima distinguishes between two kinds of twentieth-century national liberation struggles: *power versus power* and *culture versus power.*[2] He argues that power can exist only by creating fear and resentment. Power, he writes, has no soul. As a consequence, a liberation struggle based on power changes nothing at all.

However, the integrity of a people's identity and culture, Klima argues, can neutralize a power and make it look ridiculous. It is quite apparent in my own part of the world, the Balkans, that culture can be absolutely indestructible. Unfortunately, it is also readily apparent from recent events there that people in power can use protecting culture as a pretext for new forms of oppression and colonialism.

I have expressed my strong personal feelings on this subject out of respect and solidarity for what you yourselves have been trying to achieve here in British Columbia. I am well aware that the Province of British Columbia has become an important test case for the resolution of land claims. The manner by which you achieve a just and lasting settlement and the manner in which you use the territories and traditional resource rights that you recover will be studied carefully by Indigenous Peoples everywhere—and (of course) by international legal experts and the United Nations. We will all be very interested to see whether your struggle to recover your traditional resource rights results in a renewal of your distinct cultures and in a reorientation of the management and conservation of your magnificent forests and oceans.

I have read some of the historical and cultural material prepared by Gitksan and Wet'suet'en hereditary chiefs for the *Delgamuuk'w* case. What impressed me most was the way in which the entire system of chiefly titles, names, symbols, and ceremonies has been interconnected with the stewardship of the land and living resources. Everything was completely interdependent in a way that was specific to each house and clan and nation. While today's Western ways of thinking *separate* arts, religion, political organization, kinship, nature, and science, *your* knowledge systems integrated all aspects of human experience and human responsibilities.

In this way, your ancestors understood the total social and ecological effects of their actions, and, I believe from what I have read and heard, your ancestors carefully considered the full consequences before they made changes. Nothing was done without feasting the other houses—the animals and the plants and the ancestors—to maintain good relationships. This approach made your nations successful and prosperous for the long term.

If, in your struggle to regain your rights, you adopt a different relationship with your land, you may gain power but you may lose your children and grandchildren. I want to assure you today that the First Nations of British Columbia stand out because you *have* taken guidance from your hereditary chiefs and Elders and have kept them at the center of your struggle. This is your crucial strength and should never change.

We are gathered here together at Vancouver to find stronger ways of protecting knowledge and traditional resource rights. You will talk about law and legislation, about politics and self-determination, about the Canadian political system, and about the international economic system. Whatever you discuss, I would like to propose three basic principles to consider as a framework for ensuring that you do, indeed, strengthen your heritage in your efforts to regain your lands and resources.

The first principle is what I call the principle of *integrity*. By this I mean the integrity of the whole set of relationships between your nations and your territories. This includes names and chiefly titles, knowledge systems and arts, symbols and ceremonies—that is to say, all human dimensions of living together on the land as well as all of the ecological relationships between humans, animals, fish, and plants. A lawyer might refer to this concept as *non-severability*, which simply means that interrelated things should not be separated.

The principle of integrity also implies a continuing responsibility for the health of the land by maintaining and using the knowledge and practices that belong to the land. In my recent travels among North American First Nations, I have been quite taken by the extent to which land-use administration, environmental protection, human health, education, and cultural activities have evolved into separate institutional domains—separate bureaucratic departments with inconsistent goals and values. If First Nations self-government results in reproducing the same kinds of governments as the nation-states, I fear we will see the *same kinds* of results—including the packaging and sale of the land and of everything sacred and precious that is connected with the land.

The old ceremonies, songs, and names kept people tied to the land and continually reminded them of their responsibilities. Strip away the ceremonies, symbols, and knowledge from the land—or sell them off—and people will no longer feel responsible for the land. The heritage of a people is deeply rooted in their traditional territory. Heritage is not only a reflection and a celebration of a people's territory, but it is also a *management system* for the territory. Separating heritage from the land may have serious adverse ecological and social consequences. I have analyzed the concept of heritage in my study entitled *Protection of the Heritage of Indigenous People*.

A people's ceremonies, symbols, names, and songs contain their laws: the fundamental rules governing who may use the land, who may hunt the animals and fish, who may harvest the medicinal plants, and how all of these things must be done in a proper way. This brings me to a second principle for the defense of traditional resource rights.

The second principle I would like to place before you is *locality*, by which I mean that every people's territory is unique and has its own laws. The laws of the Tsimshian and the Nu-chah-nulth were not exactly alike because they lived in different territories with different ecological relationships. Tsimshian law governed the relationships between human beings and the land in one particular place, and I am certain that the Tsimshian would never think of forcing Tsimshian laws on any other peoples. Different countries have different laws. However, Indigenous Peoples, in my experience, think of their laws as inherently arising from their lands and territories—as inseparable from their territories—while it has become commonplace for Europeans to think that laws can be carried around and applied to any place and any people.

I would like to suggest that there is a very simple way of settling the legal issues surrounding Indigenous Peoples' cultural and intellectual property rights. The solution is to resolve any disputes over the acquisition and use of Indigenous Peoples' heritage according to the customary laws of the Indigenous Peoples concerned. If someone claims to have properly acquired the right to use and sell a Tsimshian song or story or house panel or medicine, let that person show that he or she has faithfully complied with the requirements of Tsimshian law!

In international law, we refer to this as the principle of *lex loci*—that is, "the law of the place." It is a very ancient principle among nations. It was recognized by the Roman Empire and still applies to disputes over contracts, the ownership of private property, and family relationships when the parties live in different countries.

The principle of locality means that British Columbia cannot properly make laws controlling Tsimshian people's heritage—nor can Canada or the United Nations. Instead, British Columbia, Canada, and the United Nations should recognize, respect, and enforce Tsimshian law. I would like to suggest, furthermore, that this principle can be found in the *Convention on Indigenous and Tribal Peoples, 1989 (No. 169)* adopted by the International Labor Organization and is implied very strongly in the United Nations *Convention on Biological Diversity*.

The third and final principle I would like to suggest here today may be described as the principle of *effectiveness*. The legal weapons you choose to defend your traditional resource rights should be genuinely effective. They must be adequate to achieve all results, and not simply be—like many principles of national and international law, I am sorry to say—just so many pretty words and promises. When you are choosing your weapons, ask yourself two key questions: Who is my real adversary? Who has real power over my adversary?

Nearly all the laws aimed at protecting Indigenous Peoples are addressed to the nation-state. They are designed to influence the actions and decisions of national government officials. In the past, of course, Indigenous Peoples were ordinarily the victims of state action, such as military intervention, forced relocation, and forced assimilation. Laws have gradually developed to restrict these abuses of state power and to compel states to compensate, assist, and protect the Indigenous Peoples they had previously oppressed. In other words, laws are aimed at the abuses and oppressors *of the past.*

As we embark on the twenty-first century, however, we are entering a new world of international economic cooperation, trade liberalization, and privatization. Nation-states are yielding more power to international trade and financial institutions, such as the World Trade Organization, and international trade and financial institutions are working hard to make the world a safer place for private enterprise and investment.

The net effect of this restructuring of international relations is obvious. Corporations—and their shareholders and investors—will gain greater global freedom and power. And as they do, corporations will assume more of the functions of the nation-state.

You can see this clearly within your own region, North America. Governments are privatizing everything from post offices and hospitals to prisons and national parks. Corporations will overshadow governments in many ways and will play a growing role in our daily lives. Many people around the world see this as an extremely dangerous trend, because they believe that corporations are selfish and undemocratic. Most of us can vote for the leaders of our states, but very few of us own shares of voting stock in multinational corporations. States are bound, in principle at least, to respect their national constitutions and the principles of human rights. Corporations are bound by law to make profits for their owners.

On the other hand, the profit motive can be used to influence the decision-making of corporations for the better. Corporations are owned mainly by the relatively rich, but they make their profits by selling to everyone. It is increasingly clear that corporations are sensitive to carefully focused consumer boycotts. It is also clear that some owners and investors in multinational corporations appreciate the fact that, *in the long term,* their investments have greater value when they respect the rights of their workers and consumers and the people who live close to their activities.

Here in the northwest coast, you are part of a very important experiment in corporate accountability. Boycotts and shareholder complaints have persuaded Home Depot, a giant in furniture manufacturing and retailing, to stop using wood from your old-growth rainforests. This bodes well for the Interior Alliance's recent campaign to persuade corporations to withdraw from lands under claim.

The draft of the "UN Principles and Guidelines for the Protection of the Heritage of Indigenous Peoples" (1995), which I have had the honor to prepare and which is under consideration of a UN seminar next week, is addressed not only to the governments of states but also to corporations, universities, museums, artists, and scientists. I firmly believe that defending your traditional resource rights in today's international environment requires the use of tools that reach directly into the conscience—and into the pockets—of the private and nongovernmental sectors.

In my opinion, then, whatever legal, political, or economic weapons you choose for defending your heritage should be fully consistent with these three principles—*integrity, locality,* and *effectiveness.* This important conference has been designed to provide a thorough review of the range of possibilities: what has worked thus far and what new weapons may work even better in the future. As you work together over the next few days, I urge you to choose wisely and, once you have chosen, to act together in solidarity.

I thank you very warmly and from the bottom of my heart for the opportunity you have given me to be present at this historic meeting and for your kind attention. I should like to conclude by wishing you every success in your noble activities and a fruitful conference.

## Notes

1. Miguel Leon-Portilla. *Pre-Columbian Literatures of Mexico* (Norman: University of Oklahoma Press, 1969), 124.

2. Ivan Klima, *The Spirit of Prague* (London: Granta Books, 1994), 110.

. . . .

*Published in* Justice as Healing *(2000) 5:2, this article on the heritage of Indigenous Peoples was presented by Dr. Erica-Irene A. Daes in Vancouver, British Columbia, at the "Protecting Knowledge: Traditional Resource Rights in the New Millennium" conference held on 23–26 February 2000. The conference was hosted by the Union of British Columbia Indian Chiefs with support from the Law Foundation of British Columbia, Legal Services Society of British Columbia—Native Programs, the University of British Columbia Museum of Anthropology, and the Canadian International Development Agency. The Union of British Columbia Indian Chiefs may be contacted at Suite 500, 342 Water Street, Vancouver BC V6B 1B6, Tel: (604) 684-0231 or http://www.ubcic.bc.ca. The editor would like to thank the Union of British Columbia Indian Chiefs and Dr. Daes for permission to publish this article.*

# Protecting Indigenous Knowledge and Heritage— A Global Challenge

*Marie Battiste and James Sa'ke'j Youngblood Henderson*

*As the authors explain more fully in their book,* Protecting Indigenous Knowledge and Heritage: A Global Challenge, *Indigenous knowledge and heritage are Aboriginal rights within the Constitution of Canada. While the source of Aboriginal rights are firmly anchored within Aboriginal jurisprudence and laws, the strongest constitutional document of Canada, namely, the Constitution of Canada, is theoretically to provide protection. Aboriginal Peoples therefore look to the Constitution of Canada to protect their knowledge, ecological relationships, and linguistic and heritage rights, even though current implementation falls far short of this promise. (MDW)*

## The Canadian Legislative Régime

In contrast with Canada's achievements in international law and constitutional reform, the federal and provincial governments and the administrative régimes have ignored Aboriginal and treaty rights. They have been creative in finding ways to avoid Indigenous knowledge and heritage, and they have not responded to Canadian constitutional reform in any significant way. Thus, Canadian legislators have not passed any new laws to protect, preserve, or enhance the rights of Indigenous Peoples to their knowledge and heritage. One reason for this passivity is the underrepresentation of Aboriginal interests in the federal parliament.[1]

Many types of intellectual and cultural property are created and protected by a variety of federal and provincial laws. Under Canada's new constitution, these laws need to be consistent with existing Aboriginal and treaty rights. The attempt to protect Indigenous knowledge and heritage in Canada is just beginning. Already, Aboriginal and treaty rights are creating challenges for the existing régime when it comes to protecting Indigenous ideas, information, and inventions as private property for a specific time.

The Canadian legal system prevents others from copying, selling, or importing a product without authorization. Although these laws are sufficient to protect individual rights or the rights of corporations when considered as individuals, they are inadequate to protect Indigenous knowledge and heritage. Scholars who have reviewed the Canadian system agree that it discriminates against the constitutional rights of Aboriginal Peoples. There are compelling interests in protecting Indigenous knowledge and heritage as Aboriginal rights and in eliminating these discriminatory régimes in Canada.

At present, Eurocentric cultural and intellectual property régimes govern Indigenous communities. Although these régimes are effective in limited cases, they do not serve the unique relationship that Indigenous Peoples have with their ecological orders, heritage, and knowledge. Indigenous thought and languages, artistic works, traditional designs, and oral traditions are not viewed as simply commodities owned by individuals. Neither are these gifts valued for the economic benefits they may yield; they are valued as integral parts of the Indigenous order.

Most legal commentators as well as the UN special rapporteur for the Working Group on Indigenous Populations[2] have concluded that the current legal system of intellectual property, based on the assumption that intellectual property is a transferable commodity, is "not only inadequate for the protection of Indigenous people's heritage but inherently unsuitable." These commentators argue for a reform of intellectual and cultural property régimes to protect Indigenous Peoples. These legal reforms must recognize the close and continuing links Indigenous Peoples have to their ecosystems, their languages, and their heritage. Such recognition is vital to a fair legal order. Indigenous Peoples cannot survive or exercise their fundamental human rights as distinct nations, societies, and peoples without the ability to conserve, revive, develop, and teach the wisdom they have inherited from their ancestors. . . .[3]

## Enhancing Indigenous Knowledge and Heritage in National Law

The United Nations' "Principles and Guidelines for the Protection of the Heritage of Indigenous Peoples" define the proper role of national legislation and governments:

25. National laws should guarantee that Indigenous Peoples can obtain prompt, effective, and affordable judicial or administrative action to prevent, punish, and obtain full restitution and compensation for the acquisition, documentation, or use of their heritage without proper authorization of the traditional owners.

26. National laws should deny to any person or corporation the right to obtain patent, copyright, or other legal protection for any element of Indigenous Peoples' heritage without adequate documentation of the free and informed consent of the traditional owners to an arrangement for the sharing of ownership, control, and benefits.

27. National laws should ensure the labeling and correct attribution of Indigenous Peoples' artistic, literary, and cultural works whenever they are offered for public display or sale. Attribution should be in the form of a trademark or an appellation of origin, authorized by the peoples or communities concerned.

28. National laws for the protection of Indigenous Peoples' heritage should be adopted following consultations with the peoples concerned, in particular the traditional owners and teachers of religious, sacred, and spiritual knowledge, and wherever possible, should have the consent of the peoples concerned.

29. National laws should ensure that the use of traditional languages in education, arts, and the mass media is respected and, to the extent possible, promoted and strengthened.

30. Governments should provide Indigenous communities with financial and institutional support for the control of local education, through community-managed programs, and with use of traditional pedagogy and languages.

31. Governments should take immediate steps, in cooperation with the Indigenous Peoples concerned, to identify sacred and ceremonial sites, including burial sites, and protect them from unauthorized entry or use.

We affirm these principles. However, there is more to discuss. . . .

## Conclusions

Survival for Indigenous Peoples is more than a question of physical existence. It is an issue of protecting, preserving, and enhancing Indigenous worldviews, knowledge systems, languages, and environments. It is a matter of sustaining spiritual links with ecosystems and communities. Unfortunately, these ecosystems and communities are often critically endangered. The awareness that the demise of Indigenous populations and the loss of their languages is causing the demise of Indigenous knowledge and the loss of biological diversity has not stopped the rush on Indigenous knowledge systems by outsiders. These outsiders have not attempted to prevent the extermination of Indigenous Peoples or their ecosystems; instead they have intensified their efforts to access, to know, and to assert control over this endangered knowledge and these endangered resources. This is such a tragic response. . . .

The protection of Indigenous knowledge and heritage represents the protection and preservation of Aboriginal humanity. Such protection is not about preserving dead or dying cultures. It is about the commercial exploitation and appropriation of living consciousnesses and cultural orders. It is an issue of privacy and commerce. The use of Indigenous knowledge for private or public profits by others under existing laws is a central issue. Other surrounding issues present numerous ethical and legal questions. Indigenous knowledge and heritage must be approached with respect and sensitivity.

Internationally, a convention protecting Indigenous knowledge and heritage with an appropriate enforcement agency is required. A declaration will not be sufficient to effect change. Nationally, such a convention must be implemented or a similar convention and law with the Indigenous Peoples could be enacted. However, these laws must be interrelated with Eurocentric legal régimes and seen as equal, coexisting side by side, protecting all humanity and its products based on their heritage.

All peoples must have equal dignity and essential worth. Their languages, heritages, and knowledge must be equally respected by public institutions and by all peoples. Their ecological order and intellectual integrity must be respected by the market economies. Equality and respect require cooperative frameworks, efforts, and innovations to protect Indigenous intellectual, cultural, and trade policies. Indigenous Peoples must be actively involved in the development of any new convention or laws. They need representatives to discuss how to move toward developing these legal régimes. Their participation will develop new sensitivities to what is sacred, to what is capable of being shared, and to what is fair compensation for the sharing of information among diverse peoples. Community-based partnerships are also needed to resolve the nature of fair compensation and the ethics of research. Public education is needed to develop an understanding of the new régimes and frameworks.

The issues associated with protecting Indigenous knowledge are deeply concerned with the structural inability of Eurocentric law to give Indigenous Peoples control of their humanity, heritage, and communities. The absence of protection of the humanity of Indigenous Peoples in international and Canadian law is disturbing. As Indigenous Peoples, we have had more than our share of adversity and tragedy because of the denial of the manifestation of our humanity. International and national law should embrace and celebrate the world's cultural and intellectual diversity for the richness and depth this diversity brings to life on earth.

## Notes

1. James Sa'ke'j Youngblood Henderson, "Empowering Treaty Federalism," *Saskatchewan Law Review* 58, no. 2: (1994) 242; Patrick Macklem, "Aboriginal Rights and State Obligations," *Alberta Law Review* 36 (1997):97.

2. Erica-Irene Daes, *Study on the Protection of the Cultural and Intellectual Property Rights of Indigenous Peoples* (1993), E/CN.4/Sub. 21/1993/28; Subcommission on Prevention of Discrimination and Protection of Minorities, Commission on Human Rights, UNESCO, para. 32.

3. Ibid., para. 1.3.

. . . .

*Published in* Justice as Healing *(2001) 6:2, this article is excerpted from the book,* Protecting Indigenous Knowledge and Heritage: A Global Challenge *by James (Sa'ke'j) Youngblood Henderson and Marie Battiste, published by Purich Publishing Ltd., Saskatoon, Canada, in 2000. The editor would like to thank the authors and Purich Publishing for permission to reprint these excerpts.*

# 28

# The United States Supreme Court and Indigenous Peoples: Still a Long Way to Go toward a Therapeutic Role

*S. James Anaya*

The United States Supreme Court has long played a major role in defining the relationship between the country's majority institutions and its Indigenous Peoples. The history of Supreme Court action regarding Native Americans has included two opposing positions. On the one hand, the Supreme Court early on recognized the "original" rights of sovereignty and property on the part of Indian tribes and has continued to do so. On the other hand, it has developed a doctrine that allows such rights to be terminated or diminished in favor of majority institutions.[1] The Court has also upheld special benefits to Native Americans conferred by the government whenever the benefits have been found to be "tied rationally to the fulfillment of Congress' unique obligation [of trusteeship] toward the Indians."[2]

Although the Court has in many instances ruled in favor of Native Americans, its approach could rarely be called therapeutic. The Court's jurisprudence in this area provides perhaps the starkest American example of the appellate judiciary serving an antitherapeutic role in majority-minority conflicts. In this brief article, I will identify particular aspects of the Court's jurisprudence to make this point. Further, I will suggest what is needed for the Court to function in a more conciliatory role.

In cases involving Indigenous Peoples, the Supreme Court usually focuses on assessing the relevant exercise of federal power. The federal government—and Congress in particular—is deemed to have "plenary power," or complete power, over Native Americans. This power is considered to be subject only to limited constitutional constraints.[3] Native Americans have whatever "residual" sovereignty and land rights the federal government—or one of the European colonial powers that preceded it—has not taken away, as well as those rights and benefits that the government has acted affirmatively to provide. Such residual rights of dominion over territory and people extend only insofar as the rights are not inconsistent with the tribes' status as "domestic dependent" communities.[4]

The Supreme Court's decisions regarding Native Americans typically do not give adequate attention to historic misdeeds or to how they relate to contemporary inequities that Native Americans experience. These undertreated factors include taking Indigenous Peoples' land through fraudulent means, duress, or force; the outright slaughter of many Indigenous women, children, and men who stood in the way of non-Indigenous settlement; and the active suppression of Indigenous religious and cultural patterns and Indigenous self-governance institutions.

The Supreme Court's narrative has acknowledged or recounted such events mainly to reinforce the dominant mythology of conquest that cast Native Americans in the role of vanquished subjects. "Every American schoolboy knows," wrote Justice Stanley Reed for the Court in *Tee-Hit-Ton Indians v. United States*, "that the savage tribes of this continent were deprived of their ancestral ranges by force and that, even when the Indians ceded millions of acres by treaty in return for blankets, food and trinkets, it was not a sale but the conquerors' will that deprived them of their land."[5]

Yet reinforcing the conquest myth obviously does not promote justice from an Indigenous perspective. For a system of law concerning Indigenous Peoples to be in any sense therapeutic, it should recognize both the wrongful nature of historic events and the suffering those events have caused. Unless the agents of the larger society acknowledge the historic wrongs that remain alive in the collective memory of the aggrieved, conflicts between the majority and any aggrieved minority are likely to persist, and animosities are likely to fester or flare. Such acknowledgments are a matter of simple dignity for aggrieved groups, and they provide a basis for treating their claims in a manner that is considered fair and just by all concerned. When a court addresses a controversy involving an Indigenous group, the history of wrongs pertaining to that controversy should be brought to light.

Supreme Court jurisprudence also fails to embrace the kind of process values that Professor Nathalie Des Rosiers finds in the Supreme Court of Canada's 1998 decision in *Quebec Secession Reference*.[6] In Professor Des Rosiers's analysis, this decision appropriately stressed the importance of using a conciliatory process. Specifically, it used a process that hears and treats with respect both majority and minority voices and viewpoints. Moreover, the outcome of the process is determined not by choosing a winner and a loser but by negotiation and mutual accommodation.[7] This regard for process, according to Professor Des Rosiers, is evident in the Court's treatment of the competing narratives of Quebec secessionists and Canadian federalists. It is also evident in the Court's finding of a "duty to negotiate" if a substantial majority of Quebec's population were to vote for secession.[8]

United States Supreme Court opinions, by contrast, have seldom supported process-driven solutions to conflicts between majority institutions and Indigenous Peoples. Instead, the Court's decision in *Alaska v. Native Village of Venetie*[9] illustrates its method of propagating the conquest myth against Indigenous Peoples, rendering them the losers in a winner-take-all contest. In that case, the power of the Alaska Native village of Venetie to levy taxes for business conducted on land owned by the village was called into question.[10] The power of Native communities to tax activities on community or tribal land is one aspect of Indigenous sovereignty that the Supreme Court has recognized.[11] In *Venetie*, the state of Alaska contested the village's taxing authority, clearly seeing the assertion of such authority as a threat to its own sovereignty.[12]

The *Venetie* case, however, was about more than taxation. The state invoked the standard frame of analysis for judicial decisions on Indigenous issues, namely, what could be regarded as the relevant exercise of federal power. The state of Alaska argued that the particular exercise of federal power in Alaska had entirely deprived the village of Venetie—and virtually all other Native communities in the state—of governmental jurisdiction over community-held lands.[13] The litigation in *Venetie* thus represented a far-reaching contest over governmental authority between the Native Peoples of Alaska and the state government, which represented the interests of the majority. The position taken by the state undoubtedly exacerbated the sense of alienation felt by Indigenous Peoples and helped consolidate majority sentiment against Indigenous claims of continuing sovereignty.

Rather than help bridge the majority-minority divide underlying the *Venetie* case, the Supreme Court widened it. In a unanimous opinion written by Justice Clarence Thomas 25 February 1998, the Court declared that federal enactments, particularly the *Alaska Native Claims Settlement Act*,[14] had rendered Venetie's lands—and, by implication, most all of the lands now held by Indigenous communities in Alaska—outside the rubric of "Indian country,"[15]—that is, not lands to which Indigenous sovereignty or governmental authority attached.[16] According to the Court, the condition of Native Peoples in Alaska had been determined by Congress, which had decided that the governmental authority belonged to the state and its majority constituency.[17] In no way did the Court validate the Indigenous voice or point of view, neither did it provide anything that would bring about majority-minority reconciliation over this issue of such fundamental importance to both Indigenous and non-Indigenous people. In typical fashion, upon declaring the Indigenous litigants losers, the Court sought to wash its hands of the matter, while reaffirming federal supremacy. It stated that any modification in the outcome "is a question entirely for Congress."[18]

Even when the Supreme Court has voted in favor of Indigenous litigants, it has held fast to the conquest myth, supporting federal supremacy at the expense of process-oriented solutions, such as those described by Professor Des Rosiers.[19] In *Kiowa Tribe of Oklahoma v. Manufacturing Technologies* (1998), the Court held that Indian tribes enjoy sovereign immunity from civil suit in transactions occurring both on and off reservation lands, whether or not the transaction involves tribal governmental activities.[20] In his majority opinion, Justice Anthony Kennedy relied on the Court's precedents, but he characterized sovereign immunity as something that had "developed almost by accident" and that Congress had left intact.[21] Thus, the Court held in favor of tribal sovereign immunity reluctantly and out of purported deference to Congress.

Justice Kennedy declared, "There are reasons to doubt the wisdom of perpetuating the doctrine of [tribal sovereign immunity]."[22] In examining those reasons, he ignored the historical inequities and considerations of self-determination. From the perspective of the Indigenous litigants, these considerations favor maintaining those attributes of Indigenous sovereignty that Indigenous Peoples have not freely given up, including Native governmental institutions' immunity from suit. But in Justice Kennedy's view, sovereign immunity is an "accident"—something Congress and the Courts unwittingly allowed to survive. Kennedy concluded the Court's opinion by inviting Congress to get on with this unfinished business and to limit or do away with tribal sovereign immunity: "Congress, subject to constitutional limitations, can alter its limits through explicit legislation."[23]

In a more recent opinion, *Rice v. Cayetano* (2000), Justice Kennedy further demonstrated a judicial tendency to conquer Indigenous Peoples, instead of supporting process-driven solutions to Indigenous Peoples' claims.[24] The decision in *Rice* rendered invalid the voting procedure for electing the trustees who govern the Office of Hawaiian Affairs, or OHA. This Hawaii state agency administers programs designed to benefit people whose ancestry can be traced to those inhabiting the Hawaiian Islands prior to European arrival in 1778.[25] Voting for the OHA trustees had been limited to people who have Hawaiian Indigenous ancestry.[26] Because of this voting limitation, Native or Indigenous Hawaiians have substantially controlled OHA, although, of course, not without differences of opinion. However, a majority of the Court considered the voting limitation an "explicit, race-based voting qualification," violating the Fifteenth Amendment to the U.S. Constitution.[27] As a result of the Court's ruling, Native Hawaiians will no longer be the ones to select OHA trustees, and Native Hawaiian control over OHA governance will give way to the dominant political winds.

The Court's decision in *Rice* has dealt a blow to redress efforts for widely acknowledged historic and continuing wrongs against Native Hawaiians. As a group, Native Hawaiians do not qualify for federal programs or statutory benefits aimed at Native Americans generally, and their status under United States law remains ambiguous.

In 1993, Congress acknowledged and apologized for historical acts that "resulted in the suppression of the inherent sovereignty of the Native Hawaiian people" and expressed its "commitment to . . . provide a proper foundation for reconciliation between the United States and the Native Hawaiian Peoples."[28] Since then, the state of Hawaii stepped up its efforts to facilitate a resolution of Native Hawaiian claims. Native Hawaiian groups have been pressing their demands with ever-greater effectiveness at the state, national, and international levels. As debate has continued over how best to resolve Native Hawaiian claims for redress of historical wrongs, the OHA has represented an existing program aimed at benefiting Native Hawaiians—a program justified by circumstances of historical origins that have not yet been adequately addressed. The state justified the voting limitation for the OHA trustees as a way to allow Native Hawaiians to determine how the program would be administered.[29]

Justice Kennedy's plurality opinion in *Rice* determining the constitutionality of the OHA voting limitation gives no weight to the historic and continuing inequities suffered by Native Hawaiians. Instead, Kennedy's finding that the voting limitation is race-based makes it seem just as harmful as the voter qualifications used in the Deep South to exclude or limit voting by

Blacks.[30] It is apparently irrelevant to Kennedy and his fellow justices that the OHA voting limitation is far from the kind of racially motivated discrimination that drove the other, now infamous schemes. To the contrary, the OHA voting limitation can be justified as part of an effort to redress the historic wrongs suffered by a minority. Justice Kennedy's opinion does invoke history, but his historical narrative ultimately reinforces the conquest myth. Although he acknowledges some suffering and historic wrongs against Native Hawaiians, the picture he gives is one of a vanquished people whose fate has been decided by an inevitable pattern of history, the outcome of which Indigenous Hawaiians must now simply accept.[31]

Rather than use the Court as a means for reconciliation, Justice Kennedy's opinion constricts the possible responses to Native Hawaiian claims, and it does so in a manner that limits creative impulse and stifles conciliatory efforts. For Justice Kennedy and the concurring justices, conquest is the presumed state of affairs, no matter how sad the Native Hawaiians' history may be. Any effort to address Native Hawaiian grievances must conform to United States constitutional constraints, which are defined and imposed without regard to those grievances or the reasons for them. According to Justice Kennedy:

> When the culture and way of life of a people are all but engulfed by history beyond their control, their sense of loss may extend down through generations; and their dismay may be shared by many members of the larger community. As the State of Hawaii attempts to address these realities, it must, as always, seek the political consensus that begins with a sense of shared purpose. One of the necessary beginning points is this principle: The Constitution of the United States, too, has become the heritage of all the citizens of Hawaii.[32]

There is no question that cases involving Indigenous Peoples raise difficult issues and that appellate judges face a daunting challenge when they confront these issues. In meeting this challenge, however, the Supreme Court has not advanced what could be called a therapeutic jurisprudence. Rather, it has propagated a demeaning myth of conquest and diminished the impact of the Indigenous point of view in the resolution of relevant conflicts. A different, more conciliatory approach is needed.

Ironically, the last sentence of Justice Kennedy's quote suggests one such approach—something like the one taken by the Supreme Court of Canada in the *Quebec Reference* case. His last sentence might be read to suggest that the Constitution could serve as a basis for a shared discourse. Assisted by the judicial process, this shared discourse could identify common values among Indigenous and non-Indigenous Peoples. These values, in turn, could guide the resolution of Indigenous Peoples' claims by engaging all those concerned in appropriate procedures of negotiation.

Unfortunately, this conciliatory use of the Constitution and the Supreme Court does not appear to be what Justice Kennedy had in mind. The Supreme Court still has a long way to go before its conduct in relation to Indigenous Peoples can be called therapeutic.

## Notes

1. See generally David H. Getches et al., *Federal Indian Law*, 4th ed. (1998).

2. *Morton v. Mancari*, 417 U.S. 535, 555 (1974).

3. *Lone Wolf v. Hitchcock*, 187 U.S. 5 53, 56 5 (1903).

4. The term "domestic dependent nations," a term that remains of dubious meaning, was coined by Chief Justice John Marshall in *Cherokee Nation v. Georgia*, 30 U.S. (5 Pet.) 1 (1831). See generally Getches *Federal Indian Law*.

5. *Tee-Hit-Ton Indians v. United States*, 348 U.S. 272, 289–90 (1955).

6. See Nathalie Des Rosiers, *From Telling to Listening: A Therapeutic Analysis of the Role of the Courts in Minority/Majority Conflicts*, Ct. Rev. (Spring 2000), 54 (discussing *ref Re Secession of Quebec* 2 S.C.R. 217 (1998).

7. Ibid., 61–62.

8. Ibid., 62.

9. *Alaska v, Native Village of Venetie Tribal Gov't.*, 522 U.S. 520 (1998).

10. Ibid., 526.

11. See, e.g., *Merrion v. Jicarilla Apache Tribe*, 455 U.S. 130 (1982).

12. 522 U.S., 525.

13. Ibid., 530.

14. 43 U.S.C. sections 1601 (1994).

15. The court applied the definition of "Indian country" found in 18 U.S.C. section 1151, which relates to the geographic scope of tribal and related federal jurisdiction. *Venetie*, 522 U.S., 526.

16. *Venetie*, S22 U.S., 530.

17. Ibid., 528.

18. Ibid., 534.

19. See Des Rosiers, *From Telling to Listening*.

20. *Kiowa Tribe of Oklahoma v. Manufacturing Techs., Inc.*, 523 U.S. 751 (1998).

21. Ibid., 756–58.

22. Ibid., 758.

23. Ibid., 759.

24. *Rice v. Cayetano*, 528 U.S. 495 (2000).

25. Ibid.

26. Ibid.

27. Ibid.

28. S.J. Res. 19, 103d Cong., Ist Sess., 107 Stat. 1510 (1993).

29. Research regarding the status of Native Hawaiian claims in the State of Hawaii and the OHA programs is on file with the author.

30. *Rice*, S28 U.S. 495.

31. Ibid.

32. Ibid.

. . . .

*Published in* Justice as Healing *(2002) 7:1, this article was originally published in* 24 Seattle University Law Review 229, © 2005 Seattle University Law Review. *Reprinted with permission. We are grateful to the* Seattle University Law Review *for permission to reprint this article.*

# 29

# Denial, Acknowledgment, and Peace-Building through Reconciliatory Justice

*Robert Joseph*

## Introduction

Attempts to address and settle injustices against Indigenous Peoples are in motion in the Anglo-Commonwealth and elsewhere. Unfortunately, concerns about the post-settlement agreements are emerging with growing frequency, and Indigenous polities are either unprepared for them or unable to resolve them. Even more alarming, little academic attention has been focused on the complex dynamics of the post-settlement development phase. Academic analysis needs to move beyond discussing the aspirational legal instruments that emerged from negotiations and toward examining specific aspects of the post-settlement development phase.

This article will briefly highlight some post-settlement tensions from the *Waikato Raupatu Claims Settlement* (WRCS), the first contemporary settlement in New Zealand for addressing the historic grievance between the British Crown and the Maori of Waikato-Tainui. In 1863, the Crown unjustly invaded the Waikato, initiated hostilities, and confiscated 1.2 million acres of Waikato land.[1] I will discuss the politics of denial and its insidious effects in New Zealand and elsewhere. Then I will look at reconciliatory justice as a dispute resolution concept, ideal, process, and strategy for overcoming the politics of denial and for resolving some of the inevitable inter- and intra-post-settlement challenges, issues, and tensions.

## I. Post-Settlement Tensions

### Implementation Concerns

Denese Henare cautioned that post-settlement implementation and development involve matters quite different from those which were important during claims negotiations and following settlement proceedings.[2] The successful post-settlement implementation of the WRCS is a complex, long-term project that has not resulted in one quick government action. Implementation is occurring in stages, giving local communities and neighbors time to adjust to the realities of new governing structures.

There are and will continue to be no assurances that the implementation of the WRCS will run smoothly and no guarantees that difficulties will not occur within and between local communities. Implementation is working in many areas and is failing in others. It has entered rapidly in some areas and much more slowly in areas that do not deem themselves ready to undertake new responsibilities.[3] Thus, settlement implementation and development is an amorphous, moving target.

### Leadership Errors

The settlement relied extensively on multiple tiers of committees, and this has placed heavy personal and institutional demands on the Tainui infrastructure at the local level. Implementing settlements locally often carries its share of conflict and criticism. Like all other governments, the Tainui governance structures—the Kauhanganui and Te Kaumarua—have made and will continue to make mistakes.[4] Occasionally, infighting, adverse options, poor investments, what is perceived as a new stratum of Tainui elite, nepotism, and other leadership struggles have emerged and will emerge. When local residents become offended, their frustration is directed toward the locus of power, only to find it at their doorstep. With empowerment comes responsibility, and the people need to collectively and individually adjust their mind-sets to accommodate the inevitable post-settlement development and implementation tensions.

The challenge for the people of Tainui, as I see it, is to adjust entrenched attitudes that hinder personal and collective development. Post-settlement development demands positive change. Nonetheless, these and other post-settlement tensions will continue to emerge at both the inter- and intra-tribal levels.

## II. The Pernicious Politics of Denial

I will now discuss the politics of denial not only to illustrate how it contributed significantly to the protracted *raupatu* [confiscation, land theft] injustice and its subsequent effects, but moreover to show how denial contributes to post-settlement injustices. The politics of denial was (and in many ways continues to be) one of the most pernicious dimensions of colonial injustices and is a significant barrier to actualizing justice. Injustices against Maori have been perpetuated through the subtle culture of denial that prevails in New Zealand society.

Denial includes various ways that people block, shut out, repress, or cover up certain forms of disturbing information or otherwise evade, avoid, or neutralize the implications of this information. Stan Cohen provides a framework for analyzing the official and popular discourse about denial.[5]

## Content: Literal, Interpretative, or Implicatory Denial

*Literal Denial.* At times, a type of denial asserts that something did not happen or is not true. The facts of the matter are being denied: "there was no massacre," "they are all lying," "we do not believe you." Such assertions generally refuse not only to acknowledge the facts—for whatever reason, in good or bad faith—but even to determine whether these claims are true or blatantly untrue. An example of literal denial is the so-called revisionist history of the annihilation of European Jews, which dismisses the entire event as a hoax or a myth.[6]

In New Zealand, for example, a controversy arose when Dr. Joel Hayward of Massey University denied the holocaust in his master's thesis written at Canterbury University in 1992. He claimed that there was no evidence of the extermination of Jews in Hitler's Germany, that gas chambers had not existed, and that far fewer than six million Jews died at Nazi hands.[7] Closer to home, a controversy arose when the University of Waikato enrolled the alleged neo-Nazi, Hans-Joachim Kupka.[8] Professor Dov Bing of Waikato University even delivered two papers at an international conference in Paris last year entitled "Holocaust Denial and New Zealand Universities" and "The Denial of Holocaust Denial at the University of Waikato."[9]

*Interpretive Denial.* More often, the raw facts are not being denied, but they are given a different meaning from what seems apparent to others. Thus, government officials responding to allegations about injustices to Maori might claim that "nothing happened." Something did happen, but "this is not what you think it is," "not what it looks like," "not what you call it." What happened is the "transfer of populations," not forced expulsion; "moderate physical pressure," not torture. In all cases, by changing words or using euphemisms or technical jargon, the observer disputes the meaning given to an event and reassigns it to a different class of events.

A further ploy of the revisionist movement to deny a holocaust combines both literal and interpretive denial: "it did not happen"; "it happened too long ago to prove"; "the facts are open to different interpretations"; or "what happened was not genocide." Referring to the Jewish holocaust, another revisionist, Dr. Frederick Toben of Adelaide University, asserted:

> Hitler fervently admired National Socialist Zionists and with their agreement tried to transport as many Jews as possible to Palestine where many were killed by religious zealots against the creation of a Jewish state. . . . [Concentration] camps such as Auschwitz were in effect transit camps where hospital and similar facilities were provided until the transport system collapsed through Allied bombing.[10]

Toben seems to insinuate that Arabs, not Nazis, killed the Jews, that the Nazi death camps were in fact medical camps, and that they were destroyed by—hence shifting the blame to—the Allies. Dr. David Irving, another revisionist historian, stated that the Auschwitz death camp was a "Disneyland for tourists"[11]—a ludicrous interpretation to say the least.

Another recent example in New Zealand was the national controversy over the use of the term *holocaust* by Associate Maori Affairs Minister Tariana Turia to the Psychological Society conference in Hamilton last year.[12] Turia stated:

> What seems to not have received . . . attention is the *holocaust* suffered by Indigenous people including Maori as a result of colonial contact and behaviour[13] [emphasis added].

This speech caused a political storm, because it was interpreted as comparing the Maori experience of colonialism to the Jewish holocaust of World War II. However, Mason Durie concluded that, although the term *holocaust* might grate on the New Zealand psyche, when you think the population of two hundred thousand Maori in 1840 was reduced to forty-two thousand in 1900, that's pretty close to a holocaust.[14]

*Implicatory Denial.* At other times, there is no attempt to deny either the facts or the conventional meaning they are given. The observer rather denies the resulting psychological or moral implications. It might be perfectly clear what is happening, but any responsibility as a citizen or neighbor to intervene is denied, usually through such rationalizations as: "it's got nothing to do with me"; "its worse elsewhere"; or "some one else will deal with it." These assertions may be perfectly justified, both morally and factually, or they may signify a denial that is an excuse for doing nothing. The facts are readily accepted, but their moral message and import are denied.

We do nothing for a number of reasons, ranging from principled justification ("they are getting what they deserve") to moral indifference ("I know what's happening, but it does not bother me"; "why should I care?") to various forms of accommodation, tolerance, and normalization ("that's just what happens in places like that").[15] A recent example of implicatory denial occurred when, in the racially charged areas of the South, the Taranaki, Stratford, and Taranaki Regional Councils refused to participate in the Taranaki Group. This group was set up on the recommendation of Race Relations Conciliator Rajen Prasad to address racial tensions in the region. The regional councils said they hadn't been sufficiently consulted, or they saw the issue as one for New Plymouth.[16]

### Organization: Personal, Official, or Cultural Denial

There is an obvious difference between forms of denial that are personal, psychological, and private and those that are shared—social, collective, and organized—and that come from the state and its official discourse. Cohen presents these differences through three possibilities:

*Personal Denial.* Sometimes we talk about what appear to be wholly individual denial reactions—actions that can be studied at the psychological level. For example, spouses may suspect their spouse's infidelities but then put aside their suspicions, or alcoholic and drug addicts may refuse to acknowledge their dependency. These variations of "personal denial" are different psychological ways of coping with knowledge.

*Official Denial.* At the other extreme are forms of denial that are public, collective, and highly organized. In more totalitarian societies, official denial

extends from particular incidents ("the massacre did not happen") to an entire rewriting of history and a blocking-out of the present. Such denial is not
a private coping mechanism; the state makes it impossible or dangerous to
acknowledge the existence of past and present realities.

In more democratic societies, official denial is more subtle—twisting the
truth, setting the public agenda, arranging leaks to the media, or expressing
selective concern about suitable victims. The "manufacture of consent" has
been exposed by scholars such as Noam Chomsky.[17] This form of denial is
not a personal matter but has been built into the ideological fabric of the
state. The study of Indigenous Peoples' rights and settlements is simultaneously a study of the official techniques used to deny these realities—not just
to observers but often to the perpetrators themselves.

An example of official denial in New Zealand occurred in 1926 when the
government finally examined the *raupatu* land confiscations through the Sim
Commission.[18] The commission was unfortunately prevented from looking
into questions of the lawfulness of the raupatu and from considering the
Treaty of Waitangi. Consequently, the Sim Commission found not that the
raupatu was unjust but that it had not been excessive, demonstrating the extent of official denial.

*Cultural Denial.* There are yet other forms of denial that are neither wholly
private nor officially organized by the state; these are called cultural denial.
Whole societies slip into collective modes of denial not dependent on a totalitarian and hegemonic form of thought control. Without being told what
to think about and what not to think about, and without being punished
for "knowing" the wrong things, societies arrive at some unwritten agreement about what can be publicly acknowledged. People will pretend to believe information that they know is false or fake allegiance to meaningless
slogans and outrageous ceremonies. This happens even more in democratic
societies.[19]

This cultural denial might be manifested, for example, as a collective denial of the past, specifically of the treatment of Indigenous Peoples in North
America, Australia, and New Zealand. Or, people act as if they do not
know about the present: whole societies may be based on forms of discrimination, repression, or exclusion that are "known about" but never openly
acknowledged.

The classic case of cultural-official denial was the colonial doctrine of *terra nullius* in Australia. Prevailing since the start of British colonization, the doctrine advocated that a country without political organization, legal codes, or recognizable systems of authority could be legitimately annexed, because the country was without a sovereign recognized by European authorities. It was a territory where nobody owned any land at all, hence where no tenure of any sort existed. Accordingly, the settlement of Australia was based on this improper legal doctrine.

This collective cultural denial was not officially challenged until Australia's 1992 High Court decision in *Mabo v. Queensland*.[20] In separate opinions, the High Court rejected the Crown's claim, because it was based on the premise that the Aboriginal lands were *terra nullius* prior to European settlement, despite the presence of Indigenous people.[21] Judge Brennan held that the common law should be interpreted according to contemporary values of Australian society:

> [I]t is imperative in today's world that the common law should neither be nor be seen to be frozen in an age of racial discrimination. The fiction by which the rights and interests of Indigenous inhabitants in land were treated as non-existent was justified by a policy which has no place in the contemporary law of this country. . . .[22]

By reinterpreting the Australian common-law property régime and ousting the previously relied upon fiction of *terra nullius*, the High Court forced Australians to challenge their culture of denial. Unfortunately, as Rangihau has warned, you cannot legislate attitudes,[23] and the pernicious culture of denial remains endemic in Australia. For example, on 26 May 1997, Prime Minister John Howard gave a public personal apology to the Aboriginal people for the injustices of past generations, but he then went on to say that Australian history was not one of imperialism, exploitation, and racism.[24]

An example of cultural denial closer to home was the coverage of Tariana Turia's comments on the Maori "holocaust" and colonization. She was labeled a "radical" minister, and the prime minister, the Right Honorable Helen Clarke, commented: "This sort of thing which causes all sorts of alarm bells to ring out in middle New Zealand is not helpful"[25]—never mind whether or not it was true. It is interesting to note that part of Turia's apology for causing the political storm addressed her use of the term *holocaust*: "I would be happy to take advice on the appropriate words to use for the horrors of my people. Whatever the words are, it will never lessen the degradation we have suffered."[26]

Another example of cultural denial is the way some people attribute contemporary Maori socioeconomic conditions and cultural pain—the result of land loss and the diminution of Maori values—to Maori laziness, an inability to cope with the "modern" world, or even to some genetic inferiority.[27] This cultural denial can also exist among Maori. The former Maori Affairs Minister Dover Samuels commented that Turia's speech was "political and cultural correctness gone *porangi* (mad)."[28]

### Time: Historical or Contemporary Denial

Historical or contemporary denial refutes the connection between then and now in official and popular discourse. In some instances, we are talking about denial of the past. Applying the concept of denial to how we respond to past injustices exposes the phenomena of collective forgetting ("social selective amnesia") and the selective refusal to acknowledge a particular historical record ("social selective remembrance"). Sometimes this amnesia is officially organized by the state. Other times, governments do not officially sponsor denial, but it is nonetheless collective and organized.

The classic example of historical denial in New Zealand (which was official denial at the time) can be found in *Wi Parata v. Bishop of Wellington* (1877).[29] In his ruling, Chief Justice Prendergast found that, on the foundation of the colony, Maori were supposedly without any kind of civil government or any settled system of law, notwithstanding evidence and case law to the contrary.[30] Accordingly, Prendergast held that Maori were "primitive barbarians" with no body politic capable of granting cession. The Treaty of Waitangi, therefore, was considered a "simple nullity."[31] Furthermore, referring to Maori custom in section 4 of the Native Rights Act 1865, Prendergast denied Maori law altogether:

> . . . as if some such body of customary law did in reality exist. But a phrase in a statute cannot call what is nonexistent into being. . . . no such body of law existed.[32]

The chief justice thus denied the existence of Maori rights under both the established doctrine of Aboriginal title and the Treaty of Waitangi. The New Zealand judiciary, therefore, had no jurisdiction to consider any Maori claims, and Maori were institutionally denied justice, identity, and citizenship.[33] At the stroke of a pen, the ancient *iwi* and *hapu* laws, customs, and institutions were extinguished, and the Treaty of Waitangi disappeared from the legal landscape through this historical denial discourse. The treaty was not resurrected until the 1970s[34] and the SOE land cases[35] of the late 1980s, which means that this official denial lasted for a century. For this reason, any refusal today to acknowledge and redress treaty injustices because they happened long ago is historical denial.

More often, historical denial is less the result of a planned and conscious campaign and is caused instead by a gradual seepage of knowledge down some collective black hole. There is no need for intentional public manipulation if we understand how whole societies collude in a shared amnesia to never talk about discreditable historical truths. This might occur both within a society and about other societies.[36]

An example of such denial can be found in the past sanctions imposed on South Africa from nations like New Zealand and Australia, both of which criticized South African apartheid policies and yet practiced oppressive policies toward their own Indigenous Peoples. It was not until the decision to allow the South African rugby team to tour New Zealand in 1981 that a large number of New Zealanders stood beside Maori not only to protest against South Africa but more important to question New Zealand's own historical and official denial of racism. The protests and ensuing riots pitted New Zealander against New Zealander on an international stage. No longer could we overlook the historical cultural denial that was endemic to New Zealand. No longer could the world be convinced that ours was a country of equality and harmonious race relations.[37]

Denial, therefore, forms a major barrier to actualizing justice, since in the denier's mind, no injustice has been done. Denial clearly has many forms. Because it excuses the failure to recognize injury in official and popular discourse, it eliminates the need to redress historical and contemporary injustices.[38] As a result, authentic measures for promoting reconciliatory justice and peaceful co-existence are neither put forward nor acted on.

## III. Reconciliatory Justice

### Reconciliatory Justice Conceptually

Reconciliatory justice[39] is critical to reaching a settlement, but it is also essential for making post-settlement Indigenous agreement processes work. These processes require an ongoing commitment to future peacemaking, and they must be sustained in deeds, not just in words. As a result, reconciliatory justice is both a pre- and post-settlement process. It strives to overcome a culture of denial and other barriers to peacemaking in the popular and official discourses of both the dominant and the Maori societies. It focuses on building appropriate relationships by recognizing and addressing past grievances. And it explores future relationships at the post-settlement governance and grassroots levels.

To a large extent, these settlement and post-settlement processes should empower Maori to create a self-sustaining infrastructure that is self-determined, self-managed, and self-governed. Post-settlement reconciliation involves, therefore, a long-term commitment. It must establish an infrastructure and a cultural-political environment across levels of society (both state and Indigenous) that empower the Indigenous Peoples with resources for reconciliation and for successful, sustainable development.

### Process, Not Event

Concretely, doing reconciliatory justice can be distilled into seven "giant steps." Such a process never ends. Forgiveness and peaceful co-existence may be achievable, but, as Paul Havemann asserts, "to forget the past is to run the risk that the culture of denial will reassert itself and allow history to repeat itself."[40] The process and outcome must help to overcome the politics of denial, to empower the powerless, and to establish a new, more appropriate relationship. The seven key steps for accomplishing reconciliatory justice—the promotion of social justice through reconciliation—include

- *recognition:* truth finding and telling the injustices;
- *responsibility and remorse:* acknowledging the injustices and apologizing for them;
- *restitution:* returning Indigenous land and the power to determine its use;

+ *reparation:* making reparations for injustices in financial terms, recognizing that ethnocidal and genocidal harms are really incompensible in this way;
+ *redesign:* redesigning state political-legal institutions and processes to empower Indigenous Peoples to participate in their own governance and the government of the state;[41]
+ *refraining:* refraining from repeating the injustices; and
+ *reciprocity:* honoring the obligation to do unto others as you would have them do unto you—to give as you have been given.

### Recognition: Truth Finding and Telling

When Maori express grievances and tell accounts of genocide and ethnocide, these accounts of suffering and systemic injustice should trigger moments of truth. During these moments, human beings should begin to understand what justice really means in light of past injustices. Maori want answers to their questions about what happened, and perpetrators and later denialists need to understand what they have done, to whom, and the effects of their actions or inaction.

Speaking and hearing the truth is, therefore, a basic requirement for reconciliatory justice and reconstructing a society based on peaceful coexistence. The WRCS grew out of a long process of truth seeking and telling through various petitions and deputations:[42] the Sim Commission (1926), the Waikato-Maniapoto Claims Settlement Act (1946), the Manukau Report (1985) of the Waitangi Tribunal,[43] and the judgment of the New Zealand Court of Appeal in the *Coal Corp* case.[44] Commenting on the preamble of the Waikato Raupatu Claims Settlement Act (1995) (WRCSA), S. Solomon noted:

> what will be achieved . . . is to get into the public record the real history of what happened to Waikato during the years before the wars, the effect of that war on our people, and the results of the land confiscations.[45]

### Responsibility: Acknowledgment

Here, the concept of acknowledgment means having the truth recognized. Acknowledgment is what happens when private knowledge becomes officially sanctioned and enters into the public discourse. This is what people want in the "truth and acknowledgment phase" of reconciliatory justice—not new information but some public recognition of what is already known.[46] As Solomon noted, "Our history will now be publicly acknowledged."[47]

Through acknowledgment, dominant groups are encouraged to recognize and confirm past and present injustices. Particular painful emotions (guilt, shame, anger) ought to be aroused, and steps should be taken to make things right. Indeed, Bruno Bettelheim commented: "What cannot be talked about cannot be put to rest, and if it is not, the wounds will continue to fester from generation to generation."[48]

Then comes the crucial link: the stage of empowerment, when people begin to recognize the possibility of "doing" justice, not just "talking" about it.

Finally, the dominant and Maori groups should be willing to do something to change things for the better. Unfortunately, while acknowledging that something happened, people fall back on neutralization techniques that continue to feed denial. They either refuse to accept the category of acts (interpretative and implicatory denial) to which harms and injustices are assigned ("genocide," "massacre," "holocaust"), or they present the harms as morally justified: "Maori weren't using the land"; "Maori were uncivilized anyway"; "it's all part of progress"; or "Maori fought the Crown and lost."

Although truth telling and acknowledging harms may be painful forms of shaming, reconciliatory justice involves reintegrating those shamed back into society on the condition that they are committed to peace-building. Accordingly, the preamble of the WRCSA acknowledges the history of the people of Tainui in their quest for justice, and it records the detailed steps of the Crown in a litany of unsatisfactory outcomes, from the petitions of the 1860s onward. In the WRCSA, the Crown acknowledged that it unjustly invaded the Waikato,[49] initiated hostilities against the Kīngitanga,[50] unjustly confiscated approximately 1.2 million acres of land from Tainui *iwi*,[51] and that the effects of the raupatu have lasted for generations.[52]

### Remorse: Apology

Receiving apologies for injustices, however old, is always an important step in the healing process and moves people toward reconciliation. Indeed, Nicholas Tavuchis's definition of a meaningful apology is instructive: "To apologize is to declare voluntarily that one has no excuse, defense, justification, or explanation for an action or inaction."[53] Hence, one of the most important aspects of the Crown's settlement offer in the Deed of Settlement and the WRCSA was the formal apology.[54]

The apology, however, must be remorseful to be effective. The person who gives the apology, the apology's wording, and even the setting in which the apology is offered are very important. Accordingly, both parties gave the wording much thought. The Crown included the formal apology to acknowledge that the people of Waikato-Tainui suffered grave injustices that significantly impaired their economic, social, and cultural development. In the apology, the Crown expressed profound regret and apologized "unreservedly" for the suffering and hardship caused to the people of Waikato-Tainui.

Importantly, the apology confirmed the validity of the Tainui claim that was borne by many generations. The Crown sought to atone for these acknowledged injustices on behalf of all New Zealanders and also apologized publicly. On 3 November 1995, Queen Elizabeth II was in Wellington, and she signed the act, thus endorsing (among other things) the apology. Solomon stated that her signing was symbolic, because on two occasions, Tainui sought help from the English monarchy—Queen Victoria and King George—to acknowledge and settle the raupatu injustice; it was their granddaughter who signed the act with an official apology.[55]

The apology was in both Maori and English, and it acknowledged that the Crown acted "unconscionably and in repeated breach of the principles of the Treaty of Waitangi in its dealings with Tainui." The importance of the apology cannot be overstated, given that it is the ultimate course to finally overcoming the political and legal denial, at least officially, that existed in New Zealand about Tainui. Furthermore, the formal apology goes a long way to restoring harmony after 132 years of pain and injustice.

The apology does not, however, mean that the people of Tainui forget the past, but it gives the Crown an opportunity to make amends and for Tainui and the Crown to move on with the healing process in a new relationship. Official denial has been symbolically overcome, but the task of achieving understanding—of overcoming cultural denial—by the settler population and even among some Maori remains to be achieved.

### Restitution: Restoring Land

Reconciliatory justice involves the restitution of what was taken to right the balance—land for land and the power to determine its use. The preamble of the WRCSA states: "Tainui pursued compensation on the established principle of '*i riro whenua atu, me hoki whenua mai*'—as land was taken, land must be returned."[56] Moreover, the Crown recognized the significance of the "land for land" principle, and both parties agreed that the Crown should make full and final restitution to Waikato in respect of the raupatu claim.[57] The act further states that the Crown holds only a small portion of the land originally confiscated.[58] Consequently, the restitution of land amounted to approximately 40,000 acres,[59] with the Crown retaining 50,000 acres of mostly conservation land, but with a permanent Tainui representative on the Waikato Conservation Board to help manage its use. Added to these shortcomings, the settlement does not restore the Waikato River to Tainui, nor have interests in sub-surface minerals been restored.

### Reparation: Compensation

Reconciliation that can lead to a culture and relationship of trust requires other reparations and adjustments to take place as well. Reconciliation must include concrete deeds; it can never be satisfied by cheap words or processes. Symbolic reparation is essential, including an apology or some other culturally appropriate intervention, but the importance of symbolism does not lessen the need for concrete measures and financial reparations.[60]

Moreover, those involved must acknowledge that ethnocidal and genocidal injustices are really incompensible in this way. Accordingly, another guiding principle of the WRCS was *kei te moni hei utu mo te hara*—"the money is acknowledgment for the crime."[61] The Crown has acknowledged the raupatu injustice and its subsequent effects. Given that a guiding principle for Tainui was land for land, which was not feasible, compensation was accepted as reparation for these incompensible harms. Redress in financial terms amounted to $170 million plus interest on the principal sum of the settlement.

### Redesign: Redesigning State Legal and Political Institutions

Reconciliation can come only after the issues have been resolved. Conflicts have to be worked out, and immediate grievances have to be settled amicably. Only then can reconciliation follow. However, settling grievances is not the end. Reconciliatory justice is a process, not an event. Settlements are not solutions but frameworks for working on solutions, because the pain and continuing effects of the raupatu and treaty injustices do not disappear overnight.

In addition, the unjust laws and institutions that perpetuate injustices cannot remain "as is," or reconciliation will not occur. Healing requires a framework, and that framework needs to be made up of institutions that allow all sections to work together. For Tainui, the power to make decisions that affect their lives was paramount. The WRCS and institutional redesign were intended to give Tainui this power.

Moreover, the new relationship established between the Crown and Tainui was based on trust, respect, and dignity. State political and legal institutions were redesigned in theory to empower the people to effectively participate in their own governance and the government of the nation-state. The statutory Tainui Maori Trust Board has been abolished, and the people of Tainui have agreed on the mode of post-settlement governance—the Kauhanganui—drawing on three representatives from each of the sixty-three marae of the settlement.[62]

The significance of this new institution is that, because the Maori Land Court does not retain jurisdiction over the Kauhanganui, it is accountable to the iwi collectively and not to the Crown, as in the past. Furthermore, according to the settlement, some of the lands returned are vested in the first Maori King, the late Potatau Te Wherowhero. Under this new tribal land title, no individual can succeed to these lands. The lands are vested in three custodial trustees and can be alienated by them only with the agreement of 75 percent of the beneficiary marae.[63] Moreover, Te Wherowhero land cannot be alienated under the Resource Management Act (1991), nor do the Maori Land Court or the Waitangi Tribunal retain jurisdiction over matters dealt with under the settlement.

### Refrain: Refraining from Repeating Injustices

Obviously, the Crown and mainstream society must refrain from repeating the injustices of the past in order for authentic reconciliatory justice and peaceful coexistence to be achieved. In addition, the models of institutional design and the norms embedded in these models must work to prevent any further external domination over iwi affairs.

### Reciprocity: Utu

Once Maori groups have been through this protracted but empowering process, I argue that the settlement group—the iwi—has a strong obligation to do unto others as they would have others do unto them, to give as they have been given to. Often people are reluctant to take on a responsibility to make right, yet this is simply another manifestation of the politics of denial. Both the Crown and the settlement group must seek not simply to restore but to transform.

Traditionally, *utu* was an integral part of Maori society. However, it included much more than simple reciprocity or satisfying the equivalent; utu meant giving greater in return.[64] Utu was not only for restoring mana but indeed for increasing mana! Moreover, traditional Maori society had—and continues to have—a collective rather than an individual responsibility, and this liability is both direct and indirect. Maori customary law thus embodies ideals, hopes, and potential as well as a longing for harmony and reconciliation. All these ideals must be incorporated collectively in the post-settlement period, forming an integral component of how society is reconstructed based on peaceful co-existence.

## Conclusion

The Waikato Raupatu Claims Settlement is an outstanding Indigenous settlement agreement, because it was and continues to be a landmark case globally for overcoming the politics of denial and restoring the balance for reconciliation between the powerful settler state and the powerless Maori. However, the WRCS is not perfect, and the post-settlement development phase is waning. Even so, it is a step toward achieving reconciliation for past injustices and reversing generations of paternalistic control, administration at a distance, and non-Tainui rule over Tainui Peoples' lives.

Consequently, I maintain that there is much to learn from the settlement process about how to make the post-settlement development and dispute resolution stages successful. The settlement was and is much more than a commercial transaction. Perhaps the present protracted governance impasse can be overcome through this same process: recognizing and acknowledging the truth; expressing remorse through an apology; making restitution and reparations for harms incurred; redesigning political institutions (including Maori); refraining from repeating injustices; and practicing reciprocity. The aim of reconciliatory justice is to make things right between adversaries and, in the words of Dworkin, "to find the best route to a better future."[65]

The WRCSA is both revolutionary and evolutionary. Such new re-

alities—whether economic, political, cultural, or social—require new approaches, which in turn call for patience, commitment, unity, mutual trust,
goodwill, and hard work. The challenges in doing justice and in making the
settlement work have in no way diminished, and it is still not too late.

*Kia ora tatou katoa*

## Notes

1. See "Maori Biographies" from the Dictionary of New Zealand Biographies,
*Te Kingitanga: The People of the Maori King Movement* (Auckland, N.Z.: Auckland
University Press, 1996).

2. D. Henare, "Post Settlement Issues," *Strategies for the Next Decade* (1997), 23.
Interestingly, an Australian government report in 1975 listed a number of Indigenous
settlement concerns that continue to emerge in contemporary Indigenous politics in
Australia, Canada, New Zealand, and elsewhere. See *Aboriginal Land Rights Commission*, Second Report, April 1974 (Canberra: The Government Printer of Australia, 1975), 6, 7.

3. K. Coates, *Degrees of Separation: First Nations Self-Government in British Columbia* (Hamilton, N.Z.: University of Waikato, 1996), 25.

4. See, for example, V. Bidois, "Mahuta Deal Axed as Tribe Seeks Cash Sale," *New
Zealand Herald* (14 August 2000); P. Yandall, "Tribal Council Accused of Blunders,"
*New Zealand Herald* (31 July 2000); K. Taylor, "Tainui Braces for $24m Claim after
Court Loss," *New Zealand Herald* (23 December 2000); K. Taylor, "Back to Square
One," *New Zealand Herald* (8 January 2001); "Tainui in Land Sale Confusion," *New
Zealand Herald* (16 January 2001); K. Taylor, "News Blacker for Tainui," *New Zealand
Herald* (20 February 2001); "Tainui Seeks Strategy to Satisfy Bank," *New Zealand
Herald* (3 March 2001), to name a few. Online at http//www.nzherald.co.nz.

5. S. Cohen, *Denial and Acknowledgement: The Impact of Information about Human Rights Violations* (Jerusalem: Centre of Human Rights, Faculty of Law and
the Harry S. Truman Research Institute for the Advancement of Peace, Hebrew
University, 1995), 19.

6. See, for example, M. Schmidt, and R. Vojtovic, "Holocaust Denial and Freedom of Expression," in T. Orlin, A. Rosas, and M. Scheinin, *The Jurisprudence of Human Rights: A Comparative Interpretive Approach* (Turku/Abo: Institute for Human
Rights, Abo Akademi University, 2000), 133–58; D. Lipstadt, *Denying the Holocaust:
The Growing Assault on Truth and Memory* (New York: Free Press/Macmillan, 1993);
and S. Totten, W. Parsons, and I. Charmy, I., eds., *Century of Genocide: Eye Witness
Accounts and Critical Views* (New York: Garland Publishing, New Garland Publishing, 1997).

7. See G. Ansley, "Australian Buys a Fight Using the Net for Holocaust Denial," *New Zealand Herald* (14 October 2000); R. Walsh, "A-Plus Equals Anger for Jewish Groups," *New Zealand Herald* (11 December 2000).

8. "Varsity Student in Race Crimes Probe," *Waikato Times* (25 July 2000); "Holocaust Student Drops Ph.D. Study," *Waikato Times* (29 June 2000); "Holocaust Denier Case Review Urged," *Waikato Times* (6 July 2000). Online at http://www.stuff.co.nz/inl//index/.

9. "Kupka Criticism Going Abroad," *Waikato Times* (29 July 2000).

10. G. Ansley, op cit.

11. Cited in Walsh, "A-Plus Equals Anger for Jewish Groups."

12. See, for example, "Minister Hammers Colonial Holocaust," *New Zealand Herald* (30 August 2000); "Holocaust Remarks Set Race Relations Office's Phones Ringing," *New Zealand Herald* (1 September 2000); "Holocaust MP Considered Quitting Job," *New Zealand Herald* (13 September 2000); and "Turia Apologises over 'Holocaust' Statement," *New Zealand Herald* (5 September 2000); "Ministerial Psycho-bable," *New Zealand Herald* (7 November 2000).

13. Turia's full speech can be located online in the *New Zealand Herald*, 31 August 2000, at http://www.nzherald.co.nz.

14. Cited in A. Gifford, A., *Nga Korero o te wa: A Monthly Summary of Maori News and Views from Throughout Aotearoa* (31 August 2000, vol. 10, no. 12), 3. The chief executive officer of the New Zealand Maori Council, Manu Paul, stated that the banning by Prime Minister Helen Clark of the use of *holocaust* in a New Zealand context was similar to Adolf Hitler's practice of "gagging the Jews and burning them off." He stated that the word *holocaust* was appropriate to describe some parts of New Zealand history, in which the Maori population declined 80 percent in a century. A. Gregory, "Clark Behaving Like Hitler, Say Maori," *New Zealand Herald* (8 September 2000).

15. Cohen, *Denial and Acknowledgement*, 25.

16. A. Gifford, *Nga Korero o te Wa: A Monthly Summary of Maori News and Views from Throughout Aotearoa* (31 December 2000, vol. 13, no. 12), 6.

17. N. Chomsky, *Necessary Illusions: Thought Control in Democratic Societies* (Boston: South End Press, 1989).

18. In 1926, the government established a royal commission to inquire into "confiscated land and other grievances" under Justice Sir William Sim, Vernon Reed, a legislative councilor, and William Cooper, a Maori of Wairoa. *Appendices to the Journal of the House of Representatives* (1928), 6, 7.

19. Cohen, *Denial and Acknowledgement*, 27.

20. *Mabo v. Queensland*, (1992) 175 C.L.R. 1. For a good analysis of this case, see H. Reynolds, "The Mabo Judgment in Light of Imperial Land Policy," 1 *U.N.S.W.L.J.*

(1993), 16, and S. Pritchard, *Indigenous Peoples, the United Nations and Human Rights* (Australia: Zed Books, 1998).

21. For an excellent analysis of the *terra nullius* fiction and its legal history in Australia, see H. Reynolds, *The Law of the Land* (Melbourne: Penguin Books, 1988); and H. Reynolds, *Frontiers: Aborigines, Settlers and Land* (Sydney: Allen and Unwin, 1987).

22. *Mabo v. Queensland* (1992) 175 C.L.R. 1, 41–2 (per J. Brennan).

23. J. Rangihau, "Being Maori," *Te Ao Hurihuri: The World Moves On*, ed. M. King, (Auckland, NZ: Longman Paul, 1981), 173.

24. Reuter, "Cheers, Jeers at Howard Apology," *New Zealand Herald* (1997), BI; A. Press, "Apologies Are Just Grandstanding," *New Zealand Herald* (1997), B3.

25. "Warning to Turia: Keep 'Holocaust' Opinions to Yourself," *New Zealand Herald* (31 August 2000).

26. "Tariana Turia's Apology," transcript in *New Zealand Herald* (6 September 2000).

27. M. Jackson, "Justice: Unitary or Separate," ed. D. Novitz and B. Wilmott, *New Zealand in Crisis* (1995), 251.

28. "Warning to Turia, *New Zealand Herald*.

29. *Wi Parata v. Bishop of Wellington* (1877) 3 N.Z. Jur. (N.S) S.C. 72.

30. In *R v. Symonds* (1847) N.Z.P.C.C., 387, the Court asserted that whatever the strength of Native title, it is entitled to be respected. Over the next thirty years, several New Zealand cases followed the Symonds approach, including the Kauwaeranga Judgment Native Land Court, 3 December 1870. Moreover, in Re Lundon and Whitaker Claims Act 1871 (1872) 2 NZCA, 41, 49, the Court of Appeal held that the Crown was bound to a full recognition of Native proprietary rights.

31. *Wi Parata v. Bishop of Wellington* (1877) 3 N.Z Jur. (N.S) S.C. 72, 78.

32. Ibid., 72, 79.

33. This state-organized official denial was further reiterated by C. J. Prendergrast in *Rira Peti v. Ngaraihi Te Paku* (1889) 7 N.Z.L.R., 235, 238–39. See A. Frame, "Colonising Attitudes towards Māori Custom," *The New Zealand Law Journal* (17 March 1981), 109.

34. The Treaty of Waitangi Act 1975. This act signified that the political and legal culture of denial articulated in Wi Parata was over, at least in official discourse.

35. *New Zealand Maori Council v. Attorney-General* [1987] N.Z.L.R., 641.

36. Cohen, *Denial and Acknowledgement*, 29.

37. See New Zealand Collection, *1981 Springbok Tour: The Issues in Black and White: A Collection of Clippings* (Hamilton, N.Z.: University of Waikato Library, 1996); T. Newnham, ed., *By Batons and Barbed Wire* (Auckland, N.Z.: Real Pictures, 1981); History Department, *Counting the Cost: The 1981 Springbok Tour in Wellington* (Wellington, N.Z.: University of Victoria, 1982).

38. P. Havemann, and B. Hocking, *Denial and Co-Existence? Indigenous Peoples in Liberal Social Democracies: The Anglo-Commonwealth and the Nordic States* (unpublished paper in author's possession, 2000), 5.

39. See generally J. P. Lederach, *Building Peace: Sustained Reconciliation in Divided Societies* (Washington, D.C.: United States Institute of Peace, 1997), 23–37.

40. P. Havemann, "Reconciliation and Discrimination: Indigenous Peoples, Colonisation and the State in the 'Old Dominions' (Australia, Canada and New Zealand)," *A Dialogue on Indigenous Rights in the Commonwealth* (Conference Proceedings, Institute of Commonwealth Studies, University of London, 23 July 1999), 55.

41. Ibid.

42. To cite some examples, in 1866, Wiremu Tamihana petitioned Parliament to return the confiscated lands to the Maori owners; in 1876, King Tawhiao met with the Native Minister, McLean, to discuss the return of *urupa* that were promised but not enacted for a century under the Waiuku Native Grants Act. In 1884, King Tawhiao led an unsuccessful deputation to England to petition Queen Victoria for grievances between Maori and the Crown including the raupatu. The following year Tawhiao appealed to the New Zealand government to establish a Maori Council of Chiefs but was denied any support. In 1907, King Mahuta drafted a petition to King Edward asking that Maori be put on the same footing as Pakeha; and in 1914, King Te Rata visited England requesting Imperial Government intercession.

43. As an institution, the Waitangi Tribunal has played a crucial role in the truth-finding and telling stages of Maori claims and has played a major role in the settlement of Treaty of Waitangi grievances. Consequently, the Reports of the Tribunal are documents for truth-finding and telling, addressing legal, cultural, and historical matters. See the database of the Waitangi Tribunal and its reports at http:// www.knowledge_basket.co.nz//topic 4/waitr>.

44. *Tainui Maori Trust Board v. Attorney-General* [1989] N.Z.L.R., 513, 528 (CA).

45. S. Solomon, *The Waikato Raupatu Claims Settlement Act: A Draft Users Guide to the Act as at 28 October 1995* (Hamilton, N.Z.: Tainui Maori Trust Board, 1995), 4.

46. Cohen, *Denial and Acknowledgement*, 29.

47. Solomon, *Waikato Raupatu Claims Settlement Act*, 4.

48. B. Bettelheim, *Freud and Man's Soul* (London: Chatto and Windus, 1983).

49. Waikato Raupatu Claims Settlement Act 1995, Clause E, Preamble.

50. Ibid.

51. Ibid, Clause F, Preamble.

52. Ibid.

53. N. Tavuchis, in V. Vicencio and W. Verwoerd, *Looking Back Reaching Forward: Reflections on the Truth and Reconciliation Commission of South Africa* (London: Zed Books and Cape Town: University of Cape Town Press, 2000), 74.

54. Waikato Raupatu Claims Settlement Act 1995, Clause 3.6, Preamble.

55. Solomon, *Waikato Raupatu Claims Settlement Act*, 2.

56. Waikato Raupatu Claims Settlement Act 1995, Clause O, Preamble.

57. Ibid, Clause S. (b) and (c), Preamble.

58. Ibid, Clause W, Preamble.

59. Tainui Maori Trust Board, *Tainui Maori Trust Board Annual Report 1995* (Hamilton, N.Z.: Tainui Maori Trust Board, 1995), 12.

60. W. Orr, "Reparation Delayed Is Healing Retarded," in Vicencio and Verwoerd, *Looking Back Reaching Forward*, 240–41.

61. Waikato Raupatu Claims Settlement Act 1995, Clause O, Preamble.

62. Waikato Raupatu Claims Settlement Act 1995, sections 27–29.

63. Ibid, section 19.

64. See R. Firth, *Economics of the New Zealand Maori* (Wellington: Government Press, 1959); R. Walker, *Ka Whawhai Tonu Matou: Struggle Without End* (Aukland: Penguin Books, 1990); and A. Salmond, *Between Worlds: Early Exchanges between Maori and Europeans, 1773–1815* (Auckland: Viking Press, 1997).

65. D. Dworkin, *Law's Empire* (Cambridge, MA: Belknap Press of Harvard University Press, 1986), 413.

## Glossary

**Hapu**: Sub-tribe, cluster of whanau kin groups.

**Iwi**: Tribe, cluster of hapu kin groups, group of people.

**Kauhanganui**: Waikato post-Treaty settlement governance entity, an electoral college Parliament model which draws on three representatives from each of the sixty-three marae of the settlement.

**Maori and Māori**: Indigenous peoples of New Zealand, not a homogenous public.

**Mana**: Prestige, intrinsic power, respect, influence, and dignity.

**Marae**: Formal Maori meeting place.

**Pakeha**: Non-Maori, literally 'stranger,' European newcomers to New Zealand.

**Raupatu**: Confiscation, land theft.

**Tainui**: A specific Maori tribal confederation in the central North Island area of New Zealand.

**Terra nullius**: Convenient international legal concept used to displace Indigenous Peoples from their lands and resources because, inter alia, they had no acknowledged Western notion of property and sovereignty, hence some lands were deemed to have no ownership and title and were therefore free to be occupied and colonized.

**Treaty of Waitangi**: Sacred compact entered into between the British Crown and

Maori rangatira (chiefs) in 1840 to allow for British immigration but also the retention of Maori chieftainship, ownership and control over their lands, forests, fisheries, and other treasures, while at the same time guaranteeing Maori the rights of British citizenship.

**Urupa**: Burial grounds, cemetery.

**Utu**: Reciprocity and beyond, increasing good actions for good and bad actions for bad.

**Waikato**: The northern and central tribe of the Tainui confederation whose lands were confiscated following the Waikato wars in the early 1860s.

**Whanau**: Family.

**WRSC(A)**: Waikato Raupatu Claims Settlement (Act), which enacted the first contemporary treaty of Waitangi land settlement in New Zealand for addressing the historic land confiscations grievance between the British Crown and the Maori of Waikato-Tainui.

. . . .

*Published in* Justice as Healing *(2001) 6:3, Mr. Joseph presented this article to the Native Law Centre, University of Saskatchewan on 17 August 2001. We are grateful to Mr. Joseph for his permission to reprint it.*

· · · ·

# Shape-Shifting Systems

30

## Thinking about Change

*Patricia Monture-Angus*

In 1967, Canada began to recognize that Aboriginal people are drastically overrepresented in the criminal justice system. This overrepresentation did not begin in 1967; it was just finally noticed then by authorities in Canada. The relationship between Aboriginal people and Canadian criminal law sanction is in actuality a historic one. A wing of Stoney Mountain Penitentiary was built to house the "rebels" of the "Métis Uprising" of 1885. The trials of Big Bear and Poundmaker are also notable. In 1897, five people from my partner's community, the Thunderchild First Nation here in Saskatchewan, were convicted of dancing offenses contrary to the Indian Act. The relationship between Aboriginal Peoples and Canadian justice is as old as the country.

Since the 1967 "discovery" of Aboriginal overrepresentation in the Canadian criminal justice system, Canadian governments (federal, territorial, and provincial) have compiled more than twenty major justice reports. Yet despite exhaustive study and numerous recommendations for reform, recent statistics demonstrate that the problem has not been solved. In fact, it continues to increase steadily every year. Moreover, according to a number of reports, the overrepresentation of Aboriginal youth in the justice system is now even greater than the adult rate of incarceration. This provides a clear warning that Aboriginal rates of overrepresentation will continue to increase in the immediate future as offenders "graduate" from youth facilities to provincial institutions to federal prisons.

The well-documented fact of Aboriginal overrepresentation within Canadian criminal justice leads to some dramatic conclusions: Aboriginal offenders are the commodities on which Canada's justice system relies. If all Aboriginal offenders were released from custody tomorrow, prisons would be empty and forced to close. Justice personnel, from parole officers to correctional workers to police officers, would be laid off. The grave majority of any such fantasized layoffs would not affect employment in the Aboriginal community. As dramatic as the figures are of overrepresentation of Aboriginal people as clients in the criminal justice system, the underrepresentation of Aboriginal people as employees within any component of the justice system is equally notable.

An important realization must follow. Aboriginal people cannot respect a justice system that ensures that the resources flow out of our communities. Our men (fathers, sons, uncles, and nephews) are taken from us. At the same time, the money paid in fines or to hire lawyers supports a system that is foreign to us. And the jobs created by the loss of our men to jails are rarely available to Aboriginal people, nor do many Aboriginal people want such jobs. Many Aboriginal people refuse to work in a system that they view as manifestly unjust. It is obvious that Aboriginal people cannot (and should not) respect a system of criminal law that oppresses us under a pretense of justice and fairness.

As many of the numerous justice reports recognize, reforms to the existing justice system have not significantly changed the Aboriginal over- or underrepresentation in the justice system. In December 1991, the Law Reform Commission of Canada noted that the energy to reform the experience of Aboriginal people in the justice system must be directed in two ways. Clearly, reforms to the existing criminal justice system must occur. These reforms will focus on "accommodating" Aboriginal culture, experience, and tradition within the existing justice system. Whether we like it or not, that system has custody over many of the citizens of our nations, and we must not forget them. At the same time, an equal amount of Aboriginal energy must be devoted to the re-creation of Aboriginal justice systems.

The re-creation of "Aboriginal justice systems" (and since they were never formal systems in the way that we know justice systems today, I hesitate to use this phrase) is an idea that must be left with the people of Aboriginal communities. The state has only one job and that is to fully respect the dreams of Aboriginal Peoples. The state cannot interfere in the development of Aboriginal justice aspirations. It is going to be a difficult journey for both

Aboriginal communities and the Canadian state. Aboriginal communities must be allowed and encouraged to develop justice initiatives at their own pace in a way that is relevant to their communities. Justice in Aboriginal communities is an Aboriginal responsibility and must be fully respected as such. The wisdom does already exist in our communities to see our dreams fulfilled.

People in Aboriginal communities have always known that the Canadian criminal justice system does not reflect our desires or our ways of being. This knowledge is older than the 1967 Canadian recognition of our overrepresentation and the concern that this recognition has caused. Justice is a concept that does not easily translate into Aboriginal languages.

As the attention paid to Aboriginal justice dreams has increased, Aboriginal people have been determined to find ways of expressing our ideas and views in the English language. This is one of the reasons that "justice as healing" conversations have increased. Healing expresses Aboriginal views on justice more clearly and accurately than any legal or justice words. Even the word *justice* has a negative connotation, because the Canadian system of justice focuses on control, coercion, and punishment. These values are quite contrary to traditional teachings. Healing more accurately describes a process that will return us to the place where we can recover Aboriginal methods of social control and social order. These methods are very much family based.

The healing focus is important for another fundamental reason. In negotiations with federal and provincial justice officials, Aboriginal desires in the justice system are becoming increasingly frustrated. Two roadblocks are erected around Aboriginal dreams: jurisdiction and fiscal restraint. Fiscal restraint requires little explanation; everyone understands that Canada faces a debt crisis.

However, the "fiscal restraint" excuse infuriates me. Just as Aboriginal people are standing up and reclaiming our rightful places in society, Canada runs out of money to assist us in reaching our potential. Canada has fully benefited from the resource base that belonged solely to Aboriginal Peoples. Canada has not taken either their treaty responsibilities or their caretaking role of this land very seriously. If Canada is bankrupt, it is not Aboriginal Peoples' responsibility. Canada's fiscal difficulties do not end their treaty responsibilities. Yet, the fiscal restraint argument requires Aboriginal people to accept that responsibility. Fiscal restraint is a 1990s phenomenon that is built on racist thinking.

Jurisdiction issues, which form the second roadblock, are not always as well understood. Government officials still have a difficult time accepting that Aboriginal people have an inherent right to govern our own affairs and that this right includes "criminal" justice. *Jurisdiction* is a legal word that means "the power or authority to act." Jurisdictional roadblocks indicate a fear on the part of Canadian officials to move toward different solutions to problems of crime and order.

Unfortunately, Aboriginal people often feel trapped by the provincial, territorial, and federal governments' ability to erect these two barricades. This is why I think healing is so important for us to talk about. Money can help us heal by providing treatment programs. However, these programs have not proved completely successful. Healing does not require money. Healing is really about being able to care for yourself, your family, and all your relations. This is why healing avoids the jurisdictional barricade as well: no one can stop us from caring!

Healing is also about taking responsibility. It is about relearning how we are supposed to be. If we do not know what our traditional responsibilities are, then the right to self-determination really means nothing. Healing is about learning to act in a good way.

There are, in fact, many areas that Aboriginal people need to heal. Foster care and residential schools have left deep wounds. Many women and children have been physically and sexually abused, as have some of our men. Some of us have accepted Indian Act rules. We need to heal from abuse, oppression, and colonization. In my mind, these things are more important than worrying about how we write down our rights in Canada's constitution.

Healing is the solution. Healing means that we are able to "turn off the tap." When we have healed, we will be able to stop our young people from running into conflicts with the law. We will also begin to understand how to accept back and forgive those individuals who are currently serving sentences in Canada's prisons. That is the biggest challenge ahead. Many of our people know how to do "time," and jail "junkies" like myself know how to get them out. What we still do not know is how to stop the revolving door of "justice" from recapturing them. We need to know how to keep our people out of institutions. Yet this step requires healing: healing our communities and healing our people by providing opportunities for healing to those who now fill Canada's criminal justice system.

. . . .

*This article was published in* Justice as Healing *(1995). We are grateful to Patricia Monture-Angus for permission to publish her work.*

# 31

# Sentencing within a Restorative Justice Paradigm: Procedural Implications of *R. v. Gladue*

*Judge M. E. Turpel-Lafond*

*Section 718.2 of the Criminal Code of Canada:*
*A court that imposes a sentence shall also take into consideration the following principles: (e) all available sanctions other than imprisonment that are reasonable in the circumstances should be considered for all offenders, with particular attention to the circumstances of Aboriginal offenders.*

## 1. Introduction

The Supreme Court of Canada's decision in *R. v. Gladue*[1] clarified the duty of sentencing judges to consider background and systemic factors in sentencing Aboriginal offenders. In this appeal, the Court had to consider the appropriate interpretation of section 718.2(e) of the Criminal Code where an Aboriginal woman, Marie Gladue, pleaded guilty to manslaughter in the death of her common-law husband. The offense took place in the town of Nanaimo, British Columbia. Ms. Gladue was one of nine children of a Cree mother and Métis father, born in McLennan, Alberta. She had been living with the deceased, Reuben Beaver, since she was seventeen years old. They had one daughter, with another child on the way when he was killed. The relationship included a history of physical and alcohol abuse. The night he died, the two had been drinking and fighting over whether the deceased was having an affair with the accused's sister. Mr. Beaver was fatally stabbed in the heart.

Ms. Gladue was sentenced to three years imprisonment along with a ten-year weapons prohibition order. She appealed her sentence, based in part on the trial judge's ruling that section 718.2(e) did not apply to her; she was "not within the Aboriginal community as such" because she was living in Nanaimo when the offense occurred. The British Columbia Court of Appeal found that the trial judge's decision was in error, however, as section 718.2(e) applies to Aboriginal people wherever they live. Nevertheless, the court of appeal upheld the trial judge's sentence, as Ms. Gladue had been granted day parole after six months of her sentence and was thought to be living in the community with appropriate supports. The Supreme Court of Canada also upheld the sentence, but provided detailed reasons on the operation of section 718.2(e) and the duty of sentencing judges to find alternatives to incarceration for Aboriginal defendants.

The *Gladue* decision is an important turning point in Canadian criminal law. The Canadian Supreme Court's interpretation of section 718.2(e) of the Criminal Code clarified that this provision is remedial in nature and not merely a codification of existing law and practice. In so interpreting the provision, the Court clearly endorsed the notion of restorative justice and a method of sentencing that emphasizes "healing." Healing is an Aboriginal justice principle that is slowly becoming merged into Canadian criminal law through the practice of circle sentencing and community-based diversion programs. The *Gladue* decision has brought the notion of healing into the mainstream as a principle that a judge must weigh in every case of an Aboriginal person, in order to build a bridge between his or her unique personal and community background experiences and criminal justice.

The Supreme Court of Canada has acknowledged that the legacy of discrimination Aboriginal Peoples face in Canada is one of the reasons they are overrepresented in the system, and, consequently, the courts must address this in sentencing. Quite apart from the unique circumstances of Aboriginal Peoples, the Supreme Court has criticized the overreliance on incarceration for all citizens in Canada. The recognition of the disproportionate representation of Aboriginal people in the criminal justice system builds on a number of recent decisions relating to criminal justice and Aboriginal Peoples. For example, *R. v. Williams* opened the door for juror challenges based on cultural or racial bias whenever there was a demonstrated potential of partiality.[2]

Other decisions at the provincial appeal level, such as *R. v. Morin*,[3] have endorsed the restorative approach for sentencing or healing circles. The implementation of the reasoning and the régime contemplated in the *Gladue* decision provide all criminal trial courts and the appeal courts with challenges and opportunities. The decision in *Gladue* explicitly builds on more than a decade of intense scrutiny of the criminal justice system and its impact on Aboriginal Peoples in Canada. Specifically, the Royal Commission on Aboriginal Peoples, the Law Reform Commission of Canada, and the Manitoba Aboriginal Justice Inquiry have each thoroughly analyzed the situation.[4]

The concise decision of Justices Cory and Iacobucci, written for a unanimous Supreme Court of Canada, includes much that is innovative. However, given the criticism over judge-made law, it is important to remember that the notion of alternatives to incarceration for Aboriginal Peoples is not the work of the Supreme Court but a parliamentary proposal that was added to the Criminal Code in 1996. Since that time, there have been various interpretations of the sentencing amendments. Some courts of appeal deem these amendments to be mere codifications of pre-1996 law, while others view them as a departure from the past. It was my own experience that, while section 718.2(e) was part of the criminal law for a number of years, it was rarely, if ever, relied upon by sentencing judges or, more important, by counsel.

With the decision of the Supreme Court in *Gladue*, this has irrevocably changed. Indeed, the criminal bar and bench are in the midst of a transition that involves grappling with the impact of the decision on a daily basis. Certainly in the Prairie provinces, the impact of *Gladue* on the administration of justice was immediate. The impact is national in scale and may in the long run transform the practice of criminal law.

This brief commentary will address procedural effects of the *Gladue* decision. The procedural effects are of immediate concern, as experience suggests many do not understand the approach to Aboriginal offenders required by *Gladue*. Moreover, it is important that counsel, both Crown and defense, take the initiative to adjust their practice to meet the requirements of the decision. For example, simply citing the decision and suggesting to a court that it should consider "the *Gladue* factors" is not acceptable. How, then, should counsel approach this decision and, similarly, what are the duties of the sentencing judge? I will examine each of these questions in turn and leave aside the more fundamental policy issues for future analysis.

## 2. Practice Implications for Counsel

The Supreme Court of Canada's decision requires the sentencing judge to consider the unique circumstances for Aboriginal offenders in all cases. A sentencing judge can be relieved of this responsibility only if counsel and the supporting agencies in the criminal justice system, such as probation and youth services, assist the court by providing a full picture of the circumstances of the defendant and the offense. The *Gladue* decision highlighted the responsibility of the judge and described it as follows:

> There is no discretion as to whether to consider the unique situation of the Aboriginal offender; the only discretion concerns the determination of a just and appropriate sentence. . . . In all instances it will be necessary for the judge to take judicial notice of the systemic or background factors and the approach to sentencing which is relevant to Aboriginal offenders. However, for each particular offence and offender, it may be that some evidence will be required in order to assist the sentencing judge in arriving at a fit sentence. Where a particular offender does not wish such evidence to be adduced, the right to have particular attention paid to his or her circumstances as an Aboriginal offender may be waived. Where there is no such waiver, it will be extremely helpful to the sentencing judge for counsel on both sides to adduce relevant evidence. Indeed, it is to be expected that counsel will fulfil their role and assist the sentencing judge in this way.[5]

Judges need to make informed decisions, drawing on information that might not normally be before the court. The role of counsel is vital and should be seen as a kind of two-step approach. First, the defense counsel needs to bring personal information about the defendant to the attention of the court. Second, the Crown will need to assist in identifying alternatives to incarceration, in some instances with the collaboration of defense counsel, so that the court understands the options. Unless defense counsel, or the individual defendant, waives this inquiry, this information will be required in all cases involving Aboriginal people.

Clearly, *Gladue* has created additional burdens on counsel. Mr. Justice Klebuc of the Saskatchewan Court of Queen's Bench adjourned a sentencing matter for several months so counsel could do their job and collect the information he required to make a sentencing decision for an Aboriginal defendant.[6] In adjourning the matter, Justice Klebuc made it quite clear that counsel is expected to do more "if we are to honor the direction of the

Supreme Court of Canada."[7] While he recognized that counsel will have to work harder, he noted that the "court can only move as fast and as far as Crown counsel and defense counsel enable it to."[8] Justice Klebuc's sentiments are undoubtedly shared by many on the bench. The work of counsel is a large part of the practical implementation of *Gladue*.

Of course, if a defendant is unrepresented, the sentencing judge takes on most of the burden. The judge must question the defendant to determine personal circumstances. This kind of information would most likely be better gleaned by counsel, since a defendant might be very guarded in the formal context of judicial questioning. Judges will appreciate the assistance of counsel, where available, so that the disposition can fully reflect the concerns of Parliament and the Supreme Court of Canada regarding the incarceration of Aboriginal people.

One of the challenges for both counsel and the judiciary will be to encourage Aboriginal people to open up to them about their experiences. The history of mistrust that has marked the relationships between Aboriginal and non-Aboriginal people in the criminal justice system makes many Aboriginal people reluctant to share experiences. Furthermore, many Aboriginal people who have experienced racism, poverty, discrimination, addictions, and family breakdown may not be at a point in their lives where they are willing to identify these issues, much less discuss them with strangers.

This will be a significant hurdle in implementing the Supreme Court of Canada's directive. It will improve with time, but initially, many defendants may waive the inquiry, so as to maintain their privacy out of mistrust. They will wonder, "Why are they asking me this information? Will it be used against me?" Strong communication skills and understanding on the part of counsel and the judiciary will be vital to open up the exploration of background experiences.

The following is a simple checklist of the types of inquiries that should be made by counsel—or the judge where the individual is unrepresented—when dealing with an Aboriginal defendant who faces incarceration:

### i) Is this offender an Aboriginal person?

Aboriginal person is defined according to section 35 of the Constitution Act, 1982, as being Indian, Métis (of mixed ancestry), or Inuit:

- If the answer is yes, determine what community or band the defendant is from.
- Does the defendant reside in a rural area, on a reserve, or in an urban center?

## ii) *What unique circumstances have played a part in bringing this offender before the courts?*

The sentencing judge *must* consider some of the following issues and factors and pose the following questions to counsel or unrepresented offenders:[9]

- Has this offender been affected by substance abuse in the community?
- Has this offender been affected by poverty?
- Has this offender been affected by overt racism?
- Has this offender been affected by family or community breakdown?
- Has this offender been affected by unemployment, low income, and a lack of employment opportunity?
- Has this offender been affected by dislocation from an Aboriginal community, loneliness, and community fragmentation?
- Has the offender been affected by residential school education?

A presentence or predisposition report might be of great benefit to the court in examining some of these issues. To sensibly ask these questions, it is helpful if counsel, or the judge as the case may be, understands the historical and societal context of these questions. For example, has a community been relocated? Has a significant proportion of the Aboriginal community moved to urban centers? What are the reasons for these developments? Many of these issues have been thoroughly studied by the Royal Commission on Aboriginal Peoples, the reports from which are valuable educational resources for those unfamiliar with the broader context.

It is critical that all parties remember that this kind of inquiry is not necessary in all circumstances but is imperative when the sentence would normally be one of incarceration. In terms of alternatives to incarceration, counsel can greatly help the court determine whether there are alternatives in the community, and whether or not the defendant would benefit, in a restorative justice sense, by participating in such alternative programming.

Counsel will need to learn about the Aboriginal community, including in the urban context, available to address the underlying problems that Aboriginal people face. In many instances, it may be that counsel will report to the court that there are no alternatives, leaving the judge to determine whether the term should be adjusted nevertheless.

Again, a simple checklist of how this information should be brought before the court might assist counsel in preparing submissions following *Gladue*:

**A. Requesting judicial notice of the systemic and background factors.** Lawyers can request judges to consider the systemic and background factors that have led to Aboriginal people being disproportionately represented before the criminal courts and in the prison system. As the Court found, systemic and background factors do help explain the incidence of crime and recidivism for non-Aboriginal offenders as well. However, the circumstances of Aboriginal offenders differ from those of the majority, because many Aboriginal people are victims of systemic and direct discrimination, many suffer the legacy of dislocation, and many are substantially affected by poor social and economic conditions. Moreover, as studies and commission reports have repeatedly emphasized, these unique systemic and background factors cause Aboriginal offenders to be more adversely affected by incarceration and less likely to be "rehabilitated" by it. Not only is the internment environment often culturally inappropriate, but also discrimination toward Aboriginal offenders is regrettably rampant in penal institutions.[10]

**B. Addressing restorative justice in sentencing submissions.** Lawyers will need to address the concept of *restorative justice* in their sentencing submissions and explain how this is relevant to the particular Aboriginal offender. Restorative justice "will necessarily have to be developed over time in the jurisprudence, as different issues and different conceptions of sentencing are addressed in their appropriate context." However, restorative justice means a philosophy of personal and community healing and "an approach to remedying crime in which it is understood that all things are interrelated and that crime disrupts the harmony which existed prior to its occurrence, or at least which it is felt should exist. The appropriateness of a particular sanction is largely determined by the needs of the victims and the community, as well as the offender. The focus is on the human beings closely affected by the crime."[11]

*C. Identifying alternatives to incarceration.* Lawyers should know what alternatives to incarceration are available in the community (or elsewhere) and should remind sentencing judges of these alternatives, especially those that are consistent with restorative justice. Lawyers should ensure that these alternatives are explored for Aboriginal offenders "wherever they reside, whether on- or off-reserve, in a large city or a rural area."[12]

The Supreme Court of Canada noted that Aboriginal people living in urban centers, even with a fragmented connection to the community, must be afforded the same restorative justice approach. This will be the greatest challenge, as judges do not always know what resources are available in a community and whether they would be appropriate for an individual offender. Judges will want to know if an Aboriginal community or urban center has alternative programs and if they are accessible through a probation order or conditional sentence of imprisonment.

The Supreme Court of Canada found that "even if community support is not available, every effort should be made in appropriate circumstances to find a sensitive and helpful alternative."[13] Further, "the residence of an Aboriginal offender in an urban center that lacks any network of support does not relieve the sentencing judge of the obligation to find an alternative. . . ."[14]

*D. Seeking reductions in the duration of imprisonment.* Even if there is no alternative to incarceration, lawyers should offer submissions on the length of the imprisonment in view of the background circumstances of an Aboriginal offender. The term of imprisonment for an Aboriginal offender may be less than the term imposed on a non-Aboriginal offender for the same offense. The Supreme Court of Canada said, "Generally, the more violent and serious the offence, the more likely it is as a practical reality that the terms of imprisonment for Aboriginals and non-Aboriginals will be close to each other or the same, even taking into account their different concepts of sentencing."[15] The sentencing judge will want to know background factors in fixing the length of sentence when imposing a sentence of incarceration.

*E. Presenting all the factors that may be relevant to healing.* Ultimately, in determining what is a fit sentence, the sentencing judge will make a holistic determination. Counsel should not forget this and should review all relevant sentencing information and material with the court. This includes considering the factors listed above and also exploring the understanding of criminal sanctions held by the offender and his or her community. "Would imprisonment effectively serve to deter or denounce this offender . . . , or are crime prevention and other goals best achieved through healing?"[16] What might be required for healing? This information is important in the sentencing process and will present some new challenges for everyone in sentencing.

*F. Addressing the need to balance public safety with the crisis of over-incarceration of Aboriginal Peoples.* Counsel will need to tailor their submissions to sentencing judges, so that they can fulfill their duty "to craft sentences in a manner [that] is meaningful to Aboriginal peoples."[17] Defense lawyers will need to understand what is meaningful to a client and convey this to the court. Although imprisonment is intended to serve the "traditional sentencing goals of separation, deterrence, denunciation, and rehabilitation, there is widespread consensus that imprisonment has not been successful in achieving some of these goals."[18] Prosecutors will need to identify how to balance public safety concerns with what the Supreme Court has called a "crisis in the criminal justice system" because of the over-incarceration of Aboriginal Peoples.

The impact of *Gladue* on counsel as a matter of criminal practice is considerable. Not only will there be additional burdens on counsel, as in the case of legal aid, but there will likely be a need for greater resources to fulfill their obligations to the court. Continuing education on the implications of the decision will be helpful. There will be a myriad of scenarios where the application of the reasoning in *Gladue* will be controversial. This will entail legal argument and more detailed sentencing submissions.

For example, consider when there are two parties to an offense: one is an Aboriginal person, the other is not. For consistency, it would be difficult to sentence one offender to incarceration and the other to a community disposition. However, these kinds of cases will need to be worked out on an individual basis with full consideration of their unique circumstances. The Supreme Court of Canada has interpreted the provision, section 718.2(e), in such a fashion as to enunciate a series of facts and policy objectives that underpin the provision, while leaving broad flexibility to judges to find the appropriate dispositions.

## 3. Impact on the Judiciary

The potential impact of the *Gladue* decision on the judiciary is arguably profound. The Supreme Court of Canada has clarified that Parliament's decision to add section 718.2(e) to the Criminal Code means that one must, as a matter of criminal law, recognize that Aboriginal people experience incarceration differently from others. While some might suggest that an Aboriginal person who receives the same sentence as a non-Aboriginal person is being treated equally, the Supreme Court of Canada has rejected this argument as fallacious reasoning. Sometimes treating different people in the same way creates inequality. Justices Cory and Iacobucci considered the argument that this treatment of Aboriginal Peoples is "reverse discrimination" against non-Aboriginal people.[19] They concluded that section 718.2(e) is not unfair to non-Aboriginal people; it simply requires judges to treat Aboriginal people fairly by taking into account their difference.

This decision will affect the judiciary in at least three fundamental ways. First, judges will need to be educated regarding Aboriginal Peoples in Canada, including Aboriginal Peoples' history, culture, and experiences of discrimination. Second, judges will need to spend more time on the sentencing process to ensure that all information is before the court that is required to evaluate a more restorative approach to the defendant and the community. Third, judicial independence will be vital in fulfilling this function, since individual judges and the judiciary may be subjected to considerable criticism and public attack for applying the *Gladue* principles in individual cases. Each of these three areas is important, and the judiciary will experience a period of transition.

The first issue regarding judicial education is probably the most significant. While "social context" education for judges has been an important feature in training judges, it has not been as consistent or as sophisticated as it needs to be to provide a fuller understanding of the situation. For example, social-context education has not always involved representatives of the Aboriginal Peoples from the regions in which the judges sit. Furthermore, judicial education is but one component of a wider education project regarding Aboriginal Peoples.

Legal education for lawyers is another important feature. The experiences of Aboriginal Peoples in the criminal justice system and the society at large should be emphasized in the university context. For example, without proper instruction, judges might not know how to ask defendants about their background and personal circumstances. Worse, they might ask for the information in a fashion that closes down the discussion, instead of opening it up. Once a judge has a narration of the personal circumstances, what does the judge do with this information, not only in terms of fashioning a sentence, but also in terms of speaking to the defendant and the broader community about its meaning? This requires a substantial degree of understanding and education outside the individual case.

For example, when I first became a judge, I was observing a colleague in youth court as part of my training. In providing reasons for disposition to a young Aboriginal person, the judge suggested that a contributing factor could be that the young person had been raised by his grandparents and not his birth parents and that this would have had a negative impact on his early childhood. After the proceeding, I explained to my colleague that for Aboriginal people, at least in my experience as Nehiyaw (Cree), being raised by one's grandparents was a special gift. Perhaps the better way to appeal to children raised by grandparents would be to explain how they are bringing shame on their grandparents by acting as they did. They were privileged to be raised by their grandparents, and they of all people should know better. While this is a small point, it illustrates how useful it is to understand Aboriginal Peoples' culture and values in order to communicate in a manner that is meaningful to the defendant.

The second issue raised by *Gladue* is the increased time required for sentencing: to take into account all the *Gladue* considerations, judges will need to spend more time in sentencing Aboriginal Peoples. This is a remark I've heard quite often since the decision, and my own experience would suggest it is true. In a busy court context, such as the situation for the Provincial Court in Saskatchewan, the additional time required to address sentencing for Aboriginal Peoples after the Supreme Court of Canada's decision will mean delays in other matters. There will soon be a need for greater resources in order to fulfill this task. It will also require patience and attention to the importance of the sentencing process.

In many ways, this shift might be long overdue and may prove to benefit the system for all defendants. We will take more time to sentence, as we should, given how significant a moment sentencing is in the criminal justice system for both defendants and victims, not to mention the broader community. One significant impact, then, is that resources will be required in the community for alternative programming, if the *Gladue* decision is to be implemented as imagined by the Court.

While the reasoning in *Gladue* is directed at sentencing, it is clearly applicable to other areas, such as breaches of conditional sentences,[20] "show cause" hearings, and parole reviews. One early concern was the application of the reasoning to the proceedings of the youth court under the *Young Offenders Act*. This was argued in Saskatchewan in the case of *R. v. A.J. & A.J.*,[21] where it was held that, while the specific provision of the Criminal Code, section 718.2(e), is not applicable to young offenders, the reasoning in the decision is applicable in terms of finding more restorative approaches to dispositions for young people. The reasoning in the *Gladue* decision is not narrowly confined to one specific component of the administration of justice or criminal procedure. It is broad and of vast significance. Presumably, it will be introduced in a variety of contexts in the future with interesting results. It would be difficult to confine a notion like "healing" to only one component of the criminal justice system—that is, initial sentencing for adults—and not to extend it beyond this to reviews of those sentences and to young people.

## 4. Impact on Aboriginal Communities

We should also consider the potential impact of the *Gladue* decision on Aboriginal communities. These communities are diverse, culturally and geographically, although they have been working toward community healing and development for some time. While the decision was greeted positively by representatives of the Aboriginal community, such as those attending a Canadian Bar Association–Indigenous Bar Association symposium on Aboriginal justice in Toronto in April 1999, the practical implications may raise some troubling problems.

For example, if judges are sentencing to community dispositions, drawing on resources in the Aboriginal community, how heavily will this tax the limited resources of the community? While the financial resources dedicated to incarceration are significant on a per capita basis, will there be an investment in the Aboriginal community to meet the growing demand for community support, supervision, and healing resources?

This is the crux of the matter from a practical perspective. The restorative turn in criminal justice might be only imaginary unless Aboriginal communities are able to engage in healing processes with support from the broader society. While personal counseling to address addictions, family distress, and the ongoing effects of residential school education are vital to healing, so too are measures to eliminate or reduce poverty and other causes of crime. My point is that restorative justice, fully envisioned, is not something that is passed to the Aboriginal community, who are directed to "fix" a problem on their own, especially if they do not have the basic tools to do so.

The sentencing practices that emerge from applying the *Gladue* decision will also interact with strong concerns in the Aboriginal community, particularly from women, that the needs of victims should not be disregarded in the healing enterprise. In considering alternatives to incarceration, the court will have to weigh whether the victim's interests are properly protected by a non-custodial sentence. This will be a strong consideration in remote communities where the victim will be living near the offender.

As it is understood in the Aboriginal community, the restorative notion of justice is not a notion that excludes victims' concerns. To the contrary, the notion is rooted in the healing of the rift and the restoration, if possible, of all those touched by the wrongdoing. This side of the equation cannot be ignored in sentencing after *Gladue*. In *R. v. J.E.A.*, the British Columbia Court of Appeal used the background factors identified in *Gladue* to reduce an Aboriginal defendant's sentence from life imprisonment for robbery and sexual assault to twenty years imprisonment.[22] They did not reduce it further, even though the defendant had a horrific set of background and personal experiences, because of concern for public safety and the experiences of the victims.

## 5. Future Challenges

As a judge in a criminal trial court in Saskatchewan that deals predominately with Aboriginal people, one often feels like Anthony Trollope's Harry Heathcote, constantly rushing about the territory trying to keep the fires abated with no control over the weather causing the hazard. The tendency is to view the problems Aboriginal Peoples experience as those of someone else's making and to view oneself as disposed to limited tools to contain the situation.

However, a more balanced view would be to see that criminal law is a critical site for mediating conflict between Aboriginal people and non-Aboriginal people in our society. Lawyers and judges working in criminal law will benefit from understanding their mediating function beyond the circumstances of any individual case. This might seem unusual, as judges tend to view the task as highly individuated. Nevertheless, the structural circumstances of Aboriginal Peoples' entanglements with the criminal justice system will help us view our position in its full context. The task of the court and the judge is to dispense justice, mindful that justice, being a human enterprise, is hardly mechanistic.

This approach assumes a more nuanced interpretation of the rule of law than has historically been the norm. For some, this would be a welcome departure, as it potentially embraces the legal pluralism that is the basis of Canada law and holds promise for a more inclusive criminal justice system. For others, it might be vigorously challenged as a departure from the formal equality of the pre-*Charter* era.

As a barometer of Canadian law, the *Gladue* decision certainly registers as a vital departure point. Applying the reasoning in *Gladue* requires a strong understanding both of how structural factors impact individual cases and of how individual experiences reflect broader historical and community events. Perhaps this is no more than the history of the common law with its dialectic of stability and change. Nevertheless, reasoning that weighs both structural considerations and specific contexts is vital to criminal justice. It is a form of reasoning that does not always sit well with the judiciary, ingrained as we are with particularizing decision-making. Nevertheless, *Gladue* is a reminder that highly particularized decisions, without regard for broader structural and historical factors, might lead to injustice.

The *Gladue* transition period will continue for some time as various courts across the land consider numerous matters in a new light. It is clear that society expects us to carefully consider the experiences of Aboriginal Peoples and to find creative responses that are appropriate to unique circumstances. The reasoning in this watershed decision will resonate throughout the criminal justice system and will spill over into the correctional institutions and youth justice system. For judges, the defendant's personal factors will need to be weighed differently in the sentencing equation. However, the exercise is still one of careful balancing and of considering the needs of the community and society in crafting a sentence that is just for all.

## Notes

1. *R. v. Gladue* (1999) 23 C.C.R. (5th) 197.

2. *R. v. Williams* [1999] 4 W.W.R. 711 (Supreme Court of Canada). Also the decision of the Saskatchewan Court of Queen's Bench, J. Barclay, in *R. v. Fleury*, [1998] 3 C.N.L.R. 160.

3. See the evaluation of this jurisprudence in D. Kwochka, "Aboriginal Injustice: Making Room for a Restorative Justice Paradigm," 60 (1996), *Sask. L. Rev.* 153.

4. The impact of the work of the Royal Commission on Aboriginal Peoples is especially evident in the decision. This commission is having a broad influence on judicial decision-making. For an analysis of this, see D. Stack, "The Impact of RCAP on the Judiciary: Bringing Aboriginal Perspectives into the Courtroom," 62 (1999) *Sask. L. Rev.* 471.

5. Ibid., para. 82–83, 227.

6. *R. v. Carratt,* unreported decision of 21 May 1999, Saskatoon.

7. Ibid., 9, lines 22–23.

8. Ibid., 10, lines 22–24.

9. Ibid., 222 and 226, para. 67 and 80.

10. Ibid., 222, para. 69.

11. Ibid., 223, para. 71.

12. Ibid., 230, para. 91.

13. Ibid., 230, para. 92.

14. Ibid., 231, para. 93.

15. Ibid., 226, para. 79.

16. Ibid., 226, para. 80.

17. Ibid., 225, para. 77.

18. Ibid., 218, para. 57.

19. Ibid., 228–29, paras. 86–88.

20. See the decision of Judge Whelan of the Saskatchewan Provincial Court in *R. v. R.J. Stewart,* 11 June 1999, which concerned a breach of a conditional sentence and applied the *Gladue* principles to that disposition. Judge Whelan held: "I conclude without hesitation that the principles discussed in *R. v. Gladue* continue to have application in a s.742.6 hearing. In arriving at the appropriate decision . . . I must consider the unique systemic or background factors which may have played a part in bringing Mr. Stewart, an Aboriginal offender, before the court. . . ." para. 20.

21. Unreported decision of Youth Court, 14 May 1999 (J. Lafond). This decision addressed whether or not *Gladue* applies to young persons, given section 20 (8) of the Young Offenders Act, which exempts Part XXIII of the Criminal Code. In this matter, it was held that, while section 718.2(e) does not technically apply to young

people, the reasoning in *Gladue* regarding systemic discrimination and alternatives to incarceration is incorporated through section 3 of the Young Offenders Act.

22. *R. v. J.E.A.*, British Columbia Court of Appeal, 15 July 1999 (J. A. Ryan for the Court).

. . . .

*Published in* Justice as Healing (1999) 4:3, *this paper was presented at the conference of the Canadian Institute for the Administration of Justice (CIAJ): "Changing Punishment at the Turn of the Century," in Saskatoon, Saskatchewan on 26–29 September 1999. It is also published in the* Criminal Law Quarterly, 1999. *We are grateful to Judge Turpel-Lafond for permission to publish her work.*

# 32

# Restorative Justice and the Youth Criminal Justice Act

## *Judge Bria Huculak*

In 1995, I wrote an article for *Justice as Healing* called "From the Power to Punish to the Power to Heal." As one of the judges who initiated circles in 1992, I wrote the article during a time when enthusiasm was high. In Saskatchewan, sentencing circles were peaking, with large numbers of circles taking place. These circles were primarily for serious offenses. Since that time, the use of circles has diminished.

There are numerous reasons for this, including lack of resources. At the same time, many initiatives involving a restorative justice framework have developed. Canada has many examples of successful restorative justice programs for youth and adults. However, these primarily deal with less serious diversion cases. Despite the *Gladue* [1999] 1 S.C.R. 207 decision and the amendments to the 1996 Criminal Code, both of which recognized restorative approaches, the impact has not been significant. Incarceration in Canada remains very high, particularly for Aboriginal people.

The Youth Criminal Justice Act, which came into force on 1 April 2003, offers a new opportunity to revisit restorative justice principles and processes. Our challenge is to move restorative justice from the margins to the center of how we do justice in Canada. The Youth Criminal Justice Act offers hope and an opportunity to change our response to crime. Whether this happens depends on a number of factors, such as community involvement, resources, and genuine will.

## Restorative Justice and Conferences

The new act provides a mechanism to respond to crime in a constructive, healing way. Many of the principles of section 3 of the Youth Criminal Justice Act are consistent with restorative justice principles, in particular holding the offender accountable through meaningful measures, instilling respect for societal values, repairing the harm to victims and the community, seeking the participation of victim, youth, families, and community in the process, focusing on reintegration and rehabilitation, respecting differences, and supporting youth.

Additionally, the measures address the needs of victims, which include treating victims with respect, compassion, and courtesy and providing them with information. Victims should be given the opportunity to participate and be heard. The measures also encourage parental support for addressing offending behavior. In these ways, the principles affirm the restorative justice focus on reintegration and rehabilitation as well as on repairing harm.

Canada leads the world in incarcerating young persons for crime, and Saskatchewan has a history of lengthy incarceration. These sentences are largely for property and system-related offenses.

The act aims to address the high rate of incarceration of youth for nonviolent offenses. Conferencing offers a way to incorporate restorative justice theory and practice. Both restorative justice and the Youth Criminal Justice Act (YCJA) seek to prevent crime and to repair the harm. It is critical that we respond to the needs of Aboriginal youth and address the overrepresentation of youth in custody. Restorative justice processes are an important way to do this. Currently, the majority of those incarcerated (80 percent) are for nonviolent offenses.

The YCJA seeks to incorporate multidisciplinary and restorative justice approaches into the youth justice system. One of the primary methods for doing this is the conference. Section 2 of the Youth Criminal Justice Act defines a conference as "a group of persons who are convened to give advice in accordance with Section 19." The types of conferences contemplated include multidisciplinary or integrated case management conferences, family group conferences, community and neighborhood accountability panels or youth justice committees, victim-offender mediation/reconciliation, and Aboriginal sentencing/healing/peacemaking circles (as well as non-Aboriginal sentencing/healing/peacemaking circles).

Most conferencing models envision a restorative justice approach that includes victim participation. Restorative justice conferences do, in fact, imply direct victim involvement, but this will *not* apply to integrated case management conferences, support circles, sentence reviews, or conferences called concerning bail. Even in these instances, though, a restorative justice framework has a role. The mandate for a conference held in accordance with section 19 of the YCJA may be to give advice on, among other things, appropriate extrajudicial measures, conditions for judicial interim release, sentences, including the review of sentences, and reintegration plans.

Section 41 of the YCJA provides that, after a finding of guilt, the youth justice court "*may* convene or cause to be convened a conference" for sentencing recommendations. In other words, the court has the authority to order a conference. If a conference is ordered, section 41(2) requires the youth court to consider any recommendations that the conference makes before imposing a sentence.

This act corrects the failure of the 1996 amendments to the Criminal Code to refer to processes. The Youth Criminal Justice Act does not specifically refer to restorative justice, but it is implicit in the principles of the act. Processes require a theoretical underpinning and skills. A restorative justice framework situates the group's discussion and its advice, whether it be a case conference or a "restorative" conference that involves the victim. Applying core values such as respect, fairness, equality, empowerment, transformation, and care, among others, is as important to case-management conferences as it is to restorative conferences. Process skills incorporating mediation, negotiation, facilitation, and collaborative decision-making are also important to the conference's success.

## What Is Restorative Justice?

Restorative justice offers a philosophical and theoretical worldview for looking at crime and wrongdoing. The theoretical framework provides a way to organize how we think, feel, and see. The restorative justice theory guides our processes and actions, while also helping us understand the processes by clarifying the concepts, principles, and values on which they are based.

Restorative justice philosophy incorporates some core values and principles. It is a harm-centered and needs-centered approach to a criminal act, which is thought of as harm to "individuals, their property, their relationships, and their communities."[1] Restorative justice philosophy incorporates both theory and processes. It is inclusive and encourages the active participation of those who have a direct interest. Its process models include sentencing/peacemaking circles, conferencing, and victim-offender mediation. The models all hold the offender directly accountable to those harmed, but they also support the offender in rehabilitation and reintegration. Values such as accountability, open communication, caring, empathy, responsibility, fairness, respect, transformation, reparation/healing, and empowerment are key to the process. Moreover, restorative justice processes take into consideration the whole context of the crime.[2]

Research in Canada on restorative justice programs shows an overall high rate of satisfaction, particularly among victims.[3] Participation in restorative justice programs increased the likelihood of completing a restitution agreement,[4] while recidivism showed a reduction of 7 percent due to restorative justice interventions. Additionally, the Canadian public looks favorably on restorative justice.[5]

## The Restorative Circle Approach

The circle model provides an example of a restorative process. A circle approach to decision-making incorporates a nonadversarial, nonhierarchical model that can be very effective. The circle is a problem-solving, consensus-building approach. It creates a safe place for participants to express their thoughts and feelings fully and truthfully, which contributes to the circle's effectiveness. By encouraging respectful listening, the circle process recognizes that everyone has something valuable to contribute. Everyone has an equal opportunity to speak, to be heard, and to have an influence in the decision.

This face-to-face discussion encourages active listening and more effective communication. As participants listen more deeply, empathy (cognitive and emotional perspective-taking) develops, which is key to the process. Those involved learn what the other is thinking, seeing, and feeling. Their active listening builds empathy, which inspires support, both tangible and emotional, for those in need. Moreover, the fact that circles incorporate multiple and diverse perspectives adds to the value of their decisions.

Some barriers to participation need to be addressed. It is necessary, for example, to manage negative emotions like anger, shame, and embarrassment. Shame and embarrassment silence people and disconnect them, making it more difficult to share thoughts and feelings. Creating a safe, supportive environment for vulnerable people to participate is important, since people are more likely to talk about painful feelings when they feel supported.

Again, restorative justice is a harm-centered, needs-centered approach. Constructive, corrective criticism does not mean moralizing, attacking participants, or shaming others. Rather, the more participants can connect with others in a constructive way, the more they build a capacity to shift negative to positive feelings and attitudes. A restorative process like circles helps participants increase their expression of positive emotions, such as support, hope, and power, and this in turn inspires them to treat everyone with respect, care, and concern. Naturally, such shifts contribute to the process's success.

A restorative circle approach encourages direct accountability, helping those charged to take responsibility and make amends. However, a restorative circle approach also looks at the social, economic, and political underpinnings of crime. For example, the circle process calls on the community to support the young person during rehabilitation and reintegration. Recent data on Saskatoon youth in custody showed that the majority of youths were not in school. A restorative circle process that adopted the goal to keep kids in school could have a tangible benefit. Accordingly, to be fully effective, restorative processes need the resources to respond to issues like nonattendance in school, poverty, addictions, dysfunctional families, abuse, learning deficits, mental health problems, fetal alcohol syndrome, and fetal alcohol effect.

## Rehabilitation and Reintegration—Not Incarceration

In 1995, I argued that fundamental change is necessary in a justice system that has failed Aboriginal people. I stated that focusing on rehabilitation as opposed to punishment provided the best hope for protecting the public. My views in 1995 remain. Fundamental change is still needed. Using a restorative justice framework as well as confronting the social, economic, and political roots of crime can go a long way toward addressing the high rates of incarceration.

The Youth Criminal Justice Act acknowledges the value of the restorative justice approach. The act offers an opportunity and challenge to do justice differently. Making this happen requires the willingness to take a chance, make a commitment, and not let the enormous opportunity pass. Educating people about the value of restorative justice will help us embrace change with an open mind and will encourage judges and others in the justice system to use this valuable tool.

Shifting from the power to punish to the power to heal remains to be done. A justice that transforms, empowers, and heals—as opposed to simply punishing—is possible. The Youth Criminal Justice Act encourages us to continue to move toward this end.

*Notes*

1. Scott Harris, 2002.

2. Howard Zehr, *Changing Lenses: A New Focus for Crime and Justice* (Scottsdale, PA; Waterloo, Ont.: Herald Press, 1990); Van Ness, 2001.

3. Latimer, Dowden, and Muise, *The Effectiveness of Restorative Justice Practices: A Meta-Analysis* (Ottawa, Ont.: Department of Justice Canada, 2001).

4. Correctional Service of Canada, 2002.

5. Correctional Service of Canada, 2002, quoting Galaway 1994, reported in Shaw and Jone, 1998; Doob, 2000.

. . . .

*This article was published in* Justice as Healing *(2003) 8:1. We are grateful to Judge Bria Huculak for permission to publish her work.*

## Alter-Natives to Non-Violence Report: Aboriginal Youth Gangs Exploration— A Community Development Process

*Federation of Saskatchewan Indian Nations*

### Preface

The approach adopted by the Federation of Saskatchewan Indian Nations (FSIN) Alter-Natives to Non-Violence Initiative (hereafter called "the Initiative") is rooted in the understanding that behaviors are the observable symptoms of feelings and emotions that are sometimes hidden from our view. The negative behaviors of youth have been assigned recognizable labels that receive prepackaged responses from systems and adults. The processes that were developed to respond to the labeled behaviors do not necessarily address the underlying problems, which may be hidden within the lives and experiences of youth. Presently, it is our understanding that the police have adopted a system of labeling some Aboriginal youth as gang members. We are uncomfortable with this, because the process seems to be subjective, and the consequences are severe. At the same time, we understand the need to manage the larger, more formal adult gangs.

The Initiative has designed a distinct First Nations response to the issues of "youth gangs." Several times this position has been challenged by a very persuasive argument about the "need to identify the number of youth gang members." However, this need has lent false legitimacy to a police gang-surveillance practice that labels and catalogs Aboriginal youth as gang members. The practice promotes the wrongful beliefs that "youth gangs" are the problem and that simple criminal justice measures will solve them.

The Initiative is compelled to respond to this shallow analysis by offering an alternative view of the problem as youth disenfranchisement from family and society. This situation leads to troubled youths who find themselves living in poverty, exposed to multiple risk factors, and then labeled as belonging to "youth gangs." Youth gangs are only one of the many symptoms of the social crisis that Aboriginal youths experience in our neighborhoods and communities. The Initiative is determined to expose the underlying causes of youth at risk and to reevaluate the language that both shapes our views and then labels youths as members of "gangs."

For the purpose of this report, the term *Aboriginal* includes all people of First Nations ancestry.

## Report Limitations

The community consultation portion of this report was limited to six urban communities and surrounding First Nations, and approximately one day was allowed for consultation in each community. We took care to record the information, but we were not able to return and share the findings with each community. We spent large amounts of time searching for funding to support the Initiative, which took away from doing the actual consultation and community development. We met with law enforcement agencies at the beginning of the Initiative, but we could have spent more time in follow-up and further consultation. We have since learned more and have more questions.

We had excellent representation from individuals who worked in communities. We also attempted to analyze the literature, and more work is required in this area. We used our funding to develop and implement a community consultation process, provide gang-awareness workshops to communities, create educational materials, and organize the youth-gang awareness camp. Our examination focused on Aboriginal youth and gangs, although we realize that adults are involved in more organized gang structures.

## Executive Summary

- The term *gangs* carries inherent dangers, and the definition of gangs needs further analysis. Currently, gangs are understood to have organizational structures ranging from loosely organized small groups to highly organized large groups with specific rules and clear lines of authority. One definition of a gang adopted by the police is "a loosely organized group of individuals who gather together for criminal activity."[1] Gangs share a common collective identity through names, symbols, signs, turf, and reputation.

Motivations for joining a gang include finding a surrogate family, identifying with peers, gaining protection, and compensating for a lack of alternatives and money.

+ Young offender facilities, correctional centers, and federal institutions are breeding grounds for gang recruitment.

+ The positive qualities of gang structures and organization need to be further researched and analyzed to assist in work with gangs.

+ The glamorized image of gangs needs to be dispelled, and young people need to be informed of the dangerous realities of gang life.

+ The FSIN Alter-Natives to Non-Violence Initiative undertook consultations and organized youth and family gatherings during the summer of 2002. These gatherings brought communities, youth, and gang members together to receive community input and to document how communities are coping with the formation of gangs. Community representatives received support by having their experiences validated, and youth were encouraged to make positive choices through awareness workshops. The work of the Initiative requires ongoing community involvement. *This is not a gang-busting project; rather, the Alter-Natives to Non-Violence plan is a harm-reduction initiative.*

+ Gangs use intimidation and violence to control their members. One testimonial attests to their loyalties and violence. A young man received a beating by his father's gang in the presence of his father, who did nothing to stop the assault.[2]

+ Law-enforcement agencies view gangs from a criminal perspective; enforcement is their focus, rather than healing and restoration. First Nations have come to understand that the solution is to restore control and dignity to First Nations communities and to provide prevention, intervention, and healing programs to help divert youth away from gang activity.

+ Our discussions with both agencies and youths revealed the need for parents to be involved in the lives of youth where it is practical and safe for them to do so. The overarching message we received is that this problem requires a combined effort to develop strategies and to create an understanding of the nature and scope of Aboriginal youth and families in crisis.

+ On-reserve communities and urban centers need to own the gang issue locally, which includes participating in developing and carrying out solutions.
+ Governments must provide First Nations communities with resources to conduct research and to develop policies and programs.
+ Reducing Aboriginal youth gangs in Saskatchewan requires a joint response of First Nations, federal, provincial, and municipal governments, and community agencies.
+ Strong community action models must be created to address community, family, and youth needs. Communities must find a way to promote awareness about youth violence and specifically youth-gang-related activity. Gang awareness initiatives must also be counterbalanced with programs promoting positive youth achievements, cultural awareness, and self-esteem-building activities, like the Alter-Natives to Non-Violence cultural camp.
+ First Nations governments and communities are committed to youth and support the FSIN in taking a leading role in coordinating a provincial strategic response. FSIN will help communities by enhancing their capacity and knowledge base for working with families and youth at risk.
+ First Nations institutions and agencies must take the lead in developing programs for youth to maintain a healthy, balanced lifestyle.
+ First Nations leadership needs to make a long-term commitment to sustaining and raising youth awareness and consciousness around gang recruitment and the conditions that contribute to at-risk youth. The voices of our most vulnerable members need to be heard. These are the children being raised in violence and intergenerational gang affiliation.
+ The consultation process has allowed us to meet with over one hundred organizations and four hundred people in six communities in Saskatchewan.
+ Through the community consultations, we identified a lack of resources to adequately respond to the gang issue. This requires discussion with governments and First Nations. Perhaps there could be a First Nations foundation created, which would be funded in part by gaming monies.

+ In 1992, the Linn Report stated that "it was said that an Aboriginal youth had a better chance of going to jail than graduating from Grade 12"; this is still true today.
+ Saskatchewan has ninety-eight thousand youth between the ages of twelve and seventeen. Approximately fifteen thousand are Aboriginal youth. Based on known risk factors—including, but not limited to, poverty, lack of opportunity for employment, institutional racism and discrimination, and a sense of hopelessness and despair—many of the fifteen thousand Aboriginal youth are at risk of being recruited by gangs.
+ Communities and youth describe a serious gang problem that is reaching crisis proportions.
+ Finally, the causes of crime are complex. For instance, the creation of new laws and new systems to manage them creates the perception that there is more crime. We are also aware that broader social factors contribute to criminal behavior.

## Purpose of the Report

The purpose of this report is threefold: First, we wanted to share the report with a wide cross-section of stakeholders, including First Nations leadership and service providers. They receive an in-depth update on the mandate they gave this office in April 2001.

Second, we are also reporting to the participants who took part in the consultation process we held in the summer of 2001.

Third, we hope we have made a compelling case to federal and provincial government agencies that substantiates the need for new and enhanced resources directed to First Nations to address the gang issue. These resources will include—but will not be limited to—coordination, policy development, and the full range of prevention and intervention services.

*Notes*

1. FSIN Alter-Natives to Nonviolence Initiative, Power Point presentation, summer 2002.
2. FSIN Alter-Natives to Nonviolence Activity Report, 2003.

. . . .

*Originally published in* Justice as Healing, *volume 8, number 3 (2003), this article is an excerpt from the Federation of Saskatchewan Indian Nations' (FSIN) Alter-Natives to Non-Violence Report. The excerpt is reprinted with permission. The complete report may be purchased by contacting: Federation of Saskatchewan Indian Nations, Health and Social Development Secretariat, Suite 200–103 A Packham Avenue, Saskatoon SK S7N 4K4 Canada. We are grateful for permission to publish this work.*

34

# The Newest Old Gem: Family Group Conferencing

## *Gloria Lee*

Family group conferencing is the newest trend in justice development and in the hope of renewing the Canadian justice system. Federal and provincial departments of justice are looking for communities that will open up this new frontier in community justice. Researchers and government representatives rush into communities that are rumored to be breaking "new ground" or exploring community involvement with "new" justice initiatives. With interest like that, it is difficult for First Nations communities not to be cautious and a little suspicious of justice prospectors coming in from various government departments. The biggest concern of First Nations people is that cultural and traditional knowledge is being exploited by both First Nations and non-First Nations researchers and developers in the journey of community healing and recovery.

Family group conferencing (FGC) has emerged from the Maori tradition in New Zealand.[1] In Canada, government representatives and researchers speak about the FGC process that has been brought to us from across the ocean and request that the First Nations people of North America adopt the principles and process of the Maori family group conferencing. The government's presentation introduces FGC and then tries to sell it by promoting the benefits of the process to the Maori of New Zealand. The initial nudging and encouraging of First Nations communities to adopt the FGC process is quickly becoming an expectation, backed by government directives springing from newly formed policy criteria for program funding.

With all due respect to the Maori people who have generously shared their knowledge and teachings with the government of their land in the hopes of benefiting Maori youth—and with kind thanks to the government of Canada and the justice departments for their thoughtfulness—the First Nations people of North America have had since time immemorial and still do have principles and processes in place to deal with disharmony within their communities, much in the same way that the Maori of New Zealand have. I am not sure whom that surprises, but it needs to be pointed out.

Implementing policy is a major concern for provincial and federal justice department representatives, and family group conferencing seems to meet their policy objective of promoting restorative justice. However, the way the government-adopted FGC process, which is said to be a restorative justice initiative, is being rationalized and implemented has several major flaws.[2]

First, a key principle of restorative justice is that it must be community driven. Here in Canada, the Maori family group conferencing process is not community-driven. The federal department of justice and the Royal Canadian Mounted Police have instigated FGC, and it has since been adopted by Social Services provincially and by Corrections Services Canada federally.

Second, First Nations people have concerns about the process being used to develop FGC. First Nations communities are being vigorously encouraged to adopt and implement the Maori process and to make alterations to fit the specific community needs, customs, and traditions of those who will use the new process.

In general, First Nations people view this approach by the government in two ways. First, it is seen as an imposition and intrusion upon First Nations communities and people. This view sees family group conferencing as an indigenization of the Canadian justice system. Paul Havemann helps make this point in his article *The Indigenization of Social Control in Canada* when he says, "[D]espite its appearance as more benign than the model of pure imposition, the integrated or indigenized model is one in which the colonizer preserves aspects of the Indigenous social control system, primarily in order to utilize its authority to support the new pattern of domination."[3]

The second view sees family group conferencing as available to be adopted into the culture of First Nations people of North America. It has been the custom and method of survival for First Nations Peoples to acquire knowledge, technologies, and tools of other places in order to improve Indigenous life, while maintaining traditional values, teachings, and spirituality. North American Indigenous Peoples have survived—and in fact thrived—because of their syncretist[4] nature; that is, their ability to adopt what is good, useful, and strong from other cultures into their own local traditions, customs, and culture.

First Nations people will develop community justice processes that are culturally appropriate and respectful, and this will be done at the request of and in response to the needs of First Nations communities themselves. This principle of First Nations community development requires adherence to Indigenous ethics, which acknowledges and respects cultural distinctiveness.

Many First Nations and some non-First Nations people, academics, Elders, as well as First Nations government representatives, researchers, artists, and others have attempted through many forms and mediums to teach various government representatives about Indigenous ethics and standards. These efforts have fallen short, most likely because of a lack of understanding of and respect for Indigenous ethics, which is necessary for doing business with First Nations communities. It is simply not enough to understand the culture and traditions of First Nations people: that will get you a degree. One must be able to adequately apply the ethics and protocol derived from a spirit and a people reaching to us from an untold but successful history.

The new government approach of using culture to administer justice to Aboriginal people is inherently problematic in terms of cultural ethics. David Lynes presents this problem effectively:

> We are now in a position to better recognize the problem inherent in such an attempt and indeed, in this very line of enquiry. These policies and procedures understood to be essential to administrative success may never be "culturally appropriate." The failure to entertain this possibility seriously risks encouraging not cultural appropriateness but the appropriation of culture—the appropriation of cultural traditions for administrative ends.[5]

I will add that the administration of justice through culture is an appropriation of culture that exploits Indigenous knowledge and spirituality in order to meet the government's bureaucratic policy and goals. However, I disagree with Lynes when he says that "culture is damaged or compromised by administration regardless of who is doing the administering."[6] Culture is damaged, even exploited, by some First Nations and non-First Nations people alike if the people fail to understand or properly apply Indigenous ethics and protocol. However, if culture is used in an ethical fashion by and for First Nations people, then the culture is not exploited but is respected and elevated by making proper use of the Creator's gift of culture. Although I remain skeptical of the ability of non–First Nations people to ethically and appropriately administer First Nations culture, I am less cynical of First Nations people's ability to make good use of our inherent right to our culture with Indigenous ethics intact.

Manipulating culture to meet policy objectives is unethical and demonstrates disregard for human rights and dignity. In this case, imposed training and program criteria that determine funding are affecting this manipulation of culture. Behind these policy criteria are concerns over the impact of the justice system on First Nations people, and these concerns are motivating the current efforts to encourage First Nations people to use culture as a framework and model for justice. But First Nations have learned to identify such opportunities and to take advantage of them. In this case, the past oppression of culture and ceremony has been alleviated momentarily and is now allowing a cultural process to develop and grow that may in fact benefit all people of Canada.

## Notes

1. Family group conferencing is a method for determining the response to crime by involving the victims, offenders, and community representatives. For American readers unfamiliar with the process, the Office of Justice Programs for the U.S. Department of Justice defines family group conferencing on its Web site as follows: "Family group conferencing involves the community of people most affected by the crime—the victim and the offender; and the family, friends, and key supporters of both—in deciding the resolution of a criminal incident. These affected parties are brought together by a trained facilitator to discuss how they and others have been harmed by the offense and how that harm might be repaired."

2. A detailed critical analysis of restorative justice policy development from a First Nations perspective can be found in Gloria Lee, "Restorative Justice: Renaissance of Aboriginal Women through the Amerindian Wholistic Perspective" (1996) (unpublished).

3. Paul Havemann, "The Indigenization of Social Control in Canada" in Robert A. Silverman and Marianne O. Neilson, *Aboriginal Peoples and Canadian Criminal Justice* (Toronto: Harcourt, Brace and Co., 1992), 113.

4. Russell Srnandych and Gloria Lee, "Women, Colonization and Resistance: Elements of an Amerindian Autohistorical Approach to the Study of Law and Colonization" in *Native Studies Review* 10, no. I (1995): 29, citing Ronald Wright in *Stolen Continents: The "New World" Through Indian Eyes* (Toronto: Penguin, 1992), 150. Wright defines syncretism as the "growing together of new beliefs and old . . . [as] a way of encoding the values of a conquered culture within a dominant culture."

5. David A. Lynes, "Cultural Spirit and the Ethic of Bureaucracy: The Paradox of Cultural Administration" (Antigonish, Nova Scotia, May 1995), 17 (unpublished).
6. Ibid., 16.

. . . .

*Published in* Justice as Healing *(1997) 2:2, this article is an excerpt from Ms. Lee's current writings on family group conferencing. We thank Ms. Lee for permission to reprint this article.*

# 35

# Family Group Conferencing:
# The Myth of Indigenous Empowerment in New Zealand

*Juan Marcellus Tauri*

## Introduction

My writing this piece for *Justice as Healing* was prompted by an article that appeared in a previous issue, namely, Gloria Lee's excellent work "The Newest Old Gem: Family Group Conferencing" (Spring, 1997). I share Lee's concern that the imported family group conferencing forum (from New Zealand) is being forced upon Canadian First Nations at the expense of their own, more appropriate justice mechanisms. For example, Lee argues that "First Nation communities are being vigorously encouraged to adopt and implement the Maori process and to make alterations to fit the specific community needs, customs, and traditions of those who will use the new process." Lee's statement of concern is both powerful and correct. Neither federal nor provincial governments in Canada should imagine that, just because family group conferencing is *supposedly* based on Indigenous (i.e., Maori) justice processes, it is therefore appropriate for Indigenes residing in their borders.

In my view, Lee correctly describes this imposition of New Zealand's "Maori inspired" family group conferencing forum onto Canadian First Nations as furthering the "indigenization of the Canadian justice system." What I want to do in the remainder of this paper is to extend Lee's argument and contend that family group conferencing signifies the indigenization of New Zealand's own youth justice system. I also want to dispel a number of misconceptions associated with the formulation and implementation of family group conferencing in New Zealand, as well as to insert a *critical Maori voice* into the simplistic discussions that surround this so-called Indigenous empowering justice forum.

## Indigenizing Criminal Justice in Neocolonial Jurisdictions

Of late, New Zealand's apparently innovative family group conferencing forum has gained immense popularity in many Western jurisdictions, including

Canada and Australia. A number of researchers and academics in the field of youth justice in Australasia have written that family group conferencing either provides a forum that empowers New Zealand's Indigenous population (namely Maori) or signals the ability of the imposed criminal justice order to *culturally sensitize* itself and effectively *utilize* Indigenous justice philosophies and practices.[1]

In this paper, I want to argue two points. First, the family group conferencing forum and its related legislation (The 1989 Children, Young Persons and Their Families Act) signifies the indigenization of New Zealand's criminal justice system rather than the empowerment of Maori. Second, rather than signifying the ability of our justice system to culturally sensitize itself, family group conferencing highlights the willingness of the state to disempower Maori by using their own justice processes while denying them a significant measure of jurisdictional autonomy.

In both Canada and New Zealand, largely negative relations exist between criminal justice institutions and First Nations. In this context, how the state's institutions disempower Maori has emerged as an important issue in Indigenous political dialogue and action over the past twenty years.[2] In jurisdictions such as Canada and the United States, Indigenous criticisms of the imposed justice order have included the restricted judicial autonomy extended to First Nations and the extent of control that the state exerts over Indigenous justice programs.[3] In Canada, the predominant thrust of initiatives has been to *indigenize* the existing justice system.[4]

Indigenization is generally described as the "involvement of Indigenous Peoples and organizations in the delivery of existing socio-legal services and programs."[5] Moreover, Paul Havemann summarizes the indigenization process as "the recruitment of Indigenous people to enforce the laws of the colonial power."[6] The indigenization program in Canada has included initiatives that actively recruit First Nations members as court workers, police officers, and prison personnel in federal, provincial, and municipal forces and institutions.[7] Other indigenizing initiatives in Canada have increasingly attempted to develop community-based sentencing and correctional alternatives for Native offenders (i.e., sentencing circles).[8]

The definition of indigenization adequately describes many of the initiatives in the Canadian jurisdiction. However, in order to understand what has occurred in New Zealand of late, we need to broaden the existing understanding of judicial indigenization. This broader understanding is necessary as a result of New Zealand's own era of indigenization, during which the state has sought to culturally sensitize not only its justice system but also all "service delivery" institutions that deal with Maori.

The indigenization of government policy, legislation, and service delivery in New Zealand began in earnest after 1978. In many ways, it was directly linked to the radicalization of Maori land and identity politics during that decade.[9] At the time, government institutions had begun to pay attention to claims from various individuals and organizations that their existing practices were viewed negatively by their Maori "clients." Partially in response to such criticisms, in 1979, the State Services Commission, Department of Maori Affairs, and the Public Service Association Working Party presented a working paper on the state of race relations within the public sector.

The report's main recommendations included actively recruiting Maori and Pacific Island individuals into public service and providing better service delivery to these two sections of their clientele.[10] These two recommendations were indicative of state sector responses to criticisms from Maori over the next two decades. During this period, the state sector chose not to make major changes to departmental practices in reaction to Maori claims of systemic bias. Instead, the state sector concentrated on *co-opting* Maori, their bicultural ideology, and their cultural practices within institutional frameworks in order to transform the *face* of state service delivery. As a result, during the 1980s, both the Treaty of Waitangi and certain "acceptable" Maori cultural values and practices were given increased prominence and importance within the public service.[11]

Throughout the 1980s and early 1990s, many government departments created a number of programs to show their commitment to the state's "treaty partner." These programs included such initiatives as appropriating a departmental Maori name (for example, our Ministry of Inland Revenue took the Maori name *Te Tari Taake*, which was affectionately translated by some Maori as "The Ministry of Take"); adopting a departmental waiata (Maori song); adding Maori motifs to departmental letterheads; and appointing a Maori Elder as an institutional patron.

The token nature of the government's sensitization program is reflected in the fact that the state's bicultural experiment to date has largely concentrated on these types of "cultural sensitivity" exercises but made no substantive organizational accommodation. Another popular initiative included organizing in-house training sessions held on *marae* (Maori meeting place) to encourage "cultural and treaty awareness" among departmental employees. By contrast, "broader issues outside the normal institutional discourse—such as entitlement of the *tangata whenua* (people of the land), closure of the socio-economic gap, empowerment of tribal authorities, and enhancement of Maori language and culture—received little attention."[12]

New Zealand's indigenization program is, therefore, not entirely comparable to what has taken place in Canada. In the Canadian jurisdiction, indigenization became concrete policy and was acknowledged as such by the state and its various agencies.[13] In New Zealand, institutional indigenization was more insidious, including initiatives undertaken in the area of criminal justice policy and practice. In the remainder of this paper, I intend to argue that family group conferencing represents both the indigenization of our criminal justice sector as well as the continued co-option by the New Zealand state of what it considers to be palatable elements of Indigenous philosophy and cultural practice.[14]

## Indigenizing Youth Justice through Family Group Conferencing

The indigenization of the New Zealand justice process throughout the 1980s included a range of measures similar to those undertaken in Canada. These measures were intended to encourage a greater involvement of Maori within the existing system. This included actively recruiting Maori as justice employees (i.e., in the police force, probation service, and corrections); establishing links between probation services, *marae* committee, *iwi* (tribal) councils, and *whanau* (family) groups; and involving Maori communities both in administering community-based sentences and providing assistance to prisoners following their release. Pratt reports further that there has been considerable effort since 1989 to inject Maori cultural practices and values into the administration of prison life through staff "sensitivity" training and cultural programs for prisoners.[15] The indigenization program established within the justice system, therefore, mirrors the cultural sensitivity exercises prevalent among state institutions.

Olsen, Morris, and Maxwell argue that the family group conferencing legislation was heavily influenced by traditional Maori justice practices.[16] For example, family group conferences were arguably designed to heal the damage caused by an offender's behavior; to restore harmony between those affected by the behavior; to encourage the participation of those who have a direct interest in either the offender or the offense;[17] to empower the victim; and to positively "reintegrate" the offender within the community.[18] Furthermore, Carol LaPrairie writes that the goals of the New Zealand conferencing forum include making offenders aware of the consequences of their behavior; moving resolution of the offense from the state to the extended family and/or local community; and facilitating victim and offender reconciliation.[19]

When we compare the goals of the family group conferencing process in the 1989 legislation with research on the conferencing process as practiced, we begin to understand that both the family group conferencing forum and the 1989 act represent the *co-option* of Maori justice practices. We can also establish that, far from providing Maori with a culturally sensitive justice forum, New Zealand's "revolutionary juvenile justice model" has done little to adequately address criticisms made by some Maori of the justice system itself.[20]

Empirical research on the New Zealand family group conferencing process to date establishes that it has failed in those areas that supposedly distinguish it as a *Maori inspired justice forum*. For example, in terms of victim attendance, Maxwell and Morris's 1993 research found that only 46 percent of the victims attended family group conferences (and only 49 percent of this group reported satisfaction with the result of the conference they attended). Also, only 5 percent of Maori family group conferences were held on *marae* (Maori meeting house). The Department of Social Welfare offices or facilities were the most common venue used.

This is an important issue, especially since one of the main goals of the act is to encourage cultural sensitivity in juvenile justice practices. The Wagga Wagga (NSW) conferencing experiment of the early 1990s, for example, held all conferences in the local police station, which raised considerable concern.[21] One commentator gave a dubious justification for this practice by saying that the police station "is a setting that favors neither victim nor offender."[22] Both Sandor and Cunneen dispute this statement in view of the historical involvement of the police in subjugating Indigenous populations throughout Australia.[23] In the New Zealand context, similar issues could be raised over the extensive use of Department of Social Welfare facilities for family group conferences involving Maori. This is a justifiable concern given the historical role that the department has played in the control and surveillance of members of New Zealand's lower socioeconomic population, of which Maori make up a substantial number.[24]

The family group conferencing process as presently practiced in New Zealand has also failed to deliver on another aim of the 1989 legislation, namely, the *deprofessionalization* of juvenile justice. Maxwell and Morris's research showed that social workers were present at 62 percent of all the family group conferences evaluated.[25] This occurred even though the 1989 legislation severely restricts their right to attend. Only when the youth is in the care of the director general of the Department of Social Welfare can social workers be present.

This is an important issue, given the Maori criticism that current justice practices give authority to those whom European standards define as experts and professionals (for example, lawyers, social workers, and police).[26] According to Michael Jackson, this practice has contributed to a situation where Maori justice practices and philosophies are underutilized and maligned in comparison to European knowledge and expertise.[27] We might argue, therefore, that family group conferencing has thus far failed to provide Indigenous Peoples, in this instance Maori, with the opportunity to be more than the passive subjects of an imposed criminal justice system.

## A Critique of the Indigenization Process

A number of criticisms can be made of the neocolonial state's attempt to culturally sensitize its institutional practice. In the Canadian context, criticism has centered on the token nature of judicial indigenization programs. Paul Havemann, for example, is heavily critical of the process. He charges that judicial indigenization serves as an inexpensive and convenient option for the government in addressing Indigenous justice concerns without seriously affecting state control of the justice arena. He argues that "indigenization serves as a cheap substitute for a measure of autonomy, self-government or, indeed, sovereignty. It assimilates Indigenous people into the imposed social control apparatus rather than autonomizing the social control apparatus for the benefit of Indigenous people."[28]

So, too, for Canadian First Nations, Finkler contends that indigenization has not provided a substantial measure of judicial autonomy. Rather, it has led to involving First Nations and their judicial practices in delivering the state's existing justice programs.[29] Therefore, we might view the government's indigenization program in two ways. First, it functions as a pacificatory project intended to contain the legitimation crises potential of radical First Nations politics. Second, it is an attempt to recolonize First Nations communities by incorporating their existing social control practices.[30]

As shown earlier, influenced in part by the radicalization of Maori politics, the recent history of state–Maori relations in New Zealand has been characterized by a continual (re)evaluation and repackaging of state policy. This development signified a legitimation crisis for the New Zealand state. Indigenization represents but one element within its program of institutional response.

Considering this point, we might best describe the development of family group conferencing under the 1989 act as an *incorporation* of Maori justice practices through the *hybridization* of New Zealand's juvenile justice system. Havemann describes hybridization as "the mixing of formal with informal justice and social service with order maintenance."[31] The family group conferencing process as practiced in New Zealand can be viewed as a hybridized social control mechanism on the part of the state, because it involves mixing formal (European) with informal (Maori) justice processes in a forum that severely restricts Maori judicial autonomy.

The fact that the most significant example of the New Zealand government's indigenization program within criminal justice has so far failed to adequately address Maori demands for jurisdictional autonomy should come as no surprise to other Indigenes. It should be remembered that we are relying on a neocolonial state to dispense *justice,* when a central element of its historical development has been the disempowerment of its Indigenous population.[32] Nor should we be surprised at the willingness of various New Zealand governments to use Maori cultural philosophies and values to (re)legitimize their institutional practices within the justice arena. As Kelsey argues, the overall aim of much of the government's institutional practice and policy throughout the 1980s was "the co-option of Maori intellectual and cultural property for cosmetic purposes by 'non-Maori' government departments."[33]

## Conclusion

In their 1995 paper, Olsen, Morris, and Maxwell contend that the family group conferencing process in New Zealand provides evidence for the ability of Indigenous justice processes to adapt to modern times and successfully modify Western justice models.

Some Maori, however, would view the situation differently. The inability of the system to deliver on many of the promises of the 1989 act represents for them a continuation of the New Zealand government's historical ambivalence toward their cultural practices, except when they can be of use to the dominant justice order. Some Maori want more than the essence of their processes and philosophies to be "recognized." They want them respected, which means allowing Maori to employ these processes as they see fit. Instead, what we have at present is a forum that utilizes Maori processes while restricting how Maori may apply them. In some ways, this has similarities to the disempowering situation described by Lee, who laments the willingness of the Canadian federal government to implement an Indigenous-inspired forum, while continuing to overlook the philosophies and practices of its own First Nations.

Finally, returning to New Zealand, for some Maori commentators, our government's "solution" to the problem of cultural insensitivity and institutional racism—namely, family group conferencing—is inadequate. Jackson, for one, argues:

> Justice for Maori does not mean the attempted grafting of Maori processes upon a system that retains the authority to determine the extent, applicability, and validity of the processes. No matter how well-intentioned and sincere such efforts, it is respectfully suggested that they will merely maintain the co-option and redefinition of Maori values and authority which underpins so much of the colonial will to control. A "cultural justice system" controlled by the Crown is [simply] another colonizing artifact.[34]

### Notes

1. See T. Olsen, G. Maxwell, and A. Morris, "Maori and Youth Justice in New Zealand" in *Popular Justice and Community Regeneration: Pathways to Indigenous Reform,* ed. K. Hazlehurst, (Westport: Praeger, 1995); G. Maxwell, and A. Morris, *Family, Victims and Culture: Youth Justice in New Zealand* (Wellington: Social Policy Agency and the Institute of Criminology, Victoria University of Wellington, 1993); J. Consedine, *Restorative Justice: Healing the Effects of Crime* (Lyttelton: Ploughshares Publications, 1995); C. LaPrairie, "Altering Course: New Directions in Criminal Justice," *The Australian and New Zealand Journal of Criminology* (special supplementary issue) (1995): 78–99.

2. See M. Jackson, *Maori and the Criminal Justice System: He Whaipaanga Hou: A New Perspective* (Wellington: Department of Justice, 1988); R. Jarvenpa, "The Political Economy and Political Ethnicity of American Indian Adaptations and Identities," *Ethnic and Racial Studies* 8, no. 1 (1985): 29–48; L. McNamara, "Aboriginal Justice Reform in Canada: Alternatives to State Control," in *Perceptions of Justice: Issues of Indigenous Community Empowerment*, ed. K. Hazlehurst (Aldershot: Avebury, 1995).

3. See K. Kickingbird, "'In Our Image . . . After our Likeness': The Drive for the Assimilation of Indian Court Systems," *The American Criminal Law Review* 13 (1976): 429–40.

4. See H. Finkler, "The Political Framework of Aboriginal Criminal Justice in Northern Canada," *Law and Anthropology* 5 (1990): 113–19; P. Havemann, "The Indigenisation of Social Control in Canada" in *Indigenous Law and the State*, ed. B. Morse and G. Woodman (Dordrecht: Foris Publ., 1988).

5. Finkler, The Political Framework of Aboriginal Criminal Justice in Northern Canada," 113.

6. Havemann, "The Indigenisation of Social Control in Canada," 72.

7. C. Griffiths, "Native Indians and the Police: The Canadian Experience," *Police Studies* 11, no. 4 (1988): 155–60; J. Harding, "Policing and Aboriginal Justice," *Canadian Journal of Criminology* 33 (1991): 363–84; Havemann, "The Indigenisation of Social Control in Canada."

8. McNamara, "Aboriginal Justice Reform in Canada: Alternatives to State Control."

9. See E. Poata-Smith, "*He Pokeke Uenuku Tu Ai*: The Evolution of Contemporary Maori Protest" in *Nga Patai: Racism and Ethnic Relations in Aotearoa/New Zealand*, ed. P. Spoonley et al. (Palmerston North: Dunmore Press, 1996); R. Walker, "The Treaty of Waitangi as the Focus of Maori Protest," in *Waitangi: Maori and Pakeha Perspectives of the Treaty of Waitangi*, ed. I. Kawharu (Auckland: Oxford University Press, 1989).

10. See P. Spoonley, *Racism and Ethnicity* (Auckland: Oxford University Press, 1993).

11. A. Fleras, "'Tuku Rangatiratanga': Devolution in Iwi-Government Relations" in *Nga Take: Ethnic Relations and Racism in Aotearoa/New Zealand*, ed. P. Spoonley et al. (Palmerston North: Dunmore Press, 1991).

12. A. Fleras, and J. Elliot, *The Nations Within: Aboriginal-State Relations in Canada, the USA and New Zealand* (Toronto: Oxford University Press, 1992), 193–94.

13. Havemann, "The Indigenisation of Social Control in Canada."

14. See J. Tauri, "Family Group Conferencing: A Case Study of the Indigenisation of New Zealand's Justice System," *Current Issues in Criminal Justice* 10, no. 2 (1998):

168–82. One of the main features of the colonial project in New Zealand through-out the nineteenth century was the gradual "silencing" of Maori justice. On this, see J. Pratt, "Citizenship, Colonisation and Criminal Justice," *International Journal of the Sociology of Law* 19 (1991): 292–319; A. Ward, *A Show of Justice: Racial 'Amalgamation' in 19th Century New Zealand,* 2nd ed. (Auckland: Auckland University Press, 1995). Legislation was introduced that ostensibly recognized elements of Maori social con-trol practice deemed acceptable to the colonizers (*The Native Exemption Ordinance 1844,* for example). The initial mood of European colonists toward Maori justice was, therefore, one of compromise and accommodation (see R. Russell, "Legal Pluralism in New Zealand Over the Last 123 Years," *Law and Anthropology* 5 (1990): 66–93. This restricted recognition of Maori jurisdiction continued well into the twentieth century, when legislation such as the Maori Social and Economic Advancement Act 1945 and its amendment the Maori Welfare Act 1962 gave Maori District Com-mittees unlimited capacity to deal with deviant members of their committees (see J. Tauri, "Indigenous Justice or Popular Justice: Issues in the Development of a Maori Justice System," in *Nga Patai: Ethnic Relations and Racism in Aotearoa/New Zealand,* ed. P. Spoonley et al. [Palmerston North: Dunmore Press, 1996a]).

15. Pratt, "Citizenship, Colonisation and Criminal Justice."

16. Olsen, Maxwell and Morris, "Maori and Youth Justice in New Zealand." Space precludes an in-depth discussion of the philosophies and practices that underpin Maori justice. See E. Durie, *Custom Law* (1994) unpublished manuscript; Consedine, *Restorative Justice: Healing the Effects of Crime*; and J. Tauri and A. Mor-ris, "Re-forming Justice: The Potential of Maori Processes," *The Australian and New Zealand Journal of Criminology* 30, no. 2 (1997): 149–67, for further discussions of Maori justice.

17. Maxwell & Morris, *Family, Victims and Culture: Youth Justice in New Zealand.*

18. T. Stewart, "Family Group Conferences with Young Offenders in New Zea-land," in *Family Group Conferences: Perspectives on Policy and Practice,* ed. J. Hudson et al. (Annandale, NSW: Federation Press, 1996).

19. LaPrairie, "Altering Course: New Directions in Criminal Justice."

20. See Jackson, *Maori and the Criminal Justice System*; Ministerial Advisory Committee on a Maori Perspective for the Department of Social Welfare, *Puao-Te-Ata-Tu (Daybreak)* (Wellington: Department of Social Welfare, 1986); P. Sharples, "Cultural Justice" in *Re-Thinking Criminal Justice, vol 1: Justice in the Community,* ed. F. McElrea (Auckland: Legal Research Foundation, 1995); and C. Wickliffe, "A Maori Criminal Justice System" in *Re-Thinking Criminal Justice, vol. 1: Justice in the Community,* ed. F. McElrea.

21. See D. Sandor, "The Thickening Blue Wedge in Juvenile Justice," in *Family Conferencing and Juvenile Justice: The Way Forward or Misplaced Optimism?* ed. C. Alder and J. Wundersitz (Canberra: Australian Institute of Criminology, 1994).

22. D. Moore, "Facing the Consequences" in *National Conference on Juvenile Justice,* ed. L. Atkinson and S. Gerull (Canberra: Australian Institute of Criminology, 1993), 204.

23. Sandor, "The Thickening Blue Wedge in Juvenile Justice" and C. Cunneen, "Community Conferencing and the Fiction of Indigenous Control," *The Australian and New Zealand Journal of Criminology* 30, no. 3 (1998): 292–311.

24. E. Poata-Smith, "The Political Economy of Inequality between Maori and Pakeha" in *The Political Economy of New Zealand,* ed. C. Rudd and B. Roper (Auckland: Oxford University Press, 1997).

25. Maxwell and Morris, *Family, Victims and Culture.*

26. See Jackson, *Maori and the Criminal Justice System*; and A. Morris and J. Tauri, "Maori Justice: Possibilities and Pitfalls" in *Re-Thinking Criminal Justice vol 1: Justice in the Community,* ed. F. McElrea.

27. M. Jackson, "Criminality and the Exclusion of Maori" in *Essays on Criminal Law in New Zealand: 'Towards Reform?'* ed. N. Cameron and S. Francis (Wellington: Victoria University of Wellington, 1990).

28. Havemann, "The Indigenisation of Social Control in Canada," 74.

29. Finkler, "The Political Framework of Aboriginal Criminal Justice in Northern Canada."

30. J. Tauri, "Justice for Whom? The State, Popular Justice Forums and Indigenous Politics" (1996) unpublished M.Phil thesis, Cambridge University, Cambridge.

31. Havemann, "The Indigenisation of Social Control in Canada," 90.

32. M. Jackson, "Justice and Political Power: Reasserting Maori Legal Processes" in *Legal Pluralism and the Colonial Legacy,* ed. K. Hazlehurst (Aldershot: Avebury, 1995); Tauri, "Family Group Conferencing."

33. J. Kelsey, "From Flagpoles to Pinetrees: Tino Rangatiratanga and Treaty Policy Today" in *Nga Patai: Racism and Ethnicity in Aotearoa/New Zealand,* ed. P. Spoonley et al., 185–86.

34. Jackson, "Justice and Political Power," 34.

. . . .

*This article was published in* Justice as Healing *(1999) 4:1. The editor thanks Juan Marcellus Tauri for permission to publish this article.*

# Commission on First Nations and
# Métis Peoples and Justice Reform
# 2003 Interim Report and 2004 Final Report

*J. Wilton Littlechild, Chair*

## Background

Chaired by Willie Littlechild, the Commission on First Nations and Métis Peoples and Justice Reform was established 15 November 2001 with a broad mandate to survey the relations in Saskatchewan between First Nations and Métis Peoples and the justice system. This mandate from Saskatchewan's minister of justice and Aboriginal affairs included the total picture: policing, courts, prosecutions, alternative measures, access to legal counsel, corrections (including community corrections), youth justice, community justice processes, and victim services. The goal of the commission was to identify efficient, effective, and financially responsible reforms to the justice system.

To carry out this job, the commissioners traveled to First Nations and Métis communities as well as rural and urban areas to hear the people's ideas for reforms. The hearings were advertised and organizations in each community were notified in advance so they could attend. In a press release, Willie Littlechild stated: "It is obvious to the Commission that there is no better place to find solutions to the problems facing First Nations and Métis people than in their own communities. Justice must be transformed to incorporate First Nations and Métis culture, traditions, and beliefs."

The commission held hearings, analyzed proposals, and made recommendations to the governments of Canada and Saskatchewan, the Federation of Saskatchewan Indian Nations (FSIN), and the Métis Nation—Saskatchewan (MNS). On 17 January 2003, the commission released an interim report of their work. The final two-volume report, entitled *Legacy of Hope: An Agenda for Change*, was released in 21 June 2004. The following are excerpts from these two reports.

## *2003 Interim Report*

### Dialogues in the Communities of Meadow Lake, Beauval, La Loche, Sandy Bay, Pelican Narrows, and Black Lake

Northern communities acknowledge problems with the justice system but also state that these problems do not occur in isolation; they are symptoms of larger social problems. Communities clearly articulated that they want to be able to develop solutions to their own problems. We were told that the laws, policies, programs, and services created in the south do not always work in the north and can be harmful.

They reminded us that "justice" does not translate directly into a First Nation language. When Aboriginal people refer to the justice system, it is often in the context of criminal justice and refers to police, courts, sentences, jails, and punishment.

> When I talk about justice, it has to be looked at with respect to not just lawbreaking. The concept of justice in Dene means a way of life; it means responsibility; it means child rearing. It's very broad and very big. You can't confine what justice means. There is no word for *justice* in Dene, and there's probably no word for justice in Cree either. Because these concepts have been imposed on us, and we're expected to follow these laws.
>
> —*Speaker at La Loche dialogue*

> Another big issue we have is the way sentencing is done. Sentencing must be done by those who know us, those who understand our difficulties at home and school or in the community. The judge doesn't know us from Adam, and yet all the powers are in his hands oftentimes, not realizing that we have come back from broken homes, suffer from addictions, and have identity problems and a loss of culture.
>
> —*Speaker at the Beauval dialogue*

For communities to effectively address their issues, they require assistance in devising, funding, and implementing programs that will serve them long term. They need the training and resources to provide remedial services to address underlying causes of social problems in their communities.

> When it comes back to justice, we must first find ourselves. We were given a law to follow. We were given a way to follow. As this lady talked, she talked about culture. That is justice. Beliefs, that is justice. A lot of that we have lost within colonization, assimilation, but we must return back to that. We have the opportunity to do that. We have Elders. And the Elders say in order for us to return to justice, we must return to our grassroots and to find ourselves. Yes, we can go around blaming other people, but it begins with us, as the Elders say. But our children, we must teach them the walk of our ancestors.
>
> —*Speaker at the Pelican Narrows dialogue*

A consistent theme emerging from the northern dialogues was the need for greater recognition of the importance of the spiritual and cultural aspect of Aboriginal cultures and traditions.

> I help my own people using my own language, and a lot of the counseling I do, I collected from Elders. I spent time with Elders for three, four years and that's why I teach the medicine wheel. I do the circle of life, the four aspects of ourselves as human beings: physically, emotionally, spiritually and mentally. And I use a lot of what I have collected from the Elders in my counseling, so people can look at the four aspects, so they can heal themselves, and they can stay balanced.
>
> —*Speaker at the La Loche dialogue*

Many speakers expressed a feeling that the existing justice system needs a dramatic facelift. They believe minor modifications and increased Aboriginal staffing will not bring about substantial improvements.

> In terms of the courts, I think, you know, we're starting
> to see movement in areas where we have Cree judges,
> Dene judges, but it's still the same system. The polic-
> ing, well, we see our own Native police officers, as well,
> being trained in Regina, being assigned certain places,
> but it's still the same system. It's the system that we have
> to reform, not as much as the people [who] work in it.
> Because the people [who] are working in that system are
> just symptoms of that system, the way they operate.

> — *Speaker at the Meadow Lake dialogue*

## Law Enforcement

Many speakers told the Justice Reform Commission about their general mistrust of the police officers working in their communities. They had concerns
in several areas.

> I'd like to see the RCMP to do their job. That's the rea-
> son why they're in the community of Sandy Bay, not to
> work for the white people but to work for each one of us
> in this community of Sandy Bay. When a white person
> calls them over, they're there right away, but the Native,
> they won't show up, not till about 24 hours after.

> —*Speaker at the Sandy Bay dialogue*

Many people said it was important to include Elders and traditional Aboriginal values in the process of healing those who have social problems that
have made their behavior unacceptable in their community. The Elders in
particular are seen as a valuable resource.

> There's some schools in reserve communities that have
> Elders going into the schools talking about traditional
> culture, ceremonies, and survival skills, and I think that
> is useful to youth as well.

> —*Speaker at the Meadow Lake dialogue*

Youth have their own voice and need to be heard on issues that impact their lives. Youth want to participate in decision-making and policy development, particularly when those decisions and policies affect them. Including young people in decisions and providing them with opportunities to take responsibility will result in enhanced services. Article 12 of the United Nations Convention on the Rights of the Child gives children the right to express their views on all matters affecting them. The rights granted under this convention are recognized in the YCJA.

> I think that, like, big ups to the Commission for setting up this stuff to happen, because slowly, our communities are catching on to listening to youth and that. I like to come to things where people start realizing that you can't make decisions about people when they're not involved in it. You're wasting your time trying to plan for people and not even asking them what they want for themselves. . . . The people [who] are sitting around this table, I just see, like, we're going to listen to each other, and, I don't know, that's just really promising.
>
> — *Youth speaking at a dialogue*

## *2004 Final Report*

### Chapter 4. Restorative Justice: Restoring Justice in Saskatchewan

*Introduction*

*Restorative justice* is a term the commission heard repeatedly in its dialogues around the province. Often referred to as necessary for justice reform, restorative justice has been defined in many ways. It involves the principles of repairing harm, healing, restoring relationships, accountability, community involvement, and community ownership. The Law Commission of Canada calls this approach relationship-based. It reflects *opintowin*, which is Cree for "lifting each other up."

> The values that are in restorative justice are more in terms of empathy, information sharing, problem-solving. It's designed to restore people to the community. It's built

around principles such as involving all parties, a sense of healing and accountability. It unites what's been divided and strengthens the community. What ultimately restorative justice is about is respecting people.

*—Participant at the restorative justice roundtable*

Justice to Aboriginal people has always been the preservation, the restoration of the primary balance within the lives of people. Justice has not been individualistic; justice has been for the collective whole. Sanctions have been used within Aboriginal communities, that is true, but that has been to maintain a balance and to maintain the harmony—to bring it back. Sanctions are used within the Euro-Canadian system to punish, to get even. As an educator, I have never known an instance where I was able to teach anyone anything by punishing him. You teach by reaching out and becoming a part of what they are doing. You engage them in the process.

*—Speaker at the North Battleford dialogue*

The current justice system is not trusted or respected by many First Nations people, because First Nations have had no say in its creation, no say in the development of its policies or laws. First Nations have had to endure the attitudes of the practitioners and, more than any other group of people, we are disproportionately affected by the system.

In terms of values, the use of the adversarial approach to resolving differences in the justice system creates winners and losers. This approach clashes with the concepts of First Nations justice, which emphasizes the restoration of social harmony in the community. Social harmony requires the building and maintaining of strong family and community relationships.

*—Speaker at the FSIN Health*
*and Social Development Presentation*

I wanted to talk about how we arrived in the provincial justice system, because we're only about 108 years old, and we're in a mess already. And justice in Indian country is respect, that's what justice is, but we don't know how to say it in our language, all we can say is justice. If we go back to our languages and try and find out what justice means, if you're Saulteaux or Cree, maybe you'll understand what justice is; it's respect for each other. Justice is not to get even, you know, he took my candy and I'll break your arm; it's not justice. You learn justice already in Indian justice, you learn it at home, and you learn it in the community. Everybody provides justice. A lot of respect and compassion for each other, justice. It isn't calling the police because you did something. That's not justice to me. So I think what I would like to find out in everybody's mind, what is justice to you? What do you feel justice is? We're so ingrained with justice, calling the cops, having a lawyer involved, having a judge involved. To me, that's not justice.

—*Speaker at the Cowesses dialogue*

The goals of the restorative justice strategy are consistent with Saskatchewan's Aboriginal justice strategy, which works to involve the First Nations communities in developing approaches to justice that are culturally sensitive, responsive to community needs, holistic in delivery, and that give authority to the community. Focusing on crime prevention, improving race relations, and building bridges within the justice system will achieve these objectives.

### Transforming Justice

The commission was invited to attend a symposium on justice coordinated by the Office of the Treaty Commissioner. During the symposium, several Elders provided instruction on the concept of justice as seen through the treaties. Professor John Borrows was invited to document the symposium. Professor Borrows referred to the need for a transformation:

It is not enough to simply reform the way in which the criminal justice system operates, if all that it implies is adding a few Indigenous elements onto the current system, however welcome they may be. It would be more valuable to talk of transformation; changing the way the system operates at all levels to take account of the Treaty relationship. Reform seems to connote taking what lies at hand and making it better. Transformation seems to imply taking what exists and making it different and even better still.

While both processes start with what currently exists, reform allows for change only within a particular scope and context, while transformation permits change of both scope and context. If you reformed a caterpillar, you would get a better caterpillar; if you transformed a caterpillar, you would get a butterfly.

Treaties are the path to the transformation of the criminal justice system, because they allow the people of Saskatchewan to start where they are, while simultaneously reorienting the entire scope and context of how they approach and achieve justice. This metamorphosis would gradually alter the reach and framework of what could be accomplished to bring about peace and order in the province.

It would [also] provide a degree of comfort for current justice personnel, because they would not change what lies at the heart of their jobs, though the range and context in which they carry out their work would be dramatically revised and expanded. They would still be expected to be good police officers, lawyers, judges, parole officers, etc., but they would be expected to practise their profession in a Treaty milieu, taking account of any change that Treaties would require.

### The Role of Healing

When speaking of restorative justice, First Nations and Métis people often say that healing is essential for individuals, families, and communities.

> I think we have to start bringing our own children back
> to the community, teaching them the culture. That way,
> they respect the land, the people, and themselves. . . .
> You have to be able to forgive and start dealing with a

lot of these issues on a personal basis, because if you don't deal with it from that perspective, then it doesn't matter how much money you get, the problem is still going to be there.

*—Speaker at the Beauval dialogue*

I hear people express their pain, the pain that they have, that they carried with them all through their lives, and the anger that is created from that pain. We talk about healing, I think that's part of healing, [not to] forget the pain and the anger. That is something that we will never get rid of, because it was an experience that we have come through, and it becomes our reference for teaching our youth, for teaching our children. The main teaching of our great-great-grandfathers and great-great-grandmothers was to listen. The first teaching, listen. And you have eyes, you are blessed with eyes, and that's to look, look around you. There [are] a lot of things around you that you can be grateful for. There [are] a lot of good role models around you that you can look up to. That's the way you learn.

The second most important teaching of our ancestors was to get along with things and people. There are lessons in the universe, and it's about the unwritten history, you know, your stories. The stories that you tell today are very important. You are important for all our children, our grandchildren, our great-grandchildren. We have a history behind us. We are history. Our history should be taught to our children by our Elders, the values, the beliefs of our people in all four directions, the unconditional love, respect, honesty, bravery, generosity, the love of nature, purity. The spirituality of our people is what has pulled us through all these trials and traumas in our lives.

*—Elder at the dialogue with Elders*
*of the Office of the Treaty Commissioner*

> I think if we can give families what they need to ground
> their family values and bring family back into the sys-
> tem, to identify with their cultural background and their
> needs, then they are the ones [who] are going to improve
> and provide opportunities and create initiatives.
>
> — *Speaker at the Meadow Lake dialogue*

## Conclusion

The restorative justice model must not be limited to the criminal justice process. All people in Saskatchewan must recognize the value of restorative justice. There is a need for all Saskatchewan people to embrace the concept of
justice with an emphasis on restoring justice, individuals, communities, and
the province of Saskatchewan.

> In closing, I guess I would go back to that [point that]
> still we will never be a part of you. [But] we're always—
> everything is—interconnected. So what I would like to
> say is that we both work together to make this process
> a process that deals with all human beings equally, not
> just white or black or blue, but for everybody, and then
> an incorporation of our traditional processes that are
> meant for the good of everybody.
>
> — *Speaker at the Treaty Four Community dialogue*

## Chapter 9: Aboriginal Justice in Saskatchewan, 2002–2021—The Benefits of Change
*Prepared by Isobel M. Findlay and Warren Weir*

Recognizing Aboriginal and treaty rights is not a privilege but a constitutional
fact to be defended by all Canadians, because all our freedoms and privileges
depend on such recognition. The general population of Saskatchewan as
much as Aboriginal Peoples remain beneficiaries of the treaties by which
our relations and realities are defined. With these historical and constitutional facts, as well as the costs and benefits of social cohesion in mind . . . we
address widespread myths and fears about Aboriginal participation in the

justice system, distinguish public perception and facts, and thereby aim to enrich public debate, facilitate decision-making, and motivate meaningful change.

### Popular Myths and Powerful Realities

If misconceptions, myths, and fears lead to oversimplified responses to justice issues and polarize opinion, they also undermine confidence in the administration of justice. No jurisdiction can operate effectively without the public trust. Nor can any jurisdiction afford the human costs of such ignorance—or the economic consequences of decisions it licenses. In this section, we address some of the most damaging myths that obscure what we all have to gain from change.

*Myth #1: Canada has and should have only one system of justice.*

In his dissenting opinion in *R. v. Morin* [1995], Justice Bayda stressed that there may be "only one system of justice," but "an objective onlooker unfamiliar with our society would be surprised to learn that was the case, were he or she to look only at the consequences or products produced by the system of justice. From the perspective of consequences, we appear to have two systems of justice."

*Myth #2: All Canadians are or should be equal before "the" law.*

"The present system fails the Aboriginal peoples. . . . [T]he current régime fails to respect the Charter's guarantees of equality and fundamental justice in a number of important respects."[1]

"Aboriginal peoples have experienced the most entrenched racial discrimination of any group in Canada. Discrimination against Aboriginal people has been a central policy of Canadian governments since Confederation. . . . In short, the current court system is inefficient, insensitive and, when compared to the service provided to non-Aboriginal people, decidedly unequal."[2]

*Myth # 3: Aboriginal Peoples are treated preferentially by the justice system.*

According to the Canadian Criminal Justice Association (2000), Aboriginal people experience overt and systemic racism within the justice system with these particular results:

+ Aboriginal accused are more likely to be denied bail.
+ Aboriginal people spend more time in pretrial detention.
+ Aboriginal people are less likely to have legal representation at court proceedings.
+ Aboriginal clients, especially in the north, spend less time with their lawyers.
+ Aboriginal offenders are more than twice as likely to be incarcerated than non-Aboriginal offenders.
+ Aboriginal Elders are not given the same status as other spiritual leaders, priests, and chaplains.
+ Aboriginal people often plead guilty because they feel intimidated by court proceedings and want them over.

*Myth # 4: The administration of justice requires jurisdictional clarity: Canada cannot afford to add jurisdictional powers to Aboriginal Peoples.*

The Constitution Act of 1867 divided powers and responsibilities on justice between federal and provincial governments (with great diversity among the latter) and even concurrent jurisdictions among municipal, federal, and provincial policing.[3]

+ "In reality, there are already many criminal law authorities in Canada. . . . Canadians do not complain loudly about the separate criminal law jurisdiction held by the military. . . . Canadians do not question the general workability of the civil and common law traditions in this country."[4]
+ Likewise Hamilton and Sinclair argue that "fully functioning tribal court systems on a variety of Indian reservations in the United States, many of them similar in size and socio-economic status" to Indian reserves in Manitoba, provides "strong evidence that separate Aboriginal justice systems are possible and practical."[5]
+ In addition, Hamilton and Sinclair find support for a separate court system in the persistence of the section 107 court of the Indian Act:

    The section 107 court remains in the statute as a vestige of the ignominious past of federal colonization and domination of reserve life. . . . The restrictions that exist in the Act are such that it offers little promise for the long-term future and is unlikely to satisfy current demands from First Nations to establish their own justice system. At most, it offers a short-term interim measure and an indication that a separate court system can function readily on Indian reserves without causing grave concerns within the rest of society or the legal community.[6]

## Notes

1. Law Commission of Canada, 1991, 16, 75.

2. A. C. Hamilton and C. M. Sinclair, *The Justice System and Aboriginal People: Report of the Aboriginal Justice Enquiry of Manitoba, Vol. 1* (Winnipeg: Queen's Printer, 1991).

3. R. Gosse, J. Youngblood Henderson, and R. Carter, eds., *Continuing Poundmaker and Riel's Quest: Presentations Made at a Conference on Aboriginal Peoples and Justice* (Saskatoon: Purich, 1994).

4. Patricia Monture-Angus, *Thunder in My Soul: A Mohawk Woman Speaks* (Halifax, Nova Scotia.: Fernwood Publishing, 1995).

5. Hamilton and Sinclair, *The Justice System and Aboriginal People.*

6. Ibid.

. . . .

*These excerpts were published in* Justice as Healing *(2002) 7:4 and (2004) 9:3. The complete reports are available by contacting the Commission on First Nations and Métis Peoples and Justice Reform, 802-119 4th Avenue South, Saskatoon SK S7K 5X2, Tel: (306) 964-1209; Fax: (306) 964-1206. The reports can also be found on the Web at www.justicereformcomm.sk.ca. We thank Isobel M. Findlay, Warren Weir and J. Wilton Littlechild for permission to publish this piece.*

# Aboriginal Legal Theory and Restorative Justice

*James J. R. Guest*

Aboriginal Peoples are attempting to remove the legal system from their communities and to replace it with culturally relevant systems of justice. Aboriginal perspectives about what constitutes justice are as varied and distinct as the various Aboriginal nations that exist throughout the world. There are, however, more commonalities than differences in how they view the basis for truth and justice. The definition of justice is not the sole domain of any single nation, Aboriginal or non-Aboriginal.

Today, three justice system models operate in Canada:

1. the main criminal justice system, which uses raw coercive force as its power base;
2. a criminal justice system that is attempting to use restorative justice processes and to remake its image after years of locking up Aboriginal Peoples; and
3. Aboriginal justice systems within communities that use respect and teaching as the basis of knowledge for living together.

In this short article, I will not address the main criminal justice system and the problems of marginalization, assimilation, and racism, since much has already been written on this subject. This article will focus on restorative justice principles within the criminal justice system and the differences in legal theory that make it difficult to implement these processes.

A number of problems have been created by attempts to integrate restorative justice approaches with the existing criminal justice system. These problems all stem from the fundamental differences between Aboriginal legal theory and Euramerican legal theory. Aboriginal legal theory uses respect and teaching as its basic tenets. By contrast, the existing criminal justice system uses raw coercive force and the threat of incarceration to convince citizens to follow its written laws. Aboriginal justice systems are more organic.

An Aboriginal justice system is flexible to the needs of the community, and its "body of law" springs from the life of the community itself.

As its main procedural element, Aboriginal legal theory involves community members in the justice system; it does not look to state intervention. Respected members of the community pass on its values and traditions to the community's children. When conflicts arise, it is community members who come forward to help ensure a speedy and peaceful resolution in keeping with the traditions of the community. While this system of justice may seem simplistic, its practice involves hard work based on a complex philosophy.

### Horizontal Structures: We're All Equal

Aboriginal societies are horizontal structures. An act of crime creates an inequality between the victim and the victimizer. Unlike the vertical structures of Euramerican justice systems, in which crime is a violation of the law of the state, all matters in an Aboriginal society are private. Aboriginal societies do not make a distinction between criminal and civil law, as the Euramerican tradition does. In an Aboriginal society, when a crime is committed, a debt is created that is owed to the victim, not to the state. Because the victimizer has lowered the victim's status, the victimizer must restore the victim's previous status—namely, of being equal with all others in the society.

The processes within the community help resolve the dispute. When the conflict concerns the community or if the dispute remains unsettled and threatens to disturb the harmony of the community, the community may take a more active role in the dispute resolution process. Conflicts spark conversations within the community. Through the process of discussion, the community comes to a consensus about what should or needs to be done. The justice process is therefore a teaching and learning experience for the entire community. There are no hierarchical structures, no mechanisms for judging, no written substantive rules that resemble a "meat chart," only a fluid process of justice.

### Justice Is a Fluid Process

In the Navajo Justice and Harmony Ceremony, the peacemaker does not ask if the existing relationship is bad or good. Such value judgments are not respectful, helpful, or truthful. Instead, the Navajo peacemaker will ask "Hashhkeeji"—is this relationship moving toward disharmony?—or "Hazhooji"—is this relationship moving toward harmony? It is important to emphasize the movement aspect of these terms. The Aboriginal belief is that all living things are in a constant state of flux, moving either toward harmony or away from it. Bright lines marking people as good or bad do not exist. There is no black and white; everything is complex, different shades of gray.

This difference in basic perceptions give rise to differing views about how best to treat "wrongdoing." In the criminal justice system, the commission of a crime is cause for labeling a person as bad. The label is established through a long and complicated series of events, from the description of the crime to finding guilt based on either an admission or the use of "objective" evidence.

In Aboriginal communities, wrongdoing is viewed as misbehavior and is the result of the person's relationship with the community moving toward disharmony. Accordingly, the way to treat the person does not revolve around labeling the person who committed the crime and subsequently punishing him or her as the court prescribes. Instead of limiting their focus to how criminal law defines the offense, Aboriginal communities broaden the scope of the justice system to address the victimization that was caused by the conflict.

Considering the underlying cause of the conflict inspires flexibility. It also allows the community to address the victimizer's misbehavior through "lecturing" (teaching) or by treating an underlying illness. The goal is to facilitate the person's healing process and to help the person feel connected to the community once again. The goal is not to seek "blind justice" through punishment in the name of general or specific deterrence.

Whereas the criminal justice system often ignores victims' plight, the inclusive nature of Aboriginal justice includes concern for victims. The Aboriginal justice system recognizes that, although victims did not "do" anything, their experiences can cause ripple effects within the community. These effects can result in cycles of abuse and self-abuse, as well as other harmful behaviors. In other words, victims may find themselves moving toward disharmony as a result of the harm they experienced. Helping people and relationships move toward harmony is the very essence of helping victims.

In the criminal justice system, the victim is put in an ambiguous spot. The victim has no say in the legal process and is pushed aside. According to the criminal justice system, the victim does not fit into the categories of good or bad. Any problems resulting from the crime are largely considered the victim's concern. Victims may even be reviled, because they have been tainted by crime. The larger society leaves victims as it found them; namely, in a different position of equality within society and on their own to deal with the aftermath of their victimization. Crime is considered an individual act on an individual person; the larger community interests are represented by the democratic state. The net result is punishment for the offender and isolation for the victim.

## Tolerance and Change

In a bipolar world of good and bad, insofar as we view ourselves as good, a change in our position or a change in our viewpoint must be bad. However, if we view the world as dynamic and ever-changing, then we might view ourselves as moving in an infinite continuum. In this continuum, we are called to constantly reevaluate our starting position in terms of preference, not judgment. This approach allows for differences. One person's preference may differ from someone else's.

According to this worldview, judgments of good or bad do not apply. Instead, the focus is on the constant flux of relationships within the community as the relationships move toward either disharmony or harmony. How to attain harmony when there is disharmony is probably the community's preferred goal. Because the community prefers harmony, disharmony in a person's life becomes relevant to the community. When disharmony affects the person's relationship with the entire community, the community's response is to lance the sore so that it might heal. The criminal justice system, by contrast, acts like an inadequate bandage. Because it prevents communities from deciding which form of dispute resolution they should use or which forum is appropriate, its "help" allows existing sores to fester and spread.

This view of an ever-changing world and our position within it inspires greater tolerance for differences among people. People are different from one another, and these differences cannot be classed as simply bad or good. This leads me to ask, does an increasingly bipolar worldview lead people to become more intolerant? Do those living with this view have a higher rate of conflict because their worldview has increasingly separated them from reality with all its shifting complexities?

The loss of one's self in society and the sense that one is becoming more and more disconnected from society cause many social ills, including suicide and crime. Anonymity and the feeling of being disconnected from the community cause crime as well. People who do not feel connected are like those who do not have a consciousness; an essential awareness is missing. The two tenets of Aboriginal communities—teaching and respect—prevent crime, because they help us remember how we are connected. Helping a person see and "empathize with the victim" may be the greatest tool in crime prevention, because it connects a person to his or her community. People who do not feel this sense of connection must be helped by teaching them how to build it.

The argument that intensifying the legal system will solve the problems of the criminal justice system is based on the idea that punishment reduces crime through specific and general deterrence. However, most criminals think they will never be caught, and those who do consider this possibility tend to weigh the pros and cons of their action and come to a rational decision that the potential profits outweigh the risks. That being so, the argument for deterrence falls apart. Punishment fails to serve as a general or a specific deterrence, because all the threats of punishment fall on deaf ears.

By contrast, restorative approaches convey to the offender the experiences of the victim. This is a necessary part of the offender's learning process, because it helps the offender link his or her actions with the consequences of those actions to the victim, the victim's family, the victimizer's family, the community, and all of his or her relations. Only as offenders understand the full consequences of their actions will thoughts equivalent to a conscience enter into their profit-risk analyses. These processes of teaching, creating an awareness of acts and their consequences, and perhaps even brainwashing in extreme cases are important in helping offenders develop an internal moral code. "Being your own person" as someone connected in a community reduces crime through a self-policing moral code. Intensifying an external legal code cannot do this.

The Aboriginal emphasis on teaching distinguishes between defining a person as having acted badly and defining a person as a bad actor. A person may act on mistaken assumptions in new situations and disturb the community's ethos. The difference in how Aboriginal and non-Aboriginal communities respond to such a case is stark. Within the Aboriginal community, the mistake would be recognized as a mistake. The victimizer's lack of knowledge would be addressed, and reparations would be made.

The criminal justice system, however, allows no middle ground between guilty and not guilty. "I did it, but . . ." is not a plea but an admission of guilt, and it carries the full weight of the prescribed punishment. "I didn't know . . ." is sure to receive the familiar rebuke: "Ignorance of the law is no excuse." The criminal justice system is malignant and completely incapable of teaching without first inflicting harm. Using mitigating circumstances to lower sentences or even using alternative sentencing does not mitigate the use of coercive force. Yet abuse, which coercion and force are, is not a precursor to learning and healing; respect is. It seems an oxymoron to state, "I sentence you to heal"—a declaration reminiscent of an exorcist crying, "I cast the devil out of you."

The differences between the two systems are profound. Whereas restorative justice naturally reflects the Aboriginal approach, its differences with the criminal justice system are so fundamental that it cannot become fully effective in that context. First, we need to realize that the existing criminal justice system is a failure. Second, we need to realize that people who commit crime can be characterized in three ways: (1) as suffering from a lack of knowledge; (2) as not acting with consideration of others; or, most seriously, (3) as not being capable of acting with consideration for others.

All three types of criminals are capable of learning. Only in the third case of career criminals, predatory criminals, or psychopaths may the teaching approach not work. These criminals may be bound to repeat their crimes. However, it could be argued that the criminal justice system fails in these cases as well. How do you protect society from those who lack consideration for other people? If you cannot teach people to respect others and to empathize with them, then incarceration may be necessary as a substitute for the Aboriginal practice of banishment. Indeed, public safety may be the only legitimate reason for incarceration. Whether issues of public safety warrant incarceration would, however, have to be decided relative to the mind-set of the individual victimizer and not according to the rules of a uniform external legal code.

Trying to institutionalize restorative justice processes within the existing criminal justice system raises many problems. For example, restorative justice processes offer holistic approaches to conflicts. Yet their use within the linear criminal justice system, which is not holistic, presents difficulties, with the result that the processes are applied inappropriately. This is not the typical excuse of "Oh, that can't work in that situation." In fact, I advocate that every type of situation can and should be addressed using restorative justice approaches—but within an Aboriginal justice system where it can be used fully and appropriately, not piecemeal, halfway, or with conflicting messages, such as trying to coerce a person to heal.

Moreover, if we try to use a restorative justice process within the linear criminal justice system, we still face issues about coercion: what size stick should we place over the head of the victimizer? No matter how restorative we try to be, this sword of Damocles defeats the open, honest, and respectful discourse that a restorative justice, holistic process requires in the first place. Victimizers, victims, and communities cannot hope to resolve their problems when the constant threat of incarceration chills the air. Whenever offenders open their mouths, they forgo the institutionalized safeguards that protect them from the full coercive effect of the criminal justice system.

For this reason, family group conferencing is probably inappropriate after a charge has been filed. Sentencing circles are inappropriate as well when there is a chance that the judge will not respect the recommendations of Elders and community members. Using restorative justice principles is also inappropriate when the actors within the criminal justice system do not understand the process or lack confidence in or commitment to its use. These circumstances raise the danger that the restorative justice processes will be thwarted and rendered ineffective.

It is very important, therefore, to consider when it is appropriate to use restorative justice processes within the criminal justice continuum. The real dangers are that

- reforms in the name of restorative justice will simply repackage and relabel the existing criminal justice system;
- these attempts will be used to deflect the criticisms by the many reports and commissions levied against the criminal justice system; and
- these attempts at reform, rendered ineffective by the criminal justice context of their use, will be incorporated in statistical data that is then used to "prove" that restorative justice doesn't work.

The most appropriate place for restorative justice processes remains within the separate Aboriginal justice systems that exist within Aboriginal communities. Granted, the diversity of Aboriginal cultures makes it difficult to generalize to this extent. However, for the purposes of this brief article, I will simply state that Aboriginal societies are marked by a horizontal social structure that supports restorative processes in ways that the hierarchical criminal justice system does not.[1]

## Notes

1. For those who would like to read further on this subject, see Rupert Ross's book, *Returning to the Teachings: Exploring Aboriginal Justice* (Toronto: Penguin Books, 1996), especially the section "Replacing the Good, the Bad and the Ugly," 122–125.

. . . .

*This article was published in* Justice as Healing (1999) 4:1 *and* 4:2. *The editor would like to thank James J. R. Guest for permission to publish his work.*

# CHAPTER 8

# *Honoring Healing Paths*

## Indian Justice: Our Vision

*Federation of Saskatchewan Indian Nations'*
*Strategic Plan for Indian Justice*

The Federation of Saskatchewan Indian Nations' (FSIN) vision of justice development is to create a justice system that restores traditional First Nations values, culture, and spirituality and is trusted and respected by all members of the First Nations community in Saskatchewan. Our focus is to ensure that the justice process is community driven.

The FSIN views the responsibility for justice as residing in the chiefs and headmen whose roles are listed in the numbered treaties and confirmed in the spirit and intent of the treaties. The chiefs and headmen are charged with the responsibility of maintaining peace and good order amongst our peoples as well as in the relations between First Nations people and non-Native people. The treaty duty to maintain peace and good order expressed in each of the five numbered treaties that affect Saskatchewan is the basis upon which all development has occurred in this province.

Our vision of the future of our justice system is that it will promote the healing of First Nations individuals, families, and communities and provide the flexibility to accommodate the cultural, geographic, and linguistic diversity of our peoples, not only on and off reserves but also in the urban setting. Strengthening our families, protecting First Nations people from injury, and restoring the traditional core values that once guided our people in regard to justice constitute the ultimate purpose of our justice initiatives.

· · · ·

*Published in* Justice as Healing *(1997) 2:3, this statement is from the Federation of Saskatchewan Indian Nations' Strategic Plan for Indian Justice. It was approved by the FSIN Indian Justice Commission, the FSIN Indian Government Commission, and the Chiefs of the FSIN at the 1–2 May 1996 Chiefs' Legislative Assembly. We are grateful to the FSIN for permission to reprint it.*

# Saskatchewan Holds Court in Cree

*Wanda D. McCaslin*

On 26 January 2001, the appointment of Gerald M. Morin to the Provincial Court of Prince Albert was announced. Shortly thereafter, Judge Morin became responsible for the development of a northern Cree court circuit. The Saskatchewan minister of justice stated, "Judge Morin is a northerner and speaks Cree. I am looking forward to his leadership in establishing the capacity for Cree language services in the Provincial Court of Saskatchewan."[1]

His extensive experience in social work, corrections, education, and the practice of law serves him well in presiding over a Cree court. As the judge within a Cree court circuit, Judge Morin reaches people in a new way by using the Cree language in the court process. Judge Morin, who holds a Bachelor of Laws, 1987, explained, "People often see an injustice when they don't fully understand the process and they feel they haven't been fully and fairly dealt with."[2]

It is hoped that by incorporating the Cree language into the court, this system of "justice" will seem less foreign to Aboriginal Peoples. Using the traditional language during the processes makes justice more accessible, as the court can explain matters using more specific terms. The Cree Court, as it is known, consists of Cree speaker Judge Morin in addition to a Cree-speaking prosecutor, legal aid lawyer, and two clerk-translators.

In an address to the University of Saskatchewan Law School on 19 November 2001, Judge Morin spoke of his respect for the law and the need for respect of the language.[3] This respect is what led him in the journey to the Cree Court. By using the traditional language, the Cree Court provides the accused, who is in conflict with the law, the opportunity to give full answer to the charge.

The court does, however, face some unique challenges concerning translation. It is a court of record, and as such, it will need to offer translations between English to Cree and vice versa as the need arises through the judicial system, translations which are not easy. Jurisprudence will need to be developed on the issue. As Judge Morin points out, "The language and words are very important and must be respected."[4] Moreover, an appeal of a Cree Court decision is a distinct possibility; therefore the precision of the interpretation will be important.

The Cree Court is a precedent-setting endeavor, since the process is rooted within the language of the Cree. It offers young people an opportunity to "see their language being legitimized within the major institutions," providing a sense of pride and belonging.[5] People are watching the positive steps of the court with hopes of further development. As such, Judge Morin presides over a new and inspiring approach in Saskatchewan courts.

## Notes

1. Saskatchewan Provincial Government, News Release "New Judge For Prince Albert" (26 January 2001).

2. B. A. Adam, "Courts Offer Cree in Northern Sask," *The Star Phoenix* (2 October 2001), A1.

3. Judge G. M. Morin, Speech to the Faculty of Law, University of Saskatchewan, 19 November 2001.

4. Ibid.

5. Ibid.

. . . .

*This article was published in* Justice as Healing (2001) 6:4.

# Peacemaking and the Tsuu T'ina Court

*Judge L. S. Tony Mandamin*
*in consultation with Ellery Starlight and Monica One-spot*

The Aboriginal Peoples of Canada's First Nations have a deep respect for their Elders that is deeply rooted in their traditions and cultures. Even today, one can see the impact of Aboriginal respect for Elders. The Tsuu T'ina Court and peacemaking initiative on the Tsuu T'ina Reserve in southern Alberta is an example of Tsuu T'ina respect for their Elders and the benefits that flow from this respect.

The Tsuu T'ina are Dene people. They number approximately 1,800 and occupy their 108-square-mile reserve southwest of Calgary, Alberta. In 1996, the Tsuu T'ina proposed establishing an Aboriginal court and peacemaking initiative on the reserve.

The Tsuu T'ina Court began sitting in October 2000. This provincial court is located on the Tsuu T'ina Reserve with jurisdiction for criminal, youth, and bylaw offenses committed on the reserve. A peacemaking program was initiated by the Tsuu T'ina and is an integral part of the justice process.

. . . .

*A group of young people had been idle and, as a result, got into trouble. They broke into the school, stole some money, and damaged school property. The loss was over one thousand dollars. The peacemaking circle decided that the youths had to pay back what they had stolen and compensate the school for the damage caused. The youths agreed with the circle to pay for the loss and damage they caused. They all found jobs and paid the restitution in full.*

. . . .

It started with a traffic case. A Tsuu T'ina member was charged with driving without insurance on reserve roads. The case went to court, and the charge was dismissed because the provincial law regarding insurance applied only to public roads. The reserve had been set aside for the benefit of the Tsuu T'ina, and the roads on the reserve are not for public use. The Tsuu T'ina Elders, however, were concerned about the behavior of drivers on Tsuu T'ina roads. They said all drivers on their roads should have insurance, because if there was an accident and someone was hurt, the person who was hurt would suffer without the benefit of insurance. The Tsuu T'ina Elders directed the chief and council to do something about this problem.

The chief and council and their advisers decided to pass a traffic bylaw. In the course of their deliberations, they determined that they had to look beyond traffic problems and address all justice issues on the reserve, whether arising from assaults, thefts, other crimes, or traffic offenses.

The criminal justice system was not working for the Tsuu T'ina as it should. The Tsuu T'ina had established their own police service and participated in a community corrections society that provided crime prevention, a court worker, and probation supervision services. Yet something was lacking. The Tsuu T'ina community was not becoming more peaceful. When the Tsuu T'ina consulted their Elders, the Elders explained the traditional approach to dealing with conflict. The Elders said that those in conflict had to be healed if they were to behave properly, and relationships between victims and offenders had to be restored. These things had to be done by the people of the community. Through such peacemaking, conflict in the community could be resolved.

The Tsuu T'ina drew on the Elders' advice, their community resources, their cultural traditions, and the experience of other First Nations and tribes to develop their concept for an Aboriginal court and peacemaking initiative.

· · · ·

*A younger woman assaulted an older woman. The two had been friends. The assault had ended the friendship. In the peacemaking circle, the younger woman apologized to the older woman, saying, "I'm sorry I hit you, but what you said to me at the time really hurt me." In this case, apologies went both ways, and their friendship was restored.*

· · · ·

The Tsuu T'ina proposal for an Aboriginal court and peacemaking initiative was accepted, along with an agreement to proceed. This agreement was signed by the Tsuu T'ina, Alberta, and the federal Department of Justice on 15 October 1999.

The Tsuu T'ina Peacemaker Court has two aspects. First, a provincial court was established on the Tsuu T'ina Reserve. The court is set up in a circular arrangement. The judge, the prosecutor, the court clerks, the court worker, and the probation officer are Aboriginal people. Some of the defense lawyers who appear are Aboriginal. The protocols of the court reflect Tsuu T'ina traditions. The court starts with a smudge—a traditional burning of sage or sweetgrass signifying a prayer for guidance. The judge wears a beaded medallion symbolizing the Tsuu T'ina Nation. The court clerks wear tabs embroidered with eagle feathers, a sacred symbol for Aboriginal people. These measures are taken so that the Tsuu T'ina will see the court as their court, their system of justice, and their wish for peace and order in their community.

Second, peacemaking was made an integral part of the court process. A Tsuu T'ina peacemaker sits across from the Crown prosecutor. When a person charged with an offense is willing to enter into peacemaking, the case is adjourned while the peacemaker coordinator assesses the case and decides whether to take it into peacemaking.

The Tsuu T'ina had asked the Elders which offenses could be dealt with by peacemaking. After deliberating, the Elders advised that any offense could be considered for peacemaking except homicide or sexual assaults. The Tsuu T'ina also decided that they would do peacemaking only if the victim of the offense agrees to participate. The peacemaker coordinator also considers other factors before deciding to accept the matter into peacemaking. Examples of cases that are dealt with through peacemaking include break and enter, theft, assaults, domestic assaults, drug possession cases, and traffic offenses.

. . . .

*An elderly lady from Morley was charged under the Tsuu T'ina traffic bylaw with driving on a reserve road without motor vehicle insurance. The peacemaking circle included an Elder from the Stoney Reserve. During the peacemaking circle, it came out that there had been a death in the family and the woman was driving around trying to complete arrangements for the funeral. The peacemaking circle asked the Stoney Elder about the Stoney traditions. He explained that, some time after the death, the family of the deceased would arrange for a ceremony where the family and friends of the deceased would say good-bye to the departed and let go of their grief. The peacemaking circle decided that the woman had to arrange for that ceremony. There was an expense to holding the ceremony, and that expense was comparable to a fine for driving without insurance but, in this case, the money was spent in a healing way. By the time the matter returned to court, the motor vehicle in question had been insured.*

. . . .

If a case is accepted into peacemaking, the peacemaker coordinator assigns the matter to a community peacemaker. He or she chooses a person who will be seen as fair to both sides. The peacemaker then takes charge of the process.

The Tsuu T'ina choose their peacemakers from the community by asking the members of every household on the reserve whom they trust to be fair in peacemaking. This process identifies people who can be peacemakers for the community. The Tsuu T'ina then recruit from these community members and provide a training that reflects their concept of peacemaking, which incorporates their traditional values, mediation training, and dispute resolution skills, as well as provides an understanding of addictions, child welfare, and family issues.

Once the peacemaker takes charge, he or she will gather together the participants. The person charged with the offense will be present, as will the victim. Family members of the offender and victim may also be involved. There is always an Elder to see that the peacemaking is conducted properly. In addition, there may be helpers or resource people. For instance, if the offense involves alcohol, then there may be an alcohol addiction counselor from the Spirit Healing Lodge. A peacemaking circle may have anywhere from five to twenty-five participants.

The peacemaking circle draws upon Tsuu T'ina tradition. Each peacemaking circle generates its own dynamics. The people present either know details about the event that happened or know the speaker—features of the circle that discourage deception and evasion. When one speaks, he or she has the attention of all those in the circle. A victim is supported in a safe environment. The offender is offered help. The peacemaker guides the process but does not take the direction away from the participants. The Elder's presence and input, derived from lifelong experience and knowledge of

Tsuu T'ina traditions, adds a further perspective to the peacemaking circle's understanding.

Peacemaking circles work to resolve the conflict, heal the offender and the victim, and restore relationships. A peacemaking circle begins with a ceremony. It may be a traditional ceremony using sage or sweetgrass, a prayer, or just a simple statement that the circle is about to deal with an important matter. When a circle is held, each person speaks uninterrupted, while the others listen. The first time around the circle, people speak about what happened. The second time around, each person says how he or she was affected by what happened. The third time around, they speak about what should be done. This may take time, and it continues until it is clear what should be done. In the fourth round of the circle, participants speak about what is agreed. Circles may take from two hours to two days, although most conclude within an afternoon.

. . . .

*A husband had assaulted his wife. The couple had a history of domestic strife because of drinking and arguments. After the husband was charged, the case was taken into peacemaking. The peacemaking circle enabled the couple to speak openly with each other and set limits for each other's conduct. The wife was able to tell her husband that she would not let him assault her again. She would call the police if necessary, and she would leave the marriage. In the circle, the husband was able to express his frustrations and tell his wife that he would not accept her verbal harassment. The husband was also able to speak about his personal unresolved grief issues. They had children, and neither wanted the marriage to break up. The husband agreed to attend grief counseling, and the couple both agreed to see a marriage counselor together. The peacemaking circle was witness and party to these agreements. After the circle, the husband took counseling. As the counseling progressed, the husband began to feel better about himself. As a result, their marital relationship has improved.*

. . . .

At the conclusion of a peacemaking circle, the person who committed the offense will sign an agreement to follow through with the resolution that was reached within the circle. It may be an apology. It may be to make restitution for damage done. It may be to undergo alcohol abuse counseling, psychological counseling, or one-on-one sessions with an Elder. The person may agree to participate in a traditional ceremony. The person may also agree to do community service, such as working for the Elders or performing other tasks. The possible tasks are as varied as the people in the circle. Often several tasks must be undertaken. Once the person completes these tasks, he or she returns for a final peacemaking circle, and a ceremony is held celebrating the tasks' completion. The matter is then returned to court.

In court, the peacemaker coordinator reports on the offender's progress. The Crown prosecutor assesses what has been done against the nature of the offense. If he or she thinks it is appropriate, the prosecutor will withdraw the charge. In serious matters, the prosecutor will agree to submit the peacemaking report for court's consideration before sentencing. Either way, the outcome of peacemaking is important in resolving the offense.

The peacemaking process allows for checks and balances. The person charged and his or her lawyer can assess whether to choose peacemaking, while the peacemaker coordinator also assesses whether the matter should be taken into peacemaking. The Crown assesses the matter at hand both prior to its referral to peacemaking and when the case returns from peacemaking. The judge not only is involved in deciding whether to adjourn a matter to allow peacemaking to proceed but also considers the outcome of peacemaking if the matter returns for sentencing.

If the offender decides not to enter peacemaking, then the matter stays in court. If the matter is not accepted into peacemaking or if the offender fails to cooperate with the peacemaking process, then the peacemaker coordinator will return the matter to court. The process is flexible.

· · · ·

*A woman attempted to steal some pills and was charged with shoplifting. She was very depressed. When asked in the peacemaking circle what skills she had, she answered that she had no skills—she had nothing. The pills were to help her cope with her depression. She had been relying on pills for a long time, and she was addicted to them. Her life was going nowhere. She hadn't finished high school. In the peacemaking circle, the participants asked her if she could cook and keep house. She said yes. They asked if she could make camp. She said yes. They asked if she could make traditional garments. She said yes. Through their questions, she came to realize she did have skills. They asked what were her dreams. She said she wanted to go to college. The circle decided she must take counseling for her drug dependency, complete high school, and then she was to go to college. She took counseling for her addiction to pills. She finished her high school equivalency and registered in Mount Royal College. Some time later she came to the peacemaker coordinator and explained she was withdrawing from college. She had two teenage daughters who needed her help and attention. She was going to concentrate on helping them, and then she would return to college. In this case, two daughters gained a mother's help at an important stage in their lives when they most needed it.*

. . . .

The Tsuu T'ina have chosen to deal with conflict in their community. They are to be commended for becoming involved in the justice process and for showing another way to deal with conflicts. By addressing offenders' underlying problems and by restoring relationships between people, the Tsuu T'ina are working to create a more peaceful and safe community.

. . . .

*This article was published in* Justice as Healing *(2003) 8:1. The editor is grateful to Judge Mandamin, Ellery Starlight, and Monica One-spot for permission to publish this work. The circle process has been used in many ways to address conflicts in communities. For a fuller discussion, see Kay Pranis, Barry Stuart, and Mark Wedge,* Peacemaking Circles: From Crime to Community *(St. Paul, Minnesota: Living Justice Press, 2003).*

# Implementing Alternative Structures
# for Dispute Resolution

*Larissa Behrendt*

The following model offers an alternative dispute resolution process based on traditional processes and the values of the Indigenous community. This model, which is to be used within Aboriginal or Torres Strait Islander communities, is not definitive but merely an exercise in developing real alternatives to the legal system. It is an attempt to use creativity and flexibility in developing legal processes whose outcomes are fair and just. It is also an example of a model that does not simply transplant non-Indigenous methods of alternative dispute resolution but rather reflects the values of the Aboriginal community itself.

Aboriginal communities are capable of determining their own methods of dispute resolution. Aboriginal people are adults, not children. One of the underlying goals of this model is to promote community autonomy. With greater community autonomy, Aboriginal and Torres Strait Islander communities are likely to move away from the structures of the dominant culture. It's also likely that they will develop dispute resolution processes that are culturally specific to their community's needs and values. The more the dispute resolution process reflects traditional community values, the more respect it will receive from the members of that community. Not only the appearance but also the reality of greater justice and fairness will be achieved.

An important benefit is that the model reinforces the values of the Aboriginal and Torres Strait Islander communities. In the situation we have now, the imposed legal system does not recognize traditional values—and in many cases directly conflicts with them—and so erodes those values.

For this reason, the model I propose can be implemented only as an alternative to litigation in the dominant culture's legal system. It is a method of dispute resolution that could be used as a prelitigation option, just as mediation and negotiation are. It does, however, operate on the premise that the government and non-Aboriginal people will make an honest attempt to implement a policy of Aboriginal self-determination and greater community autonomy.

The model also shows that there can be, and must be, flexibility in dispute resolution models, so that they can be used in the different types of Aboriginal communities.

Example 1 deals with a traditional community. These communities remain on traditional land or reside on outstations. Such communities are geographically remote. They have stronger links with the traditional laws and processes of pre-invasion society.

Example 2 deals with rural communities. These communities are displaced from their traditional land but live on the fringes of towns near their traditional lands. They are poorer than the urban communities, having fewer resources and opportunities.

Example 3 deals with urban communities. Over two-thirds of Aboriginal people live in urban areas. Very few non-Aboriginal people live within the Aboriginal community in cities, because it remains socially unacceptable in non-Aboriginal society for them to do so. These urban Aboriginal communities pose the most difficult questions for Aboriginal/non-Aboriginal relationships in Australia. Many non-Aboriginal people argue that urban Aborigines are not a distinct community, believing that the choice of Aboriginal people to live within an urban area means they have adopted the values and customs of the non-Aboriginal community. Most non-Aboriginal people in cities have little understanding of the dynamics within urban Aboriginal communities.

In fact, the Aboriginal urban community has strong cultural values that reflect traditional values. These communities remain distinct because of their socioeconomic position, their social position, and their cultural differences. Even in urban centers like Sydney, the Aboriginal community is tight-knit and has a strong communal spirit. It has networks and cultural activities, as with any distinct cultural group living in Australia. . . .

Each example of dispute resolution presented here has a proposal for resolving disputes both within the community and between the community and a non-Aboriginal interest or body.

While it is not controversial to propose that communities be responsible for resolving internal conflicts, especially in geographically remote traditional communities, it is controversial to propose that non-Aboriginal people approach the Indigenous community on its own terms. Yet this approach is essential for addressing the enormous power differential that exists between Aboriginal and non-Aboriginal people within the non-Aboriginal community. It generates a respect for Aboriginal culture and values that are otherwise ignored or demeaned by non-Aboriginal Australians. And it is no different from requiring Aboriginal people to approach conflict resolution through non-Aboriginal mechanisms. Making a non-Aboriginal person submit to the authority of an Aboriginal dispute resolution process is the same as making Aboriginal people submit to the non-Aboriginal court system.

Aboriginal people have the right to have their customs and values respected. Greater community autonomy promotes this. It also promotes the value that Aboriginal people, as an autonomous group, should have the power to make decisions. People who are outside the community should recognize this when they wish to deal with issues affecting the Aboriginal community.

Advocating this power to Aboriginal people in Australia in no way advocates equivalent power to other minority groups living in Australia. As the Indigenous dispossessed people of this land, Aboriginal people are in a unique relationship with the rest of Australia. When other cultural groups have come to Australia, their cultural differences should and must be respected. However, it can be argued that, by coming to Australia, they have agreed to succumb to the laws of the sovereign powers that exist here.

The unique status of the Aboriginal community comes from the unique possession they have as the Indigenous people of this country. Promoting Aboriginal autonomy and a greater acceptance of Aboriginal cultural values are steps toward improving the socioeconomic position of the Aboriginal community. This should be a priority for all Australians. But even if one's personal morality does not give this priority, obligations under human rights covenants demand it.

## Model for Dispute Resolution

The following model shows that alternative dispute resolution processes can be established within Aboriginal and Torres Strait Islander communities that reflect Indigenous cultural values and that are more appropriate than processes developed in the non-Indigenous community. The cultural values shaping the process include

- community;
- egalitarianism;
- oral presentations;
- cooperation;
- respect for Elders, including female Elders;
- consensus; and
- flexibility of procedure.

I believe these values are the most vulnerable ones when Aboriginal people come in contact with the dominant legal system. The cultural values of that system are antithetical and therefore erode these particular Indigenous values.

## Facilitators

A council of Elders facilitates the procedure, thereby removing the impartial, independent facilitator that other models of dispute resolution require. The council is not elected or dependent on training. Admittance to the council is decided as it was done in traditional society—by being a respected member of the community. Credentials come from experience, knowledge of customs and traditions, and commitment to the welfare of the community. Elders are male and female, and a female Elder can have more power or influence than a male Elder.

In a traditional or rural community, Elders are easily identifiable, and they probably already serve as facilitators in resolving disputes. Within urban communities, selecting Elders may seem more difficult, because so many more people qualify. But even in urban areas, the community is sufficiently tight-knit to know who the most respected Elders are. Members of the community simply know who is appropriate to include, consult, and refer to in any political or social activity. For example, an Elders' conference met to discuss community strategies over negotiations with the federal government about the *Mabo* case. Five hundred Elders attended the conference. No debate was necessary to decide who should be included in that conference; the community just knew who the appropriate Elders were.

## Arena

Proceedings need to take place in public within the community, which removes disputes from the formal environment of courtrooms and offices. Traditionally, disputes were heard outdoors and in the community of the disputants. Having the proceedings take place outside may appear to be trivial, but an outdoors setting gives the process a more relaxed and informal feel.

The venue for disputes within a community is easily determined. When there is a dispute between the Aboriginal community and a non-Aboriginal person or group, the venue should still be in the Aboriginal community. This way the power imbalance that Aboriginal people suffer within the non-Aboriginal community is somewhat diminished.

If the dispute concerns community land, holding the proceedings within the community becomes especially useful. It gives the non-Aboriginal party a chance to see the way in which the Aboriginal community respects and values the land in question. It also promotes a better understanding of the cultural values of the Aboriginal community.

## Format

The Elders control the proceedings. People involved in the dispute sit in a circle with the Elders at one part. One disputant or group of disputants sits on one side with their families and supporters around them. They face the other party or group, who also has their family and supporters present. Rather than focusing on one individual, this arrangement gives the proceedings a communal aspect. . . .

The process follows the following format.

*1. The aggrieved person, people, or party initiating a proposal states the issue.*

Some traditional dispute resolution processes start with the complainant airing the grievance. . . . Any aggrieved person can express what has upset him or her, which allows an emotional level into the process. The problem is stated, and any disgruntled parties have a chance to air their grievances.

If someone is seeking to negotiate a proposal in the forum, this first step gives the person a chance to explain what it is that he or she wants, so that the issue is clearly understood from the start.

Gone is the formality of written and oral submissions. Any person affected by the proceedings has a chance to express how he or she feels about the matter. Perhaps it sounds New Age-ish, but this process clarifies what has upset the disputants. At this point, the central way of resolving the conflict is to define the issues and focus on them.

*2. The Elders state what the appropriate law is.*

Once the issue has been established, the Elders discuss the relevant traditional law or, in an urban setting, the values of the Aboriginal community. What they say will not be the binding law, but it will help those involved understand the relevant traditional values. Aboriginal law would be binding only if legislative instruments were in place to make it so.

The Elders state the law, and whoever has something to add about it speaks. For example, Elders might explain the traditional value of land and specifically the sacred sites on an area, while other members of the community may wish to raise economic issues, suggesting, for example, that the community could permit commercial activity on the land. Again, this step gets the issues out into the open. It places importance and value back on the knowledge of the Elders. And it eliminates the ludicrous situation where anthropologists are called in to give evidence about the cultural heritage of Aboriginal groups.

*3. The other side speaks.*

The respondent then speaks. This is done out loud and without the need of supporting evidence. The family and supporters of an aggrieved person are also allowed to state their concerns or opinions.

The Elders then question those who speak. Their purpose is to narrow the argument or area of contention as well as to see if the parties can agree to a compromise or to some action of redress.

If compromise is needed, both sides know the other side's position at this stage. The scope of the conflict has been verbally expressed, and the Elders can then direct the discussions toward those issues.

*4. Others affected by the decision respond.*

Others are invited to express an opinion about the decision, which allows for a thorough airing of viewpoints. It also acknowledges that other people have an interest in the proceedings and their outcome as well.

There is no issue of standing or hierarchy. Every person has the right to have his or her opinion heard, and it is expressed in the light of what the Elders have stated about the law.

### 5. The Elders question the person or people in conflict.

This part of the process further narrows the boundaries of the dispute. Elders ask questions to help the parties get at the real issue. They also try to get the aggrieved person to describe a solution he or she would be happy with. The Elders' involvement helps an inarticulate person express his or her grievance. It also helps focus the proceedings by narrowing down the disputed topics.

### 6. The Elders work toward an agreement.

By questioning the parties and suggesting compromises, as well as by going over traditional law and the realities of post-invasion life, the Elders eventually help those involved to identify the core issues and to reach a compromise that is acceptable to both parties.

The process develops, therefore, through various stages. First, the aggrieved party describes the problem or conflict. Second, Elders speak about the appropriate laws or values to establish what the traditional and cultural values are. Third, the opposite party has a chance to express concerns. Fourth, others with an interest in the dispute are given a chance to express their interests. Fifth, the Elders ask questions and suggest ways to compromise in an attempt to narrow the issues. Sixth, the process culminates in an agreement between the parties reached by consultation and input from numerous Aboriginal groups.

The oral nature of the presentations adds to the informality of the proceedings and makes them more flexible. Emotional responses can be made and given value. Disputants have a chance to speak for themselves and to air their own grievances and feelings. This is empowering and useful, as the public expression of a grievance often goes a long way toward making an aggrieved person feel redress. It also means that written submissions and evidential rules are not required.

This is by no means a perfect process of dispute resolution. It is merely an example of how a dispute resolution process can be created that emphasizes rather than eliminates cultural values. The ideal is to have Aboriginal communities develop such processes. . . .

## Implementation

The government has the power to make room for such schemes to be established. It can delegate the responsibility of keeping order. Greater Aboriginal autonomy can also be achieved through government policy and, where necessary, legislation. These methods of implementation fall within the government's constitutional powers.

Moreover, establishing such processes is in line with the government's current policy of self-determination. Although the term *self-determination* is amorphous, it could be understood to mean, at the least, greater input in decision-making processes and, at the most, the embodiment of the necessary elements for total autonomy. . . .

### Example 1. Traditional communities

Communities that live traditionally already have traditional practices to resolve disputes among members of the community. The use of traditional methods of dispute resolution in such cases is not controversial. Living away from the non-Aboriginal community, the Aboriginal community has a certain amount of autonomy.

More controversial, though, is the use of the model in disputes between the community and non-Aboriginal people or groups. For example, when a mining company is interested in mining on land that has been returned to Aboriginal people under the Land Rights Legislation in the Northern Territory, although the community does not own the mineral rights, they do retain a veto right to mining. In this case, the mining company needs the permission of the traditional owners in order to mine the land, so they must negotiate with the Aboriginal community.

The model allows the Aboriginal community to meet with the mining company in an environment that severely diminishes the power advantages that the mining company has in the non-Aboriginal community. These advantages include the financial resources the mining company has available to them, their access to skilled legal opinion, and the fact that they live by the adversarial values embodied in the dispute resolution process, which the Indigenous party does not. Such values are alien to the Aboriginal and Torres Strait Islander disputants.

The community-based process allows the Elders and community to state the value that the land has to them and to explain the culturally different way in which the Aboriginal community views land. It also allows Elders to describe where sacred sites are and why those sites are important. This contributes to a greater understanding of the Aboriginal culture by the mining companies, who in the past have lacked such knowledge. The Elders' expressions give their cultural values credibility and enforce them.

By dealing with the community in this manner, the mining company must listen to Elders and respect their decisions. This setting also lessens the amount of interference by non-Aboriginal governments in the outcomes.

The approach has, of course, several evident problems. Such negotiations are dependent on the good faith of the non-Aboriginal disputants. In the past, mining companies have not acted respectfully toward Aboriginal communities. Instead, they have a history of deception and malice in their dealings with them. In 1963, for example, Aboriginal homes at Mapoon were burned to make way for mining interests.

Another problem is that a non-Aboriginal litigant may not see how a council of Elders will not be biased. Such distrust shows an ignorance of the wisdom of Elders. Some Aboriginal communities have, in fact, allowed mining on their lands when they have seen that it will benefit the community as a whole in some way. They have more control over what areas are mined; the community can also ensure that sacred sites are protected and the ecological balance is maintained. Communities often decide that they need the economic benefits of mining parts of their land. If this is done with cooperation and consent, Aboriginal people have been quite willing to negotiate....

Those who wish to deal with a self-determining community should do so by approaching the community with deference to its values and customs. Wherever possible, negotiations and disputes should be resolved by using that community's dispute resolution mechanisms. If the mining company wanted to negotiate with non-Indigenous landowners, they would use the non-Indigenous legal system. So, too, if they must negotiate with the Aboriginal community, it should be on Aboriginal terms and through the legal system of the Aboriginal community.

*Example 2. Rural Communities*

Rural communities are smaller in population than urban communities, and they are marginalized in the areas where they exist. Communities may be on old missions or on the fringes of town. As in traditional communities, respected Elders are easily identifiable. They run grassroots community organizations and know tribal groups and customs. They are also involved with community affairs and, as in traditional communities, are probably already involved in settling disputes within the community. . . .

Here again, the process affirms community autonomy and promotes community unity. Because opinions and reasons are heard publicly, the decision-making process has a communal aspect. For example, the model allows the community to hear all opinions about how resources should be allocated, and it also allows grievances to be publicly aired against those who are hoarding resources. After listening to community opinions and decisions, those involved can make a decision. Because decisions about where money will be spent is the result of community consultation and consensus, they are more likely to be carried out with cooperation.

A problem arises if younger members of the community have become too imbued with non-Indigenous values and do not have respect for Elders. This is more likely among young people who have lived away from the community in non-Aboriginal society. In these cases, the community has methods for instilling respect for the Elders' authority.

For example, as in traditional society, people who are disrespectful to Elders face public accusations of their disrespect as well as community pressure to redress their rudeness. If they fail to comply with the community's standards and values, they will be socially ostracized. Although mobility to and from Aboriginal and Torres Strait communities is much easier now than in pre-invasion days, the closeness of Indigenous communities makes social pressure to conform extremely powerful.

A rural community can also use the model when it has a conflict with a non-Indigenous group or interest. . . . Again, the main problem in implementation is likely to be the unwillingness of the non-Aboriginal party to submit to the jurisdiction of the Aboriginal community or to comply with a decision made through the process in good faith. Not only will the procedure be seen as biased, but also the non-Aboriginal party will not wish to give up the advantage they have in the power imbalance that exists between

Aboriginal and non-Aboriginal groups in the wider Australian society. For this reason, the model will be useful only for non-Aboriginal parties who are sincere about wanting the Indigenous community's approval and cooperation in their ventures.

*Example 3. Urban Communities*

Urban Aboriginal communities have large populations that come from different tribal groups. Despite this diversity, they have a strong sense of community that allows their cultural values to flourish, even though most members of the community have contact with the non-Aboriginal community through schooling or work.

As in rural communities, Elders are still easily identified because of their involvement in community affairs and for the wisdom of their counsel. The Aboriginal community knows who to invite to speak at functions and who to consult for community decisions. Elders are already involved in resolving disputes within the Aboriginal community. For example, disputes within the community may arise over the use of property within the community. . . .

The advantage of keeping internal disputes away from the non-Aboriginal community is that it prevents non-Aborigines from seeing any discord within the community. Non-Aboriginal people are quick to label any type of internal dispute as evidence that the Aboriginal community is incapable of running its own affairs. When the community controls its internal disputes effectively, it proves that the community is more than capable of resolving whatever conflicts arise in its administration.

In some cases, a person's traditional Aboriginal values may have been eroded by contact with white people. But even in urban areas, the Aboriginal community is close-knit. Social pressure is still a powerful force and can help people restore their sense of cultural values.

Here again, the model can be used to resolve disputes between an urban Aboriginal community and a non-Aboriginal community or interest, as, for example, in the case of a dispute with a non-Aboriginal community over a housing project. By and large, non-Aboriginal communities will not want Aboriginal people moving into their neighborhoods, and so white backlash is likely. They will pressure local and state governments to prevent the Aboriginal community from developing the project.

Although non-Aboriginal residents have no legal remedy if Aboriginal people buy land in their area, some kind of dispute resolution procedure can still be useful. If the process is successful, it will allow the parties to live together with greater tolerance.

The model offers several benefits in this situation. It allows grievances to be aired publicly, and it allows the disputants to come face to face. Since a dispute of this kind is often based on ignorance, a process that brings together disgruntled non-Aborigines with Aboriginal families may be useful in eliminating negative stereotypes. By having to acknowledge the powers of the Elders and seeing the cultural values of community and cooperation, non-Aboriginal people may find their prejudices diminishing.

Given the blatant racism of most segments of Australian society, this may seem like a naive suggestion. Nonetheless, a lot of racial hatred is based on ignorance. If the ignorance is destroyed, so is the hatred. It cannot be assumed that non-Aboriginal people are necessarily bad. Some are simply uninformed.

Besides not wanting to submit to the Aboriginal community's jurisdiction, non-Aboriginal people may balk at recognizing the urban Aboriginal community as an entity. Two common non-Aboriginal misconceptions are that Aboriginal people who live in urban areas either are not real Aborigines or have somehow lost their cultural values. These views are again based on ignorance. Most non-Aboriginal people do not know the nature of the urban Aboriginal community, and so they are in no position to judge.

However misguided, such misperceptions can pose barriers to recognizing the Aboriginal community as an entity. When these misperceptions arise, the dangers are twofold. Either non-Aboriginal people will not seek compromise or cooperation from the Aboriginal community in their ventures, or they will gain the approval of a few token members—people who do not represent the Aboriginal community's opinions or interests.

In sum, this culturally based model for resolving disputes has profound advantages for Aboriginal communities. It reinforces the communal nature of decision-making. It empowers the Elders and the community, it strengthens traditional and cultural values, and it affirms the community's autonomy.

· · · ·

*Published in* Justice as Healing *(1998) 3:3, this article is an edited excerpt from chapter 6 of Ms. Behrendt's book* Aboriginal Dispute Resolution: A Step Towards Self-Determination and Community Autonomy *(Australia: Federation Press, 1995). The editor wishes to thank Ms. Behrendt and Federation Press for permission to reprint it.*

# 42

# Mapping the Healing Journey: First Nations Research Project on Healing in Canadian Aboriginal Communities

*Phil Lane Jr., Michael Bopp, Judie Bopp, and Julian Norris*
*Four Directions International and the Four Worlds Centre for Development Learning*

Six Canadian Aboriginal communities generously participated in intense consultations on the subject of healing in First Nations communities. These community-based consultations brought together program leaders, key volunteers, and the core healing teams from each community. The communities also participated in a national consultative meeting held in Winnipeg 14–15 January 2002. These communities (listed in alphabetical order) are

+ Eskasoni First Nation on Cape Breton Island, Nova Scotia;
+ Esketemc First Nation, otherwise known as Alkali Lake, British Columbia;
+ Hollow Water First Nation in southeastern Manitoba;
+ Mnjikaning First Nation at Rama, Ontario;
+ Squamish First Nation near Vancouver, British Columbia; and
+ Waywayseecappo First Nation in southwestern Manitoba.

In each of these communities, key healing personnel and community volunteers gave many hours and, in some cases, days of their time. They grappled with very challenging and difficult questions related to the ongoing healing work in their communities and to the requirements of the road ahead, leading to sustainable well-being and prosperity. The following report is based on what these communities have shared of their experiences.

## I. Introduction and Background

For hundreds of years (in some cases as many as three hundred years), Canadian Aboriginal communities have experienced wave after wave of debilitating shocks and traumas that left whole nations of people reeling and broken. These shock waves came in many forms:

- diseases (such as influenza, small pox, measles, polio, diphtheria, tuberculosis, and later, diabetes, heart disease, and cancer);
- the destruction of traditional economies through the expropriation of traditional lands and resources;
- the undermining of traditional identity, spirituality, language, and culture through missionization, residential schools, and government day schools;
- the destruction of Indigenous forms of governance, community organization, and community cohesion through the imposition of European governmental forms, such as the Indian agent and the elected chief and council system, which systematically sidelined and disempowered traditional forms of leadership and governance and fractured traditional systems for maintaining community solidarity and cohesion; and
- the breakdown of healthy patterns of individual, family, and community life, manifested in alcohol and drug abuse, family violence, physical and sexual abuse, dysfunctional intimate relationships, neglected children, chronic depression, anger, and rage, and greatly increased levels of interpersonal violence and suicide.

The trauma originating from outside Aboriginal communities eventually generated a wide range of dysfunctional and hurtful behaviors (such as physical and sexual abuse) that became recycled generation after generation inside communities. Descendants who are as many as three to five generations removed from the externally induced trauma—namely, the great-great-grandchildren of those who were originally traumatized by historical events—are now being traumatized by patterns that continue to be recycled in families and communities today.

The result of all this trauma is a wide range of personal and social dysfunction that has many symptoms.

*Individuals:* Individuals find they can't maintain intimate relationships, can't trust or be trusted, can't work in teams with others, can't persevere when difficulties arise, can't function as parents, can't hold a job, and can't leave behind harmful habits, such as alcohol and drug abuse or family violence. Of course, we now know that all these "can'ts" can be reversed through healing and learning processes.

*Families:* When individuals who are stuck in harmful patterns enter family life, the family becomes a generator of trauma and dysfunction, as patterns of addictions and abuse are passed on. Basic human needs for safety, security, love, and protection are not met, and the family system is no longer able to provide the foundation for healthy community life, as it once did in traditional societies.

We note that many Aboriginal communities are considering returning to the clan system and to clan-based government. This can be viable only if Aboriginal families are able once again to develop high levels of trust, intimacy, cooperative behavior, and effective communication, which in turn involves adhering to a system of life-promoting, life-enhancing values, beliefs, and moral standards.

Again, we now know that families can learn, heal, and overcome a long history of intergenerational trauma and dysfunction through hard work and a lot of love and support from others.

*Communities:* Aboriginal communities that have been traumatized display fairly predictable patterns of collective dysfunction. These patterns include rampant backbiting and gossip; perpetual social and political conflict and infighting; a tendency to pull down the good work of anyone who arises to serve the community; political corruption; a lack of accountability and transparency in governance; widespread suspicion and mistrust of others; a chronic inability to unite and work together to solve critical human problems; competition and turf wars among programs; a general sense of alienation and disengagement from community affairs (a sense of "what's the use?"); a climate of fear and intimidation surrounding those who hold power; and a general lack of progress and success in community initiatives and enterprises, which often seem to self-destruct.

We now know that these patterns, like their counterparts at the individual and family levels, can be transformed through community healing and development. We also know that Aboriginal nations cannot move forward as long as the pattern of recycling trauma and dysfunction generation after generation is allowed to continue. Something is needed to interrupt the cycle and to introduce new patterns of living that lead to sustainable human well-being and prosperity.

### The Aboriginal Healing Movement

Since the early 1980s, an increasing number of Aboriginal communities have been struggling with the challenge of healing. Most early efforts focused on the pernicious pattern of alcoholism that was destroying so many lives. But as more and more communities had some success with their efforts to stop the drinking, they gradually realized that alcohol and drug abuse were only the tip of a very large and complex iceberg, the bulk of which remained hidden beneath the surface of community life.

Aboriginal healing programs sprang up across the country, addressing such issues as addictions, sexual abuse, parenting, family violence, depression, suicide, anger and rage, and eventually the residential school syndrome.

With these many varied programs came a wide variety of approaches. Strategies to promote "healing" ranged from residential treatment programs (based on a variety of treatment models), one-on-one counseling programs, personal growth workshops, retreats, and traditional practices, such as sweat lodges, healing ceremonies, fasting, prayers, and the application of traditional teachings. As this study goes to press, more than a thousand Aboriginal healing programs are operating on reserves and in cities and towns across Canada, and many more programs include a healing component.

### Background to This Study

While a great deal of innovative work is clearly going on related to individual and societal healing in Aboriginal communities, there have not been many comprehensive attempts to map all the concepts, experiences, and practical work necessary for this healing process. For example, in the 1996 Canadian government's report of the Royal Commission on Aboriginal Peoples entitled *Gathering Strength*,[1] the commissioners say, "Healing, in Aboriginal terms, refers to personal and societal recovery from the lasting effects of oppression and systematic racism experienced over generations." While this description tells us something about the origins of dislocation and disease in Aboriginal communities, it does not tell us how to promote the recovery process.

A comprehensive "map" of the healing process may not exist partly because healing is such an integral part of all the development efforts, whether they focus on alternative justice, recovery from addictions and sexual abuse, economic development, or education. Healing work is going on in many contexts and is shaped by different programs. In each program, healing is important. When specific initiatives have focused on different aspects of the healing work, they have naturally developed particular types of expertise.

In addition, clear and generic definitions, principles, and processes may not have been elucidated thus far because communities need to develop their own models and processes—ones closely linked with their own cultures, resources, and needs. . . . Healing work needs to be intimately linked to relationships with Elders and other cultural leaders, as well as to ceremonies, systems of personal development, and ways of restoring healthy relationships within families and communities. As a result, how specific communities or nations design and implement their healing programs will vary greatly.

On the other hand, Aboriginal Peoples across Canada seem to share some basic principles—such as the principle that healing comes from within as well as the principle that the healing of individuals and the healing of communities go hand in hand. The general consensus is certainly that healing work involves overcoming the legacy of past oppression and abuse. In practice, this usually means transforming inner lives, family and community relationships, as well as the social and environmental conditions in which people live. In other words, healing means moving beyond hurt, pain, disease, and dysfunction and establishing new patterns of living that produce sustainable well-being.

Despite these common characteristics, however, a clear and comprehensive portrait of the healing process would be highly valuable to communities. For example, what does individual and community healing mean in the context of Aboriginal communities? How does healing relate to developing well-being and prosperity? And how can healing and development efforts best be nurtured and supported? . . .

## II. Summary of Findings from Reviewing the Literature

In reviewing the literature on healing, we looked for answers to three questions:

1. What is healing?
2. What has been tried?
3. What works? . . .

*What Is Healing?*

Healing has various definitions. For example:

- *Gathering Strength,* the RCAP report, states that "good health is not simply the outcome of illness care and social welfare services. It is the outcome of living actively, productively, and safely, with reasonable control over the forces affecting everyday life, with the means to nourish body and soul, in harmony with one's neighbor and oneself, and with hope for the future of one's children and one's land. In short, good health is the outcome of living well."[2] . . .
- "Healing may therefore be strategically described as a process of removing barriers and building the capacity of people and communities to address the determinants of health."[3] . . .
- Healing is about being aligned with natural spiritual law. That alignment can happen swiftly, but the healing process itself takes a long time. The major part of the unresolved suffering that needs to be healed actually belongs to the ancestors. By healing themselves, each generation heals their ancestors.
- Choctaw wisdom keeper Sequoyah Trueblood reflects on his healing experiences: "Being 'healed' means living in peace, living in acceptance, and not judging anyone. Thus, with the residential school experience, healing means to come fully into acceptance of what took place and fully forgiving everyone who was involved. The only way to resolve the pain that comes from living in the past is acceptance and forgiveness. I tried all different kinds of healing, but I didn't feel like I was healed until I saw all the things that had happened to me as a great gift."[4] . . .

The literature includes many maps and models that describe different ways of understanding the healing journey for individuals and communities and identifying the stages or elements within that journey. For example, in the field of trauma and abuse recovery, many researchers and practitioners state that the first stage begins with creating a safe place, because it allows the recovering person to tell his or her story. Telling one's story is a fundamental need for those who have suffered abuse, and it is an essential first step in the healing journey. . . .

*What Has Been Tried? What Works?*

In the past twenty-five years, the "Aboriginal healing movement" in Canada has included a wide range of experiences, programs, and activities, such as

- participation in traditional healing and cultural activities;
- culturally based wilderness camps and programs;
- treatment and healing programs;
- counseling and group work; and
- community development initiatives.

The literature exploring this broad experience is just beginning to emerge as a recognizable stream. Compared to the literature relating to the colonial experience and its legacy, the community healing literature remains somewhat fragmented and diverse. While a growing amount of literature focuses on these areas of experience, few authors have attempted to integrate the fields. In this section, we summarize some key initiatives and lessons. . . .

*Traditional Healing and Cultural Activities*

*Cultural healing practices.* Cultural healing practices are playing an increasingly strong role in the community healing movement. Traditional practices have been invigorated at the community level and participation has increased tremendously. Cultural components delivered by Elders and cultural specialists are now commonly found within most government institutions serving Aboriginal people, such as schools, colleges, the justice system, the health care system, and other institutions. Culturally based curricula and models are widely used within treatment and healing programs. The community healing movement and the cultural renaissance have grown hand in hand over the past three decades.[5]

*Culture as treatment.* A variety of factors—such as the prohibition of traditional practices, the movement from traditional territories to urban centers, the development of an intertribal Indigenous identity—have led to a growth in cross-cultural healing models and practices, many of which have been adopted from Plains cultures. As Aboriginal cultures have undergone massive transition, so too have many healing practices. Within a "traditional" context, diagnosis, treatment, and healing are often clearly defined. Within a "transitional" context, however, the whole field has shifted, and traditional healing systems have had to adapt. The "Culture as Treatment" model advocated by groups such as the Round Lake Treatment Centre is often highlighted as a "best practice."[6] The approach appears to be particularly effective and may be found in various forms coast to coast. In some cases, it appears to have displaced local healing models.

In some areas of the country and within some Aboriginal communities, traditional healing practices remain very strong. Some traditional "treatment centers" are being run with no external funding, no staffing, and no administrative structures. They are undocumented, often operating at the homes of Healers. Many people, both within the literature and anecdotally, attribute their healing to participation in traditional cultural practices.

*Contemporary healing practices.* Contemporary healing practices are centered around ceremony but offer a structured way of life that involves fellowship, community, economy, spiritual practice, education, and a profound sense of meaning and belonging, which funded programs can never fully replicate. For example, a growing number of people are involved in Sundances. The Sundance itself lasts for only a few days in the summer. However, participation often requires a multiyear commitment to an annual schedule that involves fasting, regular sweat lodges, Sundance meetings, medicine gathering, feasts, preparation, participation in particular ceremonies, and other forms of involvement. It is a whole way of life, and few—if any—treatment "follow-up" programs come close to being as complete or rigorous. . . .

*Outcomes of traditional healing.* Considerable anecdotal evidence attests that traditional healing practices have profound effects. For example, in a study of traditional healing with Aboriginal sex offenders in prison, therapists identified traditional practices as beneficial and noted changes in those who participated in them. "Among the key areas of change that therapists saw were a general increase in openness to treatment, a greater ability to accept feedback, an enhanced level of self-disclosure (general and offense-specific), a decrease in hostility and resentment, the development of trust and empathy, and a greater sense of grounding or stability."[7] A therapist quoted in this report stated: "Having attended some Sweats, I do know that, during the ceremony, people are able to talk about their own victimization because of the safe and secure nature of the Sweat."

The same study identified conceptual and cultural differences between a "Western" treatment model, which is essentially medical and is described by therapists, and an Aboriginal healing model, which is described by Elders and traditional Healers. The study identifies several key areas of perceived conflict between the two worldviews. For example, whereas the primary focus of the Western model is cognitive and behavioral, the primary focus of the Aboriginal model is spiritual and emotional. Whereas the Western style of treatment is clinical and confrontational, the Aboriginal style is nurturing and non-confrontational. And whereas the Western orientation to the offender is guarded and suspicious, the Elder-based model is more trusting and caring. . . .

### Summary and Conclusions

Our brief assessment of the available literature shows a number of trends.

1. The literature on Aboriginal personal and community healing is just beginning to emerge as a recognizable body of work, and this trend will most likely increase over the next few years. Important work remains to be done to draw together the lessons and insights from existing resources and to make them more widely available to practitioners in an accessible and practical way.

2. "Healing" within a Canadian Aboriginal context refers to a cluster of ideas, activities, events, initiatives, and relationships that happen at every level, from the individual to the intertribal. This cluster has drawn extensively on models and experiences from around the world. It is also developing its own unique models, methods, language, and analyses, many of which are just beginning to enter mainstream dialogue. We can describe this cluster as the "Aboriginal Healing Movement."

3. The healing movement is generating interconnected outcomes on many levels. These outcomes are hard to track and measure, especially using existing (culturally patterned) models and tools. Specific program interventions at the community level clearly have a direct impact on individuals, but so does the emerging climate of revitalization within communities. This revitalization movement includes the burgeoning activities associated with the

growing cultural renaissance; the emergence of a growing number of inspirational Aboriginal role models at the local and national levels; the increasingly confident and positive portrayal of Aboriginal Peoples and issues within the growing Aboriginal media; the resolution of key land claims; self-government initiatives; and many other currents of collective healing.

4. The interconnected nature of this movement makes it somewhat difficult to isolate and measure specific outcomes of specific interventions. Yet the interconnected healing movement offers clear lines of action for promoting healing and development. Specifically, interventions must adapt to and mirror this holistic and multilevel process, precisely because it is the reality of how healing actually happens. Moreover, according to the literature, existing mainstream systems are just beginning to engage with this healing movement. They are opening themselves to the possibility of being transformed through their interactions with Aboriginal healing processes and by their own efforts to understand and support communities on their healing journeys.[8]

5. Almost everything has been tried when it comes to models of healing. Basically, almost everything works for someone, and nothing works for everyone. From an Aboriginal perspective, specific models are less important than the larger context in which they take place. Indigenous perspectives on healing lie at the heart of the Aboriginal healing movement and have been the quiet engine of many significant initiatives. In this larger context, Aboriginal communities have adapted many methods and models to suit their own cultural and social reality. These Indigenous perspectives are not specific healing models in the way that specific counseling or therapeutic techniques are. Rather, they provide the frameworks within which such techniques find their meaning and best use.

6. Traditional healing has itself undergone change. Healers have adapted techniques, medicines, and models to meet the new challenges they face. A growing number of Aboriginal practitioners engaged in the healing movement are drawing on traditions that combine elements of both traditional and contemporary practices. In some cases, these blended practices have come to be presented as "traditional," since they have been increasingly incorporated into the language and experience of the healing movement.

7. The most promising specific initiatives seem to be those that actively transform patterns of "disease" and dysfunction within a person or group's actual

social context. Community-based treatment, systemic counseling approaches, participatory learning, and research activities are examples of initiatives that work on individuals and groups within their everyday worlds. These healing initiatives treat patterns of thought and action as emerging from these worlds, instead of viewing problems as existing on their own, disconnected from a social or life context. The disconnected approach to problems is often the implicit rationale behind sending someone away for treatment.

8. Young people—the largest and fastest growing sector of Aboriginal society—seem to carry the symptoms of community and cultural disruption most acutely. Prevention, healing, and development efforts are not keeping pace with this reality. The literature is clear on this point: unless young people are specifically targeted for healing initiatives, they are destined to repeat and even amplify the self-destructive behavior patterns of those who came before them.

9. Many authors highlight the important role played by catalytic, cross-disciplinary community workers. These individuals can organize and focus existing initiatives, support and sustain integrated approaches, and serve as cross-pollinators of strategies, ideas, and success stories. . . .

## Part IV: Voices from the Communities

During our visits to the six communities, we explored three big questions.

1. What is healing? Do people ever get healed? What are the results?
2. What is the healing journey? What happens at various stages of the journey? Which obstacles arise? What can be done to overcome them? What really works? What doesn't?
3. What is the healing future? What is the goal or destination of the healing journey? What needs to happen at the later stages? What is the relationship between healing and nation building?

In this section we present a summary of what we heard in these important discussions. . . . The full text of the community consultations can be found in the individual site visit reports. In the material that follows, individual speakers are not identified by name but by community.

## What Is Healing?

*Eskasoni:* Healing is a process, a journey. There is rarely a definite beginning or end to it. It's not because we are all broken or because we want to be perfect. It's because we want to be healthy individuals in a healthy community.

*Esketemc:* Healing is mental, emotional, physical, and spiritual development. It's all in the medicine wheel. And it's not just an individual thing either. It's also political, social, cultural, and economic development.

*Mnjikaning:* The term "healing" can also be called "reviving," "rebuilding," or "re-creating."

*Squamish:* Healing means having a clear mind, having a spiritual way of thinking, freedom from rage, anger, and hurt, and believing in the Creator, in yourself, and in other people.

*Waywayseecappo:* Healing is many things. It is processing and moving beyond hurt feeling, yes. But healing is also economic development. Education is healing. Getting out of poverty and out from under welfare is healing. Healing is anything that helps people become more unified and more able to be well and to prosper.

*Hollow Water:* Much of what used to be described as "healing" is now viewed as "decolonization therapy" by the CHCH team. The legacy of the colonial assault on the community and culture includes people who are out of balance, destructive values dominating community life, a mind-set of dependency, and community systems that help to perpetuate the previous three issues. Community healing as decolonization therapy involves articulating the principles that promote health and balance for the community, supporting people to move back into balance, basing all community systems on healthy balanced principles, and taking full responsibility as a community for the journey.

## What Are Some of the Issues for Which Healing Is Needed?

*Hollow Water:* Traditionally the Elders taught young people about the teachings, so that by the time they were able to create themselves, they understood something about life and their place within creation. The influence of the Elders and the teachings were understood to be an obstacle to assimilation by the colonial system and this influence and connection was therefore systematically disrupted and severed. This disruption plays out most fully in the emotional and spiritual life of the people today and is the reason that relationships, sexuality, and religion are the areas that seem to be most out of balance today.

*Eskasoni:* We have a complicated web of issues we are struggling with—alcohol and drugs, gambling, sexual abuse, family violence and the full spectrum of residential-school-survivor issues related to parenting, emotional withdrawal, and slow, burning rage (to mention a few).

*Squamish:* Our programs are part of the problem. We have "programitis." We have no common money and common goals, no common vision and no integrated plan. We have separate as well as overlapping services, and we are often enabling people more than we are helping them to heal.

*Esketemc:* You can't really heal the people unless you can create security related to food, clothing, and shelter. Unless we can address our real economic development challenges, complete healing remains out of reach.

*Waywayseecappo:* We have many healing issues. A big one (identified in a recent study) is family violence. There's lots of denial about this, but it's a huge problem. While we know that there is a lot of sexual abuse, that issue has not been opened up and addressed. If you count the binge drinkers, almost every household is living with alcohol and drug abuse as a constant pattern of life. When you count the young people (who are around 60 percent of the population), the numbers go way up. Maybe 90 percent of the kids are using.

*Mnjikaning:* The community does not want to hear about the really tough issues like sexual abuse, because this means facing their pain and doing the hard work of making changes.

### What Is the Healing Journey for an Individual?

*Waywayseecappo:* A healthy person has something to get up for in the morning.

*Mnjikaning:* When you are healing, your confidence and self-esteem are getting stronger. Your fire gets bigger, and you start feeling worthy and using your voice more. You respect yourself and the people around you more. You can look at people who have hurt you with understanding. Healing gives us some understanding of why people are the way they are.

*Squamish:* Healing means having a clear mind, having a spiritual way of thinking, believing in the Creator, in yourself, and in other people and freedom from rage, anger, and hurt. As people are healing, they become more and more functional. Anger, fear, and despair gradually leave them and are replaced by feelings of hope, caring for others, compassion, and love. As the grip of negative feelings loosens, people feel less and less paralyzed and more able to think clearly, to see themselves as effective agents of change in their own lives, and more able to take responsibility for their own choices.

*Eskasoni:* Spirituality is the main foundation ingredient to healing. Religion is not the same thing. We use prayers, sweats, and traditional gatherings—anything to keep the spirit alive. . . . A big part of healing is attaching meaning to past losses and pain. You have to reorient the meaning of past events so it is positive. . . . One size does not fit all. People are different and their healing needs are very different. We differ according to how we were hurt, but also according to gender, age, the type of family we come from, etc.

*Esketemc:* Healing circles are needed to hear the pain and the stories of victims. Often they focus on offenders. Both are important. . . . Our responsibility is to get by our own feelings in this generation and to face the rest of the world . . . to say there is our land, our heritage. It's not just that non-Natives hurt our feelings. They took our lands and shattered our culture. Now we have to pick up the pieces and carry on. "So pony up," we say. I don't want my granddaughter to go on fighting, and we're not going to pass it on.

*Hollow Water:* The healing process seems to go in cycles. There are periods of great movement and apparent growth and periods when nothing seems to be happening or when things get worse again.

### What Are Other Dimensions of the Healing Journey?

*Squamish:* Many adults are still so wounded that they are unable to parent or to provide, and yet raising the next generation of children to be healthy (without recycling the pain and abuse) is a vital requirement for healing the nation. This is a central healing challenge for the Squamish people for which viable solutions need to be found.

*Waywayseecappo:* Our governance system is making and keeping us sick. It sets people against each other. Since our (recent) election, the women have been split. Old friendships were broken. We're going to have circles to try to heal this. Right now the governance system is adversarial, so we fight and become disunited. Our current system encourages nepotism and corruption. We have $3 million for social programs, but it's all split into pieces, and program managers protect their piece.

*Eskasoni:* Four to five years ago, bootleggers were banned here, but this law was never enforced. The community gathered and worked together to bring about change, but the public institutions and leadership they trusted to carry out the community's decision managed to avoid really dealing with the problem. Corruption in high places is a major obstacle to healing and really is part of what needs to be healed.

When this sort of systematic undermining of the community's will and intention happens, people get discouraged about their own ability to make a difference or to bring about change. They are less and less willing to get involved in anything controversial, more passive, and more inclined to wait for and depend upon others to solve community problems.

The reality is that many people feel helpless and powerless to change an environment that they know is slowly grinding them down. There's lots of discontent, but also a strong fear to speak up. We are afraid those in power will come down on us somehow, like when we need something fixed or when we need a house for one of our children. They control our access to services and programs that may be our "right" to have, but they still control everything. So many of us remain silent. We are ruled by our own fear.

*Mnjikaning:* Our chief and council are not currently fully committed to a clean and sober leadership. For the most part, the community is asking for our leaders to commit themselves to being healthy role models, and there is also some impetus from the National chief. . . .

Money is still flushing through our community. Our community is just too small to sustain a lot of businesses (economy of scale isn't there). There are other barriers to entrepreneurial activity. For example, if a business begins to be successful, the council might take it away from you.

*Hollow Water:* In essence, the healing process involves the community as a whole taking ownership of problems and their solutions. The tendency to view particular problems as belonging to particular departments, programs, or outside agencies is itself part of the problem. The "program mentality" that people develop can itself be hazardous to the healing process. People enter programs as change agents, wanting to make a difference in their community. Gradually they learn to conform, "to not rock the boat," and lose some of the qualities that originally motivated and made them effective.

There is a tendency for programs to lose sight of their goals and do everything they can to justify the continued existence of the program. There is frustration that the very systems designed to serve people become systems that are no longer accountable and responsive to community needs.

*Esketemc:* Recovering our traditional justice circles is healing. Dealing with the emotional pain and scars of residential school is healing. Rebuilding our economic security and creating real opportunities for wealth-creation is healing. Helping our young people to find a better path in life than the one we took is healing. Rebuilding our traditional clan system is healing. All of these things are necessary because these are the things that were taken away from us, and we need all of them in order to recover our true strength as a Nation.

*Eskasoni:* The structure of government funding related to healing is another major obstacle for us that stands in the way of developing a coherent long-term program. We are forced to spend a major part of our time and energy trying to access funds (or accounting for funds received). There are many small pots of money, and we have to act like a chameleon—always changing the appearance of our mandate in order to get funding. These funds include Building Healthy Communities, NNADAP, the Healing Foundation and Brighter Futures. But there is no core funding that supports the essential long-term work of building and maintaining a coherent initiative. The big problem is that the government doesn't work together internally.

### What Has Worked for You in Promoting Healing for Individuals, Families, and the Community?

*Hollow Water:* Healing processes often require support from outside the community as well as the effective mobilization of the resources inside the community.

*Waywayseecappo:* An important key to the healing journey resides with the leadership. They have to work out a plan for the community that supports the work that needs to be done. We need a comprehensive healing and community development plan that includes healing, housing, governance, economic development—all of it. . . . We have learned that healing doesn't stop. There is recovery, but it takes a long time. The long-distance runner that trips doesn't give up. Why is that? Because of self-motivation and confidence. We have to support our people for the long run, for years. This means they will need training, lots of encouragement, and long-term support, until they have self-motivation and confidence.

*Esketemc:* So, in order to heal, you need a vision of what you want out of life, a plan to get there, and the help you need (it could be healing, training, access to funding, or just the support of friends, family, and community). Each person needs a plan. Each family too. Then you have to get everyone together to make a community plan that will support the realization of everybody's hopes and dreams.

*Mnjikaning:* As helpers in the community's healing journey, we need to keep coming to work. We need to keep listening and then to act. We need to have empathy. We need to walk our own talk. . . . Healing comes from living within the teachings and ceremonies. All of our programs are based on respect for ourselves and for others. We also need rites of passage ceremonies to safeguard young people as they enter the second stage of their lives.

*Squamish:* Other approaches besides talk-based therapeutic approaches are important to include in the repertoire of strategies used. Some of these include breath integration work, cultural activities, an art-based approach, and fun-orientated social activities. All of these (and many more approaches) can be effective in combination with more conventional approaches.

*Eskasoni:* We go right into homes. Mi'kmaw-speaking staff work closely with all the family members. The whole family is considered to be "in the program"—not just a troubled teen or struggling mother. We involve aunties and siblings and Elders in supporting the new behaviors we are trying to instill. We may go into a household three times a week. Sometimes we take over family management for a few hours and model new behaviors. We provide help and guidance (for example, parenting approaches). Sometimes we bring a problem person in for counseling and gradually reintegrate him or her back into family life. Mom and Dad may be in counseling with different counselors than children or youth. But we do case conference, so we have a coordinated view of the whole process. Lots of times, someone just needs physical help. People are poor. They have no phone, no vehicle, and sometimes for a single mom, the pressure is just too much. They can call their worker, and we will help drive them to the store, or just stop over and have a talk. Being there for people—really being a friend and support—is an important part of what it takes to help a family heal. . . .

## V. Lessons about Healing and the Healing Journey

What are some of the lessons learned about healing in Aboriginal communities? Above all, we heard that healing is possible for individuals and communities. Both appear to go through distinct stages of a healing journey. The healing journey is a long-term process, probably involving several decades. Healing cannot be confined to issues such as addictions, abuse, or violence. Healing interventions and programs have the most impact when they take place within the context of a wider community development plan.

Community healing requires personal, cultural, economic, political, and social development initiatives woven together into a coherent, long-term, coordinated strategy. Such a coherent strategy requires integrated program development, funding delivery, and ongoing evaluation. Healing is directly connected to nation building. At some point, community healing activities and movements towards self-government and community development begin to merge and join forces.

### What is Healing?

1. Healing is a process of development aimed at achieving balance within oneself, within human relationships, and between human beings and the natural and spiritual worlds. It has to do with choosing to live in harmony with the basic values and teachings that are at the core of Aboriginal (as well as other) cultures. "Healing" actually describes a wide range of initiatives, impulses, and efforts occurring at the level of individuals, families, communities, organizations and institutions, and the nation.

2. The concept of healing in Aboriginal communities focuses on well-being rather than on sickness. It focuses on moving the population toward wholeness and balance. It includes all levels of the community, from individual to nation, and embraces politics, economics, patterns of social relations, and the process of cultural recovery. . . .

The important point that Aboriginal people keep making is that their way of life—which was an integrated system of many dimensions—was taken away, and if healing doesn't mean restoring some form of life that can support human well-being, then what does it mean?

3. There are two distinct impulses within the community healing process. "Healing as recovery" essentially involves moving away from the pain and suffering experienced by a community in crisis. "Healing as wellness" involves moving towards and maintaining healthy patterns of life.

4. The healing journey may well take generations. It took generations for many communities to internalize the pain and trauma they now carry, and it may take generations to move past them. Healing is possible, however, and although there will always be a need for programs to help people heal from pain and suffering, which is an inevitable part of life, as well as to learn skills for healthy living, the type of intensive healing work that is required now will not necessarily always be needed.

Currently, there are some special situations (such as the legacy of residential schools and years of colonialism) that require intensive healing work. In time, this work is likely to shift from recovery to rebuilding new patterns of life.

5. Healing requires decolonization. At this point in history, the healing journey has a lot to do with overcoming the legacy of dependency and dysfunction that are the result of decades of colonization, missionization, and residential schools. The term "healing" refers to restoring human and community integrity and well-being that were destroyed by the aftermath of such historical trauma. It is certainly not confined to restoring mental health and ending dysfunctional behaviors such as abuse, addictions, and violence, though it does, of course, include these things. Those working on the front lines sometimes describe community healing as "decolonization therapy."

### The Community Healing Journey

1. The healing process seems to go in cycles. There are periods of great movement and apparent growth and periods of stagnation and retreat. This is true of any learning endeavor, from an individual mastering a new skill to an organization reorienting itself around new principles. It is very important for those leading and supporting healing to understand the learning process.

Often what seems to be stagnation and retreat is actually a plateau on which important consolidation and learning takes place. The periods of rapid growth are invariably preceded by long periods where "nothing much happens." Learning how to track these cycles is an important step in itself, so that people can gain an appreciation for the type of work that must be done at various stages of the journey.

2. Periods of rapid growth and development are often triggered by a crisis of some sort. If properly managed, such crises can create opportunities to mobilize people for rapid learning and coordinated action. Once the crisis loses its edge (either because the issue is dealt with to a significant extent or because people become discouraged, apathetic, bored, etc.), the healing process can really bog down as well. Because the healing work has become organized around a series of crises, it can be very difficult to shift gears in order to take advantage of new opportunities to mobilize the community to take responsibility for its problems.

### The Individual Healing Journey

1. People can heal, change, learn, and grow. Inspirational and effective leaders of healing processes nationwide are living testaments to the possibility of transformation. Program initiatives across the country clearly demonstrate the life-altering power of engaging individuals (no matter how unhealthy they may be) in a process of long-term, systematic transformation that leads from dysfunction to wellness.

2. Personal and community healing journeys go hand in hand. The leaders of the healing movement have to pay careful attention to their own wellness or they will not be able to work effectively in their communities. At the same time, progress with the general wellness levels in the community gives leaders the courage to continue and eventually the human resources they need to build on.

3. It is not possible to talk about "healing" or the "healing journey" in one simple definition. We can, though, talk about the attributes that someone acquires through personal healing. For example, healthy people do not need to control others, are not crippled by fears from the past, and have gained skills to look after themselves. They have strong confidence and self-esteem, respect themselves and others, and can listen to what others say about them without taking it inside.

4. It is also possible to talk about healing in terms of the medicine wheel. Healing involves the whole person—body, mind, spirit, and feelings. It involves the whole individual, the whole family, the whole community and the whole nation. It involves the whole cycle of life from childhood, to the time of youth, to our adult years, and on to Eldership.

5. People only begin their healing journey when they are ready and that is often when they hit bottom. In other words, when people are in danger of losing something (i.e. their freedom, their relationship, their children, their job), they are ready to work on healing. We have to be ready to work with people when they are ready (not in our time frames and on our terms).

6. Every recovering individual needs to have a dream (i.e. a vision and a plan) that lays out a pathway to a better future. The dream grows as people go further on their healing journey. For some the dream may entail getting more education and training. For others it may mean having access to credit or investment dollars. For still others, it may mean building viable partnerships or obtaining needed support and approval from the community leadership.

### Elements of the Healing Journey

1. Many different healing methods and modalities have been tried in communities. The lessons, both from community experience and the literature, is that many ways are of value. Nothing works all the time or is appropriate for everyone. Body therapies, breath-work, spiritual healing, energy work, individual and group counseling approaches (of which there are more than 200 different documented forms), participation in traditional healing ways, participation in religious activities, recreation, skills training, arts and music, support groups, relaxation techniques, and mind/body practices all have something to offer. Skilled helpers in communities are aware of the multiple

entry points available and are able to guide different people to a modality that will be helpful for them.

2. A major piece of the healing journey is understanding the past. What happened to us? What choices did we make that led to the layers of hurt? What was done to us? What did we lose? What did we use to have that we need to recover or rediscover?

3. "Forgiveness" is a controversial concept, given the justice-related issues connected to the legacy of residential schools. Nevertheless, forgiveness is an essential part of healing. Unless people learn to forgive (not forget), they are still holding onto feelings that hurt them. The healing journey requires taking full responsibility (as individuals, families and communities) for the work that needs to be done to overcome that legacy.

4. Often it takes a crisis (such as a disclosure of abuse on the part of a prominent person) to help the community overcome its denial that a problem exists and to recognize the need for healing.

## VIII: Lessons about Healing as the Rebuilding of Nations

### *Linking Healing and Economic Development*

1. Healing is inseparable from social and economic development and nation building. While everyone knows this intellectually, most communities have experienced a functional separation between healing activities on one side and the work of political development, economic development, housing, and even human resource development (training and education) on the other.

2. The orientation to nation building constitutes a new emphasis in perspective within the Aboriginal "healing community" across Canada in the past few years. During several previous national studies conducted by Four Worlds, there were always a few people in every community who made vague references to the linkages between healing and community development, but now those linkages are front and center in everyone's minds. In the past, many communities always had a conceptual divide between those who advocated for economic development and those who advocated for healing as a solution. Now many leaders in community healing say that economic development and political reform are healing and need to be actively pursued as part of the healing agenda.

3. The economic dimension and particularly the addiction of many communities to the welfare system need to be included in our analysis of community healing. The lack of productive work opportunities, structurally enforced poverty, and hopelessness on the one hand and the capacity of individuals and communities to move beyond patterns of hurt and dysfunction into constructive processes of development on the other are directly related. Some of the most pressing healing issues are being addressed when people have enough income to meet their basic needs with dignity and can participate in society without shame.

4. The stable funding base of the healing movement needs to be greatly expanded. One way to do this is to link healing directly to economic development by working with those in recovery to create businesses that provide a living wage to workers and a steady income (i.e. the profits of the business) to healing programs.

### The Need to Transform Structures and Systems

1. Communities need an integrated holistic system that provides critical pathways for healing, personal growth, and learning and that significantly improves the social, economic, and political life of the person, the family, and the community. In other words, as individuals become more healthy, they need a range of opportunities open to them that lead to better housing and greater levels of economic security and prosperity. They also need a significant increase in their capability (i.e. power and capacity) to participate in planning and creating the future.

2. "Healing" needs to go (conceptually) far beyond ending hurt and dysfunctional patterns. It also needs to include building new patterns of life that are healthy and pursuing visions and dreams of possibilities. Restoring balance to a people and society that were thrown out of balance by what happened to them in the past must return the people to a form of life that goes well beyond meeting the basic minimum requirements for survival. "Healing as restoration" must include creating conditions for people and their society to support and enhance the realization of human potential.

3. Recovery needs planning. Healing is much more than an individual journey into sobriety or personal wellness. It is the rebuilding of a nation. You don't rebuild a nation without systematic long-term work. You need a plan.

A "Nation's Reconstruction Plan" should simultaneously address a number of levels:

   a) addressing the dreams and aspirations of individuals;
   b) transforming the current political system;
   c) developing a sustainable economic foundation;
   d) recovering language and culture; and
   e) preparing future generations of children (to name a few important areas).

4. Creating and implementing such a comprehensive plan requires resources and sustained support over a number of years. The attempt by some to limit the definition of "healing" to exclude almost all of the above (in the interest of restricting legal liability) is extremely troubling and problematic when viewed from the standpoint of nations in recovery.

5. If recovery doesn't mean gaining back all of the collective capacities that were lost (e.g. taken away by the process of residential schools), then what does it mean?

### The Role of Spirituality and Culture

The renewal of spirituality in general and Indigenous cultural forms of spirituality in particular is central to the healing journey for most Aboriginal communities. When communities have been forcibly separated from their own spiritual roots for a long enough time, a lack of vision and coherence at the core of community life set in. This lack of vision and cultural coherence makes it difficult for them to "see" any pattern of life for themselves other than the ones in which they are currently enmeshed. On the other hand, rekindling spiritual and cultural awareness and practices can greatly strengthen the coherence and vitality of a community healing process.

## IX. The Individual Healing Journey

### Stage 1: The Journey Begins

The healing journey of individuals often begins when they come face to face with some inescapable consequence of a destructive pattern or behavior in their life or when they finally feel safe enough to tell their story. They may have spent a significant part of their lives unaware of the damaging pattern or denying that it is destructive, or they may have believed that the rewards of the behavior outweighed the costs. But when they find themselves in jail, facing legal consequences, pregnant, without their spouse, fired from work, tired of living this way, having lost their kids, in grief because someone close died, engaged in a spiritual awakening, or confronted by others, they feel a desire to change the way things are. They realize the answer must be to stop the behavior.

At this point, people often enter some kind of treatment/therapy/ support group—or they may do it alone. Either way, they begin their healing work. Often people make many attempts to start their healing but retreat into denial and pain. However, when the threat of consequences outweighs the fear of opening up and trusting others, or when people feel "sanctuary" (i.e. a sense of safety) in the relationship they develop with those working to support their healing, then the journey can really begin.

Usually the first steps involve telling their story, at first just to get it out and later to understand how the story is related to the pain and dysfunction in their lives. It can be very hard to stop the behavior, and the consequences of stopping may seem worse than continuing. People may go through many cycles of relapse and recovery. They may become stuck in this cycle for years—even a lifetime. The cycle will continue until they address the primary forces driving the cycle—that gave rise to and maintain their patterns of dysfunction and addiction. Cycles of addiction are hard to break for two main reasons.

1. Substance abuse is usually a whole lifestyle, and most addicts are part of an addictive subculture. Whether addicts get involved with the substance and then progress to the lifestyle or gain a sense of belonging within the subculture and find that substance abuse is the price of entry, their lives become oriented around a culture of addiction. Within this addictive subculture, the addicts' basic human needs are met—albeit in a way that has high costs. Their friends and family, their group membership and sense of belonging, their activities, their daily routines, their diet, their social role, their sense of purpose and order, their dress, their language, their sexuality, their rituals, symbols and music, their livelihood and much more are shaped by the addictive subculture. Their whole world and identity are bound up with it. "Quitting" is like trying to get out of a moving vehicle. Treatment is not simply

competing with the intoxication experience; it must provide an alternative pattern of living. Many people learn this the hard way when they return home from treatment centers.

2. Once the addictive behavior stops, traumatic feelings and fearful consequences often surface. Feelings of shame, worthlessness, anger, rage, grief, loneliness, guilt, depression, and sadness may have festered and been building up for years. Once addicts "quit," they become aware that such feelings dominate their inner landscape. They are likely to face terrifying ordeals— confronting abusers, being confronted by victims, accepting one's inner nature or calling, and taking responsibility for one's life. They may have no effective coping strategies to replace the addictive behavior itself.

A vicious cycle can ensue in which the addiction is used to treat the symptoms brought about by the withdrawal from addiction or just the complexities and stresses of daily life itself. The healing journey seldom means returning to a previous healthy life. It is a rite of passage that requires separating from the old identity, a period of learning, guidance and support, and forging a new identity, new patterns of life, and new relationships.

### Stage 2: Partial Recovery

At this stage individuals have mostly stopped their addictive behavior, but the driving forces that sustained it are still present. Now the journey involves struggling to uncover the roots of trauma from the past that caused the pain and dysfunctional behavior. It can be slow and painful work, but it can also be tremendously exhilarating. While the recovery is precarious, people often experience enthusiasm, excitement, and renewed energy. They are doing something with their lives. They make discoveries about themselves. They may join new communities within which they gain acceptance and which rewards them for participating in the healing process. A new vision of possibility emerges.

During this transition stage, people need a lot of support. Many become involved in healing communities of some kind, whether they be therapeutic (such as Alcoholics Anonymous or community treatment programs), religious (such as church groups), or focused on traditional cultural ways. These groups often meet many needs that were previously met by the addictive lifestyle, and people may fully and wholeheartedly immerse themselves in this new "culture" (in some cases for the rest of their lives). The culture of recovery replaces the culture of addictions.

## Stage 3: The Long Trail

Once someone has reached a hard-won sense of stability, it takes a great deal of courage, discipline, and motivation to continue the healing journey. The momentum begins to wane, the length of the journey becomes apparent, support may drop off ("she's just obsessed with healing!"), opposition may be encountered ("Why can't he just let sleeping dogs lie?"), and people want to get on with their lives.

Many people stop doing the healing work once the pain becomes bearable or life seems manageable. Yet this can be a dysfunctional stability. The old behavior no longer dominates ("I'm sober"), but the consciousness that generated it still exists. This consciousness may come out in what seems to be less drastic or destructive ways. It may manifest in unhealthy and compulsive relationships with people, work, food, tobacco, or gambling.

Ultimately, this stage is about developing a new identity and life pattern, and it involves long, slow work. There may be long periods of stagnation, enlivened by periods of growth and change. There will be many mistakes made and many lessons to be learned. New strategies and patterns will be tried. Some will fit and some won't. Each person must find his or her own way through. It is hard to walk this path alone. Many things can help a person keep going: renewal experiences, supportive community, guides and mentors, participating in a disciplined path (such as traditional ceremonial cycles and activities), and ongoing education. Much of the work is invisible because a person is building new foundations and putting down new roots.

## Stage 4: Transformation and Renewal

Ultimately, the healing journey is about the transformation of consciousness, acceptance, and spiritual growth. This stage of the journey is no longer about dealing with the demons of the past. It is drawn forward by a higher vision. People feel a conscious determination to build their lives and community around life-enhancing principles (spiritual laws, original teachings, healthy virtues, etc.). A conscious articulation of the vision motivates and draws them. The experience of the hurt self diminishes, and the experience of a universal self grows.

As people's consciousness becomes more fully aligned with life-enhancing principles, their outer lives also naturally go through profound changes. New relationships emerge. New pathways of expression and service to the community become important parts of an emerging pattern of life. At this stage, people no longer need the "culture of recovery," and so their participation in "healing" activities declines. Nevertheless, the self-centered focus of addictions has been replaced by a much more outward-looking orientation to serving others. A personal identity of dysfunction is replaced by a much richer, deeper identity anchored in culture and community.

## X. The Four Seasons of Community Healing

Based on our consultations with the six partner communities, combined with the knowledge and experiences of many other communities, we learned that community healing processes seem to go through distinct stages or cycles as well. These four distinct stages are

  stage 1: beginning the journey (thawing from the long winter);
  stage 2: gathering momentum (spring);
  stage 3: hitting the wall (summer); and
  stage 4: moving from healing to transformation (fall).

Taken together, these stages form one "map" of the healing process, which can be useful for both understanding the current dynamics of a community process and determining future actions and priorities. These stages are, however, only approximate models of complex real-life events. They are not "the truth," although there is truth in them. When, for example, the six partner communities reviewed this model, some people observed that the cycle could just as easily begin in the spring, since the stages do not take place in a linear way. They are more like ripples unfolding in a pool, where each new circle contains the previous ones. The important thing is that the healing journey with its stages forms a cycle.

As each stage progresses, those involved develop their understanding and power to transform current conditions. This development is primarily driven by a dynamic cycle of action and reflection that generates learning.

*Stage 1: Winter—Beginning the Journey*

This stage is characterized by the experience of crisis or paralysis that grips a community. Most of the community's energy is locked up in maintaining destructive patterns. Dysfunctional behaviors arising from internalized oppression and trauma are widespread, yet community members may view this state as "normal."

In this scenario, one of two things may happen:

1. Key individuals begin to question and challenge the status quo, often making significant shifts in their own lives. Their personal journeys often include service to their community, as they begin to reach out to other individuals to provide support and to initiate healing activities and crisis interventions. These activities are often undertaken at great personal sacrifice, since these individuals frequently encounter intense and very real opposition from within the community.

2. Programs are another way that community healing gets started. Frustrated with their inability to affect the scale of crisis that they find themselves facing, existing programs and agencies begin forming alliances in the community to develop a wider strategy. Often interagency groups are formed, and these networking groups begin to plan collaborative interventions and initiatives.

Both starting points have a similar effect. "Healing" becomes part of the community agenda. Core groups begin to form that are focused on health, sobriety, wellness, and other healing goals. These groups start laying the foundation for an alternative reality, often with significant support from outside the community in the early stages. Another essential source of support and inspiration at this stage are key Elders who have kept the cultural ways alive.

*What is driving this stage?*

One or more of the following types of people provide the energy for this beginning period:

- dedicated individuals (often women) who are responding to their awareness that things are bad and that there is an alternative;
- leaders and staff within programs who have been given the task of addressing the consequences of some aspect of the "crisis";

♦ visionary and courageous political leaders within the community who create a "climate enabling for healing."

All three types of people are essentially responding to a particular problem (alcohol abuse, suicide, etc.).

*Community consciousness: how is the nature of the situation perceived?*

The crisis condition is often denied at the community level. Those driving the process view their main task as one of creating an awareness of the need for healing. This awareness may be largely focused on the outward face of the problem (e.g., "alcohol is what is holding us back").

*What types of action are being taken?*

At the beginning, much of the activity is focused on personal healing and engaging in revitalization experiences. Around these activities, informal core groups and networks for mutual support begin to form.

*What are the results and indicators of success?*

People begin their own healing journeys. A growing number of people seek help for a particular issue or problem. Success and failure are measured in stark terms, such as drinking or not drinking.

*What are the restraining forces?*

Restraining forces often come from within the community itself. These range from a denial of the issues to overt and intimidating opposition directed at key individuals.

*What is being learned?*

The mechanics of the individual healing journey are being mapped out and modeled.

### Stage 2: Spring—Gathering Momentum

The second stage seems like a thaw. Significant amounts of energy are released and become visible, and positive shifts occur. A critical mass seems to have been reached, and the trickle becomes a rush as groups of people come together to go through the healing journey that was championed by the individuals in stage 1. These are frequently exciting times. Momentum grows, and significant networking, learning, and training starts happening. The spirit is strong.

New patterns of organization also begin to emerge. A recognizable network focused on healing begins to develop that is legitimized by the community, often with political support. The healing process begins to take visible form as programs and organizations. This stage often witnesses a lot of volunteer energy, but professional organizations also emerge. People start changing how they see the "problem," as they experience a gradual shift from a sickness to a wellness model. Their focus also shifts from concern about the presenting problems to a desire to address the underlying core issues and traumas.

The second stage is characterized by great hope and optimism. People have the sense that if enough individuals and families can begin the healing journey, then the "problem" will be "solved." Those driving and involved in the process invest huge amounts of time and energy in the community healing movement. Opposition still lingers, but it is generally overshadowed by the enthusiasm being generated.

*What is driving this stage?*

A growing awareness of the scope and scale of the problem within the community gives this stage its energy. The lid has come off the box, and it becomes very hard to put it back on. The growing momentum makes it easier for people to "get on board."

*Community consciousness: what is the nature of the situation?*

Community members begin to recognize the underlying issues (such as residential school trauma, sexual abuse) and understand how these issues give rise to the presenting problems. Moreover, they accept that the deeper solution lies with addressing these "root causes."

*What types of action are being taken?*

More and more people go through treatment and become involved in programs, services, healing gatherings, and other revitalizing activities.

*What are the results and indicators of success?*

Not only do an increasing number of people commit to a path of sobriety and wellness, but they also feel a growing sense of hope, momentum, and transformed vision. People now believe that community healing is possible.

*What are the restraining forces?*

A lack of community services and trained service deliverers constitutes a significant limit. Given the growing demand, service providers may have trouble working together. The community may be lacking in resources. It may also lack political support or have only a token showing of public endorsement. Finally, resistance to healing by groups within the community may continue to pull against the momentum that has been built.

*What is being learned?*

The process of individual healing becomes more clearly articulated, and a recognizable pathway with local relevance begins to emerge for people to follow.

### Stage 3: Summer—Hitting the Wall

At this stage, the path gets heavy, and those involved can feel as if the healing movement has hit the wall. Frontline workers find themselves increasingly tired, despondent, or even burned out, and the healing process seems to be stalled. While many people have done healing work, many more seem left behind. The workers start feeling overwhelmed, as they begin to realize that not only individuals but also whole systems need healing.

These systems (education, governance, economics, justice, etc.) may already be developing new initiatives. In some cases, though, these initiatives can appear to be becoming institutionalized and to be losing the spark and hope they had in stage 2. In other cases, even though awareness has begun to shift, old patterns persist for lack of new—and culturally relevant—models and strategies. The honeymoon stage is over, as the community begins the difficult work of transforming deeply entrenched patterns and reconstructing a community identity to replace the one forged in oppression and dysfunction.

Stage 3 is often characterized by a series of paradoxes:

1. The community's relations with organizations, agencies, and forces outside the community are being transformed. They often experience far more openness and find that the prevailing climate has shifted. Outside support is much greater and more available than in the past. At the same time, however, support and collaboration within the community itself may have actually decreased. The reason is that old patterns have begun to re-emerge, and a "healing fatigue" has set in.

2. Just when a significant number of adults have sobered up and worked hard to gain control over their lives, a new and seemingly worse crisis starts breaking out among the youth. Youth crime is on the increase. Alcohol use is replaced or augmented by drug use.

3. Among the adults, new addictive patterns seem to replace alcohol abuse. Gambling is becoming a serious social issue, along with prescription drug abuse and other self-medicating behaviors. People begin to realize that drinking covered up many other things, and community secrets begin to emerge. Despite increased sobriety, things actually seem to be getting worse.

4. Those on the frontlines notice that quite a few people appear to be "dropping out" of the healing movement. Community members don't get involved or show up like they used to. At the same time, a new group begins to emerge, namely, a relatively healthy group of people within the community whose energy is focused on their own lives and the lives of their families. No longer engaged in the "culture of addiction," they prefer to spend time on family activities and live their lives, rather than to be so actively involved in the "culture of recovery."

What feels like a wall may in fact be a long plateau. Not much seems to be happening on a plateau. Yet though it may seem as if you aren't going anywhere, a period of plateau is actually when the foundations for all future advances are being laid. Hindsight will reveal the significant advances made during this stage. Community norms are shifting; "bad" isn't as bad as it used to be. More people are engaged in positive activities. Capacity is growing within the community, as more people gain access to training, education, and employment. Often a cultural and spiritual revitalization has been developing parallel with the healing process, both shaping and being shaped by it.

As stage 3 develops, a new analysis emerges. People begin to realize that "healing" alone is not enough and never will be. Healing from the hurts of the past does not build the future. A growing community awareness recognizes the need for decolonization—decolonizing thought patterns and structures—and the need to address structural obstacles to development, such as Indian and Northern Affairs Canada rules, racism, poverty, and other obstacles. The realities of the economies of scale become apparent. A small community can only do so much to address such things by itself.

*What is driving this stage?*

Stage 3's organizations and initiatives have grown out of the previous stages. Healing becomes increasingly institutionalized, as professional capacity develops within the community. A key challenge for this stage, in fact, is maintaining community participation. Also driving the process (although not necessarily overtly) are the agendas of funding agencies, which provide the material support for the healing initiatives.

*Community consciousness: what is the nature of the situation?*

Complex and competing patterns of analysis emerge, and people rarely stop long enough to take a hard look at the current situation. Feelings of despondency and frustration exist side by side with a realization that progress is being made. People struggle with the nagging question: "Is this as good as it gets?"

*What types of action are being taken?*

Specific program initiatives develop, and the community gains increasing control over the programs and services that affect community life. More and more community members become trained to develop and run initiatives, and expertise grows.

*What are the results and indicators of success?*

The community increasingly supports and participates in healthy activities. More people seek education and training opportunities that lead to self-employment. The climate has definitely shifted, and negative behaviors, such as public drunkenness, family violence, or sexual assault, are no longer tolerated or considered "normal."

Public policy (i.e., local band government rules and practices) has also shifted toward legitimizing healthy standards of behavior and supporting healing efforts. As a result, new programs and services have been created to assist individual and family healing.

The community now has a greater awareness and acceptance of traditional cultural values, and traditional approaches are being incorporated into community initiatives and activities.

*What are the restraining forces?*

Dealing with the pain and suffering of community members day after day begins to weigh on frontline workers and key volunteers, draining their energy and vision. Plus, old tensions, conflicts, and habits that were put aside unresolved during the excitement of stage 2 generally reemerge at this stage. The momentum and support for healing slows once the overt crisis is over and a new dysfunctional stability emerges. Uncertain of how to deal with the dysfunctionality but pressed by needs on all sides, community workers feel pressure to "produce results" rather than work on reflecting and refining their approaches. Few viable models exist for how to work holistically, and community agencies are hampered by an inability to function easily together.

Outside forces impose restraints as well. Political agendas and in some cases corruption and other networks of vested interests may oppose the momentum for healing. Funding comes in isolated pockets and may require considerable energy and creativity to harness in ways that serve the community's healing agenda. Too little funding for too short a period comes with too onerous sets of strings and reporting requirements.

While workers cope with these bureaucratic realities, new forms of social problems emerge, especially among the growing number of youth.

*What is being learned?*

A great deal of individual learning, training, and skill development goes on. However, this learning often falls short of extending the shift to the whole institution. Intense demands make it hard for people to take time to reflect on the considerable learning they've experienced and apply it to the broader levels of systems and institutions.

### Stage 4: Fall—From Healing to Transformation

In stage 4, further significant changes in consciousness take place. The sense of healing as "fixing" shifts to healing as "building," and the focus on healing individuals and groups shifts to transforming systems. The sense of ownership for systems grows, and community members develop the skill and capacity to negotiate effective external, reciprocal relationships. People feel more responsibility, as the impetus for healing moves from programs and government to civil society. Indeed, civil society emerges within communities and the Aboriginal community at large, and healing becomes a strand in the nation-building process.

The leaders of the healing movement in stage 2 now enter a new stage in their personal lives. As they approach Elderhood, their analysis and vision matures and deepens. They shift their focus from putting out fires to building new and healthy patterns of life, and their own families and networks often begin to reflect these new patterns in significant ways. Often these individuals begin to search for new partnerships, alliances, and support for addressing larger scale issues.

*What is driving this stage?*

The driving energy for this stage often comes from a wider vision or context of activity. For example, people realize the limitations of current approaches, or community members increasingly participate in the larger economy. Even wider factors serve as drivers, such as the increased interconnection of the Aboriginal community, shifting macro-political agendas, or broader sociocultural forces (such as increased urbanization, youth culture, or the Internet).

*Community consciousness: what is the nature of the situation?*

Community awareness shifts to a more systemic analysis and from "healing" to nation building and transformation.

*What types of action are being taken?*

Communities form networks and alliances with other groups, and they increasingly take over programs and services. They design and deliver locally relevant training as well as consciously modify mainstream programs to fit their local needs. Community economic development ventures are now used to partially fund their development initiatives.

*What are the results and indicators of success?*

Success is gauged by the community's increased control over the fundamental patterns that shape community life, as communities claim greater responsibility in all areas affecting them.

*What are the restraining forces?*

Various restraints confront stage 4. The scale of the ongoing effects of trauma and suffering among community members remains a challenge, while competent leaders often get "siphoned off" into industry, academia, and government. On top of this, political systems continually stir up division and disunity within communities. Governments haven't caught up with the holistic analysis that communities have come to understand through their healing process. More than that, existing policies and rules are geared to maintain dependency and external (non-community-based) decision-making.

*What is being learned?*

Learning, like healing, is constantly evolving and is dependent on experience. For communities, the story is still unfolding. . . .

### *One Nation's Healing Journey: Esketemc First Nation (Alkali Lake, British Columbia)*

Esketemc is famous across the Indigenous world for its successful struggle to overcome community alcoholism. In the mid-1980s, the community made a dramatic shift from a situation in which virtually every man, woman and child over twelve years of age was a practicing alcoholic, to one in which ninety-five percent of the population practiced sobriety. The community did not stop there. They went on in their healing process to address high levels of physical and sexual abuse and many other challenges. Much of what was learned in this struggle was incorporated into a comprehensive training program called "New Directions Training," which has been shared in many community settings across North America.

The Esketemc Healing Committee not only represents all the band programs engaged in healing but also consists of many of the original "spark plugs" to the Esketemc healing movement. Most of the veteran team has been active in the community-healing journey since the early 1980s, and many are well known across North America for their training and healing work carried out in hundreds of Aboriginal communities. . . .

What the Esketemc team wanted to explore in depth largely related to the relationship between community healing and the social and economic development dimensions of nation building. Clearly, in the minds of Es-ketemc people, the healing process in their community has run into a kind of "glass ceiling."

From their point of view, it doesn't much matter how "healthy" commu-nity members become, how emotionally competent, how free of addictions and abuse, how spiritually connected to their own identity and values, how clear thinking in articulating the future they want for themselves and their Nation, how willing they may be to work hard and even sacrifice for the realization of the vision—none of this is enough when you have to live in-side a repressive political and economic system that keeps Aboriginal people powerless, poor, and unemployed.

The Esketemc people have demonstrated that while it is certainly pos-sible to emerge from trauma and tragedy to become physically and spiritu-ally whole and to have family and community relationships that are largely positive and healthy, governmentally imposed limits to the people's devel-opment potential constitutes a very serious obstacle to keeping the next generations remotely healthy. In the minds of the core healing team, there is a clear and present danger that unless a way through these obstacles can be found, many of the wellness gains Esketemc has made will be lost within a generation.

## Notes

1. *Gathering Strength,* report of the Royal Commission on Aboriginal Peoples, vol. 3 (Ottawa: Canada Communications Group, 1996), 109.

2. Ibid., 34–35.

3. J. Bopp, M. Bopp, and P. Lane, *Community Healing and Aboriginal Social Se-curity Reform: A Study prepared for the Assembly of First Nations Aboriginal Social Security Reform Strategic Initiative* (Lethbridge, Alberta: Four Worlds, 1998).

4. Sequoyah Trueblood, interview.

5. See Wayne Warry, *Unfinished Dreams: Community Healing and the Reality of Aboriginal Self-Government* (Toronto: University of Toronto Press, 1998), 240.

6. See Maggie Hodgson et al., *The National Native Alcohol and Drug Abuse Program Final Report* (Ottawa: Health Canada, 1998), 43.

7. Joan Nuffield, ed., *Issues in Urban Corrections for Aboriginal People* (Ottawa: Solicitor General Canada, 1998), 75–76.

8. See, for example, Warry, *Unfinished Dreams*, 257.

. . . .

*Published in* Justice as Healing *(2002) 7:3, this article presents excerpts from the 2002 final report of a First Nations Research Project on Healing in Canadian Aboriginal Communities that was conducted by Four Worlds International in conjunction with the Aboriginal Healing Foundation and was released by the Solicitor General, Canada. The complete report may be obtained online or by writing to: Aboriginal Corrections Policy Unit, Solicitor General Canada, 340 Laurier Avenue West, Ottawa ON K1A 0P8 or www.sgc.gc.ca. The report is also available on the Four Worlds website: www.fourworlds.ca. The editor would like to thank Phil Lane Jr., Michael Bopp, Judie Bopp, Julian Norris, Four Directions International and the Four Worlds Centre for Development Learning for permission to publish this work.*

. . . .

# Closing Reflections

43

## Digging Deeper: Challenges for Restorative Justice

*Denise C. Breton*

The desire to publish these articles from the newsletter *Justice as Healing*—produced by the Native Law Centre at the University of Saskatchewan—was one of the original motivations for founding Living Justice Press, a nonprofit publisher devoted to restorative justice, and for three basic reasons:

1. to present Indigenous voices speaking directly about their knowledge and experiences of restorative justice;
2. to help expand the restorative justice work to addressing historical harms and systemic injustices; and
3. to offer perspectives that invite transformation both as persons and as peoples, whether Native or non-Native.

The first reason for publishing this book is that the restorative justice movement traces its origins to Indigenous cultures worldwide, yet few books about restorative justice present Indigenous voices speaking directly about their traditional ways of responding to harms and creating harmony in their communities. Furthermore, based on the distinct experiences that Indigenous Peoples have had with the restorative justice movement and its practices, Indigenous voices offer both insights and critiques that are highly instructive and that deepen the global restorative justice dialogue.

The second reason for doing the book concerns the direction of the restorative justice field itself. Many people of color are challenging the restorative justice movement to expand its focus from dealing with the symptoms of

*Digging Deeper*   409

communities in pain (individuals in trouble or incarcerated) to dealing with the deeper social causes, specifically colonization, racism, and their ongoing legacies of degradations and harms.

Given the spirit of restorative justice, this challenge makes sense. Restorative justice involves much more than what happens to individuals after a harm has occurred. Crime and conflict reflect what is going on in communities as well as in society. Moreover, what people experience today grows directly from what happened in the past—the choices made by individuals and by society through our institutions.

## The Restorative Justice Movement's Development

If we consider the movement's development in relation to the criminal justice system, restorative justice proposed to the dominant society of the 1970s an alternative paradigm for dealing with harms one-on-one. In Canada, the United States, and Europe, victims began to meet offenders, offenders heard the stories of victims, and both experienced change as a result. The common humanity that often emerged from these meetings—from sharing stories, listening and being heard deeply, and working together to make things right—challenged the model of punishment as an adequate or effective way to deal with experiences that were already full of pain on all sides. Seeds were planted for finding different responses to harms.

In the decades since, the restorative justice movement has grown worldwide. Many practices for achieving more peaceful, satisfying resolutions for those affected by harm are now being used, including victim-offender mediation, group conferencing, and peacemaking circles. While the meaning of restorative justice as a theory and practice is increasingly being debated as the movement grows, many of those involved are coming to understand restorative justice as a philosophy and a way of life—more than a technique or process. It is seen as a completely different paradigm for being in relationship, whether the relationship is with those close to us or those we don't know, with individuals, groups, peoples, or nations, and with humans or others of the natural world. Something so simple as bringing together "victim" and "offender" is shifting our whole way of being—or, perhaps more accurately, it has the potential to do so.

While those of us raised in Euramerican society have by and large not experienced a healing, peacemaking paradigm as the dominant model shaping our institutions, it is not new to many Indigenous Peoples. For many of these cultures and communities, restorative justice suggests ways of being that have been practiced for millennia. Over the past centuries, the ways of the invaders of Native homelands have been imposed on Indigenous Peoples, interrupting traditional methods of restoring balance and harmony. Yet the traditional ways have been learned over many generations, often through hard experiences. As a result, Indigenous traditions embody a deep wisdom about what works and what doesn't if we want to be in a good relationship with each other and the world around us.

The articles in this book either express or in some way interact with Indigenous wisdom about how to be in good relationship. Many voices are Indigenous, yet there are also other voices, as those of us raised in non-Native societies begin to come to terms with our history and its ongoing legacies. A growing number of people in the restorative justice movement are considering these larger historical issues, since restorative justice is equipped as few disciplines are for addressing them. We realize that focusing the restorative justice work exclusively on individual crimes, most of which are related to addiction or poverty, without addressing the collective crimes that shaped how we got here (genocide, slavery, land theft, racism, and colonialism) is like straining at gnats while swallowing camels. Yet confronting our history is a painful and difficult process.

## The Challenges to Confronting Our History

How could it be otherwise? Even to raise the subject is a challenge, not only because our history on this continent is so horrendous but also because it has been so selectively told. Many if not most facts are generally unknown, which means that the history is not part of our everyday awareness of how we came to have the lives that we do. Neither are we who are white accustomed to seeing ourselves in the kind of light that our untold history sheds.

For these reasons, to name more fully what has happened and to explore our responsibilities today often elicit emotional responses. White people in particular express concerns about feasibility before any discussion begins, a preference for "putting the past behind us and dealing with now," and negative judgments about "people who blame the past for their problems." Charges of "white bashing," "white self-hate," or "white liberal self-flagellation" are quick to follow. These reactions reflect not only how hard it is to raise the subject of historical harms in good, effective ways but also how easy it is to dismiss serious efforts to do so.

Nonetheless, the history is what it is, and the consequences remain what they are. It is an unfortunate and terrible fact that Euramericans in North America have caused mass suffering, enslavement, and death to peoples of color for the purpose of controlling their land, labor, and resources for many centuries. In the United States, *holocaust* and *genocide* are the words that truly name what has happened here. And these patterns continue today. Many Native homelands are toxic from military testing, uranium mining, agribusiness, and corporate pollution. Death rates from cancer and infertility rates are disproportionately high on many reservations. Whites now own or control millions of acres of reservation homelands, and the U.S. Supreme Court still invokes the infamous "Doctrine of Discovery" to deny tribes jurisdiction over tribally owned land within their historical reservation boundaries.[1] The mechanisms of genocide have changed, but the agenda to eradicate Natives as Peoples and inherently sovereign nations and to steal and keep their lands remains.

Moreover, those who benefit multigenerationally from this agenda—as those of us who are Euramerican do simply by living here, our ancestors having come here of their own accord to find new homes—have not as a people confronted these wrongs, acted to right them, or changed the agenda. Quite the opposite. Genocide, theft, and oppression have been justified by the dehumanization of others, compounding past wrongs with more injustices. The criminal justice system, for example, is filled with the direct descendants of those who suffered immense harms, perpetrated as national, state, and local policies for the material gain of whites.

Today, many of us who are white do not confront the extent to which people of color continue to be degraded by being denied things we take for granted—educational opportunities, jobs, promotions, bank loans, apartments, justice on any level, as well as everyday respect. As Paul Kivel explains in his classic book on the subject, *Uprooting Racism: How White People Can Work for Racial Justice*, discriminatory patterns are matters of public record, and their effects are multigenerational.[2] These violations are symptoms of our longstanding collective failure to respect others as fully autonomous, inherently self-determined peoples and nations possessed of lands, resources, knowledge, and heritages that are theirs and not ours to control.

That I raise these issues—as many others (white and non-white) do as well—does not mean that I hate myself or white people, or that I wish to engage in "blame and shame." I do not believe all white people are bad, or that all Native people—or people of color—are good. Neither am I less concerned about the millions of white people who are poor, unemployed, undereducated, addicted, incarcerated, and treated as "less than."

I raise these issues because I believe that Euramericans as a people have the capacity to do better in our relationships with peoples who are different from us, and that we have acted in harmful ways for reasons that we can change but have yet to change. I write from self-respect and a respect for others, whites included. I also write from hope that we can be more than we have been. Who we are as a people is at stake. According to restorative justice values, respecting Euramericans as a people involves affirming our moral strength to hold ourselves accountable for our harms, just as we show respect for others by expecting accountability from them, including those whose access to resources is far more limited than ours and whose harms are of far less consequence.

## Blame—Not Conducive to Healing

The fact that other peoples have committed genocide often comes up at this point. Unfortunately, this is quite true, and yet what conclusions do we draw from this? Does this fact, for example, lessen our responsibility? The fact that many people steal does not lessen a particular offender's responsibility to those whom he or she has robbed. Does it make our having committed genocide more acceptable? Does it give us moral permission to forget our history and ignore its consequences? Does it mean that committing genocide is just part of human nature and we may as well accept it?

Those who raise this point probably would not say "yes" to any of these questions. After all, we believe in the appropriateness of holding the Nuremberg trials, South Africa's Truth and Reconciliation Commission, the trial of former Yugoslav President Slobodan Milosevic, and the Rwandan genocide trials. As a global community, we do hold people accountable for genocide, no matter how often it has occurred in history. I suspect the fact that other peoples have committed genocide arises because we as white people feel blamed and accused, and we have a hard time dealing with these feelings.

Naturally, feeling blamed and accused is quite unpleasant, and it *is* difficult to deal with these feelings well. Our gut reaction is to try either to get ourselves off the hook or to minimize our responsibility by spreading the blame. Restorative justice—as I understand it, and I know others may understand it differently—does not use blame or accusation for emotional punishment as the backbone or muscle of the restorative process. There are several reasons for this.

First, restorative justice processes do give offenders opportunities to confront the human faces of their harms and readily subject them to all the intense emotions that go with these experiences. Yet these experiences and the painful remorse that offenders often feel is not for the purpose of punishing them but for connecting them with the realities of what they have done. It is the connecting that spurs their transformation, and it is an essential part of the healing process.

The pain they feel as a result of connecting with others is not, therefore, about punishment but about healing and transformation. Their pain might be analogous to the pain of a wound that's healing. The pain exists not to punish our bodies for having cuts in them but to send information to our brains about reconnecting torn tissues so our bodies will mend. Pain does not equal punishment, or every mother would be punished during childbirth, as would every athlete during training or every foot that we sat on too long. Instead of categorizing the pain of connecting as punishment, we could understand it as a natural phase in healing, growth, and transformation.

Second, restorative justice emphasizes how important it is for offenders to admit what they did. Yet blame and accusation make it harder for perpetrators to do this. Instead of eliciting healthy shame—also referred to as appropriate guilt for a particular action or deep remorse for having caused hurt to others—blame and accusation tend to generate toxic shame, which makes us feel no good for who we are. As is often said, toxic shame condemns the actor, rather than the action, and it pervades society—racism being one form. The process of healing harms begins when those involved accept responsibility, yet thanks to a culture awash in toxic shame, blame and accusation trigger opposite responses—the self-defensive responses of toxic shame. Making excuses or justifying ourselves, we feel more isolated rather than more connected.

To minimize these reactions, many restorative justice processes keep the focus on the actual harms and on finding ways to rectify them. The work is practical without being emotionally punishing, mindful that it is part of our human condition to make mistakes, even terrible ones. As much as possible, restorative justice processes address the harm head-on *and* avoid attacking the good in human beings that provides a basis for positive change.

Blame and accusation are not particularly useful for a third reason. Individual actions or specific events grow from whole systems: relationships, families, communities, societies, peoples, and the interconnected histories of each. Restorative justice is holistic in its approach, and from a holistic perspective, responsibility is shared, as Chief Justice Yazzie, Ada Pecos Melton, and other authors have emphasized in their articles. Blaming one person seduces us into ignoring the larger dynamics that gave rise to hurtful conduct. For example, nailing one white person for racist conduct fails to address the white mindset and programming that affects all whites and keeps racism going.

Douglas Stone, Bruce Patton, and Sheila Heen argue this point from a communications perspective in *Difficult Conversations: How to Discuss What Matters Most*. The question "whose fault is this?" is not nearly as helpful or constructive, they find, as asking: "How have we each contributed to this situation, and how can each of us, by taking responsibility, act differently now?"[3]

Because blame and accusation are so ingrained, though, it is hard for those of us who are white to hear about our history with Native Peoples and not have toxic emotions kick in. Yet when they do, our capacity to listen shuts down, as does our commitment to rectifying the wrongs. This reaction poses a considerable obstacle to dealing with America's history of racism, colonization, and genocide. And it is why a restorative justice approach can be so helpful: restorative justice reframes the job at hand. The aim is not to condemn or emotionally punish white people but to call on our self-respect as a people to hold ourselves accountable for our past and to make things right as much as possible in our present. The focus shifts from blame, accusation, and punishment and toward developing self-respect, mutual respect, and a shared commitment to making things right.

Restorative justice suggests not only how to do this but also that doing so can be transformative for those on both sides of harm. From a holistic view, harms hurt everyone. Unhealed, they function like festering sores. They don't go away on their own, because they exist to reveal something fundamental about our ways of being together that need healing and that will bless everyone if we do heal.

Many of us wish that our forebears could have found the moral and spiritual strength either not to commit these harms in the first place or to come together with those who were hurt to make things right. We do not want our descendants to have the same regrets about us, neither do we want them to bear the burden of our failing to make things right. Again, it is not a negative impetus but a positive, constructive, and holistically inclusive one that makes us seek healing, even though the task seems overwhelming.

## Core Healing Practices of Restorative Justice

Restorative justice offers hope that healing ways can be found. Precisely because colonization through racism is so central to how our society came to be what it is, confronting these realities is central to its larger healing work. Those of us engaged in restorative justice have an opportunity to apply what we have learned about healing harms in individual cases to healing these historical, systemic roots of suffering. For example:

+ Having learned the importance of *hearing the stories*, we can listen to the accounts of what has happened in the lives and histories of Indigenous Peoples and peoples of color, as well as create public forums for this truth-telling. Truth and reconciliation commissions, for example, can be powerfully healing.
+ Valuing the importance of holding people *accountable for harms inflicted*, we can practice this value by holding ourselves accountable for how we got to where we are as a society. Doing this can mean many different things, but they all start with an attitude shift—a wholehearted commitment to mending the harms and their consequences.
+ Having learned that *heartfelt and remorseful apologies* are essential to the healing process of both victims and offenders, we can work to replace the national policy of racist colonization with a national policy of apology—officially acknowledging that what happened and continues to happen is racist and wrong.
+ And, having learned that apologies are just the beginning of the

real job of *making things right*, we can show that we are committed
to righting our wrongs in more than words. As with any crime,
making things right involves deeds: restitution, returning stolen
property, reparations for harms done or resources exploited, and,
in the process, listening to those harmed and finding out from
them what they need to have done for the wrongs to be made right.

The restorative justice field has learned that these practices help heal relationships by helping individuals change their paradigm of how to be in
relationship. On a collective level, these same practices can help heal the
deeper causes of harms by helping us do the work of decolonization; namely,
changing our paradigm of how to be in relationship with other peoples and
nations.

## Our History and Our Inner and Outer Obstacles to Rectifying It

Yet non-Native people like myself face many obstacles to taking such steps
of restorative justice in regard to our history and its legacy today. These obstacles, embedded in the dominant society and hence in us as members of
that society, stand between where we are now and the kind of people and society many of us hope we could be. Precisely because these obstacles keep the
harms and their rectification off our collective radar, they warrant attention
if we want to move in restorative directions.

The obstacles are, of course, complex, but we could group them into two
broad categories. One set of obstacles is inwardly focused through the socialization we have received. The other set is more outwardly focused in our
material interests and how we pursue them. As obstacles to choosing a path
of social healing, the mind-set, values, and behaviors of racism and colonization pervade both areas.

The inner obstacles largely come from our socialization into a society that
ranks people according to race. Our social programming has trained us to
identify with the status quo and to defend our favored positions. Since we
have been raised to internalize the role of colonizer, our default behavior is to
act from this social script in blatant and subtle ways. When we look at realities
from perspectives other than the "master narrative" of white supremacy and
domination—as the decolonization literature refers to the racist colonizer

paradigm—we feel uneasy, out of our authorized script, and even personally threatened. Our self-image and position in society depend on our keeping our one-up status intact.

As we begin to uncover all the ways that this social programming affects how we think and behave, however, it's not uncommon for us to experience guilt, shame, grief, and even identity issues—"Am I the good person I thought I was?" As Robert Joseph discusses in his article, we may also experience various forms of denial to offset these unpleasant emotions. From psychology, we understand these dynamics, and we also know that such responses can play essential roles in personal and social change. Whenever these reactions arise, we face a choice: Shall we continue to identify with our programming and defend it, or shall we stay open and allow ourselves to be transformed?

Some of the most difficult inner obstacles arise, though, when we are not aware of the programming. Insofar as we are unaware of the ranking categories installed in us, for example, we are less likely to notice all the ways they affect our interactions, even though those on the receiving end notice right away. Or, unaware of how we have been socialized to be colonizers, we may also consider only the racism side of the racism-colonization duo and believe that the solution is to like everybody as people—the color-blind idea. We assume (or hope) that this one-on-one emotional shift by whites is sufficient for racism to cease to affect people and for the injustices to go away.

Certainly a shift away from racial hatreds is a positive step, and certainly it is good to realize that we share a common humanity beyond our skin color, ethnicity, ancestry, or nationality. Yet though these views express nonracism, the sentiments do not adequately address the actual injustices. For example, they don't deal with the realities of colonization, which include the history of how we came to have the lives that we do—who did what to whom, who benefited, who lost, and whose descendants benefit or suffer now as a result. They don't acknowledge the many ways in which people of color still endure damaging and dehumanizing racial stereotypes. Neither do they challenge the institutions that perpetuate race-based ways of ranking people and allocating power, decision-making, land, and resources accordingly.

Insofar as we don't confront these issues and work to rectify them, we also tend not to confront why it is that prisons are filled with people of color or why poverty remains greatest among Indigenous communities and communities of color. The assumption is that the reason must have to do with "them," not us. Those who are poor or in prison must be society's "bad apples." Indeed, the bad-apple concept is a core premise of the current criminal justice system: society will improve if we root out the bad apples among us.

Yet the bad-apple concept is a well-designed misdirect of our programming. Blaming individuals or groups diverts our focus away from the dominant paradigms and institutions, not to mention the bare facts of who did what to whom and the consequences of these historical realities today. The bad-apple approach is not a holistic way of responding to harms, because it does not consider the systems or processes that generated the harms—and has done so over generations. Whether applied to whites or to people of color, the concept protects vested systems, keeping their histories invisible and their power hierarchies unchanged.

As I write, for example, many white Americans are stunned by the deaths of six white deer hunters allegedly shot by Chai Vang, a Hmong hunter. He told relatives that racist language was directed at him and that as he walked away, he was shot at. While Mr. Vang faces charges alone in a courtroom, one thousand people attend a memorial service for the hunters who died. At the service, one white woman referred to a bumper sticker that reads, "Save a deer, shoot a Hmong"—a variation of another bumper sticker seen here in the Midwest, "Save a fish, spear an Indian."

Whatever happened in those Wisconsin woods, we have an opportunity to use this tragedy to look at our society's dominant paradigm. Its lethal nature is evident not only in the hunters' deaths but also in the bumper stickers, which espouse that access to resources should be race-based—"for whites only"—and that violation of this rule means death. Whether Mr. Vang suffers from post-traumatic stress disorder, as some have suggested, is less of an issue than the social realities that presumably triggered his trauma, moving this Laotian refugee and former California National Guardsman away from healing and toward heightened trauma. If we dismiss either Mr. Vang or the hunters as bad apples, we miss an opportunity to help change the collective paradigm that lies at the root of this tragedy.

Historically, though, our habit as a people has been to avoid such opportunities and for reasons that involve our material interests. As in this case, these reasons involve who lives where, who hunts where, and who controls which resources. Indeed, our interests pose the second set of obstacles impeding our readiness as a people to act on restorative justice values. Racially programmed ways of thinking blur the link between our good fortune and others' lack of it. Connecting the dots seems threatening, since to do so could seriously rock our boat.

Critical race theory, however, brings this link into unmistakable focus. It argues that racism is not fundamentally about liking or disliking people; it's about justifying injustices and the histories that created them. Again, it's about colonization: stealing land and resources and then using laws and force to maintain exclusive control of them. What drives racism and keeps it in place is a win-lose model of politics and economics.

On this analysis, it goes without saying that "race" is a social construct and not a biological reality. Power advantages engage prejudices around natural human differences in order to control who wins and who loses. The differences among us are not actually the issue; the issue is that others have things we want, and we use their differentness to justify our taking what they have by force. In the winner-take-all worlds that follow, one group systematically profits at another's systematic expense. Mass crimes—crimes committed by one people against another—are made acceptable multigenerationally.

In our hemisphere, Euramericans have, as we know, embraced this race-based win-lose paradigm unreservedly. But again, as Chief Ted Moses observes, whites frequently declare the realities of our paradigm's past and present off-limits for discussion. To talk openly and undefensively about our history challenges our programming: it challenges our one-up status, at least from a moral and spiritual point of view (the inner obstacle), and it challenges the claims we have made on land and resources (the outer obstacle). As long as we obey the no-talk rule, the terrible realities of racism and colonization exist like elephants standing in our living rooms that we pretend aren't there.

The metaphor comes from the field of recovery from addictions. A person's addiction may govern the dynamics in a family—it's the elephant filling the living room—but instead of talking about this, everyone acts as if everything is okay. Arguably, genocide and holocaust are committed by addicts—people addicted to wealth, power, conquest, cruelty, and violence. And the illness has been extreme. Besides the outright massacre of Native Peoples by the millions, white men have cut off Native women's breasts so they couldn't feed their babies; white women have grabbed Native babies and killed them before their mothers' eyes; and civilians and soldiers have slaughtered nearly to extinction a "people of the natural world"—the Buffalo People—so that Native Peoples living up and down the Great Plains would starve.

Unnamed and unchallenged, such behaviors settle into our collective psyche and influence what we accept as a norm. In our past, genocide was overtly the law of the land, but in our present as well, prisoners are routinely dehumanized and tortured, civilians are bombed, and starvation is used as a weapon of mass destruction. Beneath a veneer of civility, the assumption we as whites seem to have inherited is that we can and must be ruthless with others—particularly peoples whose skin is darker than ours—in order to secure the way of life we want.

Typical of addictive processes, though, no matter how blatantly destructive such "norms" may be, they are protected by taboos against talking about them. Naming the realities and challenging their acceptability threatens the prevailing order. The charges of "white bashing" or "white self-hate," for example, reinforce the no-talk taboo whenever people (non-white or white) try to address the holocaust elephant standing in the middle of American society. According to the taboo, it's okay to talk about Germany's elephant or South Africa's, Rwanda's, or Sudan's, but not our own.

Yet the realities of our cultural paradigm's history exist as irrefutable facts. Our governments, our courts, our academics, our religious leaders, and our citizenries all acknowledge them—at least in their broad lines: we have stolen land and resources and kept them; we have a history of exploiting labor without respect for human rights; we retain hundreds of billions of dollars stolen from treaty-created trust funds; we have not paid reparations for harms committed; we have terrorized peoples of color with every social, economic, and political mechanism; and we have killed en masse those of the racially dehumanized groups whose existence obstructed our gain. Nor are these behaviors only of the past.

These are incredibly hard realities to face. Yet the longer we go without addressing them, the more the communities involved become polarized, and the longer addictive patterns pass as acceptable. Those of us who are white tend to think that the terrible things happened long ago and don't affect us now. We do not see ourselves as complicitous in mass crimes against peoples. But for many of the surviving descendants, the wholesale murder of their people, the theft of their homelands, and the degradation and enslavement of their ancestors remain fresh in their memories as if these events happened yesterday, and why not? Their lives are continually shaped by their consequences—as are ours.

Many of us whites readily acknowledge that these things not only happened but also are terribly wrong. That being so, though, where is our resolve to right them? No rectification has been made. One on one, we experience each other as good, well-meaning people. Collectively, though, we have a problem. Our integrity as a people is not up to speed with where we want it to be or where we strive to be personally. Again, this is not to blame us but to state a problem.

For example, we have had no "truth and reconciliation" process for the holocausts here. Even something as basic as Senator Bill Bradley's 1987 bill to return the Black Hills to the Oceti Sakowin Oyate did not pass. And no movement among whites to rectify the 1877 theft of the Black Hills has ever developed, despite the rulings of both the Court of Claims and the United States Supreme Court that blatant theft occurred. The 1985 Claims Court stated:

> A more ripe and rank case of dishonorable dealing will never, in all probability, be found in our history, the duplicity of President Grant in breaching the Government's . . . obligations to keep trespassers out of the Black Hills, and the pattern of duress practiced by the Government on starving the Sioux to get them to agree to the sale of the Black Hills.[4]

## Programming and Its Smokescreens

Confronting this problem we whites have as a people, we invariably wonder why we suffer this "shameless"—shameless in the full and precise John Braithwaite sense[5]—lack of commitment to making things right, at least as far as Native Peoples and other peoples of color are concerned? Knowing the immensity of wrongs, why do we let their effects hurt generation after generation? Worse, why do some white people today say that we should have "finished off the Indians when we had the chance," as Tim Wise, the anti-racist author, activist, and director of the Association of White Anti-Racist Education (AWARE), reports having heard two white, power-dressed businessmen bemoaning in an airport lounge?[6]

I have not known how to answer these questions when they have been put to me. I still don't know. There are no justifications or excuses, yet there are dynamics, and unraveling these, perhaps we can begin to break the destructive patterns. Certainly the fact that we have never been held accountable for our genocide contributes to our current mentality. Why haven't we held ourselves accountable? Presumably because of our programming. We are carefully programmed to think in ways that "justify" our "unjust" actions, and this programming begins early.

For example, I remember hearing the Laura Ingalls Wilder books about nineteenth-century pioneers moving westward being read to me as a child, and I remember "Ma" saying more than once, "The only good Indian is a dead Indian." I realize now, as I didn't then, that not all advocates of genocide wear Nazi uniforms and get tried for war crimes; some wear calico frocks and get immortalized in children's classics.

True, the account of white pioneering in the United States would not be complete without Ma's support of genocide, since the two have gone hand in hand. "Pa" did not share Ma's feelings about Native Peoples, but he was nonetheless proud of his insatiable desire to "go west." His assumptions were that he as a white man could go wherever he pleased; that the land was his for the taking without concern for those who have lived here since time immemorial; that there were no terrible costs being paid by others for his relentless westering; and that such views about pioneering formed a noble American ideal. If he felt bad for the plight of Native Peoples, his feelings did not alter his assumptions or his actions. In Ma and Pa, genocidal racism and colonization were truly married. Yet white Americans continue to embrace the *Little House* books uncritically—a Google search calls up long lists of clubs devoted to them—indicating how far we are from confronting the realities of our history, much less rectifying the wrongs involved.

How about other white fathers of the period: what were some of them doing 150 years ago? In a presentation during the 2004 Dakota Commemorative March, Dakota scholar Dr. Chris Mato Nunpa recounted one aspect of the racist colonization that occurred here in Minnesota: "*The Daily Republican* newspaper in Winona announced on Thursday evening, 24 September 1863, that the bounties on the heads of Indian men, women, or children killed by whites increased to $200 per death. Whites killed Natives, collected the bounty money, and then used it to buy land." Similar bounties were placed on Native people's lives across the United States and in Canada. As I sit here a stone's throw from Fort Snelling—the site of a concentration camp for 1,700 Dakota women, Elders, and children during the severe winter of 1862–63, in which hundreds of Dakota died—I wonder if the land I live on was originally bought by these means.

Once again, such realities are incredibly painful to face, and the easier route is obviously to avoid them. To help us do that, our cultural paradigm has provided smokescreens—more programming—to rationalize our horrendous history or to minimize it. For centuries, racial stereotypes, hatreds, and Darwinian attitudes about "superior" and "inferior" have formed the leading smokescreens, serving both to justify the "gains" and to hide their ill-gotten nature. The smokescreens have made the injustices seem, if not just, at least appropriate according to "nature" as our hierarchical, win-lose model defines it. By dehumanizing those we have wronged, our programming makes us feel no commitment to making things right with them.

For many, the smokescreen of racial hatreds is wearing thin. Its gradual dissolution does not, however, mean that the core—the racist colonization that determines who makes the decisions and controls the power and resources—has changed, evidenced by the fact that these huge wrongs remain so unrighted. In correspondence, Harley Eagle observes:

> In the dismantling racism training that I am a part of with Mennonite Central Committee, we talk about how racism often changes when one of these smokescreens is exposed. We point out how early nineteenth-century entertainment often portrayed African American folks as backward and dumb. When that stereotype was exposed, it morphed into portraying them as criminals. There are many more examples that are easily pointed out. My thoughts around this pertaining to the restorative justice movement and Aboriginal folks is [that] without addressing the "economic and historical injustices," what happens is that we morph the concept of Aboriginal teachings as uncivilized, evil, and backward into noble, romantic, wise, and useful. All true and nice, of course, but without the deeper understandings, it becomes frustrating, condescending, paternalistic, and hurtful to Aboriginal folks. Needless to say, in the long run it does not nurture genuine, mutual, transformative relationships.

To treat an emotional smokescreen as if it were racism's whole reality is to avoid addressing racism's root in colonization—the systemic racism that decides who wins and who loses, whose loss gets repaired and whose loss is ignored. We unwittingly promote the paradigm of racial oppression by acting as if it doesn't exist, simply because we personally no longer engage in the particular smokescreen of racial animosity.

In other words, until we confront our paradigm's melding of colonization with racism, other smokescreens for racism will step in to keep the power hierarchies in place, albeit under different guises. Criminalizing African Americans, especially young men, and then legally disenfranchising those who have been imprisoned is an obvious example of a retooled smokescreen that perpetuates racist colonization.

The other example of a retooled smokescreen that Harley Eagle cites—that of romanticizing Native cultures—shrouds those of us who are white in a "feel-good" fantasy about our relationship with Native Peoples, as if the relationship could be righted without first "making things right." This fantasy is, of course, not shared by those whose land has been stolen, whose relatives suffered genocidal attacks, whose families struggle with racism and oppression every day, and whose inherent self-determination, nationhood, and peoplehood are not respected.

Dr. Edward C. Valandra comments, for example, that reconciliation between Natives and non-Natives is not about singing "Kumbaya" together; it's about official apologies, land return, restitution, and reparations. These are the litmus tests for American whites and our governments that demonstrate precisely how committed we are to being in a good relationship with Native Peoples. Without these actions—the expected behavior among respected equals of making proper restitution in order to establish good relations—the claim that racism and colonization are things of the past is insulting.

So far, we have not begun to pass these litmus tests. Land return alone poses a major stumbling block. As one white person put it, "We certainly can't give back all the land that was stolen, or we wouldn't have a country anymore, not to mention all the innocent losers in such transactions." The issue of culpability aside, First Nations have various ideas about how land return might be negotiated. Their proposals for land return are very different from what many whites assume.

As far as I can tell, First Nations are not proposing that they do to us what we did to them; namely, to throw us off the land altogether at genocidal gunpoint. According to some proposals, land return means returning jurisdiction, and within a First Nation's jurisdiction, whites can own land and leave it to children for as long as we please. However, if whites ever wish to sell land, the First Nation reserves the right of first refusal. Whites would, of course, have to abide by the laws and authority of the First Nation, just as we would if we chose to live in France or England.

## An Issue of Paradigms

Pondering these issues, I find hope in critical race theory's analysis. What we face is fundamentally an issue of paradigm. Like all humans, we whites have the potential to do great harm or great good. Which of these potentials we develop and act upon depends on our cultural paradigm. If we were intrinsically flawed beings, innately greedy and selfish, then there would be no hope for us. But if it is our cultural software that is flawed—that sends us down these racist, oppressive paths—then we can change it and liberate ourselves from ways of being that are arguably destructive to us as well. A win-lose, reward-punishment model is not our only option, and any group of people who relies on this model is likely to behave as ruthlessly and irresponsibly as we have done.

So yes, our colonize-by-racism, white supremacist boat needs rocking. Yet changing paradigms does not mean we are going to drown. The people we have elected to carry out our collective will have spent billions, even trillions of dollars on wars and incarceration, both of which are violent and cause more violence. These are the tsunamis engulfing our society. They give witness to the massive resources we have illegally appropriated—resources that we are using in harmful rather than healing ways.

Instead of making this choice, we can elect people committed to investing these resources in putting things right, making restitution and paying reparations for harms, and decolonizing. Among other things, decolonizing means doing what it takes to build respectful relations with other peoples and nations—peoples and nations who are not us (not white or Euramerican), and more important, have no desire to be us, like us, assimilated with us, or subsumed under us. The fact that Native people drive cars, wear jeans, use computers, and carry cell phones in no way diminishes their inherent self-determination as separate, distinct peoples and nations.

In other words, we have the choice to make real peace by shifting our paradigm of what it is to be in relationship as peoples. No matter how deeply programmed we have been, we can devote ourselves to undoing this programming. Addressing how we got to where we are collectively and doing what it takes to "make things right" may well prove the single most effective way to make a genuine cultural paradigm shift—a shift that will bring our healing, transformation, and hence liberation as well.

## Turning Off the Faucet

For a book on restorative justice, is it necessary to expand the work to these broader dimensions? Is this a direction that the movement can feasibly go? As one restorative justice practitioner commented, "There are so many harms today that need healing; we are overwhelmed as it is. We cannot take on past wrongs too." Today's harms *are* overwhelming, but a strong argument can be made that harms have proliferated and continue to multiply because we have neglected to come to terms with how we got here.

Surveying our past from a paradigm perspective, more than "liberty for all," "might makes right"—colonialism and its win/lose brutality—has operated as the de facto paradigm in founding the United States and choreographing its rise to power. "Might-makes-right" policies decimated the tens of millions of Native people who lived here when Columbus arrived.[7] The four million Africans who represented 35 percent of the population in 1860 had their own horrific experiences with "might makes right," as have Asian, Latino, Chicano, and many other ethnic groups since.

Today, as many observe, a paradigm of "might makes right" continues. Not having challenged this method or rectified its effects, our people still support it at the polls. The dehumanizing treatment and torture of Iraqi and other prisoners illustrate how racism and conquest go hand in hand. Indeed, the U.S. war in Iraq has been a painful trigger for many Native people, calling up raw memories of invasion, occupation, massive civilian deaths, and cultural devastation. Such patterns are not likely to go away as long as the paradigm behind them is deemed successful and brings multigenerational rewards that are never challenged.

Here is where restorative justice comes in. Merely knowing that immense harms have occurred does not mean we know how to right them or are committed to doing so. Knowledge is a first step, but we need a restorative, healing process to help us take the next step and the one after that—to overcome the inner and outer obstacles one by one.

For example, an early step of the restorative justice process by most everyone's definition requires that perpetrators of harm take responsibility for what has happened; otherwise destructive patterns are not likely to change. As a white person who benefits from past harms and who participates in the society that perpetrates them, I—along with many others—want to take responsibility for what has happened, because then I can be part of changing the patterns. Again, accepting responsibility and holding myself accountable are not about blame; they're about healing.

As people join in taking responsibility, the restorative process of righting harms often morphs into the more fundamental task of transformation. A harm is a symptom of something out of balance, something not working— in this case, our cultural paradigm. In interconnected social systems, when something isn't working for one person, it's usually not working for others as well.

So it is with our cultural paradigm: racist colonization hurts not only people of color but whites too. In attempting to dehumanize others, we are dehumanized. Sacrificing our morals, ethics, and spiritual integrity—our humanity—for material gain carries a price, and this price is passed down through the generations as well.

The moral and spiritual toll that this takes on us is inescapable. Many whites are swamped with material possessions and yet are deeply unhappy. Harley Eagle observes, "When I think of [the economic roots of racism], to me, it screams of the need for white folks to focus on 'white privilege' and to expose its harmfulness not only to the 'others' and the environment but also to the Spirit and Soul of white folks. White folks do harm to themselves when they buy into (pardon the pun) the values, worldview, and paradigm on which capitalistic economics are built."

The call to address these harms gives us opportunities to change the patterns. Harms serve as wake-up calls for us to shift our personal and collective paradigms and to let ourselves and our institutions be transformed in the process. Yes, the restorative process is about making things right with respect to specific harms, but it is also about much, much more. It is about inviting whoever is willing to go on a healing path that leads to whole-person, whole-community, whole-paradigm, whole-culture, and whole-people change.

This is what we in America's dominant white society have not yet done with our past, and because we have not done it, these harms and their legacies pervade our present. The core belief system responsible for past harms has not been collectively challenged by a restorative process that involves facing the magnitude of hurt inflicted and doing what it takes to make things right. As a result, the harms of today are like water spilling over the side of an overflowing tub, and the unhealed harms of the past are like the faucet turned on full blast. We can keep mopping up the floor—a truly overwhelming task—but the simplest and most efficient response may be to turn off the faucet.

## Compelling Issues for Non-Natives as Well

The third reason for publishing this book is the obvious number and depth of issues that the articles raise not only for Natives but for non-Natives as well, especially those involved in restorative justice. The authors invite us to rethink the criminal justice system, of course, but in the process, they also make us think about historical harms and what steps we as peoples should take to right them. Looking further, they make us think about our paradigm—how a win/lose model that culminates in "might makes right" has shaped our core notions of law and government.

Yet the issues don't stop there. Our cultural paradigm of coercion and win/lose affects not only how we approach law and justice but also how we approach relationships, families, child-rearing, schooling, business, health, inter-nation relations, the natural world, and religion. If Native people experience coercion as disrespectful, don't we as well? If so, what is our society, control oriented as it is, doing to us—all of us, not only those caught in the criminal justice system or oppressed by racism and colonization?

Regarding the work of transformation, the articles also raise the question of where we as whites can go to find healing traditions, considering that our cultural paradigm is so unhealthy and that we are so disconnected from our own Indigenous origins. What ways can we rely on for our healing? I am a Breton Celt in ancestry, for example, but I was not raised in the cultural wisdom traditions that my ancestors living in Scotland, Cornwall, Ireland, and Bretagne knew before the Romans invaded. All of Europe had Indigenous cultures, and these embodied more healing, peacemaking ways than the history of European wars, battles, and barbarisms would reveal. Our history as Indigenous European Peoples and cultures has been told selectively as well.

According to Riane Eisler, author of *The Chalice and the Blade*, the genocidal destruction of Indigenous European "partnership societies"—peaceful, nonhierarchical societies that respected both genders—began roughly six thousand years ago and has continued ever since, including Hitler's killing of Gypsies. The eighteenth century, for example, marked the end of three hundred years during which Christians burned perhaps a million women as "witches," all but destroying Europe's ancient "wise woman" tradition through "gendercide."[8] Having lost our own healing traditions and gained instead centuries of trauma and addiction, where do we go for healing now?

Obviously, each of us can do the anti-racism, decolonization work, both personally and with others, which is a start in the healing process. But further, perhaps there is a purification ceremony that is ours as Euramericans and adapted to us as a sacred way—a way that can serve our transformation. Perhaps our healing, purifying ceremony is to go straight into the fire of confronting these wrongs and then to stay in the heat of doing what it takes to make things right. Sweating in this heat may not signify our demise but our healing and transformation—our rebirth. If we long for our humanity and integrity as a people, which has unfortunately gotten so lost during these centuries in a mad rush for gain, perhaps we can find ways back to it—sacred ways, since healing harms and broken relationships is very sacred.

In short, the issues raised in this book are by no means for Native Peoples alone but concern us all. Restorative processes typically discover that a specific harm represents the tip of an iceberg and that the scope of the healing work is far greater than it first seemed. Because harms impact the whole community of the victim and reflect the whole community of the victimizer, many more people than the immediate victim and victimizer are called to participate in healing. The challenge, of course, is not to get overwhelmed by the magnitude of work before us. As those involved in various forms of activism have found, one approach is to do whatever is ours to do wherever we are and to seek guidance from whatever sources sustain us.

### Restorative Justice as a Holistic Way of Life

For those who find the idea of restorative justice liberating and a way of being that inspires hope, we publish this book offering Indigenous perspectives on justice as healing in order to help expand the restorative justice work to these broader dimensions. As you have seen, the articles have varied greatly in how they consider these larger challenges.

Some have given critiques. They have challenged the way the criminal justice system frames "the problem" and gone on to address the systemic, historical, and paradigm issues, including racist colonization. Some have challenged the core notion of law as it has been used historically in European and American societies. Other articles have challenged the restorative justice movement itself, pointing out that restorative practices have more than once appropriated Indigenous traditions as a way to maintain the "same old, same old" racist-colonizer model of domination and control.

Along with critiques, the articles have offered visions and examples of how we can be together in a good way. They have presented the healing worldviews and philosophies of different Indigenous traditions, as well as shown how traditional healing ways are being adapted to the needs and circumstances of communities today.

And the articles have discussed how the prevailing criminal justice system—in Canada, at least—is acknowledging its failure to address the needs of Indigenous people in any significant or constructive way and is slowly changing its policies and practices. From a judicial perspective, the landmark case is the 1999 ruling of the Canadian Supreme Court in *R. v. Gladue*, which, in the words of Judge M. E. Turpel-Lafond, "clarified the duty of sentencing judges to consider background and systemic factors in sentencing Aboriginal offenders."

In short, the articles have helped articulate what restorative justice can mean as a holistic way of life. They engage us in doing the difficult, painful, and complex work of decolonizing and making things right, because to do so is healing and ultimately sacred on so many levels. To support us in doing this work, restorative justice appeals to what lies deepest in us, namely, our profound capacities to change, to relate to each other in respectful, healing ways, and to do what it takes to make things right—precisely when this seems hardest to do. The challenge now is to apply the capacities we have developed with individuals and groups to healing our societies and nations. To use the overflowing tub metaphor, the articles invite us to turn off the tap.

· · · ·

We are most grateful to the Native Law Centre, housed at the College of Law at the University of Saskatchewan, Saskatoon, Canada, for its ten years of publishing the *Justice as Healing* newsletter. We are honored by this opportunity to share their decade of profound work with the American audience. We are immensely grateful to Wanda D. McCaslin, the newsletter's editor, and to Dr. James Sa'ke'j Youngblood Henderson, the director of the Native Law Centre, for their great generosity in working with us in producing this book. It has been a joy and a privilege, and we have learned so much from engaging with them on this project.

We are exceedingly grateful to renowned Dakota Elder, professor, and writer Dr. Elizabeth Cook-Lynn for her generosity in taking time from her demanding schedule to write a foreword to this work, based on her decades of Native studies scholarship. We also want to thank Harley Eagle and Dr. Edward C. Valandra, who have contributed their wisdom and experiences most generously to Living Justice Press as advisers in this endeavor. We deeply appreciate those who have taken time to comment on this book and review it; your efforts help our small independent press enormously. And we are most grateful to you, our readers, for the time you have taken to ponder these deep and challenging issues.

## Notes

1. The most recent example is the U.S. Supreme Court's ruling in the *City of Sherrill v. Oneida Indian Nation of N.Y.* case (2005), in which Justice Ruth Bader Ginsburg invoked the Doctrine of Discovery to deny the Oneida Nation's assertion of sovereignty over 17,000 acres that they repurchased within their ancestral homelands. Conceived at the time of European invasion, the Doctrine of Discovery claims European/American title to land "discovered," regardless of the Native Peoples in actual possession of the land since time immemorial. The Doctrine of Discovery justifies land theft by whites in the same way that the British doctrine of terra nullius has done, as Robert Joseph discusses in his article.

2. See Paul Kivel, *Uprooting Racism: How White People Can Work for Racial Justice* (Gabriola Island, BC: New Society Publishers, 2002). This is an excellent book for any white person wanting to do anti-racism work.

3. Douglas Stone, Bruce Patton, Sheila Heen, *Difficult Conversations: How to Discuss What Matters Most* (New York: Viking Penguin, 1999), 58–82.

4. Edward C. Valandra, "The Lakota Land Return Policy: Examining the Rhetoric of South Dakota's White Opposition," *Turtle Quarterly*, Fall–Winter (1994): 18.

5. John Braithwaite's concept of reintegrative shaming argues that offenders need to feel shame in order to change. Evidently, this is what we whites as a people seem to lack. Braithwaite is not referring to the toxic shame that makes us ashamed of who we are, the kind of shame that racism tries to impose. Instead, he is talking about healthy or constructive shame, which involves feeling regret, remorse, loss of face, and inner pain for having caused harm to others. We feel this constructive shame most in the presence of our families and communities. In communities, the function of shame is to help community members muster the moral fiber to do what it takes to "make things right," for then they can be reintegrated with the community.

Perhaps we white Americans have not felt constructive shame for the atrocities committed by our relatives in our names and for our benefit—not enough to rectify them at least—because we lack a sufficient sense of our connectedness. Thanks to the dominant paradigm, we see ourselves as occupying the top of a social and natural world hierarchy. Like the offenders who commit crimes from a sense of isolation, we experience ourselves as cut off from the natural and human communities. In Chief Justice Yazzie's words, we act "as if we have no relatives." Along with the benefits to victims and communities, doing what it takes to make things right rebuilds an offender's sense of connectedness. So it could do for us as a people as well. See John Braithwaite, *Crime, Shame and Reintegration* (Cambridge: Cambridge University Press, 1989).

6. Tim Wise, "Didn't We Get Rid of Those People Years Ago? Reflections on Empire and Uppity Indians," *CounterPunch*, 9 February 2005, P.O. Box 228, Petrolia, CA 95558. Tim Wise is the author of two new books: *White Like Me: Reflections on Race from a Privileged Son* (Brooklyn, NY: Soft Skull Press, 2005) and *Affirmative Action: Racial Preference in Black and White* (New York: Routledge: 2005).

7. See, for example, Ward Churchill, *A Little Matter of Genocide: Holocaust and Denial in the Americas, 1492 to the Present* (San Francisco: City Lights, 1998) and David E. Stannard, *American Holocaust: The Conquest of the New World* (Oxford: Oxford University Press, 1993).

8. No one knows how many women were killed by the Inquisition during these 300 years. Some say the numbers were as low as 60,000, while others estimate into the millions, some believing as many as nine million people were killed, some of whom were men. Many towns were left without any surviving women at all. Elder women who passed on the Indigenous European, "pagan," healing wisdom traditions were particularly targeted, but little girls could be suspected, tried, and burned as well. *The Malleus Maleficarum (The Hammer of Witches)*, published by Catholic inquisition authorities in 1485–86, expressed the misogynist paradigm: "All wickedness is but little to the wickedness of a woman. . . . What else is woman but a foe to friendship, an unescapable punishment, a necessary evil, a natural temptation, a desirable calamity, a domestic danger, a delectable detriment, an evil nature, painted with fair

colours. . . . Women are by nature instruments of Satan—they are by nature carnal, a structural defect rooted in the original creation." See Anne Llewellyn Barstow, *Witchcraze: A New History of European Witch Hunts* (San Francisco: Harper San Francisco, 1995); also Robin Briggs, *Witches and Neighbors: The Social and Cultural Context of European Witchcraft* (New York: Penguin Books, 1998).

# Index of Persons and Peoples

# Index of Subjects

## A

Aboriginal Healing Foundation, 15,
25–26, 28n.2
Aboriginal healing movement, 372, 375,
377–78
Aboriginal Peoples, in boarding schools,
*see* boarding schools; and Canadian
criminal justice system, 3–5, 275–79,
333–36; and common principles in
healing, 373; and community healing
in action, 184–88, 190–95, 369–407;
and conceptions of justice, 61–64,
99–107, 121–33, 141–59, 275–79; and
dispute resolution model, 356–67;
and Elders, 202, 359–67; and *Gladue*
decision, 280–95; and Healing Foundation, 25–28; and healing movement, 372–74; and justice system,
324–36; and legal theory, 337–44;
and over-representation in prisons,
80, 275, 281, 288; and participation in
justice system, 66–67; and racial discrimination, 5, 29–58, 77, 80, 221, 226,
227–28, 249–50, 281, 284, 286, 289,
306, 334–35; and restorative justice,
337–44; and "reverse discrimination,"
289; and systematic attack on cultures, 369–70; and worldview of, 88,
90, 96, 108, 135–36, 142–46, 340, 377,
431; and youth, 61–64, 114, 197–201,
210–211, 221, 275, 290–91, 296–306.
*See also* Native Peoples
abuse, 62–63, 115, 137, 172, 185, 224; in
boarding schools, 15, 25–28, 204;
by corporations vs. nation-states,
237–38; cycles of, 339, 370–71; from
colonialism, 13, 23; and criminal justice system as, 342; of human rights
of Indigenous Peoples, 225–30; and

need to heal from, 278, 369–73. *See
also* sexual abuse
accountability, 142, 213; and Christian
view of, 103; and colonizers, 36;
and corporations, 237–38; of Euro-
americans, 413, 416; for genocide, 413,
422–23; as about healing, not blame,
413–416, 428; and offenders, 110,
115–16, 118, 182, 187–88, 191, 195, 296,
298–300; of offenders' relatives, 110,
115; of perpetrators of harm, 44, 110,
115; and social context, 300
adversarial justice, 63, 108, 118, 164, 188,
207, 220, 329, 363–64, 383; and nonadversarial circle process, 299
alcohol abuse, 126–27, 370–71, 381; and
crime, 131, 352; recovery from, 405;
and Wounded Knee massacre, 34;
and youth, 300, 381, 401
alternative justice systems, 78, 206–211; in
Canada, 314–15; to incarceration, 283,
285–87, 291; and Lake Babine Nation,
78; successes and failures of, 196–205
Alter-Natives to Non-Violence Report,
302–306
Americans. *See* colonizers
anarchy, 66
anti-Indianism compared to anti-
Semitism, 51n.2
apology for harms, 44, 109, 115, 210–11,
262, 264–65; by churches for residential schools, 26; as essential to healing
process, 50–51, 264–65, 416; by governments, 249, 259; as no substitute
for restitution, 266, 416–17
appropriation of Indigenous cultural
values and practices, 221–22, 240–44,
308–311, 313–20
assimilation, 4–5, 89, 197, 380–81; as

decolonization, 380, 387; and healing
journey of, 388, 396–405; and healing
of as nation building, 224, 379, 386,
390–92, 404, 406; and importance
of staying connected to, 170–73; and
justice systems, 102, 324–36, 337–39;
and role in problem-solving, 129, 135,
163–64, 177–82, 196–205, 207–211,
337–44, 356–67; and spiritual foundations, 102, 392; taking responsibility for healing, 383–384; and transformation, 404–405; and Wiping of
the Tears Ceremony, 44–45. *See also*
clan, relatives, tiospaye
Community Holistic Circle Healing
Program (CHCH), 89, 91, 102–103,
184–95, 380
community justice programs, 196–205,
206–211, 324; and state involvement
in, 308–311
conflict resolution. *See* dispute resolution
conquest myth, 246–48, 250
consensus, 69–70, 128, 131, 135, 164, 199,
299
courts, 65, 70, 110–115, 117, 124–32, 358;
and Indigenous need and demand for
separate system, 138, 327, 334–36; and
legal pluralism, 74–75; and working
with community circle programs,
177–78, 180–81, 186–88, 191–95,
200–205, 207–211, 223. *See also* adversarial justice, Cree court, *Gladue* decision, peacemaker courts, Supreme
Court of Canada, tribal courts, U.S.
Supreme Court, and youth courts
court rulings, 68–69; in relation to community circles, 177–78
Creator, 99–103, 105, 142–44, 154, 213;
and victimizers as out of balance
with, 213
Cree court, 223; and use of Cree language
in, 347–48
crime, and addressing underlying cause
of, 16, 216, 302–303, 325, 339–40; and

Haudenosaunee approach to, 141–59;
and infrequency of among Iroquois,
141; and Indigenous response to,
108–119; and Navajo response to,
121–33; and preventing, 297, 341
criminal justice system, 3–4; and Aboriginal over-representation in,
275–76, 281, 288; and contrasted with
Indigenous ways, 61, 99–106, 118, 222,
277, 329–30; and decolonizing the,
6, 8; and economics of, 66–67, 201,
275–76; and establishing separate
Indigenous systems, 78, 276; and
failure of, 163, 164, 206–207, 276; history of, 65–66; and Indian participation in, 66–67, 76, 222, 276, 326;
and indigenization of, 220, 221–22,
309–311, 313–20; and Indigenous self-
determination, 205, 218, 220, 276, 325;
and myths about Aboriginal people
in, 334–36; as power-over approach,
87; as protecting powerful elites,
63–64, 68, 71, 74; and reforms of, 276,
308, 324, 331; and restorative justice,
117–18, 337–44; and transformation
of, 331; and youth, 296–301. *See also*
adversarial justice, courts, sentencing
cultural appropriation, *see* appropriation
cultural paradigm, as one of racist colonization, 426–29
cultural programming, 18–19, 414–15,
417–27
culture, as treatment, 375–76
customary law, 71n.4, 74, 77, 78, 108, 111,
113–14, 236, 260, 268

# D

Dakota Death March, 1862, 15, 30, 46, 56
Darwinian model, 32, 69–71, 424
death penalty, 161; and Haudenosaunee
philosophy of, 150–51, 153–54
*Declaration on the Rights of Indigenous
Peoples*, 73, 227–28, 229
decolonization, 51, 54; as changing

Wounded Knee massacre, 33–35. *See also* holocaust, UN on genocide

*Gladue* decision, 207–208, 221, 280–95

Great Law of Peace, The, 141, 145–46, 147–53, 155

# H

harmony, 7, 24, 108, 130, 210, 268, 286, 338–39, 411; in communities, 15, 90, 108, 110, 116, 130, 155, 164, 168–69, 207, 329, 338–39; and desire for vs. practice, 43; and hozho, 130, 133; and Hozhooji Naat'aanii or the "Justice and Harmony Ceremony," 90, 124, 128, 130, 133, 338–39; as meaning of justice, 100–102, 105–106, 108–109, 130, 135, 138–39, 167–69, 210; and moving toward or away from, 338–39; and role of apologies in restoring, 265

harms, 7; and colonizers, 16, 29–53, 217, 264, 415–430; and communities, 89–90, 221; and criminal justice system response to, 103, 219–22; and dealing with past and present ones, 8, 13, 264, 409–34; and decolonizing, 89; and denial of, 264; and genocide, 35, 262; and healing from, 8, 90, 128–29, 168, 415–17; and healing roots of, 8, 16, 18, 89, 416; as hurting everyone, 415–16, 427–29; as incompensible, 266; and Indigenous responses to, 90, 215, 221–22; and legacy of, 8, 13, 225, 409–410, 412, 418–19; and reduction of, 304; and repairing, 88, 118, 297, 328; and reparations for, 266; and restorative justice, 15, 296–300, 409, 414–417; and shared responsibility for, 87, 89, 415; and trauma, 29; and youths' view of, 62–63

healing, 3–8, 87–88, 98–99, 121–33, 221, 222–24, 278–79, 342–43, 350, 369–407; and Aboriginal programs for, 372–79; and blame, 413–16, 428; from colonialism and oppression, 13, 15, 54, 63, 72n.7, 89, 215–16, 370–73; in

and with community, 89–91, 138–39, 164, 184, 221–24, 373; and community journey of, 396–405; and community voices on, 379–86; and culture, 375–77; and decolonization, 51, 89; and definition of, 374, 377, 380–81, 386–90; and Elders, 373; of Euramericans, 429–30; and forgiveness, 115; and *Gladue* decision, 281, 286, 291–92; as holistic, 16; and Hollow Water, 184–95; and incarceration, 67, 213; and Indian law, 69–70; and Indigenous principles of, 87–88, 98–99, 108–109; and Indigenous worldview of, 90, 99–106, 108–109; and individual journey of, 392–96; and justice as, 3–8, 81, 99–106, 121–33, 198–99, 277; and mapping the journey of, 224, 369–407; and nation building, 390–92; and official apologies, 264–65; and practices of, 375–79, 385; from programming, 18–19; from punishment to, 3–4, 90–91, 161–65, 217–18; and reconciliation (or conciliation), 27, 40, 43, 45–46, 266–68; and relying on traditions for, 215–216; from residential schools, 25–26; and restorative justice, 331–32, 416–17, 427–29, 430–31; and revitalization, 15; and sentencing, 221; and Si Tanka Wokiksuye Ride, 44–45; and spirituality, 137–38, 374, 376–77, 380, 382, 386, 392, 401; and taking responsibility, 278; and traditional methods of, 116, 144, 156n.11, 375–77; and youth, 296, 304. *See also* The Aboriginal Healing Foundation, Aboriginal healing movement, healing circles

healing ceremony, elements of, 124–28; and Euramericans need for, 430

healing circles, 89, 91, 177–82, 200–201, 204, 209, 281; and need for, 382. *See also* circles, peacemaking circles, sentencing circles, talking circles

healing contract, 185

and Declaration on Rights of, 73, 225–30; and decolonization, 7–8; and denial of genocide of, 254–61; and indigenization, 314; and lack of equal status in legal systems, 77; and law, 88, 219; and legal pluralism, 79; and legal positivism, 218–20; and over-incarceration of, 220–21, 275; and protecting resources, knowledge, and heritage of, 216–17, 231–44; and racism toward, 5, 77, 216, 258; and restorative justice, 409, 411, 415–17; and right of self-determination, 80–81, 216, 222, 229; and rights of, 225–30; and settlement agreements, 253–54, 258, 262; and syncretist nature, 309; and teaching of relatedness, 7; and terra nullius, 273; and UN, 73, 226; and U.S. Supreme Court, 217, 245–52; and worthiness of for compensation for suffering, 49–50. *See also, for example,* Aboriginal Peoples, healing, traditional law

individual healing journey, 392–96

individual, 70, 87, 154, 417–18; and collective responsibility, 268; and community and nation healing, 373–81, 381–86; and criminal justice system, 3, 103–104, 340; and free will, 156n.9, 156n.10; and healing, 392–96; and Indigenous justice system, 168, 329–30, 360; and Indigenous view of, 70, 88–89, 105–106, 109–110, 135; and kinship relations, 109–110, 147–48; and ownership of cultural property, 241; and rights, 80–81, 81n.1, 83n.5, 146; and reintegration into community, 149; and social theory of, 3, 6

injustice, 412; of criminal justice system, 207; and denial of, 217, 254–61; of Euramerican concept of law, 217–19; to Indigenous Peoples, 217, 253–54; to Oceti Sakowin Oyate, 29–53; and racism and colonialism, 417–31; and reconciliation after, 262–69; and sen-

tencing, 293; and settlement process, 253–69; as systemic, 409

intellectual and cultural property rights, 234–44

interconnectedness, 55, 101, 144, 154, 234, 333, 377–78, 404, 415, 428

international law, and Indigenous self-determination as peoples, 79, 216, 225–30; and international rights, 227–28; and "law of the place", 236; and legal pluralism, 76; and protecting Indigenous heritage, 240–344

Iraq war, 29–30, 47, 50, 427

Iroquois. *See* Haudenosaunee

## J

judges, 103, 127, 292; and Aboriginal view of, 325, 327; and Cree court, 347–48; and education of, 289; and meeting young people, 62; and Navajo concept of, 124, 126; and role in Anglo courts, 124–26; and sentencing circles, 70, 163, 177–78, 188, 191–95, 202–203, 206, 296, 300, 343; and sentencing post-*Gladue*, 207–208, 221, 280–93, 431; and Tsuu T'ina Peacemaking court, 351, 354

judgment, Indigenous concept of, 105; as not conducive to healing, 187, 213

judicial indigenization, 314–15, 318

jurisdiction, and foreign over Indigenous, 61; and Indigenous autonomy, 277–78, 314, 318–19; and Indigenous nations over non-Indigenous people, 69, 364–67; and land return, 425; and Maori land court, 267; and Native nations over land, 247, 412; and separate, 335; and state vs. community over criminal, 65; and tribal justice systems, 110

justice (because this is the subject of the entire book, these citations are those that relate to an Indigenous paradigm; critiques of the dominant paradigm of justice can be found

# About the Native Law Centre

*University of Saskatchewan, Saskatoon, Saskatchewan, Canada*

The fundamental objective of the Native Law Centre is to assist in the development of the law and legal system in Canada in ways that preserve and sustain Aboriginal and treaty rights. As a national law centre, it seeks to provide ways in which the aspirations of Aboriginal Peoples can be achieved in the Canadian legal system and to make the law more accessible to Aboriginal people.

In existence since 1975, the Native Law Centre is Canada's principal research program for Aboriginal law and lawyers. Its research activities involve researching, organizing, and analyzing the structures of rules and court decisions directed toward Aboriginal Peoples in Canada and globally. It focuses not only on the legal doctrine but also on the broad concepts of the purpose underlying this area of law in the post-colonial world.

Through various activities, the Centre attempts to achieve the following goals:

- to encourage more Aboriginal people to consider law as an area of study;
- to encourage law schools to provide academic support for Aboriginal students;
- to provide an avenue for publication of scholarly research on Aboriginal issues;
- to encourage scholarly research by Aboriginal researchers, scholars, and lawyers;
- to make information on Aboriginal legal issues widely available.

The Centre undertakes a number of activities in fulfilling these objectives, including:

- our Program of Legal Studies for Native People;
- publications (e.g., *Canadian Native Law Reporter; First Nations Gazette*);

- *Justice as Healing: A Newsletter of Aboriginal Concepts of Justice;*
- research initiatives;
- library;
- scholarships;
- our Young Professionals International program, which sends Aboriginal students abroad.

*Justice as Healing* is a newsletter that deals with Aboriginal concepts of justice founded upon our knowledge and language and rooted in our experiences and feelings of wrongs and indignation. The title refers to jurisprudential traditions in Aboriginal thought and society. After the Aboriginal experience with colonialism, racism, domination, and oppression, we are returning to justice as healing as a foundation for contemporary remedies. While there is no one single theory of Aboriginal justice, the common theme remains the necessity of using our knowledge to heal our people and ourselves.

**The Native Law Centre**
University of Saskatchewan
101 Diefenbaker Place
Saskatoon, Saskatchewan S7N 5B8 Canada
Telephone: (306) 966-6189 • Fax: (306) 966-6207
Web site: http://www.usask.ca/nativelaw/index.html
Email: Wanda.McCaslin@usask.ca

# About Living Justice Press

*A nonprofit, tax-exempt publisher on restorative justice*

Living Justice Press (LJP) seeks to increase public awareness of the principles and practice of restorative justice through publishing, which includes a larger rethinking of what justice means in every aspect of our lives—from home to school to work to courts of law to relations among peoples and nations. We create books that are accessible and useful to individuals, families, and community groups as well as to professionals in the field. To this end, LJP books are clearly written, attractively produced, affordably priced, and responsive to the information needs of all those interested in the restorative justice movement.

Our debut book, *Peacemaking Circles: From Crime to Community* by Kay Pranis, Barry Stuart, and Mark Wedge, was on the "Top Five 2004 Bestseller List" of the Conflict Resolution Network Canada. Receiving excellent reviews, *Peacemaking Circles* is being used extensively by tribal courts and First Nations communities, law schools, colleges (for courses ranging from philosophies of life to dispute resolution to criminal justice), churches, law enforcement and probation departments, schools, youth centers, families, and, of course, community justice programs across the country and around the world.

Thank you for the time and thought you have given to our publications. We are also deeply grateful to those who have chosen to support us financially. Because publishing is so expensive, and because we try to keep the price of books as low as we can, we could not make them available without your support. Above all, we appreciate your telling your family, friends, colleagues, and communities about our books, because that is how books get into the hands of those who need them. Thank you.

We invite you to add your name to our mailing list, so we can inform you of future books, and we look forward to hearing from you.

2093 Juliet Avenue, St. Paul, MN 55105
Tel. (651) 695-1008 • Fax. (651) 695-8564
E-mail: info@livingjusticepress.org
Web site: www.livingjusticepress.org